D1757373

The Colonial Heritage of French Comics

Contemporary French and Francophone Cultures, 17

Contemporary French and Francophone Cultures

Series Editors

EDMUND SMYTH
Manchester Metropolitan University

CHARLES FORSDICK
University of Liverpool

Editorial Board

JACQUELINE DUTTON
University of Melbourne

LYNN A. HIGGINS
Dartmouth College

MIREILLE ROSELLO
University of Amsterdam

MICHAEL SHERINGHAM
University of Oxford

DAVID WALKER
University of Sheffield

This series aims to provide a forum for new research on modern and contemporary French and francophone cultures and writing. The books published in *Contemporary French and Francophone Cultures* reflect a wide variety of critical practices and theoretical approaches, in harmony with the intellectual, cultural and social developments which have taken place over the past few decades. All manifestations of contemporary French and francophone culture and expression are considered, including literature, cinema, popular culture, theory. The volumes in the series will participate in the wider debate on key aspects of contemporary culture.

MARK McKINNEY

The Colonial Heritage of French Comics

LIVERPOOL UNIVERSITY PRESS

First published 2011 by
Liverpool University Press
4 Cambridge Street
Liverpool
L69 7ZU

Copyright © 2011 Mark McKinney

The right of Mark McKinney to be identified as the author of this book
has been asserted by him in accordance with the Copyright, Designs and
Patents Act 1988.

All rights reserved. No part of this book may be reproduced, stored in a
retrieval system, or transmitted, in any form or by any means, electronic,
mechanical, photocopying, recording, or otherwise, without the prior
written permission of the publisher.

British Library Cataloguing-in-Publication data
A British Library CIP record is available

ISBN 978-1-84631-642-5 cased

Typeset by Carnegie Book Production, Lancaster

PRINTED AND BOUND by CPI GROUP (UK) LTD, CROYDON, CR0 4YY

*To the memory of my father,
to his granddaughter, Louise,
and to her mother, Valérie*

Contents

Acknowledgments

Several people at Miami University helped this work along in many crucial ways: Jonathan Strauss, Chair of French and Italian; all my departmental colleagues, who have heard and commented on my presentations in the Irvin works-in-progress series; Juanita Schrodt, administrative assistant for the department, for her obliging help with many tasks; Matthew Gordon (History and Near Eastern Studies) for expert advice on a bit of Arabic; and David Keitges and the colleagues who awarded me a Hampton Grant in 2006, allowing me to undertake research at the Centre National de la Bande Dessinée et de l'Image in Angoulême.

Colleagues at other universities have also greatly enriched this study and my understanding of *bande dessinée*. In particular, I am deeply grateful to Fabrice Leroy (University of Louisiana at Lafayette), Wendy Michallat (University of Sheffield), Ann Miller (Leicester University) and Matthew Screech (Manchester Metropolitan University), who carefully read my work and provided generous, expert and thought-provoking feedback at crucial junctures, enabling me to significantly improve my analysis. Responsibility for choices, biases and any remaining mistakes in this book is, of course and as always, my own.

Other specialists of *bande dessinée* (and of many other scholarly domains) have encouraged, inspired and otherwise contributed to my work in many ways over the years: Laurence Grove (Glasgow University), president of the dynamic, path-breaking International Bande Dessinée Society, based in the U.K.; Hugo Frey (Chichester University); and the many other comics scholars I have met at ICAF and IBDS conferences. Their feedback on my work on those occasions has been most useful, and their own scholarship has been very inspiring.

I am grateful to Pascal Lefèvre (Katholieke Universiteit Leuven), who kindly put me in contact with The House of Alijn, Ghent; and to Patricia A. Morton (University of California, Riverside), who helpfully suggested where to look, at the CAOM, for information I hoped to find on the Exposition coloniale internationale of 1931. My analysis is especially indebted, in many ways, to her study of the Exposition. Raphaël Taylor generously spent several hours gathering materials from his fantastic library of Tintin scholarship to share with me.

I also thank the organizers of panels and conferences where I read early versions of pieces of this work, and panel participants and attendees for their helpful comments: the International Comic Arts Festival (2000, 2002); the Colloquium on Twentieth/Twenty-First Century French Studies (2002, 2005); and the Kentucky Foreign Language Conference (2003).

Others have kindly provided expert advice: Alec G. Hargreaves (Florida State University) wisely counseled me on how best to steer this project into print. Years earlier, my professors and mentors, Jonathan Ngaté and Philip E. Lewis, at Cornell University, inspired and guided my study of (post-)colonialism. Earlier in my university studies, Dina Sherzer, Pierre-Etienne Cudmore and Hal Wylie, at the University of Texas at Austin, encouraged my learning about French popular culture and francophone literatures from Africa and elsewhere.

I thank the many cartoonists who have taken the time to share their thoughts with me. Several cartoonists especially have taught me much about the art and business of *bande dessinée* over the years: j'adresse mes remerciements chaleureux à Farid Boudjellal, José Jover (Tartamudo), Xavier Löwenthal (La Cinquième Couche), Séra, and Slim.

Anthony Cond and his staff, at Liverpool University Press, have been extremely supportive of this project from beginning to end. I deeply appreciate their contribution to it.

Without the enormous help from the staff members of several archives and libraries, this project would have been far poorer: Monica Sweeny and Ed Via in Inter-Library Loan at MU; Gilles Ciment, Catherine Ferreyrolle, Jean-Pierre Mercier, Catherine Ternaux, and the rest of the staff of the Cité Internationale de la Bande Dessinée et de l'Image (CIBDI), Angoulême, where I did research in 2006; Aurore Grégoire and other staff members of the Centre Belge de la Bande Dessinée (CBBD), Brussels, where I have done research several times over the years; the staff of the Centre des Archives d'Outre-Mer (CAOM), Aix-en-Provence, where I conducted research in 2010; and Sébastien Rembert, of the Archives départementales des Vosges, for having provided some very helpful information on an *image d'Epinal*.

This project also benefitted from the helpful assistance of many booksellers in France and Belgium. I especially thank Michel Denni and Isabelle Morzadec, of the Librairie Lutèce and the French comics pricebook, the *BDM*, for dipping into their vast knowledge and suggesting many helpful leads over the years. In the final weeks of my work on this book, Michel Denni helped me discover the elusive identity of two cartoonists.

Several publishers, cartoonists and rights holders very generously gave permission to reproduce the illustrations in this volume. I wish to thank Yvan Alagbé (Frémok); Clément Baloup and Mathieu Jiro; Jacques Ferrandez, Christel Masson and the Editions Casterman; Pascale Guilbaud and Delagrave Edition; Grégory Jarry and Otto T. (Editions FLBLB); Michel Lieuré of Hyphen-Comics, Paris; Larbi Mechkour; Jean-François Richez and the Editions Larousse; Greet Vanderhaegen and Sylvie Dhaene at The House of Alijn, Ghent.

My friends Sylvie Durmelat and Derek Letourneau, and their son Léo, generously hosted me during ICAF conferences where I presented material in this volume. Sylvie also kindly shared advice and suggestions about this project, and encouraged me to complete it.

My American and French families have contributed immeasurably to this project. I thank les Dhalenne and the McKinneys for their kind and always generous support. Valérie Dhalenne read the entire manuscript, weeding out many errors of analysis and expression. Her thoughtful insights have enriched this volume vastly. I thank her and Louise for their unflagging help throughout these many years of work on the manuscript.

List of Illustrations

Figures

Plates

1 Accompanied by Zig and atop an elephant, Puce arrives in Mysore, India, to claim his colonial inheritance. From Alain Saint-Ogan, "Présentations à la cour" [Presentations to the court], in *Zig et Puce aux Indes*, vol. 6 (Grenoble: Glénat, 1995), p. 7, frame 1. Rights reserved: Zig et Puce de Alain Saint-Ogan / Greg / Hyphen-Comics Paris.

2 A version of the voyage into the center of the French empire during the 1931 Exposition coloniale in Paris. From Alain Saint-Ogan, "A la coloniale" [At the colonial exposition], *Le coup de patte*, no. 7 (27 June 1931), p. 18.

3 French children Luce and Colas visit the French West African section of the 1931 Exposition coloniale in Paris. From *Luce et Colas aux colonies* [Luce and Colas in the colonies], illus. René Giffey (Paris: Delagrave, 1931), n.p. © Librairie Delagrave 1931, Paris.

4 Zig and Puce are the captives of fierce Moroccan Rif fighters. From Alain Saint-Ogan, "Zig et Puce chez les Rifains" [Zig and Puce with the Rifains], in *Zig et Puce*, vol. 1: *En route pour l'Amérique!* [Off to America!] (Grenoble: Glénat, 1995), p. 10, frame 4. Rights reserved: Zig et Puce de Alain Saint-Ogan / Greg / Hyphen-Comics Paris.

5 Zig is crowned king of some African cannibals, after having impressed them with his juggling talent. From Alain Saint-Ogan, "Zig et Puce: Le roi des cannibales" [Zig and Puce: King of the cannibals], in *Zig et Puce*, vol. 1: *En route pour l'Amérique!* (Grenoble: Glénat, 1995), p. 6, frame 12. Rights reserved: Zig et Puce de Alain Saint-Ogan / Greg / Hyphen-Comics Paris.

6 A hostile depiction of voodoo in a popular, colonial-era children's comic. From Alain Saint-Ogan, "Zig et Puce: Un embarquement imprévu" [Zig and Puce: An unforeseen boarding], in *Zig et Puce millionnaires*, vol. 2 (Grenoble: Glénat, 1995), p. 11, frame 4. Rights reserved: Zig et Puce de Alain Saint-Ogan / Greg / Hyphen-Comics Paris.

7 "Le voyage impérial" [The Imperial Voyage], a children's game commissioned from Alain Saint-Ogan by the Vichy government in 1943. Pasted into Alain Saint-Ogan's scrapbooks (SOC 44.108–9). Image © CIBDI, Angoulême.

23 Saint-Ogan sends his characters on a trans-African itinerary that recalls the route followed by the Croisière noire. From Alain Saint-Ogan, "Zig et Puce: Furette avale les kilomètres" [Zig and Puce: Ferrety eats up the kilometres], in *Zig, Puce et Furette*, vol. 7 (Grenoble: Glénat, 1996), p. 19, frame 5. Rights reserved: Zig et Puce de Alain Saint-Ogan / Greg / Hyphen-Comics Paris.

24 A fictionalized adaptation of the official account of the Croisière noire. From Henri Pellier, *Avec la Croisière noire*, part 1 (Paris: Librairie Larousse, 1928) ("Les livres roses pour la jeunesse," no. 449), p. 7.

25 The fictional "Mission John Citron" is a parody of Citröen's African car expeditions. From Jean Bruller, "Chapitre XXIV: Où M. Lakonik est cru fou pour la deuxième fois" [In which Mr. Lakonik is thought mad for the second time], *Le mariage de M. Lakonik*, pref. Thierry Groensteen (Angoulême: Centre National de la Bande Dessinée et de l'Image, 2000 [1st ed. 1931]), p. 34, frame 3.

26 The Pieds-Nickelés pass themselves off as the French Minister of Colonies and his aides, on a visit in French West Africa. From Louis Forton, *Les nouvelles aventures des Pieds-Nickelés*, vol. 10: *La vie est belle* (Paris: Société parisienne d'édition, 1949 [1st ed. 1933]), p. 3, frame 2.

INTRODUCTION

The Colonial Heritage of French Comics

White man's loot: patrimony, tradition and inheritance

French-language comics, or *bandes dessinées*, are celebrated today the world over for their artistry and their playful humor, and more recently – in some cases at least – for the willingness of their creators to depict troubling and controversial topics, including French and Belgian colonial injustices and crimes. Series such as "Bécassine," "Tintin" and "Spirou" have delighted many generations of children, and continue to do so. These classic comics are part of a tradition that extends back decades or even centuries, depending on the criteria used to define the medium. Some of its most accomplished cartoonists trained professionally as artists, including at schools of fine or decorative arts (e.g. French cartoonists Pinchon and Saint-Ogan), whereas others (e.g. Belgian cartoonist Hergé) were essentially autodidacts. Swiss, Belgian and French cartoonists have helped raise the medium to new and unprecedented levels of accomplishment and visibility in the cultural field. There is no denying the artistry in the personal and collective styles that these cartoonists have developed, and, generally speaking, the visual appeal and narrative sophistication of their publications. However, certain dimensions of the comics tradition and current production are disturbing, and it is on some of these that I focus in this book.

Dreams of getting rich from colonial loot have long been a staple of European fiction, including comics, as key works in the *bande dessinée* canon illustrate. *Zig et Puce aux Indes* [Guy and Flea in the Indies] (Saint-Ogan 1995f), the sixth volume in a once wildly popular series by French cartoonist Alain Saint-Ogan (1895–1974),[1] was first serialized 29 March 1931 to 20 March 1932, and then published in book format in 1932.[2] It begins with a colonial variation on the dream of receiving an unexpected windfall inheritance from a rich relative who has died: Puce, a French boy of modest means, is informed that he is the sole beneficiary of a distant cousin descended from Onésime Puce, a Napoleonic officer (*capitaine de hussards* [hussar captain]) who – after the defeat of the French emperor in 1815 – had moved to India and become the ruler of the state of Mysore by unseating the autocratic raj. Although there are many references throughout Saint-Ogan's "Zig et Puce"[3] comics series to contemporary colonial history, this fictional story conjures up earlier colonial epochs, including the period when Napoleon dreamed of conquering India and driving out the English (Ferro 1994: 98–103).[4]

The history of the French colonial presence in India was, in part, the story of French mercenaries or *aventuriers* [adventurers], some of whom hired themselves as military advisors to Indian rulers (Le Tréguilly 1995).[5] Contemporary French officials described these mercenaries and advisors generally as incompetent wastrels (Le Tréguilly 1995: 56–7). Before arriving in India, some had been French common-law prisoners or dissolute aristocrats, punished by expulsion to the colonies, but who deserted after arrival in order to earn a better living, they hoped, as advisors or "partisans." The latter made up the small European nuclei of mercenary armies serving some Indian rulers. Nonetheless, a few *aventuriers* appear to have been industrious and reasonably competent, especially Charles-Benoît Le Borgne, known as the Comte de Boigne (1751–1830).[6]

De Boigne and other French soldiers and *aventuriers* in India no doubt helped inspire Saint-Ogan's story about Onésime Puce. Another model for his story may have been Soliman Pacha (Joseph-Anselme Sève), a Napoleonic officer who arrived in Egypt in 1819 and was hired by Mohammed Ali, the country's ruler, to train his army (Solé 1997: 62–3; cf. Mitchell 1991: 36). Soliman Pacha was eventually named Major-General of the Egyptian army. According to Dominique Petitfaux (in Saint-Ogan 1995a: 45), who edited two re-publications of Saint-Ogan's Zig et Puce, in 1906 the young Saint-Ogan traveled to Cairo with his family and stayed there for approximately six months, while his father worked as editor-in-chief of *L'étendard égyptien*, a newspaper.[7] Perhaps Saint-Ogan learned about Soliman Pacha at that time. Neither de Boigne nor Soliman Pacha replaced the rulers whom they served, as Saint-Ogan's fictional Onésime Puce does, after the jealous raj's attempt to execute the popular French officer provokes a revolt by the Indian army. However, Saint-Ogan clearly drew on the history of French military advisors and *aventuriers*, of which de Boigne and Soliman Pacha were two of the most successful examples, and on the allure of "imperial adventure" (Said 1994b: xxiii) in distant, exotic lands such as India.[8]

Moreover, through the connection between the expatriated Napoleonic officer and his young descendant, the story exhibits an imperialist link between colony and metropolitan center, the former providing wealth to the latter. Edward Said argues that this has been a significant motif in European prose fiction from the nineteenth century (1994b: 58–60). When Puce learns about his ancestor and inheritance, Saint-Ogan visually emphasizes the imperialist relation between the colonial metropolis and distant colonies governed by France by inserting a small map of India, showing Puce's Mysore next to genuine French colonial possessions (*comptoirs*) in southern India – Mahé, Pondichéry and Karikal (Saint-Ogan 1995f: 4).[9] After Puce arrives in India (Plate 1), a corrupt Indian Finance Minister and a conniving (French?) lawyer, Maître Harang, plot to overthrow him to obtain his newfound wealth. The plot thereby suggests the fragility of French colonial claims on the region, and sends the boys on the road again. The plot fails and the plotters are crushed by a rampaging elephant, in a slapstick sequence that concludes with the boys fleeing, pursued by a whole menagerie of animals, including two snakes – with their fakir snake-charmer – a sacred cow and two elephants. These characters (the animals and fakir) were typical exotic elements in subsequent French and Belgian comics set in India, including the Tintin stories (Douvry 1991: 68–71).

Another classic *bande dessinée* story has similarities to the inheritance tale in *Zig et Puce aux Indes*. Its author, Hergé (Georges Remi, 1907–83), greatly admired Saint-Ogan's work. His *Le secret de la Licorne* [*The Secret of the Unicorn*] and its sequel, *Le trésor de Rackham le rouge* [*Red Rackham's Treasure*] also recount a tale of colonial adventure, wealth and inheritance. Hergé first serialized his two stories beginning in June 1942 and February 1943, respectively. Hergé and his work, especially his Tintin series, have played a key role in French comics and popular culture, and therefore deserve critical analysis here. His *Tintin au Congo* [*Tintin in the Congo*], first published 1930–1 and still in print, has been widely cited as an influential example of colonialist ideology in comics. Hergé explicitly marked the trope of colonial inheritance as French, perhaps to better sell his books to a French audience, but maybe also in recognition of his debt to French comics. Thierry Groensteen has convincingly demonstrated that Hergé borrowed many elements from Saint-Ogan's Zig et Puce series over a period of several years (cf. Sadoul 2000: 123). Although Groensteen (1996a: 16) discusses one element taken from Zig et Puce that Hergé adapted in *Le secret de la Licorne*,[10] he does not mention the fact that the theme of a colonial inheritance appears in both. This is perhaps because of his stated desire (1996a: 13) to mostly set aside ideological or political issues – such as *pétainisme*, antisemitism and colonial racism – in his research on Saint-Ogan, including the profusely illustrated, co-authored book, *L'art d'Alain Saint-Ogan*, published under his imprint, L'an 2 (Groensteen and Morgan 2007). Groensteen (1996a: 13–15) does clearly state that he finds "[a] certain idea of the world"[11] in the Zig et Puce series: a vision that collects and uncritically represents the stereotypes and prejudices of the artist's time. Groensteen briefly illustrates this with examples suggesting both colonial racism against black Africans – specifically, at the Exposition coloniale internationale in Paris (6 May–15 November 1931) – and exoticizing clichés about other groups, including the Japanese. I propose that textual traces of these troubling matters in comics deserve serious and sustained investigation, because they inform the content *and the art*: whether in the art deco style of Saint-Ogan or in Hergé's clear-line drawing, the colonial grotesque (including a focus on black bodies as material excess or deformation – fat lips, large eyes and prominent teeth) is a recurring counterpoint to the stylization of white characters, which may be humorous but is rarely grotesque in the same way.[12] Moreover, just as the colonial "adventure" lies at the heart of the Tintin series (Halen 1993a: 147–85; Miller 2004) – as it does for Saint-Ogan's comics – so also the transfer of colonial wealth is fundamental to the reality principle that Hergé progressively worked out (cf. Fresnault-Deruelle 1979; Barthes 1985). This principle, Groensteen (1996a: 17) argues, fundamentally distinguishes the work of Hergé from that of Saint-Ogan, who often included elements from the fantastic and science fiction in his comics.

In *Le secret de la licorne*, Captain Haddock rediscovers some family heirlooms that once belonged to an illustrious ancestor, François, le chevalier de Hadoque: his chest, sword, hat and handwritten memoirs. Haddock recounts their story to his reporter friend Tintin, in a well-known passage during which a portrait of Hadoque falls onto the head of Haddock, who literally takes the place of his ancestor within the portrait. For Benoît Peeters (2002b: 28), this passage embodies the triumph of dynamic comic strip narrative over the stasis of painting. Peeters's form-based interpretation is useful and convincing, but I also read this comic-book passage as a *mise-en-abîme* of how the cartoonist reappropriates the (visual) inheritance *of colonialism* to construct his comic book. To a certain degree this is not surprising – Ann Miller (2007: 125–46) reminds us that meta-representation plays a significant role in comics. I read much of the two volumes by Hergé as an allegory of his salvage operation on colonial history and representation.

The rest of this episode recounts Haddock's active quest to retrieve the lost treasure of his ancestor. He retraces the voyages made by Hadoque, first to the Caribbean site where his ship sank, then to a tropical island to which he escaped, and finally back to Europe, to his ancestor's castle. Tintin and Haddock discover the locations of the shipwreck and island to which Hadoque escaped by assembling three pieces of parchment, the first of which Tintin discovers by chance in a model boat purchased in a European flea market. The model ship and two identical ones had been created by or for Hadoque, who had left the three parchments hidden in them as clues to the whereabouts of his inheritance. By the end of the voyage, Haddock has salvaged much of the cargo that Hadoque had been transporting when his ship was attacked by pirates (Hergé 1974: 14):

> Nous sommes en 1698. *La Licorne*, un fier vaisseau de troisième rang de la flotte de Louis XIV a quitté l'île St-Domingue, dans les Antilles, et fait voile pour l'Europe avec, à bord, une cargaison de... de... enfin, il y avait surtout du rhum...

> It's 1698. *The Unicorn*, a proud vessel of the third rank in the fleet of Louis XIV has left Saint-Domingue island, in the Caribbean, and is sailing toward Europe with, on board, a cargo of... of... well, there was mostly rum...

Haddock's recounting of this story from an earlier colonial period informs us that Hadoque may have engaged in the slave trade, which structured commerce between Europe, Africa and the Americas.[13] Although Hadoque is never described as the captain of a slave ship, the triangular trade typically involved the transport of slaves from West Africa to the Americas, including the French colony of Saint-Domingue (the western side of the island), renamed Haiti after slaves revolted there during the French Revolutionary period.

On the other hand, the slave trade also involved ships traveling not in a triangular fashion, via Africa, but instead directly from the French mainland to the Caribbean colony and back. These trips "en droiture" transported manufactured goods, which French colonies were forbidden to produce and were required to import from France (Pétré-Grenouilleau 1998: 27; Guillet 2009: 116). The return voyage from Saint-Domingue conveyed colonial goods (especially sugar) produced by slave labor, often as deferred payment installments for slaves who had been brought by ships involved directly in the triangular commerce (Pétré-Grenouilleau 1998: 39; Guillet 2009: 24–31). However, the fact that Hadoque's ship is in the fleet of Louis XIV suggests that this may not have been the case, because ships involved in commerce, including slave trading, were generally part of commercial ventures.[14]

Nonetheless, even if Hadoque were not involved in the slave trade, his cargo of rum suggests that it is logical to view him as participating more or less directly in the slave-based colonial economy that raised the sugar cane crops from which the rum would have been produced.[15] We may read Haddock's stammering description ("une cargaison de... de..." [a cargo of... of...]) as a textual marker of what has become unspeakable about his ancestor.[16] This has implications for the way in which slavery is treated in subsequent books by Hergé, especially *Coke en stock* [*The Red Sea Sharks*] (Hergé 1986), and for the meaning of related colonialist terms in the repertoire of swear words and insults shared by Hadoque and his descendant, Haddock (e.g., anthracite, *cannibale*; see Sadoul 2000: 113–15): they point to the shameful secret of colonial slave trading in the fictional pre-history of Haddock and his friend Tintin.

Another colonial inheritance in *Le secret de la Licorne* and *Le trésor de Rackham le rouge* is the treasure that Hadoque took from Red Rackham. The pirate had confiscated a case of jewels from a Spanish vessel three days before attacking Hadoque's ship, *La Licorne* (Hergé 1974: 21).[17] Here again, the historical context strongly suggests a specific interpretation of Hergé's story: in real life, slaves would have extracted the jewels from the mines of Spain's American colonies.[18] When Tintin and Haddock reconstruct Hadoque's story and retrace his trans-Atlantic itinerary, they produce significant wealth in two ways. First, they enable Professeur Tournesol to test the submarine that he invented.[19] Then, after Tournesol sells his invention to the government, he in turn offers to finance Haddock's purchase of his ancestor's castle. There, Tintin and Haddock finally discover Red Rackham's treasure, hidden by Hadoque in the secret compartment of a religious statue. The castle and hidden treasure furnish the capital that provides a social promotion to Haddock, thereby completing his transition from a sodden and ineffectual captain of a cargo ship to something like a wealthy nobleman (cf. Apostolidès 1984: 149–61, 250–7). Logically, this colonial inheritance must also fund the subsequent, world-wide travels of Haddock and perhaps of Tintin too, although this is never explicitly stated in the series. Moreover, the ancestral castle of Haddock anchors the series geographically: the protagonists depart from there on their globe-trotting adventures and return when they are done.

Clearly, the colonial inheritance is multi-faceted in both Zig et Puce and Tintin. It provides wealth in each, but only in the latter is it transformed into an enduring source of capital, whose bloody colonial origins are conveniently erased. By contrast, in *Zig et Puce aux Indes* Puce loses his colonial inheritance, which frees the protagonists to continue their wide-ranging adventures.[20] The colonial inheritance changes social status in both series: Puce temporarily becomes a wealthy rajah, and Haddock permanently joins the landed gentry. Most importantly, it is a rich source of storytelling: even today, colonialism remains a major source of narrative (as "adventures") in French and Belgian comics (Miller 2004).[21] So in both works, European characters must actively pursue their inheritance, by travel in time (the ancestor's story is re/collected, retold) and space (a pilgrimage to the colony and back).[22] The comics of Saint-Ogan and Hergé continue to tell readers many colonial stories, both about the French colonies already mentioned and about other (ex-)colonies, including Djibouti, Egypt, Haiti, North Africa, Senegal and the Belgian Congo. These comics constitute a colonial inheritance in themselves.[23] One of the greatests debts that Hergé owes Saint-Ogan is, therefore, a colonial one, extending from the narrative, geographical trope of colonial inheritance – found first in *Zig et Puce aux Indes*, and then in *Le secret de la Licorne* and *Le trésor de Rackham le rouge* – to the imperialist, eurocentric mapping of the world in the other volumes of the Zig et Puce and Tintin series.

We may gauge colonialism's importance in French and Belgian comics by examining the theme of inheriting a colony or its wealth from a family member. My two examples show that the trope can be traced back in comics to at least 1931–2, and it still occurs in contemporary versions. The "inheritance plot" also features in prose fiction (Williams 1975: 174–6, 285; Williams 1995: 200; cf. Said 1994b: 84–97), from which these cartoonists may have borrowed it. The trope of colonial inheritance also provides insights into the comics of Saint-Ogan and Hergé, viewed by many as the founding fathers of modern French-language comics. It expresses a geographic relationship between an imperialist metropolis and its colonies, and is one among several recurrent "structures of location and geographical reference" (Said 1994b: 52), including the "voyage out"[24] – the trip to the colonies – with which the "inheritance plot" generally occurs in comics. In other words, the colonial inheritance triggers a voyage that occurs in colonial space and/or time and is an imperialist "ceremony of reappropriation" of the colony by the colonizer (Said 1994b: 144). Analyzing the colonial inheritance allows us to compare the representation of colonialism in comics at the height of the modern French colonial empire with narratives about it produced today, after the formal independence of most French colonies. It thematizes the ways in which colonial history and culture constitute an inheritance for cartoonists and comics readers today, as well as for French society as a whole.

Within the contemporary comics industry, a variety of factors exist that have contributed to a partial contestation and critical re-evaluation of colonialist and imperialist traditions and tendencies in French comics: anti-colonialist and anti-imperialist activities by cartoonists and comic-book publishers, especially after the Algerian War; a weakening of (self-)censorship; an increasing number of cartoonists and even some comics publishers from historically colonized groups; beginning in the 1980s, a growing group of small publishing houses willing to take risks by publishing the work of cartoonists with new outlooks, including anti-imperialist ones; and the appearance of a broad range of new character types and plots, reflecting new multi-cultural realities within contemporary France (and beyond).

Constructing a comics tradition and market has involved the accumulation of cultural capital and the extraction of value from past works, recuperated from forgotten corners of past production, dusted off and transformed, while their authors are elevated and monumentalized, sometimes literally (e.g., the statue of Hergé in Angoulême). There are striking similarities and significant differences between this cultural recuperation and that of camp: both involve "the *recreation of surplus value from forgotten forms of labor*" (Ross 1989: 151; original emphasis) embodied in products of popular culture. In *bande dessinée*, value is often recovered from works created at an earlier stage of development of the medium and the field, a period that was saturated with colonial ideology and representations. However, critics often focus primarily on the stage of development of the great artist in these works, the features that they share with a general period style in art (art deco in Zig et Puce), their defining features from classical schools of comics aesthetics (the clear-line style of the *école de Bruxelles* [Brussels school], around Hergé; or the *style atome* of the Marcinelle group and *Spirou* magazine), and similar artistic criteria that are carefully pried away from the art, ideology and history of colonialism. Fans may participate directly in this recuperation, or may simply retrieve and re-read stories that they read as children, enjoying their familiar narrative structures and nostalgically reliving their childhood. However, they may also bask again in the comfort of an earlier France (or Belgium), whose global position was defined by its imperial power and was expressed in comics through colonial adventure, for example. Publishers often recreate value from works sought by fans and celebrated by critics for these reasons.[25] Therefore, one often finds less of a suggestion here, in the (re-)construction of the comics tradition, than in the "necrophilic economy" of camp (Ross 1989: 152) that what one recuperates might exhibit middle-brow "bad taste." For most fans and critics of comics, "comic books are not self-evidently kitsch but are a cultural form with as much value as [or more value than] painting or prose" (Beaty 2007: 76). Partial exceptions to this tendency include so-called second-degree comics (even called "third degree,"[26] or "nth degree"[27]), for example by Yves Chaland, who ironically rearticulates, lampoons, but also revels in, colonial-era clichés from *bande dessinée*, while simultaneously paying homage to the great cartoonists (Hergé, Franquin, etc.) who had used them earlier – before Europe's colonies began to achieve formal independence – but often less ironically (cf. Lecigne 1983: 109–15; Quella-Guyot 1991: 15; Delisle 2008: 153–75). A second-degree approach to colonialism in comics generally produces a very ambivalent and ambiguous vision of the colonial past and of its relics that tends toward the approach in camp. This ambivalence or ambiguity comes in part from the absence of a clearly articulated critique of the historical substance and context of an earlier work, a past master, or a now-outdated style. The second-degree comic often lampoons the latter in a decontextualizing mode both playful and half-admiring ("What a great artist, at least for his time! And now let's play around with his style, whose tropes have since become clichés and a bit ridiculous!") And this despite the fact that ideology, historical context and form are inextricably intertwined in the *ligne claire* [clear line] drawing school of Hergé or Edgar P. Jacobs, for example: its clear-ness, its legibility, is to a considerable degree an imperialist, orientalizing, eurocentric manner of reading the world (Miller 2004; 2007: 17–18; 2009a).

However, for many, the appropriate attitude toward great cartoonists and favorite comics of the past – regardless of their relationship to colonialism – simply remains an unmitigatedly reverential one. This is essentially what Luc Boltanski (1975) argued, but without regard to colonialism, in his analysis of the role of cultural capital in the emerging *bande dessinée* field in an article published in the first issue of the *Actes de la recherche en sciences sociales*. More recently, in *Unpopular Culture: Transforming the European Comic Book in the 1990s*, Bart Beaty provided an updated and wide-ranging Bourdieusian analysis of comics creation and marketing, as a struggle for the production and control of cultural capital, which turns in part around conflicting definitions of the artist and comics. In a separate, related analysis (2008), he showed how some alternative comics publishers reissued and recast specific past works as patrimony inherited from certain (generally male) cartoonists: a cultural capital claimed by these publishers and their associated artists. Beaty accurately connects this activity with key comics institutions and events, including the "Prix du patrimoine" [Prize of the patrimony], distributed annually since 2004 at the Festival International de la Bande Dessinée at Angoulême, and the "patrimoine" section of *9e art* (a scholarly publication of the Cité internationale de la Bande Dessinée et de l'Image [CIBDI], the French national comics museum and library, in Angoulême).[28] To this, one can add the list of "lacunae" recognized by the French Centre National du Livre (CNL): classic comics deserving a publishing subsidy of up to 60 percent.[29] Some such works, and books subsidized by the CNL in other categories, have been nominated for the "Prix du patrimoine." Although not all works on the CNL's list are French, the majority are. CNL support of French comics patrimony is typical of the French state's approach to cultural heritage, for example, in architecture, film and literature (Miller 2003: 136–7; 2007: 65–6).

Related canon-forming, which can include a nationalist bias, takes place through colloquia, museum exhibits and publications. This activity is often celebratory, as Boltanski (1975: 42) has argued, and tends to focus on works deemed great and on consecrated cartoonists, whose medium is described as a "ninth art" (the source of the name of the journal *9e art*). Beaty (2008) shows that this celebratory attitude structures the narrative of standard, published histories of French and Belgian comics, excluding a broad range of old and new comics, often because of lower sales: for example, older, serialized comics never republished in book form, and recent comics that lie outside of best-selling genres or modes such as science fiction and heroic fantasy. He argues that the comics field was restructured in the 1990s by cartoonists promoting a logic of artistic autonomy and distinction through mutual recognition by other, like-minded cartoonists and connoisseurs (Bourdieu's "autonomous principle") to counter the dominant economic logic of mass production and sales (Bourdieu's "heteronomous principle"; Miller 2007: 28–32).

Scholars have contributed cultural capital to the emerging field (Boltanski 1975), whether by supporting best-selling authors, works and genres, or, instead, artists and publications pursuing a logic of artistic autonomy. They have done so partly by publishing interpretative and theoretical, often semiological, works focusing to a large extent on formal aspects of the medium (Boltanski 1975: 42; Miller 2007: 43). This activity too is often celebratory, and – to the extent that it participates in a "culture savante" – can be sacralizing (Boltanski 1975: 38). Much *bande dessinée* scholarship tends to constitute and consecrate the comics tradition as an artistic patrimony, based on a pre-determined set of aesthetic or artistic criteria (e.g., the use of speech balloons), and sometimes on nationalist or regionalist concerns: for example, the designation of the Swiss cartoonist Rodolphe Töpffer or of the American Richard Felton Outcault as the initiator of modern (Western) comics (Miller 1999). By contrast, it generally avoids serious analysis and critique of the ideological, social and historical aspects of comics, and of related (anti-)aesthetic effects. I freely acknowledge my debt to prior scholarship on the medium, but believe it necessary to re-evaluate the comics tradition in political and historical terms that cut across genres and modes, as well as artistic and economic logics. A celebratory and sacralizing approach in comics scholarship may be strategically useful in attempts to reorder the general hierarchy of cultural production, or at least the place of comics scholarship within the university (where comics are generally ignored, or classified as a debased cultural form). However, it can become a hindrance too, when the comics and cartoonists that are offered up as exemplary are deeply complicit with racism, colonialism and imperialism. An obvious example of this is Hergé and his oeuvre, which is marked by antisemitism, colonialism and racism.[30] Revealingly, scholars working on Hergé's comics generally reckon with those features partially, and only when confronted with critiques produced from outside the world of "Tintinolatry," ones that either eschew the proper celebratory attitude and sacralizing tendency (Kotek 1995; Benoît-Jeannin 2001, 2007), or inject some critical insights into a generally positive account (Assouline 1998).

Pierre Halen (1993b) has analyzed one such dimension of comics patrimony that tends to be glossed over or ignored in publications focusing on technical and aesthetic aspects of the medium: the republication of colonial-era works, such as comics in the "Péchés de jeunesse" [Youthful sins] collection of Dupuis: for example, *L'héritage* [The Inheritance], a Spirou and Fantasio story by Franquin (vol. 1 of the "Péchés"); and the Blondin and Cirage series, by Jijé (vols. 3, 9 and 17). In an essay on representations of Africa, especially the Congo, in French-language Belgian comics, Pascal Lefèvre (2008) argues that Halen mistakenly attributed this republishing activity to a nostalgia for the colonial era; instead, Lefèvre says that it is simply part of a general trend to reissue works considered to be classic, without regard for their subject matter or ideological orientation. Although it is true that this general tendency – designating, repackaging and republishing "classics" – does exist in the comics industry and is a significant factor in the republication of objectionable colonial-era works (cf. Beaty 2007, 2008), Lefèvre is mistaken to dismiss the convincing connection that Halen establishes between colonial nostalgia in newer works and the republishing of earlier, colonialist comics. We may also recall the religious and political conservatism of the main comics publishers in Belgium, Casterman and Dupuis (and the new owner of the latter, Média Participations). Their ideological slant has certainly influenced their editorial policy and must have attenuated or prevented a strong critique of colonialism (e.g., in prefaces to new editions) in comics that they had previously published to promote colonialism.

The strong support that mainstream Belgian and French publishers gave to colonialist comics before formal decolonization began has been prolonged in recent years by the pro-colonialist agenda of smaller comics publishers, including occasional ones, such as the Cercle Algérianiste. In France today, Les Editions du Triomphe, which specializes in comics and children's books, republishes some of the most religiously and politically conservative and colonialist comics of the past, including Jijé's *Charles de Foucauld* (1994). That book, originally serialized 9 April–10 September 1959, had been previously published by Dupuis in its "Figures de proue" [Figure-head] series, alongside other colonialist comics biographies first serialized in the 1940s and 1950s in the popular *Spirou* magazine: *Stanley*, by Joly and Hubinon (1994), and *Baden-Powell*, by Jijé (1990). Triomphe commissioned and published a re-colored edition of *Charles de Foucauld* and has reissued other old series with colonialist episodes, including: "Oscar Hamel," by Frédéric-Antonin Breysse; "Frédéri le gardian [*sic*]," by Robert Rigot and Raymond Labois; and "Fripounet et Marisette," by René Bonnet. Moreover, Triomphe has commissioned brand new colonialist books and series, including *Avec Lyautey de Nancy à Rabat* (Cenci and Koch 2007) and a four-volume series on the French Foreign Legion (Philippe Glogowski and Marien Puisaye). These elements – along with many others that I will cite throughout my study – demonstrate that there is both an uncritical interest in older, colonialist works shared by many in French (and Belgian) society, and an aggressive, reactionary nostalgia for colonialism among certain individuals and entities, such as Triomphe, which is a traditionalist Catholic publisher aligned with the cultural and historical agenda of segments of the political far right. Some of the French and Belgian comics patrimony – republished by Triomphe and other, more mainstream, publishers (Dupuis, Glénat, etc.) – is indelibly tainted by colonialism.

The scholarly study of colonialism as it relates to comics in general, and to French *bande dessinée* in particular, has grown over the past few decades, though more slowly than the topic deserves, given the importance of their relationship to culture, and especially popular culture. In *Imperialism and Popular Culture* (MacKenzie 1986), historians examine the links between imperialism, popular culture and the British empire, but none of the studies there focuses much on comics. Nonetheless, there are parallels between them and my analysis of French comics. For example, MacKenzie (1986: 7–8) observes that the imperialist Wembley Exhibition of 1924–5 "was featured, admiringly, in almost every children's annual for 1924 and in the weekly comics. Billy Bunter and his chums went and their excited reactions to the imperial pavilions were faithfully reported by Frank Richards in *Magnet*."[31] I analyze similar phenomena in the French context during that era. An earlier, landmark study of imperialism in comics is *How to Read Donald Duck: Imperialist Ideology in the Disney Comic* (1984; first published in Spanish in 1971) by Chilean Ariel Dorfman and Belgian Armand Mattelart, which should be read in conjunction with Dorfman's related study of Babar in *The Empire's Old Clothes: What the Lone Ranger, Babar, and Other Innocent Heroes Do To Our Minds* (1983). In *Comics: Ideology, Power and the Critics* (1989), Martin Barker critiques the analysis of Dorfman and Mattelart. These studies all inspired and inform my own work on comics. One can also find here and there individual book chapters, journal articles and some unpublished university theses on racism, colonialism and imperialism in French-language comics,[32] as well as – finally – a book in French: Philippe Delisle's *Bande dessinée franco-belge et imaginaire colonial: Des années 1930 aux années 1980* (2008).

Imperialism and colonialism in comics

... colonization, contrary to the manner in which it was and still is commonly treated, is not a marginal element in French history, nor in the history of European ideas... it is constantly inscribed with virulence in the very heart of that history, of those ideas, often to the point of influencing them in a decisive manner. (François Maspero, quoted in Benot 2001: 5)

We are at a point in our work where we can no longer ignore empires and the imperial context in our studies. (Said 1994b: 6)

The quotation by Maspero comes from a study of colonial massacres by the French army and illustrates a primary theme of my study: colonialism is not an incidental or secondary aspect of French culture or of European thought (Said 1994b: 35, 60–1). Maspero knows this well, having personally witnessed the violence of colonialism in France (especially during the Algerian War, 1954–62) and having worked against it, both as a radical publisher and a writer. Colonialism and imperialism are also central to French-language *bandes dessinées*.

They not only recur in the comics production of Saint-Ogan and Hergé, but are also present in other foundational works and authors. Serialized in 1905, *Sam et Sap* (Candide and Le Cordier 1908) has been called the "first French comic" because of its early use of speech balloons – it tells the tale of an African boy and a monkey adopted by a French family.[33] And reaching back even further, we find the imprint of French colonialism on one of the earliest works drawn by another founding father of European comics, the Swiss artist Rodolphe Töpffer: *Histoire de Monsieur Cryptogame*, first sketched in 1830, the year that the French army conquered Algiers, where Töpffer's story is partially set (Kunzle 1990a, 2007; Töpffer 2007: 640–1).

Edward Said's *Culture and Imperialism* makes a powerful case for the importance and even the centrality of imperialism and colonialism in Western European culture in general. I borrow here, with a few modifications, Said's definitions of "imperialism" and "colonialism": "'imperialism' means the practice, the theory, and the attitudes of a dominating metropolitan center ruling a distant territory; 'colonialism,' which is almost always a consequence of imperialism, is the implanting of settlements on distant territory" (1994b: 9). On closer examination, the notion of distance needs to be given more complexity. Many lands colonized by France were indeed very distant from the *métropole* [metropolis; metropolitan center]: for example, its Caribbean and Pacific Ocean colonies, as well as sub-Saharan Africa and Indochina. By comparison, France's North African colonies were much closer, in geographical terms. The varying degrees of physical proximity and distance no doubt had an impact on how French people perceived the colonies (Goerg 2002: 88, 96–7). Over time, France invested heavily to reduce the separation between the colonies and the *métropole*, especially through improvements to communication and transportation that connected them: telegraph, radio, postal service and telephone; sea, land and air travel. Moreover, although Said is no doubt referring here to physical distance, the concept of mental, or felt, distance is important too. Here also, France devoted considerable resources to bringing its colonies closer to French culture, for example through education and propaganda (Blanchard and Boëtsch 1993: 198–9; Pierre 1993; Goerg 2002), while also maintaining its colonial others in subordinate positions (Fanon 1986, 2002; Memmi 1985). The fact that certain colonies – including Algeria, Guadeloupe and

Martinique – eventually were incorporated administratively into French territory as *départements* (roughly, "states") brought them closer to the *métropole* in significant ways. French comics can teach us much about these and related issues.

So why has so little scholarly attention been paid to comics, and especially these aspects of them? Here too Said's work is illuminating. The late Palestinian critic's major scholarly focus on artistic forms high in the cultural hierarchy – especially works of prose fiction and poetry by European artists considered to be masters – means that he neglected the hidden mass of the cultural iceberg: representations of, and debates about, colonialism and imperialism in popular cultural forms, which daily affect far more people than do the works that he studied (Bancel 2003). Said is generally unconcerned with less elite forms of culture and even seems to dismiss them outright, when he apparently adopts the viewpoint of Masao Miyoshi: "Japan's contemporary verbal culture is austere, even impoverished – dominated by talk shows, *comic books*, relentless conferences and panel discussions" (1994b: 330; my emphasis). The mixed media nature of comics, as verbal-visual cultural artifacts that do not easily fit into any already established academic discipline, may also help explain this attitude. In any case, like many other countries around the world, Japan has a long history of comics production (Schodt 1986). Although Said may have had strategic reasons for focusing on imperialism and colonialism in high culture, we can analyze these themes in other artistic forms, to gain insight into the workings of imperialism and colonialism (cf. Said 1994b: 108–9). True, toward the end of his life, Said (2001) finally recognized the value of comics that offer a critical view of colonialism and imperialism, in his introduction to Joe Sacco's *Palestine*.

Putting together the two themes of proximity versus distance and elite versus middle-brow or popular forms of culture helps us investigate how colonialism and imperialism are connected to French comics. French institutions such as the state and the Catholic Church have used comics to diminish the psychic and physical distance between ordinary French people (especially children, as future adult citizens) in mainland France and French colonies. Comics helped bridge the physical distance between France and its colonies, in part by circulating in both spaces: they were exported to French colonies, so they were read by both French children and young colonial subjects, although probably in different ways (cf. Hunt 2002). They were used to foster familiarity with the colonies among French children (Holo 1993a, 1995). They may have also inspired children to travel to the colonies upon reaching adulthood, thereby emulating the French protagonists of many of these fictions, who visited the colonies. French officials still connect France with its (former) colonies through comics: for example, through government-sponsored visits by cartoonists to French cultural centers abroad, and by Francophone cartoonists from (former) colonies to France. Cartoonists have not always served as docile propagandists, even at the height of France's colonial empire: for example, Louis Forton's "Pieds-Nickelés" [Slackers] series, about a French criminal trio, occasionally mocked French colonial aspirations, although it simultaneously reproduced colonial structures of representation (see Chapters 2 and 4, below). Outright resistance to, or critique of, colonialism was absent from most of the mainstream French comics of that period.

Critically re-evaluating the imperialist and colonialist pre-history of today's comics produces a form of cultural genealogy. This is a major aspect of my own inquiry, but some French cartoonists also engage in it to varying degrees. Critical genealogy has been an extremely productive means of interrogating cultural phenomena. Said (1994a: 41) famously cites Raymond Williams and Michel Foucault as providing helpful models, but also points out that they mainly avoid dealing with imperialism in their investigations (cf. Said 1994b: 14; Robbins 1995: x). By contrast, in *Orientalism* and *Culture and Imperialism*, Said reconstructs genealogies of colonialist and imperialist cultural formations. Some have criticized shortcomings in his genealogies and archival work: for example, the way in which, in *Orientalism*, he represents Western relations with the Orient in unchanging terms, from antiquity to the present (Rodinson 1989). Nonetheless, if we bear in mind its potential pitfalls, critical genealogical investigation can be a valuable heuristic tool for piecing together the emergence and transformation of imperialist and colonialist themes, tropes and imagery in French comics. In this book I produce a critical genealogy of comic-book representations of some key events in French colonial history, which have been the object of extensive public debate and scholarly research in recent years, although most scholars have completely ignored these themes in comics,[34] despite their long presence there: the Exposition coloniale internationale of 1931 in Paris, a capital moment in French colonial propaganda (Chapters 2 and 3); and the Croisière noire, a

1924–5 Citroën road-trip across the African continent that made a huge publicity splash in France at the time and left a long-lasting mark on its culture (Chapter 4).

In my investigation, I interrogate other genealogical activity, including the nationalist construction of a French comics canon. Various institutions, events, publications and critics have founded that canon on the production of Saint-Ogan, for two stated reasons: he is one of the first French artists to systematically use speech balloons in his comics – specifically, in his Zig et Puce stories;[35] and that series was the first modern French comic strip to be enormously successful.[36] Connecting subsequent developments in French comics to Saint-Ogan is a common type of genealogical activity, with parallels in other cultural areas – it involves structuring a newly invented (artistic or cultural) tradition around a figure designated as a founding father, as part of an "attempt to establish continuity with a suitable historic past," one that will legitimize the tradition (Hobsbawm and Ranger 1989: 1; cf. Said 1994b: 32; Beaty 2008). Hergé and his work have served the same purpose in Belgium (McKinney 2007b), but Hergé has also been adopted as a second founding father of French-language comics, and as the first and most illustrious artistic son of Saint-Ogan (Groensteen 1996a; Groensteen and Morgan 2007). Comics by Saint-Ogan and especially Hergé have been extremely important in building the contemporary comics scene, as is suggested by the fact that the most prestigious prizes at France's most important comics festival, held yearly in the southwestern French city of Angoulême, were first named "Alfreds" (1974–87), after the penguin mascot of Zig and Puce, and then "Alph-Arts" (beginning in 1988), after the Tintin comic book that Hergé left unfinished at his death (Groensteen 2007b: 85).[37] This in itself seems relatively harmless, but it should give pause to anyone familiar with the politically conservative and colonialist politics of the works of these cartoonists. Equally important is the influence that these works still exert on cartoonists and readers in Belgium and France. For example, in *Jeux d'influences: Trente auteurs de bandes dessinées parlent de leurs livres fétiches* (Barbier et al. 2001), several authors cite Hergé and Saint-Ogan as formative sources of inspiration.[38] Some comics by today's artists refer reverentially to colonialist works by Hergé, or are loosely inspired by them. Other allusions to colonialist comics classics have a more critical, contestatory edge.[39] However, only a relatively small amount of critical attention has been devoted to the imperialist ideologies that structure the narratives of Saint-Ogan and Hergé.

In this study, I construct an alternative genealogy by showing how Saint-Ogan, among others, provided a colonialist and imperialist model with a long influence in French comics, beginning with Hergé. The following chapters analyze a major way in which the colonial tradition is kept alive: by republishing colonial-era comics with imperialist themes. The manner in which such colonial-era artifacts are repackaged by publishers and framed by editors in recent decades is significant. Accusations of colonialist and antisemitic racism in his works dogged Hergé during his lifetime and continue today, in spite of repeated efforts by Hergé, his inheritor, his publisher, critics and other readers to foreclose or sidestep a substantial investigation of this topic from the beginning right through to the end of Hergé's career, including the continuities, contradictions, mutations and breaks in colonialist and racist representation. Despite significant progress in this area,[40] we still lack a fully documented, book-length study of this topic, in part because the author of such an analysis would be unable to gain access to the Hergé archives in Brussels. The repeated raising of questions about such themes in Hergé's work contrasts with the relative lack of critical attention to similar features of Saint-Ogan's work, despite striking similarities in the careers and publications of the two artists. In Chapter 1, I question the celebratory manner in which original versions of Saint-Ogan's comics have been republished in recent years, with little attention to the colonialism and racism that pervade them. I show that colonialist and imperialist preoccupations remained present in Saint-Ogan's comics throughout virtually his entire career; they cannot be considered marginal to the production of this founding father of modern French comics.

Therefore Saint-Ogan's work offers several advantages from my perspective: although it has been far less studied than Hergé's work, it was seminal in its time and continues to inspire cartoonists; it has been canonized by key comics institutions (the Angoulême festival and the CIBDI) and critics; it has been the object of two recent, extensive republishing projects; and it is less jealously guarded than Hergé's comics, which are carefully overseen by his widow, her second husband, their Fondation Hergé, the lawyers they employ, some of the best-known critics and theoreticians of comics, and many fans (cf. Dayez 2000; McKinney 2007b). By contrast, I was able to obtain critical material in the summer of 2006 for my study of Saint-Ogan by examining his scrapbooks, held by the CIBDI; by all accounts it would have been impossible for me to obtain similar access to Hergé's archives at the Fondation Hergé. Saint-Ogan's scrapbooks have since been digitized by the CIBDI and posted on its website, which is in itself emblematic of the great symbolic value vested in Saint-Ogan and his work.

I begin Chapters 2 and 4 with an analysis of important episodes in Saint-Ogan's Zig et Puce series, now far less well-known than the Tintin comics of Hergé, despite the fact that the Frenchman Saint-Ogan was once enormously popular and inspired the younger Belgian cartoonist. As part of my critique, I draw on several important studies of colonial-era exhibitions in France and Belgium, but also of colonial-era expeditions abroad (especially the Croisière noire [the Black Journey]), in order to demonstrate the pertinence of these events to depictions of colonialism produced today, although this connection is seldom made in studies of colonial culture.

To readers familiar with French-language *bande dessinée*, the inclusion of some of the artists, series and individual works here will be unsurprising, given their current or past popularity, importance to the development of the medium, and association with colonial themes, whereas others may constitute less-expected choices. For example, colonial themes featured often in the Pieds-Nickelés stories, which were serialized for many decades. Book compilations of these stories are still republished even today, but it is mostly the stories drawn by Pellos (René Pellarin, 1900–98), from 1948–81, that are remembered and returned to print. The earlier ones, including those by the creator of the series, Louis Forton (1879–1934), have mostly been forgotten and have not been republished as extensively in recent decades, although historian Jean Tulard (2008) celebrated Forton's works in a short monograph. The Pieds-Nickelés were serialized beginning in June 1908 in the ninth issue of *L'épatant*, a weekly children's magazine published by La Société parisienne d'éditions (SPE), owned by the Offenstadt brothers (Gaumer and Moliterni 1994: 227, 500). *L'épatant* and other SPE publications were decried by the Catholic press as vulgar and harmful to their youthful readers, a position surprisingly shared by Communist journalist and cinema critic Georges Sadoul (Fourment 1987: 161–7), among others. Many young readers of these periodicals were no doubt from the working class, given their content and price (*L'épatant* cost 5 *centimes* in 1908, and 30 *centimes* in 1931), although one of their better-known readers, Jean-Paul Sartre, was from an upper-middle-class background:

> every week I wanted to have *Cri-Cri*, *L'épatant*, *Les vacances*, *Les trois boy-scouts* by Jean de la Hire, and *Le tour du monde en aéroplane* by Arnould Galopin, which were published in instalments on Thursdays: from one Thursday to the next, I thought about the Eagle of the Andes, about Marcel Danot, the boxer-with-iron-fists, about Christian the pilot, much more than about my friends Rabelais and Vigny. (from *Les mots*, quoted in Fourment [1987: 166])

The self-reported print runs of *L'épatant* were considerable: more than 200,000 in 1934 (Fourment 1987: 167 n1). Even when the large-scale publication of translated American comics began to undercut the sales of other French children's magazines, the combined weekly sales of the SPE publications, including *L'épatant*, was still a million copies (Fourment 1987: 169).

The "Bécassine" series, another classic children's *bande dessinée*, was scripted mainly by Caumery (Maurice Languereau, 1867–1941) and illustrated primarily by Joseph-Porphyre Pinchon (1871–1953). Frequently republished in book form and widely disseminated even today, it first appeared in the initial issue of *La semaine de Suzette*, a girls' weekly published by Henri Gautier and Maurice Languereau, which was launched in February 1905 (Fourment 1987: 211; Couderc 2000: 13–14). According to Marie-Anne Couderc (2000: 15), the magazine was aimed at the "moyenne bourgeoisie" [middle class] (it cost 10 *centimes* in 1905 and 35 *centimes* in 1928). Like the Pieds-Nickelés, the Bécassine series contains many colonial references. However, it is unlikely that many readers of Bécassine today know that Pinchon published other comics with colonial themes, such as *Frimousset directeur de jardin zoologique* [Frimousset director of a zoological garden] (Pinchon and Jaboune n.d. [1933]), which depicts a human zoo of Africans in Paris. Similarly, few scholars who study French colonial exhibitions have connected one of the two artists (Pinchon) who created a poster for the 1906 colonial exhibition in Marseilles to the cartoonist who drew most of the Bécassine comics. And how many readers of the classic *Le silence de la mer*, a famous prose story about the Nazi occupation of France written by French Resistance writer Vercors, are aware that – under his real name Jean Bruller – he published a comic book containing spoofs of a colonial exhibition and a colonial expedition (it was reissued by the CNBDI; Bruller 2000)? I analyze work by other established French artists, such as Pierre Christin and Annie Goetzinger (joint creators of several comics with colonial references), Jacques Ferrandez (author of a multi-volume series on French Algeria) and Joann Sfar (who produced the "Rabbi's Cat" series), as well as artists who are less well-known, but whose work provides fascinating insights into contemporary attitudes toward colonialism: for example, alternative cartoonists Jacques Armand (Jean-Jacques Martin) and Bergouze (Philippe Bernalin); Pied-Noir activists Evelyne Joyaux-Brédy and Pierre Joux; Clément Baloup and Mathieu Jiro, who depict anti-colonial activists in interwar France; New Caledonian cartoonists Bernard Berger and JAR; and Algerian-French cartoonist Larbi Mechkour. All of these cartoonists, and many others, have depicted at length, or sometimes simply alluded to, French colonial expeditions such as the Croisière noire (or their avatars), or a (post-)colonial exhibition. They thereby make connections between France's colonial past and its present, the far-flung French empire and the colonial metropolis.

Toward the beginning of *Bande dessinée franco-belge et imaginaire colonial: Des années 1930 aux années 1980*, Delisle (2008: 13) makes an important observation:

> "Classical" Franco-Belgian *bande dessinée* sometimes alludes to the depiction of colonization in the heart of Europe... The famous colonial exhibition organized in Paris in 1931 serves, in fact, as the starting point and framework for some fifteen plates of "Zig et Puce," published in *Le dimanche illustré.*
>
> But this type of allusion remains rather exceptional. The relations between *bande dessinée* and the colonial imaginary run for the most part through adventures that unfold outside of Europe.

That is certainly true, but I show that the voyage out and the voyage in, the colonial empire within France (and Belgium) and the one beyond it, are inextricably linked in comics and cartoons. The 1931 Exposition brought many colonized to France to work at the exhibition: these included black Africans in military units of colonized soldiers, such as the ones lampooned by Alain Saint-Ogan in a drawing published in *Le coup de patte* (Plate 2). Although the Croisière noire (1924–5) preceded the 1931 Exposition, most of the contemporary expedition stories inspired by it in *bande dessinée* that I have found were published from 1931 onwards, suggesting that the Parisian Exposition helped make the earlier expedition popular in France.[41] This is especially striking in the case of the Pieds Nickelés and Zig et Puce series, where a lengthy colonial Exposition sequence, serialized during the 1931 event, was followed the very next year by an extended colonial expedition episode set in Africa.[42] This exhibition–expedition ordering may be partly due to the fact that a special section of the Exposition was devoted to the Citroën expedition, helping to popularize the latter. It is also possible that further research will bring to light more comic-strip stories about the Croisière noire that were published before the 1931 exhibition. However, an ideological and geographical, imperialist logic also connects the exhibition to the expedition in the anachronistic order I have described: the event in Paris was designed to inspire an outward movement, both mentally and physically. The organizers of the colonial exhibition clearly stated that by importing fragments of the colonial empire into the capital, they hoped to foster a movement outward by the French, toward the colonies. In fact, the Exposition (and similar events, which preceded and followed it) powerfully disseminated colonial ideology and representations throughout French culture at the time, including comics and other forms of children's literature. An example of this is found in *Luce et Colas aux colonies* [Luce and Colas in the colonies] (1931: n.p.), a large-format, illustrated children's story published in October, not long before the exhibition was to close, which depicts the voyage out to the colonies that the Parisian event was designed to inspire. If the social class of the children in the story was meant to mirror that of its audience, it was no doubt aimed at young readers from well-to-do families. Although not a comic book, the work does contain striking, full-page color images by celebrated French cartoonist and illustrator René Giffey (1884–1965).[43] It opens with a visit by the white French girl–boy duo, Luce and Colas, to the Exposition in Paris, where we see them gazing awestruck at an African in the French West African section (Plate 3): "Ils ont visité l'Exposition coloniale et c'est ce qui les a décidés à s'en aller voir, chez eux, tous les peuples dont ils n'ont eu, là, que des échantillons" [They visited the Exposition coloniale and that is what convinced them to go off to see, in their own homes, all the peoples of whom they only had samples there]. In successive vignettes, they then travel by plane and boat to Morocco, Madagascar, Tahiti, Martinique, Angkor and Bombay, before returning home to France. In each exotic location, they find real-life examples of the colonial places and peoples that they had first glimpsed in Paris, and learn to play their appropriate colonial roles with both indigenous aristocrats and workers: for example, we see them eating with a Moroccan dignitary, and later, wearing colonial helmets, being carried around by Malagasy adults in a sedan chair.[44] The narrator describes this for his young metropolitan readers: "Le 'filanzane' n'a pas de moteur, ni de chevaux, il est porté par des 'bourjanes,' c'est-à-dire des indigènes qui sont des domestiques" [The 'filanzane' does not have a motor, nor horses, it is carried by 'bourjanes,' which is to say by natives who are servants]. In Angkor, Luce mistakes the real temple for its imitation: "Oh! s'écrie Luce tout étonnée, on a volé cela à l'Exposition Coloniale, Colas" [Oh! cried Luce all astonished, someone stole that from the Exposition coloniale, Colas] (cf. Andrew and Ungar 2005: 308–9). This introduces the theme of mistaken identities and simulacra, often found in French comics about expeditions and exhibitions, and which is bound up with both the contact between European selves and colonized others that these events produced, and with (adults' notions about) the learning process of children and their role-playing in games. In this case, Colas quickly puts the original and the copy in their proper place: "Mais non, grosse bête, dit-il fort irrévéren-cieusement, c'était une copie que tu as vue à Vincennes. Ici, c'est le vrai." [No, no, you big silly thing, he said very irreverently, that was a copy that you saw in Vincennes. This is the real one.] However, when they return to France, planning to make an illustrated travel book about their adventures (i.e., *Luce et Colas aux colonies*), they discover a new disordering of their world, when they find there the same types of exotic animals – including an African gazelle and a Madagascan maki – that they had just seen on their trip, as well as "[u]ne Martiniquaise qui ressemble à Palmyre" [a Martinican woman who looks like Palmyre], a black *doudou*[45] figure who had fed them and told them traditional folktales in Martinique. In fact, their well-traveled uncle Guy has brought the animals and the woman back to his estate in France, thereby inspiring the children to plan to go off again and do the same, under his guidance, once they will have finished their book. This suggests a recurring cycle of colonial travel out and back, sparked by the colonial exhibition, as well as the domestication, accumulation and exploitation of colonized resources – including people, nature and exotic stories – which the exhibition had put on display.[46]

CHAPTER ONE

Colonialism, Imperialism and Racism in Saint-Ogan's Publications

Archeology and nostalgia in and around comics

Why read "Zig et Puce" today? Aside from the historical interest of the series, and the surprise of finding there some bold things that creators of *bandes dessinées* have only rediscovered recently, today's reader cannot remain untouched by the extraordinary gaiety of these stories. There emanates from this body of work an optimism, a joy for life that one can hardly find elsewhere. (Petitfaux, in Saint-Ogan 1999a: 63)

Today the [Zig et Puce] series is only visited under the influence of an archeological passion or of nostalgia. (Groensteen 2007a: 7)

What is the posterity of Alain Saint-Ogan, and especially of his series Zig et Puce [Guy and Flea]? As I stated earlier, Groensteen (1996a) has demonstrated that Hergé (Georges Remi) borrowed numerous elements from Zig et Puce for his now better-known Tintin series. Dominique Petitfaux (1985: 12; 1995: 18), an editor of Zig et Puce, affirms that Saint-Ogan, not Hergé, is the "founding father" of French-language comics. For readers unfamiliar with Saint-Ogan's work, I offer a few more significant indications of the place of honor that Zig et Puce has occupied in the world of French comics over the last few decades. There is of course the naming of the original Angoulême festival prizes after Alfred, the mascot penguin of Zig and Puce. Although Saint-Ogan was unable to actually attend the first festival, in January 1974, because of ill health, he was its president (Saint-Ogan 1995f: 56; Groensteen 2007b: 85). The French national comics museum, in Angoulême, held an exhibition on "Saint-Ogan l'enchanteur" in January 1995 to commemorate the centennial of his birth. Groensteen, then the museum's director, curated the exhibition and dedicated the first article of the first issue of *9e art* (1996a), the national comic center's scholarly annual publication on comics, to an analysis of "Zig and Puce." With Harry Morgan, he later wrote and published *L'art d'Alain Saint-Ogan*, described as "the first work dedicated to this giant of the ninth art" (Groensteen and Morgan 2007: back cover). The importance of Zig et Puce is also underlined by the fact that Greg, a well-known Belgian cartoonist, continued it from 1963–9 in an updated form authorized by Saint-Ogan.[1] Various cartoonists, including Hergé, and other public figures have paid homage to Saint-Ogan and his series (Saint-Ogan 1999a: 64; 2001: 57–63; Barbier et al. 2001: 86–7, 122). With the help of Florence Cestac, Petitfaux edited Zig et Puce in a republication by Futuropolis, a seminal alternative comics publisher founded in Paris during the 1980s.[2] This version contributed to the establishment of a canon of mostly Western classic comics, and appears to have been aimed principally at a restricted audience of cartoonists and adult comics connoisseurs. It was in black and white, in a collection devoted to classic comics (entitled "Copyright"), with each volume containing a compilation of two or three stories (Cestac 2007: 55–8, 94, 98). Subsequently, Glénat, a major French comics publisher, reissued the entire Zig et Puce series from 1995–2001, in 18 volumes, edited again by Petitfaux (Petitfaux in Saint-Ogan 1997b: 63–4; Saint-Ogan 2001: 3). This most recent version, on which my analysis is based, appears to be directed more at children and adolescents, and is potentially available to them in libraries and bookstores throughout France. Most of the volumes are slightly expanded versions of the original books,[3] in color, and sold at the price of most French hard-bound comics (12 euros in 2010).

Saint-Ogan began serializing Zig et Puce in *Dimanche-illustré* [Sunday Illustrated] in 1925. Saint-Ogan's comic strip and its characters had a phenomenal success, beginning in 1927 (Petitfaux 1985: 15).[4] Spin-off products, especially of Alfred the penguin, were mass-produced, and stuffed-toy Alfreds were brought along as good-luck charms during flights by well-known aviators, including Charles Lindbergh (Saint-Ogan 1961: 87–8; Saint-Ogan 1988: 36; Greg, in Saint-Ogan 2000: 54). Famous French personalities, including singer Mistinguett and President Gaston Doumergue, were photographed holding toy Alfreds (Petitfaux, in Saint-Ogan 1995a: 46; Saint-Ogan 1995b: 45; SOC[5] 12: 70–1, I: 15). Petitfaux

(1985: 15) also reports that "sixteen albums [of Zig et Puce] will appear between 1927 and 1952 [...] These albums were translated into many languages (Dutch, Spanish, Portuguese...) and the series was published in eleven foreign countries (Belgium, the Netherlands, Spain, Italy, Canada, Brazil..." The serialized version of Zig et Puce was widely diffused in France: the print run of *Dimanche-illustré* was 325,000 in May 1925 and rose to over 500,000 in 1930 (Petitfaux 1985: 15; cf. Bellanger et al. 1972: 516). Saint-Ogan's comics and cartoons appeared in other successful publications too: for example, he edited *Cadet-revue*,[6] a bi-weekly children's publication that began with a print run of 9,000 copies in 1933 and reached 70,000 by 1939 (Fourment 1987: 213).

Zig et Puce was launched during a period when the French authorities were working hard to generate popular enthusiasm for colonialism. It is therefore not surprising that the cartoonist drew a significant amount of thematic material from colonialism from early on. The first episodes of Zig et Puce recount how the main protagonists, two working-class Parisian boys, attempt to reach the promised land of America, where they hope to make their fortune (*Zig et Puce*, vol. 1: *En route pour l'Amérique*, Saint-Ogan 1995a). In the first volume they only manage to pass momentarily through New York City harbor, but their persistent efforts take them to a variety of port cities (Le Havre, Tangiers, Antwerp, Toulon) and far-away places around the world, including sub-Saharan Africa, Morocco's Rif mountains, Spain, the North Pole, Japan, Holland, the Bering Strait, the USSR and Warsaw. The exotic appeal of distant lands certainly influenced Saint-Ogan's choice of destinations (Groensteen 2007a: 13). However, from the beginning and frequently throughout Zig et Puce and in other publications, he made extensive use of specifically colonial destinations and imperialist images, themes and events, including the Parisian Exposition coloniale internationale of 1931 and the Croisière noire of 1924–5. Here I survey imperialist, colonialist and racist features of Zig et Puce and other published work by Saint-Ogan. I suggest how judgments about Saint-Ogan's career, publications and art might change when one includes this dimension, instead of ignoring, discounting or recognizing but marginalizing it, as has often been done.

Republishing Zig et Puce raises questions about disseminating colonialist ideology and representations. For example, why republish colonialist comics today? More importantly, why make them widely accessible to children and adolescents? And if one does that, then in what ways – for example, with what contextual material? I explore these and related issues here and in subsequent chapters. One can deduce a partial response to my third question from the editorial material that Petitfaux included in the volumes. Glénat provided room for several types of materials extraneous to the stories themselves: 17 out of the 18 volumes contain from one to nine pages of additional text and images (71 pages total, or about four, on average, for each of the volumes). These range from editorial comments by Petitfaux (48 pp.), to cartoon and text homages to Saint-Ogan by other cartoonists – including Hergé, Albert Uderzo and Enki Bilal – and writers (7 pp.), republished interviews by Saint-Ogan (6 pp.) and Greg (4 pp.), and bibliographical information about the original serial and book publication of the stories (6 pp.). This would have been an ideal place to contextualize the comics in order to show readers, especially young ones, the links between the fictional works and the historical realities of colonialism and racism. For the most part, Petitfaux did not take this opportunity, and his few attempts to address the issue are troubling. He also provides material related to my first two questions. For example, he justifies his republishing project in part by arguing that "Alain Saint-Ogan, the starting point for Hergé, is indubitably the father of francophone *bande dessinée*" (Saint-Ogan 1995a: 48), which he reaffirms again later: "The chronology shows clearly that the first founding father [of francophone *bande dessinée*] is Saint-Ogan [...] Hergé considered him to be his master [in May 1931]" (Saint-Ogan 1999a: 61).[7] For Petitfaux, the books should be reissued because of their foundational status, as well as the optimism and "joie de vivre" that they exude (my first epigraph, above).

In my second epigraph, Groensteen accurately lists two reasons for re-reading Zig et Puce today: an archeological pursuit and a nostalgic return to the past. He is especially interested in uncovering the artistic contribution of Saint-Ogan to French and francophone *bande dessinée*, so his own project is archeological in that sense. My goal in re-reading Saint-Ogan and his proponents is archeological too, but it is significantly different from that of Groensteen, who – although he has helpfully recognized and briefly described some aspects of the colonialism, racism and exoticism of Zig et Puce – has mostly bracketed those dimensions off from his archeological examination of Saint-Ogan's art. By contrast, I wish to uncover the colonial and racist bases of French comics, including those by cartoonists designated as founding fathers. This is necessary, first and foremost, because it helps me to determine what remains of colonialism and racism in French comics today, and thereby to gauge how far *bande dessinée* has been decolonized, and to what extent it remains a colonialist cultural formation. Obviously, when colonialist comics are republished and sold today, the colonial violence that they express through word and image, symbol and narrative is recirculated and at least partially reactivated. Republication usually occurs without the inclusion of a critical apparatus to help readers, both young and old, recognize the violence for what it is: colonialist and white supremacist representations that were produced within a cultural and historic context that is not completely past and done with, but instead lingers on, and is even actively maintained and fostered in new forms today. Recognizing how this occurs through comics constitutes one of the necessary steps toward stemming that violence.

My archeological project also helps shift the analysis of *bande dessinée*, including works by recognized masters of the ninth art, such as Hergé and Saint-Ogan, toward a more holistic evaluation of the art itself: what would happen if one asked, throughout a scholarly study of such artists, how much their art work and entire published *oeuvre* depend on colonial, imperialist and racist terms and structures? This has rarely been attempted for the great artists of twentieth-century *bande dessinée*,[8] whereas it has for classics of prose fiction (e.g., Miller 1985) and for master painters (Porterfield 1998). I attribute this lacuna to several interrelated causes, including the relative newness and fragility of comics studies as a scholarly field, especially in countries (Belgium, France, Switzerland)[9] where francophone comics are mainly produced and consumed (for example, the dearth of university specialists, courses, or peer-reviewed outlets dedicated to such scholarship); the consequent lack of necessary critical distance between much existing scholarship and its object – including distance from publishers and other institutional structures that produce comics for profit or promote them for prestige; and a need to defend *bande dessinée* as a legitimate art form that deserves serious and sustained study. This encourages scholars to set aside features of *bande dessinée* that are seen as delegitimating, and to focus instead on aspects viewed as praiseworthy or at least innocuous, such as their technical or formal elements.

Moreover, critiquing features such as colonialism is often a foul and disheartening task, but also a necessary one. We must understand how *bande dessinée* functions as an art form, but cannot properly do so without determining how even its foundational works and, in concrete examples, their formal features are marked by colonialism, imperialism and racism.

Nostalgia is the second motivation for re-reading Zig et Puce that Groensteen mentions. Unfortunately, an unreflexive, commemorative stance on colonialist comics such as Zig et Puce can foster or fail to counter a pernicious form of imperialist nostalgia. For Renato Rosaldo (1989), imperialist nostalgia is primarily Westerners' regret for traditional, non-European societies that are disappearing because of colonialist and imperialist incursions. Rosaldo's definition is extremely valuable, in part because it self-critically shows that a person who memorializes disappearing cultural traditions and mourns their destruction is often responsible in some way for the phenomenon: for example, an anthropologist or ethnologist, whose interactions with a traditional society help erode its culture.[10] By contrast, imperialist nostalgia associated with the uncritical republication of Zig et Puce and similar comics is more distant from the process of cultural destruction. It is a neo-imperialist nostalgia, because the person or group indulging in it celebrates the imperialism-soaked products of an earlier colonial period primarily as evidence of a time of *insouciance* [carefree-ness]. Petitfaux professes an interest in (comic-book) history: "Zig, Puce and Alfred have probably now come to the end of their adventures: henceforth they belong to History" (Saint Ogan 2000: 52). Unfortunately, he never calls for, or offers, a thorough, critical, historical investigation of imperialist ideology or antisemitism in the series – quite the contrary in fact. History for him seems mostly to mean (re)constructing a tradition of French (and Belgian) comics, and specifically consecrating Saint-Ogan's series as a foundational fiction in the canon. This stance is problematic because it ignores or even celebrates the pervasive colonial ideology that Saint-Ogan translated into comics. The "extraordinary gaiety [...] optimism, [and] joy for life" that Petitfaux finds in the series is exactly predicated on the self-confidence of popular imperialism. If that is lost or shaken today, it is to a considerable extent because of anti-colonial resistance and the dismantling of French empire in the formal sense, although France has maintained imperialist hegemony over many francophone countries and regions in more or less obvious and direct ways (Verschave 2001). One form of (neo-) imperialist nostalgia today involves uncritically celebrating the relics of the era when French colonialism was at its zenith and the feeling of carefree dominance to which they still bear witness. It involves downplaying or ignoring the violent and exploitative nature of imperial and colonial rule. French critics of imperialism have reacted to imperialist nostalgia expressed today at the very highest levels of French leadership and to recent negationist historiography on French colonialism.[11]

Nonetheless, Petitfaux did respond to incriminating accusations made in a different kind of foundational text, in the first critical article to appear in the first issue of *9e art*. In it, Groensteen (1996a: 13), then director of the Musée de la bande dessinée at the CNBDI, refers to important criticisms of Saint-Ogan's series:

> Hergé has been accused of depicting Africans as large, naive children, but this "Dupond vision" was already fairly tame compared to the way that Saint-Ogan treated men of color, whether it be the Senegalese bandits of the second and third episodes, the cannibals at the Exposition coloniale (in *Zig et Puce aux Indes*) or even the simian people living on the dark side of Venus, about whom Zig declares: "These black creatures don't inspire confidence in me!" (*Zig et Puce au XXIe siècle*).
>
> I will not bring Saint-Ogan to trial here on ideological grounds – he certainly was not politically savvy (his attitude under Vichy is proof of that). Moreover, one should not single out this or that passage with unpleasant connotations, without acknowledging the fact that, under the pencil of the Parisian artist, the entire world is only a collection of commonplaces and *images d'Epinal* [comics broadsheets], rolling along all the stereotypes and prejudices of the period.

Groensteen is right about the fact that Saint-Ogan's depiction of blacks is problematic. Still, my approach to Saint-Ogan's work differs from Groensteen's. For example, I would dispute the argument that Saint-Ogan was not politically savvy: I draw exactly the opposite conclusion, based in part precisely on his conduct during and after Vichy, which he cannily rewrote and rearranged in his memoirs (Saint-Ogan 1946, 1961, 2008; cf. Delporte 1993). Petitfaux responded to Groensteen's criticisms in his own editorial comments (Saint-Ogan 1999c: 53; cf. Saint-Ogan 1998b: 64):

> It would therefore be an error to see a racist and xenophobic author in Saint-Ogan. He probably was not very interested in politics (the

proportion of his drawings connected to that is infinitesmal), and he gives the impression of only having a superficial understanding of it.

For Petitfaux, it is precisely and paradoxically because Saint-Ogan's work contains all the stereotypes and prejudices of his time that the issues of racism and xenophobia are moot, with respect to the artist or his work. To buttress this argument, Petitfaux reiterates Groensteen's assertion that Saint-Ogan was uninterested in politics and understood little about it. The editor's framing or definition of politics excludes, for example, the clear connections between Saint-Ogan's series and imperialist propaganda, including the 1924–5 Croisière noire and the 1931 Exposition coloniale. Moreover, Petitfaux's argument rests on two faulty assumptions: first, that Saint-Ogan was simply an undiscriminating channel, with no artistic control or choice of material or perspective. In his foreword to Fredrik Strömberg's *Black Images in the Comics: A Visual History* (2003: 12), African-American cartoonist, novelist and professor Charles Johnson attributes the numbingly repetitive production of racist imagery of blacks by generations of white American cartoonists to "intellectual and creative *laziness*":

> Personally, as a black cartoonist, I don't buy the idea that an artist is merely a creature of his time, a *tabula rasa* inscribed with the bigoted beliefs of his *Zeitgeist*. That, if you think about it, is no more than the flimsiest excuse for a lack of invention, daring, or innovation in one's compositions – the artist, in effect, is content to uncritically work with *received*, pre-fabricated imagery and ideas minted in the minds of others (like Joel Chandler Harris, the Plantation School writers and illustrators, or Margaret Mitchell's *Gone With the Wind*).[12]

As Johnson correctly argues, it "is the very *point* of art, comic or otherwise: to put us 'over there' behind the eyes of Others." Any serious, extended study of the art of Saint-Ogan, for example (or of Hergé, or any other master cartoonist who produced colonialist art), should therefore critically and thoroughly analyze the extent to which his art bears the stamp of "intellectual and creative *laziness*." Both Groensteen (1996a: 17) and Petitfaux (e.g., in Saint-Ogan 1995e: 61–3; 1999a: 61–3; 1999b: 52–4) have indeed noted a certain kind of laziness on Saint-Ogan's part, which is related to the laziness that Johnson describes: Saint-Ogan had a tendency to recapitulate his own narrative paradigms. But no one has yet analyzed in detail how colonialism, imperialism and racism permeate Saint-Ogan's works, continue in various ways throughout his entire oeuvre, and are paradoxically productive, in an artistic sense: they enabled him to produce – albeit lazily – certain artistic and cultural effects.

Petitfaux's second mistaken presupposition is that we could only expect Saint-Ogan to have reproduced the prejudices and stereotypes of his time, because none of his contemporaries contested these types of imagery and narrative, or was capable of doing so. Yet, at the time, the 1931 Exposition coloniale was the target of protest and criticism in Paris – by nationalist Vietnamese students and workers, French Communists and Surrealists, as scholarly publications in French and English have shown (Hodeir and Pierre 1991: 111–34; Lebovics 1992: 98–110; Norindr 1996: 34–71; Morton 2000: 96–129). We know, from Saint-Ogan's contribution to a parody of a cover from the French communist newspaper *L'Humanité*, that already in 1931 he was perfectly aware of strong criticisms against French imperialism and the Exposition coloniale (see Chapter 2). He could have taken a critical position against colonialism and imperialism. It is probable that such a stand would have been very costly in professional and economic terms: it could have deprived him of significant publishing outlets, although it might also have opened other ones to him, no doubt much less mainstream and remunerative. I turn now to what Saint-Ogan did publish.

Pedagogy of empire: the repetition of colonialist schemas and motifs throughout Zig et Puce

> Saint-Ogan believes in the educational mission of young people's literature and allows his readers to learn or to study a few scraps of culture, while having fun. (Groensteen 2007a: 10)

Some have argued that although Hergé borrowed extensively from Saint-Ogan (especially at the beginning of his career), he evolved artistically from repetition to genuine innovation, and ideologically from colonialist racism to sympathy for victims of imperialism – although the latter part of this evaluation of Hergé and his work has been convincingly disputed (Benoît-Jeannin 2001, 2007; Frey 2008a). By contrast, Saint-Ogan's artistic evolution is almost the reverse: he injected a strong dose of modernity into French-language comics early on, but then stagnated artistically throughout the rest of his career (Groensteen 1996a: 17; Petitfaux, in Saint-Ogan

1999a: 61–3). However, an important dimension of that repetition has mostly been left unexplored: the rearticulation of colonial and imperialist tropes throughout Zig et Puce (Appendix 1). This involves a crucial dimension of modernity, namely the profound reordering of human existence brought about by European imperialism, including the slave trade, colonialism and resulting migrations (Gilroy 1993). Saint-Ogan often structured episodes of Zig et Puce around visits to past and present French colonies of various administrative types (colony, protectorate, etc.): the Caribbean waters near Cayenne and Martinique;[13] the Congo;[14] Madagascar;[15] Mahé;[16] Mauritania;[17] North Africa;[18] Oubangui;[19] Senegal (Dakar and the interior);[20] Upper Volta;[21] the côte [française] des Somalis [Somali coast][22] and its capital, Djibouti;[23] as well as former French colonies or imperial conquests – Egypt,[24] Haiti[25] and Mexico.[26] In addition, there are allusions to Mahé, Pondichéry and Karikal (in India),[27] Lebanon[28] and Indochina.[29] Taken together, these recreate the map of French colonial possessions around the globe to a considerable extent.

Groensteen is right to observe, in this section's epigraph, that young people learn(ed) bits of culture in amusing ways when they read Saint-Ogan's work, but it is often the culture of the French colonial empire. We saw in the Introduction that in *Zig et Puce aux Indes* the French colonies offer exotic spectacle and adventure (French empire as a far-flung playground), but also wealth and a (temporary) sense of ennoblement for the boys. Occasionally throughout the series (vols. 1–2, 7, 15), Zig and Puce encounter soldiers from France's colonial army or its police forces, who save the boys and their bird, just as these "forces of (colonial) order" would do for the colonial settlers and possessions they were sent to defend. The first volume of Zig et Puce depicts menacing Moroccan Rif fighters, whom French soldiers, commanded by Lyautey, then Pétain, were fighting (Saint-Ogan 1995a: 10) (Plate 4).[30] French soldiers rescue the boys in the desert after they have escaped from their captors. When Zig and Puce are captured by convicts who had escaped from the *bagne* [prison camp] in Cayenne (French Guyana), French policemen again save them (Saint-Ogan 1995e: 55–6; cf. Chauvaud 2009: 124–5). The boys stumble upon a French naval contingent as it is raising the flag to symbolize that it is taking possession of Clipperton Island. The naval commander is only too happy to repatriate the lost boys and their penguin to Toulon, the home port of the navy, whose colonial connections are inscribed on its topography – one frame shows a street sign in Toulon for the "rue d'Alger" [Algiers street] (Saint-Ogan 1996a: 34–7; cf. the cover of *Zig, Puce et la petit princesse*).[31] French imperialist power is represented elsewhere through the flying of the French flag in the colonies (1995b: 24–6; 1996a: 34; 1999b: 41, 43) and, occasionally, the depiction of French settlers or other French civilians in colonies, in Tangiers (1995a: 12), Mahé (1995f: 15, 19) and Djibouti (1999c: 13). Rivalry between imperialist powers, shown in some recent French comics,[32] is relatively rare in most of the works produced during the twentieth century that I analyze here; instead, one generally finds benign coexistence. In addition to their encounters with their American friend Dolly and her relatives, Zig and Puce often meet other Europeans or Americans during their visits to colonies. For example, they sell fake medicine to a gullible Englishman in Tangiers (1995a: 12), negotiate the future profits of a possible diamond find with white South Africans (1995d: 40–8) and encounter British colonizers in Port Saïd (1996a: 18). Saint-Ogan missed an opportunity to critique colonialism in the Americas in an episode where Zig and Puce earn money by briefly working alongside blacks for a white cotton plantation owner in Honduras (1995e: 26). At one point Saint-Ogan gently pokes fun at colonial quibbling: when negotiations between French and British colonial authorities in the Caribbean bog down because of separate colonial jurisdictions, Zig and Puce ignore the administrative red tape and independently look for Dolly in the British Bermudas (1995e: 56–8). The peaceful coexistence of rival European powers in Saint-Ogan's series may be due to the historical context of its creation: by then, European countries had mostly finished dividing up the colonized world between themselves. On the other hand some overtones of imperialist rivalry are discernible in *Zig et Puce aux Indes* (see below, Chapter 2). And in an ominous episode of imperialist collusion, the boys catch plotting spies and hand them over to American police officers in the Panama canal zone (1995e: 26–8).

Colonialist, racist and imperialist ideology – specifically, white supremacism – is especially pervasive in the paternalistic relationships that Zig and Puce establish with the apparently primitive indigenous peoples that they meet abroad. Dark-skinned local populations are almost always represented as naive and therefore easily outwitted and dominated by the plucky and inventive French boys. This fits the paradigm whereby colonial-era comics often presented imperialism and colonialism as a picaresque adventure and a great game (cf. Harlow and Carter 1999: 165, 352–60). Encounters with cultures thought to be inferior are regularly expressed in fetishistic, religious terms, similar to the representation in Hergé's *Tintin au Congo*: for example, on the latter's notorious final page, where Africans and their dogs lament the departure of Tintin and his dog Snowy, and even worship statues of them.[33] Early in the first volume of Zig et Puce, black Africans are already depicted as cannibals and are extremely gullible. Gérard Pigeon has astutely analyzed how Zig and Puce easily trick the Africans, first by smearing themselves with black shoe-polish (Saint-Ogan 1995a: 6–7; Pigeon 1996: 137–41). When the polish washes off in the rain, Zig uses his juggling skill to quickly convince the Africans that he is a sorcerer, so they crown him king (Plate 5).[34] The episode recalls minstrel shows and echoes the commodity fetishism attributed to Africans in advertisements for shoe polish and cleaning products in colonial-era France (Bachollet et al. 1994: 90–103; Berliner 2002: 150–5) and England (McClintock 1995: 207–31).[35] Pigeon shows how the colonialist ideology of this multi-page sequence is composed of racist humor, the hierarchical representation of religious and ethnic differences (three groups are depicted: animists, Muslims and *évolués* [semi-Europeanized Africans]), and the white supremacist order into which African differences are violently integrated – the groups fight each other for the chance to be ruled by a French boy, Zig. I would add that this imputes to the Africans the initiative for the imperialist divide and conquer strategy, often used by the French and expounded by Lyautey,[36] and still considered a model by a recent French foreign minister.[37]

In fact, Zig et Puce is rife with images of black Africans as cannibals and, generally, as sources of racist humor (in 14 of the 18 volumes). The recurring, though usually brief, appearances of Cocoa and Cacao, in almost half of the volumes (vols. 6–9, 11, 14, 16–17), give continuity across the series to Saint-Ogan's vision of black Africans. They are visually grotesque, simplistic, child-like and emotional (Saint-Ogan 1995f: 29; 1999a: 51). They eventually become half-civilized, but there are titillating suggestions that they may yet revert to their savage state (see below, Chapter 2). This provides a rationale for continued surveillance of them and restrictions on their independence. It also helps justify their subaltern position as domestic servants in a European socio-economic order. In Zig et Puce, other blacks are similarly associated with popular spectacles, as examples of grotesque difference within European space: for example, a unnamed black boxer in Antwerp is apparently reworked later as Cous-Cous-Ramoli [Mushy Couscous],[38] a Senegalese wrestler, described as potentially a cannibal (Saint-Ogan 1995a: 28; 1998b: 54–5). Later, "Futifu, le nègre-nain" [Futifu, the Negro-dwarf], traveling by ship to Australia, where he is to appear in exhibitions, is mistaken for Alfred, the penguin (1995c: 16), much as Greg reported that Saint-Ogan had compared Josephine Baker to a stuffed toy representing the same penguin character ("Seen from behind, they both had a lot of similar characteristics"; Saint-Ogan 2000: 54; cf. Saint-Ogan 1961: 87; 2008: 87).[39] Most other Africans and African-Americans in the series are not individuated as much as "Futifu, le nègre-nain," but are always grotesque and usually naive. Moreover, Alfred is in many ways the black sidekick of the series, playing a role equivalent to that of black human characters in other French children's comics of the era. It is therefore no surprise to find him used as an advertising icon for domestic products, including cleaning materials and shoe polish, that are often associated with black people in European advertising.[40]

Similarly, in two volumes of Zig et Puce, dark-skinned Easter Islanders are temporarily fooled into thinking that Alfred, perched atop Zig, is their god Maké-Maké, at least until the penguin dives off to catch a fish and thereby ruins the disguise (Saint-Ogan 1997b: 20; Saint-Ogan 1997c: 14; cf. Groensteen 2007b: 62). A related episode occurs in the penultimate volume (published ten years later), when Zig and Puce visit the planet Venus, where they first encounter a white race of Venutians, living in a technologically sophisticated society. However, on the dark side of the planet, members of a primitive, black Venutian race – described as "nègres" [Negroes] – attack Zig and Puce, until one of the Venutians decides that Alfred is their god (Saint-Ogan 2000: 27–8; cf. Groensteen 1996a: 13; Groensteen 2007b: 51).[41] In these instances, Zig, Puce and Alfred escape by manipulating the superstitions of gullible local peoples. However, the voodoo priest and worshipers whom the threesome encounter while visiting Haiti are not fooled or impressed by them (Saint-Ogan 1995b: 11); instead, voodoo is portrayed as hostile to the European boys and their bird, which is typical of European mass-media depictions of that religion, according to Ella Shohat and Robert Stam (1994: 202–3) (Plate 6). In a few rare instances, black *évolué* characters use grammatically correct French (for example, the rulers of Haiti).[42] However, in general the idea that the darker-skinned peoples encountered by Zig and Puce are more primitive than the French boys is reflected in their speech: most use stereotyped pidgin French, especially the term "y'a bon" [that be good][43] (cf. Siblot 1991; Met 1996; Pigeon 1996). The expression is probably best remembered today as part of the advertising slogan printed alongside an image of a Senegalese rifleman from the French colonial army on tins of Banania, a French breakfast food (Garrigues 1991; Bachollet et al. 1994; Rosello 1998: 4–7; Donadey 2000). In three volumes of Zig et Puce (nos. 1, 2, 7; see Appendix 1), the presence of anonymous black soldiers in crowd scenes helps to illustrate the importance of "la plus grande France" [Greater France], specifically the value of sub-Saharan Africa to the French as a potential reservoir of soldiers to defend the "mère-patrie" [mother-land] in times of crisis, such as during the First World War (Dewitte 1989: 157–69; Berliner 2002: 9–36). Although some recent publications still perpetuate colonialist images of African soldiers in the French colonial army, others rework such characters to contest colonial ideology.[44]

In Zig et Puce there is an evolution that coincides revealingly with general trends in colonialist thought and propaganda. As I mentioned above, one finds at the beginning of the series the menacing image of Rif fighters, who were resisting European hegemony in North Africa when the strip was first published. Later images of North Africa are far less threatening, although occupying French soldiers are still regularly depicted, alluding to the reality of the military force on which colonialism ultimately rested (Saint-Ogan 1999b: 43). A high point of colonial propaganda and popular enthusiasm for the colonies in the early 1930s (Girardet 1995: 175–99) is reflected in the two comic-book episodes of Zig et Puce based on the 1931 Exposition coloniale in Paris and the 1924–5 Croisière noire (and similar expeditions; see Chapters 2 and 4, below). Later, the real threat that nationalist movements posed to the French colonial order just after the Second World War may be one basis for a manichean story about a war between black and white races, "Zig et Puce en Atlantide" [Zig and Puce in Atlantis] (serialized 1946–7; republished in Saint-Ogan 1998a), which ends with a nuclear explosion from which Zig, Puce and their friends barely escape. Of course, recent events, including the atomic bombing of Japan by the United States military, are also reworked in the story (Petitfaux, in Saint-Ogan

1998a: 46), which nonetheless may also be a textual example of the virulent racism of the threatened colonial order that France quickly tried to shore up after the end of the Second World War.

An archive of prejudice: empire in Saint-Ogan's work beyond Zig et Puce

Colonialism, racism and imperialism in Saint-Ogan's work are by no means limited to the Zig et Puce comic-book series. For reasons of space I cannot explore these in detail here, but his scrapbooks (*carnets*) are rife with examples, which makes them a valuable colonial archive deserving careful analysis (cf. Stoler 2006). As Groensteen (2007b) documents in his bio-bibliography of Saint-Ogan, from early on in his career the cartoonist published many newspaper cartoons, and later he even worked as an editorial cartoonist (Saint-Ogan 1974a). Much of this material in the scrapbooks is troubling for today's readers. Those interested in exploring this issue further are invited to compare this fundamental aspect of Saint-Ogan's work with Groensteen's bio-bibliography, where the comics theoretician reproduces a few of the relevant illustrations (Groensteen 2007b: 33, 36, 46–7, 51, 62).

Two samples of this colonial, racist material will have to suffice here. As Groensteen (2007b: 44) tells us, "Beginning on 5 August [1931], [there was] a new competition illustrated by Saint-Ogan for *Le petit journal*, on the theme of the French colonies" (this guessing game followed another one by Saint-Ogan, also published in the *Petit journal* in 1931, with some colonial riddles; see, for example, SOC 22.129, 22.133; cf. Groensteen 2007b: 43). Two of its illustrated clues are republished by Groensteen (2007b: 46).[45] One, captioned "La musique adoucit les moeurs" [Music has charms to soothe a savage breast] (Figure 1), was set in the French colony of Guinée (SOC 23.257), and the other, "La Justice poursuivant le Crime" [Justice pursuing Crime], in French Guyana (23.253; in the scrapbook, the answers to the 25 colonial riddles – i.e., the names of the colonies represented by the captioned images – are penciled in under each clipping, perhaps by Saint-Ogan). The caption of the former suggests that the heavily caricatured Africans (half-naked, with huge lips and eyes) are savages in need of civilizing. Some of them are about to be attacked by wild animals (a snake and a jaguar, or a similar big

Figure 1 "Music has charms to soothe a savage breast": colonialist violence in a guessing game drawn by Saint-Ogan. A snake (left) and a jaguar (right) threaten Africans at a jazz [*sic*] session in Africa (Guinée). From Alain Saint-Ogan, "La musique adoucit les moeurs," *Le petit journal* (1931), pasted into Alain Saint-Ogan's scrapbooks (SOC 23.257). Image © CIBDI, Angoulême.

wildcat). "La Justice poursuivant le Crime" depicts an escapee from a prison camp in the French colony being pursued by three colonial officers.

My second example is a racist caricature that Saint-Ogan drew for an ongoing feature in *Le coup de patte*: a book review entitled "Avant les quais: 'Critique par la bande'" [Before the banks: "Criticism through comics"] (Figure 2). The cartoonist's invented subtitle is as demeaning as the visual illustration and includes a clichéd representation of the speed of blacks: "Histoire de nègres: Y'en a très bon!" [Negro story: It real good!].

Saint-Ogan's personal archives are also antisemitic, although in quantitative terms there is much less antisemitic than colonialist material in his scrapbooks – and probably in his publications. On the other hand, Saint-Ogan's antisemitic material is as viciously racist as the colonialist material, although in predictably specific and different

Figure 2   A colonialist caricature of a black in a book review illustrated by Alain Saint-Ogan. From Alain Saint-Ogan, "Avant les quais: 'Critique par la bande'" [Before the banks: "Criticism through comics"], *Le coup de patte*, no. 2 (23 May 1931), p. 25.

ways. The CIBDI has republished a complete facsimile version of Saint-Ogan's scrapbooks online. The 82 volumes constitute an archive of prejudice that retraces the itinerary of a founding father of French comics.

CHAPTER TWO

French Colonial Exhibitions in Comics

Introduction: propaganda for empire

> [T]here is an [...] obstinate assumption that colonial undertakings were marginal and perhaps even eccentric to the central activities of the great metropolitan cultures. (Said 1994b: 35)

Prominent critics, historians and activists have argued that comics have disseminated colonialist and imperialist narratives and imagery.[1] On the other hand, many comics fans and critics maintain that certain works associated with European colonialism – especially early ones, such as Hergé's *Tintin au Congo* (1930; in Hergé 1973) – are either semi-sacred, canonical texts and artistic masterpieces that consequently should be exempt from political and historical criticism, or else that they are marginal within the artist's output and so should be excused away as aberrations or juvenile mistakes. Sometimes critics argue that these publications are typical products of an earlier time that did not conform to the so-called politically correct norms of today, or something artists produced because they were asked to: the easily influenced cartoonists were simply the conduit of their time, or were subordinate to a patron or artistic director.[2] They may argue that the aesthetic value of these comics or their foundational status in the tradition are of paramount or even exclusive importance, but they also continue to assert that colonialist ideology and imperialist history are "marginal and perhaps even eccentric to the central activities of the great" French-language comic strip artists and, by implication, to popular culture in France and Belgium. The refusal to confront the colonialist, imperialist and racist aspects of this work is primarily due to four factors: (1) the desire to defend national culture and identity in comics and graphic novels;[3] (2) the wish to protect the reputation of comics as a whole, a medium already considered by many to be a marginal or juvenile art form at best; (3) a felt or perceived need to construct childhood (when colonial comics were first read), or more generally the past, as a time of innocent, joyful pleasures, even if that past included violent, colonial aspects;[4] and (4) a strong desire by critics to defend the great artist, whose work they venerate. For a combination of these and other reasons, critics of French-language comics often ignore or downplay the verifiably colonialist and imperialist nature of significant portions of works now considered to be classics. In fact, there is no valid or convincing reason for setting aside or minimizing these historical and ideological aspects, because the latter remain an integral part of the work being analyzed. The art work bears potent markers of colonialism, racism and imperialism, which cling to it and are reactivated in various ways within a France that is still today strongly determined by empire, its aftermath and its current mutations.

There is a paradox in my choice of the quotation from the late Palestinian scholar, activist and cultural critic Edward Said as an epigraph to this chapter, because Said usually focused on the great works and canonical authors of European high literature, as opposed to popular culture, which is nonetheless a key area for disseminating and contesting imperialism (Norindr 1996: 18). Yet in his preface (2001) to a re-edition of Joe Sacco's graphic narrative *Palestine*, Said acknowledged the book's value because it is aimed at an adult audience and critiques imperialism. It is important for critics to carefully analyze and determine the value and meanings of comics marketed to adults and to children, including ones that critique imperialism and those that are colonialist, imperialist and racist. Comics are valuable cultural documents, partly because they provide clues to how society teaches its young about the world and about history (Ferro 1992). Moreover, by following certain motifs through time, we can measure to what degree this still chiefly popular art form has changed, and hence gather clues about the evolution of society as a whole. For this purpose at least, evidence from popular culture may be more useful than material gleaned from more highly regarded cultural and artistic forms or works (Schneider 1982), which may reach fewer people or be mainly consumed by adults, who have already formed a stable worldview, and not by children, who are still forming theirs. In fact, comics are widely read in France by both children and adults, and constitute a significant portion of the book market there. In addition, although comics are still sometimes unjustly viewed as having little aesthetic or cultural value, Said's preface to Sacco's volume and the growing acceptance of the term "graphic novel" [*roman graphique*] suggest that the status of comics is fast evolving, partly because significant numbers of cartoonists, some of whom have been formally trained as artists, are targeting and reaching an adult audience.

Transmission of memory through a tradition: colonial exhibitions and human zoos

In this chapter and in Chapter 4 I analyze how Alain Saint-Ogan closely adhered to the contours of French imperialist propaganda in two extended narrative sequences: one, *Zig et Puce aux Indes* [Guy and Flea in the Indies] (1995f), about the 1931 Exposition coloniale internationale, held in Paris; the other, *Zig, Puce et Furette* [Zig, Puce and Ferrety] (1996a), in which Zig and Puce retrace a version of the real-life Croisière noire road trip across the African continent in 1924–5. However, Saint-Ogan is not the only French cartoonist to have drawn and published comics about these two emblematic colonial events. At least 29 comic strips, books or series represent, or refer to, a (post-)colonial exhibition or human zoo (Appendix 2) (I count each series as one example here – e.g., once for all references in multiple volumes of Bécassine). One of the earliest stories, published circa 1867–8, is *Les mésaventures de M. Bêton* [The Misadventures of Mr. Ninny] by Léonce Petit. It represents savage and colonized others at a Parisian fairground sideshow, in an apparent precursor of human zoos such as those at the Jardin d'acclimatation in Paris beginning in 1877, when exotic animals were exhibited along with 14 Africans (Schneider 1982: 128).[5] A well-known early exhibition comic, the initial episode of Christophe's "Famille Fenouillard" [Fennely Family], was first serialized in *Le petit Français illustré* on the occasion of the 1889 Exposition universelle in Paris.[6] The tradition of comics depicting colonial exhibitions and human zoos was perpetuated after the original events were over, and was eventually renewed in at least three ways: (1) the continuing republication of colonial-era comics referring to exhibitions, which have remained in print virtually uninterrupted from their original publication to the present (the Bécassine series); (2) beginning in the 1980s, the republication of other colonial-era exhibition comics; and

(3), also from the 1980s, the creation and publication of new comics that allude to or represent colonial-era human zoos and colonial exhibitions, or otherwise rework the theme of exhibiting (formerly) colonized others. I analyze the renewal of this tradition in Chapter 3.

Of the 29 examples, 16 were originally published before formal decolonization began. Four of the 16 have been commercially republished once or more since 1962: "La famille Fenouillard à l'exposition"; three Bécassine volumes (counting as one example); *Zig et Puce aux Indes*; and *Le mariage de M. Lakonik* [The Marriage of Mr. Lakonik] (reissued by the CNBDI, now CIBDI). Two other comics have been reprinted in studies of colonial imagery: "Visite de la famille Cocardeau à l'Exposition universelle de 1867" and "Coco, Banania et les poissons volants (Conte de l'exposition coloniale)." The colonial-era exhibition comics vary greatly in length, from three frames to 61 pages. The amount of space dedicated to the exhibition also differs from one text to another: the 1931 Exposition coloniale is depicted in a single frame of *Bécassine aux bains de mer* [Bécassine at the Seaside] (Caumery and Pinchon 1982: 9; first ed. 1932),[7] first serialized in *La semaine de Suzette* (17 December 1931), whereas Louis Forton spent 20 pages on the same event in "Les Pieds-Nickelés" [The Slackers], serialized for ten weeks, at two pages per week, in *L'épatant* (30 July–8 October 1931). Finally, some of these works, especially the short strips (e.g., "A l'exposition" [At the Exposition]), are wholly about a colonial exhibition theme, whereas others integrate it into a larger story, or otherwise include it as one episode among several. These factors make comparisons tricky, although not impossible or unfruitful. Taken together, these comics and other related material demonstrate that colonial exhibitions were very strongly anchored in the popular and juvenile areas of French culture at the time. The repeated republication of some of the colonial strips and stories about colonial exhibitions – especially in Bécassine and Zig et Puce – has helped to maintain and renew public awareness of the events among readers of French comics, including children (who grow up and remember their childhood readings), cartoonists (who learn from the work of earlier artists) and comics collectors (who accumulate, circulate and discuss colonial-era publications). Contemporary cartoonists have also been inspired by the critical work on colonial exhibitions and human zoos by historians and cultural critics such as Sylviane Leprun, Catherine Hodeir, Michel Pierre, Pascal Blanchard, Nicolas

Bancel and Sandrine Lemaire. The last three, and their organization, the Association pour la Connaissance de l'Histoire de l'Afrique Contemporaine [Association for the Knowledge of the History of Contemporary Africa], have played a major role in disseminating information about these colonial events and their historical context to the French public over the last few decades.

This body of *bandes dessinées* raises many questions about the place of colonialism in French society today. For example, how did comics created during and about colonial exhibitions, and the cartoonists who created them, fit into colonial culture? Did these cartoonists have any other (artistic) connections to the colonies? How are colonial exhibitions and expeditions represented in French literature and popular culture today? By 1962 most of France's empire had gained independence, at least in name. What are the relationships between recent representations and those produced before 1962? What is the importance of the colonial past (and present) to the groups and individuals most closely associated with or affected by colonialism, especially ethnic minority groups and the descendants of colonial settlers, soldiers and adventurers? In this chapter and the two following I analyze the two episodes by Saint-Ogan and construct a genealogy of colonial exhibitions and trans-African automotive expeditions in French comics by comparing depictions of them in works by Saint-Ogan and his contemporaries with representations of these and similar events in comics published from 1962 to the present. I thereby demonstrate the continuities, but also the breaks and shifts, in colonial iconography within a popular medium.

Visits to colonial exhibitions by children, cartoonists and their characters

> Indeed, it is essential to emphasize the fact that the "supplying" of these "natives" [to official exhibitions and other colonial spectacles] closely followed the overseas conquests of the Republic, received the permission (and sometimes the assistance) of the colonial administration and contributed to the colonial enterprise of France. (Blanchard, Bancel and Lemaire 2002: 68)

Historians of French colonialism generally agree that the Paris Exposition coloniale internationale, held 6 May–15 November 1931 in the Bois de Vincennes, was a landmark attempt to build French popular support for colonialism. The Exposition welcomed eight million visitors (Hodeir and Pierre 1991: 101), and its organizers made a special effort to reach out to young people, to encourage them to support the colonial effort – as then Minister of Colonies Paul Reynaud explained in a letter to French youth printed in a special 32-page issue entitled *Aux colonies! Suivez le guide* [To the colonies! Follow the guide], which *Benjamin*, an illustrated children's magazine, published for the 1931 exhibition: "The colonies are not only made to enchant our dreams: it is possible to live a life there that is larger than in the old countries [i.e., Europe]. The Exposition coloniale will have reached its goal if, through it, many of its young visitors will feel the colonial vocation being born in them."[8] For example, during the summer of 1931, ten thousand children from primary schools attended the exhibition, whose organizers helped bring special caravans of schoolchildren on visits. The Exposition organizers coordinated with the national school system, which had made the study of the French empire obligatory in primary schools, beginning in 1923, and in secondary schools from 1925. Youth periodicals, including *Benjamin*, joined in the propaganda campaign.[9]

The Exposition was also visited by artists who played a key role in bringing French colonialism and imperialism to children – and in bringing children to this exhibition – through cartoons, comics and the children's magazines in which they were published. At least three cartoonists who produced exhibition comics also contributed extensively to colonial exhibitions in other ways: Joseph-Porphyre Pinchon, his friend Raymond de la Nézière and Saint-Ogan. This is significant because of the popularity and longevity of comics series by Pinchon and Saint-Ogan (especially Bécassine and Zig et Puce), the general prominence of French colonialism and imperialism (including via colonial exhibitions) in their comics, and the overlap between comics by all three and their other, official or commercial, contributions to colonial exhibitions. In the case of Pinchon and de la Nézière, direct work on colonial exhibitions was also a long-lasting family affair: for example, each had a brother who produced officially commissioned work for one or more colonial exhibitions. Pinchon, best-known today for his artwork on the Bécassine comics series, must have visited the 1931 Exposition, as well as earlier colonial exhibitions. He was paid for illustrations to an official guide for the 1931 Exposition,[10] and illustrated the special issue of *Benjamin* dedicated to the Exposition (*Aux colonies! Suivez le guide*), including its cover and centerfold. The latter is a map of the exhibition, entitled "La famille Amulette à l'Exposition" [The Amulette Family at the Exposition], that depicts several of the characters from a comics series, drawn by Pinchon, scripted by Jaboune (also known as Jean Nohain; born Jean-Marie Legrand) and serialized in *Benjamin*. The characters are training a panoptic gaze on the Exposition, consuming the imperial spectacle as a commodity, much as real-life visitors to the Exposition did at the panoramas and human exhibitions (Plate 9).[11] Jaboune was editor of *Benjamin* at the time of the Exposition, and Pinchon was its artistic director (Abelé 1988: 17; Germain 1992: 33–9). Pinchon trained professionally as a painter, and although he specialized in depicting French hunting scenes, his artistic formation and production included a colonial dimension from early on. He and Joseph de la Nézière, Raymond's brother, created an official poster for the 1906 colonial exhibition in Marseille.[12] Pinchon won prizes at various colonial exhibitions, including one that sent him abroad: "The happy candidate who won the competition for travel scholarships organized during the colonial exhibition in 1906 [in Marseilles], he is awarded the gold medal and a travel scholarship for the Indies"; "[i]n 1922, he receives the Grand Prize of the colonial exhibition in Marseilles, in 1931 the *hors-concours* diploma of the Exposition coloniale in Paris and, in 1937, the diploma of honor at the Exposition internationale in Paris" (Abelé 1988: 11, 17). Upon his return from the trip to India, he was for a time a costume designer and then the artistic director of the French national theater company at the Opéra in Paris (1908–14; *Dans l'ombre de Bécassine* [2007]). A "M. Pinchon," no doubt the visual artist Joseph-Porphyre (not his sculptor brother Emile), created dioramas for the Algerian exhibit at the Exposition nationale coloniale de Marseille, held 16 April–19 November 1922.[13] According to Roger Benjamin (2003: 105), "gigantic paintings [i.e., panoramas], along with dioramas and *tableaux vivants*, proved among the most popular attractions of the universal and colonial exhibitions" (cf. Leprun 1986: 48–59). Benjamin Findinier (2007: 57, note 16) describes another colonial competition in which Pinchon participated: "Finally, let us remember that Joseph-Porphyre Pinchon had himself won, in a field of 233 competitors, in 1928, the 5th prize in a competition of posters for the Exposition coloniale [of 1931] (*L'affiche*, IV, no. 43, juillet 1928, p. 105. *Renaissance*, no. 9, septembre 1928, p. 304)."

Pinchon's younger brother, Emile Léon Clément Pinchon (1872–1933), contributed dozens of large bas-reliefs (278.6 by 420 cm), made of a plaster mix, to the 1931 Exposition coloniale: "a cycle of more than forty tableaux, a monumental sculpture of grand dimensions integrated into an architectural work, covering a surface of close to 500 square meters" (Findinier 2007: 50–1).[14] They portrayed indigenous workers from various colonies, integrated into the French imperialist economy, for example "Vulcanisation of latex (rubber)," set in Indochina; "Colonial woods: moving of billets," set in black Africa; "Husking of rice in Indochina"; and "Phosphates of Morocco: Mining work."[15] These four bas-reliefs were donated to Noyon in 1937 by Emile's wife and now hang in its town hall,[16] but the full series was made for, and first displayed in, the Cité des informations (the main information center of the Exposition).[17] During the Exposition, the visually striking sculptures, hanging one after another with intercalated texts on the walls of the Cité des informations, somewhat like a *bande dessinée*,[18] were designed to play a role that overlapped with the one played by children's magazines such as *Benjamin*, and the comics and cartoons associated with them – a visual-textual pedagogy of empire:

> The entire set, "arrayed in a frieze in the manner of the metopes and triglyphs" – and which will receive the commentary of René Seguy, head of the administrative services of the Cité des informations, must be understood as an object lesson designed to educate the public and show the development of colonial riches to its advantage. (Findinier 2007: 51)

Findinier (2007: 57) views the parallel, commissioned work that the Pinchon brothers did as an artistic dialogue: "The Exposition of 1931 can therefore, in many ways, be viewed as an *encounter*, a true locus of exchange between the two brothers." There is in many ways a continuity between this official artistic production by the two brothers, and Joseph-Porphyre's work on children's cartoons and comics that represent French colonial culture, including colonial exhibitions and human zoos: for example, the association of the colonized with the natural world, including natural resources (indigenous characters labor to extract them for the French in the bas-reliefs of Emile) and wild, exotic animals (these too figure in his tableaux). Exhibition comics and cartoons – including ones for adult readers, such as those by Albert Dubout in a special issue of *Le rire*

(23 May 1931)[19] – made similar associations, but generally in the mode of the humorous colonial grotesque, and often via references to African cannibalism (the colonized as wild, savage others).

These overlaps and distinctions between different domains of colonialist art only begin to suggest how much artists, including cartoonists, were integrated into French colonial culture and its organized exhibitions. For example, the de la Nézière brothers both participated in the 1922 colonial exhibition in Marseilles:[20] Joseph was a Commissaire-adjoint for the Moroccan exhibition, and responsible for "all the decorative and artistic portions of the Moroccan Exposition." His individual artistic contribution included a 32-meter-long diorama, representing "a general view of Fez, taken from the height of the Casbah of the Merinidian sultans, in the setting sun" (Artaud 1923: 123). Raymond, his cartoonist brother, contributed a historical frieze highlighting France's imperialist incursions in Syria (Artaud 1923: 275). Many other French painters and artists produced commissioned art for the 1922 Exposition, or had their work exhibited there: for example, the president of the Société des artistes coloniaux [Society of colonial artists] was the artistic advisor for the Madagascan pavilion (Artaud 1923: 209); and André Joyeux produced friezes for the Indochinese pavilion, representing everyday life in the colony, and his painting *Danse du dragon* [Dance of the dragon] hung in the exhibition of the Société des Orientalistes français [Society of French Orientalists] (Artaud 1923: 181, 198, 356). Joyeux (1912) had drawn and published *La vie large aux colonies* [Living Large in the Colonies], a collection of caricatures, some racist, of social and ethnic types in French Indochina, especially Saïgon, where he worked as an art school director (republished in Vann and Montague 2008; cf. Vann 2009). Despite obvious differences in form, tone and audience, the painted friezes at the colonial exhibitions could be seen as functioning much like colonialist comics (by Pinchon and Raymond de la Nézière) and collections of caricatures (by Joyeux) published by the same artists: they were sequences of related images representing the colonized and their countries as exotic and subaltern, and highlighting French imperialist achievements in colonized spaces. Joseph de la Nézière again played a role in the 1931 Exposition coloniale in Paris, as described in its published report: "As for J. de la Nézière, to whom painting, colonial fine arts and the Exposition coloniale itself owe so many works in excellent taste, he celebrated the penetrating charm of Cambodia in two very pretty and fresh landscapes" (Olivier 1932–4, vol. V, part 1: 433). The two paintings mentioned here were exhibited at the Palais des Beaux-Arts in the Exposition. His other contributions to the Exposition included dioramas in the exhibition buildings for Cameroon and Togo: two scenes represented African ethnic groups, and three were of wild animals.[21]

Saint-Ogan also visited the 1931 Exposition: in the first of his two bio-bibliographical datebooks and photo albums, the artist logged at least ten visits.[22] He produced imperialist propaganda for colonial events, both under official commission from the French government (e.g., a "Voyage impérial" board game and a flyer glorifying Lyautey's accomplishments in Morocco, both for the Vichy government; Plates 7 and 8)) and in association with private enterprises (e.g., a "Concours colonial" [Colonial competition] for Ovomaltine).[23] Despite these interlocking connections, colonialist children's comics and cartoons represent today a relatively neglected dimension in the scholarly study of French imperialist culture.

Saint-Ogan mocks the anti-imperialists

Studies of the Exposition coloniale of 1931 have focused to a large extent on its architecture, the official publications and grand designs of its organizers, the protests against it by the Communists, the Surrealists and colonized activists, and the place of the exhibition in the collective memory of the French.[24] Close attention to the roles of comics and cartoonists can also make a contribution to our understanding of anti-imperialist critiques of the exhibition and reactions to criticism. For example, Saint-Ogan contributed drawings and perhaps text to a parody of *L'Humanité*, the newspaper of the French Communist Party (PCF).[25] The fake front cover of the daily was published in the satirical, anti-Communist and antisemitic *Le coup de patte* (no. 5, 13 June 1931, pp. 20–1), to which Saint-Ogan was a regular contributor, and which published paid advertising for the Exposition in several issues.[26] The parody lampoons Communist opposition to French imperialism and to the Exposition coloniale (Figure 3):

> L'impérialisme français, qui dispute l'os d'un secours à ses chômeurs affamés et diminue le salaire des mineurs et des "textiles," inaugure à coups de millions son Exposition coloniale. Pendant ce temps, il

séquestre notre camarade Dache, enlevé par sa police de bandits, et le cache chez les zouaves.

Il le jette en pâture aux assassins qui ont déjà décapité quatre révolutionnaires annamites coupables d'avoir tué 132 femmes du Prabang, une paille!

Des villages sont bombardés à coups de siphons [sic], pillés par la Légion [étrangère] à Co-Am, Hoc-Mon, Duc-Hoa et Honno, Ben-Luc, Ben-Mou-Yeu.

Travailleurs frères! Le *Secours Rouge* a déjà demandé de votre action bien des efforts, de votre bourse bien des gros sous!

[French imperialism, which wrangles with its famished unemployed over a shred of assistance and lowers the salaries of the miners and "textiles" (i.e., textile workers), throws money right and left to inaugurate its Exposition coloniale. Meanwhile, it sequesters our comrade Dache, kidnaped by its police of bandits, and hides him among the zouaves.[27]

It throws him to the assassins who have already decapitated four Annamite revolutionaries guilty of having killed 132 women in the Prabang, a mere detail!

Villages are bombarded by siphons, pillaged by the (Foreign) Legion in Co-Am, Hoc-Mon, Duc-Hoa and Honno, Ben-Luc, Ben-Mou-Yeu.

Brother workers! The *Red Assistance* has already asked you many times to lend a big hand, and to pull from your pockets many big bucks!]

This directly quotes and deforms text found in *Le véritable guide de l'Exposition coloniale*, a pamphlet produced for the counter-Exposition, which was an event created by the Communists and the Surrealists:

Les "prix-de-revient-fort-bas" (coolies payés à 50 sous par jour) se révoltant, *Homberg et Cie* font guillotiner, par leur bourreau *Pasquier*: 4 Annamites le 4 mai 1930, puis 13 le 17 mai, 5 autres le 20 novembre 1930 et 5 encore en février 1931.

…3.000 détenus, bientôt 600 déportés à *Cayenne*…

…Des villages bombardés par les avions, pillés par la Légion à *Co-Am, Hoc-Mon, Ben-Thuy, Duc-Hoa, Ben-Luc*, etc…[28]

[The "very-low-cost-price" (coolies paid 50 *sous* a day) are revolting, (so) *Homberg and Co* have their executioner *Pasquier* guillotine: 4 Annamites on 4 May 1930, then 13 on May 17, 5 others on 20 November 1930 and 5 more in February 1931.

…3,000 detained, soon 600 deported to *Cayenne*…

Figure 3   A published parody of the French Communist daily paper *L'Humanité* displays Alain Saint-Ogan's awareness of Communist criticism of the 1931 Exposition coloniale in Paris. From *Le coup de patte*, no. 5 (13 June 1931), pp. 20–1.

...Villages bombarded by airplanes, pillaged by the (Foreign) Legion in *Co-Am, Hoc-Mon, Ben-Thuy, Duc-Hoa, Ben-Luc*, etc...]

One of three illustrations in the parody, all unsigned but unmistakably by Saint-Ogan, depicts "Dache, le perruquier des Zouaves victime de l'impérialisme français" [Dache, the wigmaker of the Zouaves (and) victim of French imperialism]. This satirical document is proof that the cartoonist was aware, during the Exposition, of criticisms formulated by the PCF in *L'Humanité* and elsewhere against the event and against French imperialism. At the same time, Saint-Ogan was participating in the promotion of the official event and its ideology. He knew of the Vietnamese uprising against French rule and that it was brutally suppressed by air attacks ("Villages are bombarded by siphons") and, on the ground, by the French Foreign Legion ("pillaged by the (Foreign) Legion"): in fact, unarmed peasants were mown down by machine guns mounted on airplanes – at least 10,000 Vietnamese were killed by the French (Biondi and Morin 1993: 168–74). Saint-Ogan's contribution to this parody participates in a right-wing colonialist discourse in favor of the Exposition and its ideology, and resolutely against the radical critique.[29]

On the other hand, the French Communists and Surrealists apparently ignored the scandalous exploitation of Kanak during the Exposition (Dauphiné 1998: 112). It has also been argued that they were not very effective in reaching or convincing the French public about their ideas.[30] However, Saint-Ogan was certainly familiar with basic aspects of their critique. This document proves beyond doubt that his support of the Exposition and its ideology – in Zig et Puce, two competitions (in *Benjamin* and *Le petit journal*), and a live show by the Théâtre du Petit Monde based partly on his strip (see below) – cannot be convincingly defended as whimsical, light-hearted fun by a cartoonist who was apolitical, naïve or simply uninformed (this is what his editor, Dominique Petitfaux, tries to argue, in substance).[31] On the contrary, this document demonstrates that Saint-Ogan substantially knew what he was doing when he did it. My critique of colonialism in his comics, cartoons and other artistic activities cannot reasonably be dismissed as an anachronistic imposition of present-day norms on the past. On the contrary, Saint-Ogan, called the "founding father" of French-language comics, was well aware of the far-left critique of French imperialism that existed in his own time, and publicly ridiculed it.[32]

Harnessing the colonial carnivalesque:
comics as a tool of imperialist indoctrination

Saint-Ogan is exemplary in his support of French colonialism, but Petitfaux does not adequately address this fact in his comments in the republished Glénat edition of Zig et Puce. For whatever reason, the generally well-documented editor did not tell readers about the considerable place that colonial exhibitions and, more broadly, colonial imagery held in Saint-Ogan's work, just as he offered us a very incomplete picture of antisemitism in the cartoonist's production. My search of Saint-Ogan's scrapbooks, held by the CNBDI in Angoulême, produced a great quantity of such material. Saint-Ogan supplied the drawings, and perhaps the text, for a competition in *Le petit journal*, in which contestants guessed the names of 25 French colonies depicted in cartoons that served up a variety of colonial material, including caricatural and otherwise problematic ethnographical information about the colonized (e.g., colonial eroticism about Ouled Naïl women, in Algeria) and humor at their expense.[33] Competition entrants could win "one of 2,500 prizes of a total value of 300,000 francs." First prize was a fifteen-day vacation on the French Côte d'Azur for two. Several advertisements for the competition – including a large color handbill – feature the grotesque, tall African cannibal figure from the Zig et Puce episode set in the Exposition coloniale. Another advertisement shows an open-jawed crocodile set to bite the bottom of a naked black African boy or man. The same image appears in one of the drawings of the competition, depicting the French Sudan (cf. Nederveen Pieterse 1992: 43–4). This type of cruel humor is found in other colonial-era advertisements (Bachollet et al. 1994: 128). Yet other advertisements for the colonial contest depict a scene from Madagascar closely resembling an image in the Zig et Puce episode based on the Croisière noire (SOC 23: 245, 248–9). *Le petit journal* printed a letter of congratulations from Maréchal Lyautey on the contest, along with a photograph of him.[34]

This suggests that the colonial carnivalesque was not problematic for the organizers of the exhibition when it was yoked to a positive, didactic project about colonization, much like the Exposition episode in Zig et Puce (see below). In this way, the economic interests of the paper (selling copies) and the imperialist interests of the Exposition organizers were simultaneously served by Saint-Ogan's game.

Moreover, in *Benjamin*, a children's magazine that Saint-Ogan later directed (during the Vichy period), his characters Mitou, Toti and Serpentin (a boy, girl and dachshund) featured in an advertisement for a 1931 "Concours colonial" for Ovomaltine, a children's malt chocolate drink mix produced by a Swiss company.[35] An advertisement for the competition listed the cities around the world where Ovomaltine had factories and agencies. Children were to pick out the ones located in French colonies or protectorates, and list by order of preference the colonies that they wished to visit. Prizes included a phonograph, a typewriter, a crystal radio, Waterman pens, mechanical pencils and subscriptions to a "Mitou, Toti et Serpentin" publication. *Benjamin* (no. 81, 28 May 1931, p. 1) too published a letter of thanks from Maréchal Lyautey for its support of the Exposition, including the special issue dedicated to it.

In 1937, Saint-Ogan recycled parts of his *Petit journal* guessing game for the colonial section of the Exposition universelle in Paris: eight drawings each represent a colony to be identified, exactly as in 1931. The front cover of *Cadet-revue* (15 July 1937, no. 110), edited by Saint-Ogan, features a cartoon drawn by him. It has caricatures of various nationalities and ethnic groups (including a black man) dancing together at the traditional ball for the national holiday of 14 July, suggesting an international celebration of "la plus grande France," i.e., France and its colonies. As with magazines such as *Benjamin* in 1931, *Cadet-revue* in 1937 published other material related to the colonial exhibits, including an illustrated story and a strip ("A l'exposition" [At the Exposition], by Michel Lefebvre).[36] Saint-Ogan also belonged to an organizing committee for the 1937 exhibition.[37] His contribution to, and representations of, colonial exhibitions did not end there. For example, he published full-page color cartoons inspired by the 1931 Exposition and entitled "A la coloniale" [At the colonial (Exposition)] in the humor magazine *Le coup de patte*, described in ironic terms by one of Hergé's biographers as a "périodique de droite à l'antisémitisme bon teint" [a right-wing periodical with good-complexioned antisemitism] (Assouline 1998: 257).[38] In keeping with the populist, right-wing politics of the magazine, three drawings show scenes in which average, white French visitors to the exhibition are put at a disadvantage by VIPs: a wealthy bourgeois in a chauffeur-driven limousine and government ministers.[39] Another illustration shows two huge-lipped, unarmed black soldiers in uniform leaving the Exposition, above an ironic caption, "La farouche armée noire" [The fierce black army] (Plate 2). In fact, colonial soldiers assisted Saint-Ogan in a direct and tangible manner, in a show related to his comics that was performed at the Exposition coloniale.

Saint-Ogan's scrapbooks also include newspaper articles and illustrations (photos) – from *Comoedia*, *L'Echo d'Alger*, *Excelsior* and *L'Illustration* – describing theater productions by Le Théâtre du Petit Monde, directed by Pierre Humble. Child actors played the roles of Zig, Puce and Alfred, as well as Bicot and Suzy, two characters in the French version of the American comic strip "Winnie Winkle," by Martin M. Branner.[40] The comic-book stories were adapted for the stage by "Mlle Th. [Thérèse] Le Notre." The troupe traveled to Algeria and officially participated in celebrations of the Centenaire de l'Algérie française [Centennial of French Algeria] in 1930, with performances in the Algiers Opera, and in Oran and Philippeville.[41] The Algerian tour was sponsored by the Commissariat général des Fêtes du centenaire.[42] Madame Bordes, the wife of the gouverneur général d'Algérie, attended the performance of "Zig et Puce," and invited the child actors up to her theater box. Algiers schoolchildren, no doubt mostly French, were invited to a free matinee of "Zig et Puce."[43]

The following year, Humble's theater company again put on a show partly based on Saint-Ogan's characters and on Bécassine, this time at the Salle des fêtes de l'Exposition in the Cité des Informations of the Exposition coloniale in Paris. This production shows how much the comics by Saint-Ogan and other cartoonists were freely adapted to serve a major purpose of the Exposition – the colonial indoctrination of French children. Saint-Ogan's scrapbook includes a page from the official program of 5–12 June 1931: the 11 June playbill of the "Premier gala de l'enfance" [First children's gala], an extravaganza again orchestrated by Pierre Humble.[44] The first part of the program consisted of the projection of a "film documentaire et attractif" titled *La conquête de l'empire colonial français* [The conquest of the French colonial empire]. This was followed by "Le tour du Petit-Monde en Quatre-Vin...cennes" [The tour of the Little-World in Eighty Scenes/Four Vincennes] (cf. Hale 2008: 109), "a review in 2 acts and 10 tableaux by Mr. Valentin Tarault."[45] Characters included Saint-Ogan's Zig, Puce, Dolly and Alfred, as well as Bicot and Suzy.[46] The second act consisted of various "attractions for children," including songs interpreted by the six-year-old Gaby Triquet (billed as "the smallest Singer of the world") in the role of Bécassine, according to a review article published in *Benjamin*.[47] This section was followed by a ballet by skaters, and then a three-part "enchanting voyage across greater France," presented by the "Colonial Native Troops" ("Senegalese, Malagasy, Indochinese Colonial Contingents"): "In the Far East: the Mandarin, his Attendants, his Warriors, the animals. In Madagascar: the Great Island, the Queen Ranavalo, her Court, her Dancers. In black Africa: the Naba of the Mossi, his Retinue, his Griots, his Tam-Tam drums."[48] In this last part of the gala, the African colonial troops "from Sudan and Niger [are] dressed in costumes learnedly reproduced, Mr. P. Humble tells me, by Mrs. Marchand, the wife of Colonel Marchand."[49] Humble went on to pay homage to the military officers with whom he collaborated: "All of these colonial soldiers, he adds, are part of the troops of the Parc Saint-Maur, and their participation is made possible thanks to the obliging assistance of Commandant Décugis, Colonel Delayen, General Verdier, who kindly honored us with their benevolent aid." Scouts and spahis served as ushers at the event.[50] It was successful enough to be produced as a matinée on several Thursdays, at least through the end of September (the Exposition closed on 15 November 1931).[51] These performances of the Théâtre du Petit Monde in Algeria (1930) and Paris (1931) constitute a significant form of colonial propaganda aimed at children and derived from comics. Although the organizers of these colonial exhibitions considered this juvenile propaganda to be an important part of the events,[52] historians of the 1931 Exposition have mostly overlooked them and have concentrated on other important dimensions of the event instead.[53]

As part of its general propaganda campaign for the Exposition, the French state allocated eight million francs to retirement and pension funds of the press, to encourage its members to report on the Exposition and reward them for doing so.[54] Exposition organizers used additional sums to purchase targeted advertising. For example, 200,000 francs were used to pay for advertisements in publications such as *Le petit journal*,[55] where Saint-Ogan's colonial guessing game ran. Moreover, the Commissaire général of the Exposition signed a separate contract with a newspaper consortium that included the *Dimanche-illustré*, where Saint-Ogan serialized Zig et Puce and its Exposition episode. The contract, worth 400,000 francs, made clear that although the sum was nominally to pay for advertisements of specified length in the publications and for other forms of publicity (e.g., outside advertising on an "écran lumineux" [luminous screen] at 1 Boulevard Haussmann), the publications were also to include ongoing coverage of aspects of the Exposition in all categories:

> It is well understood that this classified advertising will have as its corollary the free insertion, in the newspapers and magazines listed above, of illustrated articles and of artistic, literary, tourist and economic news about the Exposition.
>
> To make your job easier, the General Commissariat will put at your disposal, on your request, all the necessary documentation.[56]

Saint-Ogan's Exposition coloniale episode in Zig et Puce may have been, therefore, a form of government-subsidized publicity designed to heighten the interest of young readers in the Exposition and encourage them to visit it. The popularity of Zig et Puce was then at its zenith, making it an ideal vehicle for imperialist propaganda.

The 1931 Exposition especially has come to occupy an important place in histories and critiques of French colonialism published by academics and scholars in France, the United States, the United Kingdom and elsewhere.[57] True, Charles-Robert Ageron, an eminent French historian of colonialism, argues – in a seminal essay on the Exposition published in Pierre Nora's anthology, *Les lieux de mémoire* – that its contribution to building support for colonialism within the French public has been exaggerated. Instead he situates the apogee of public support well after the Second World War. He argues that through "forgetting, ignorance, nostalgia, and even, among some, political astuteness or manipulation [l'habilité politicienne]," the Exposition had taken on a mythological status in the French collective memory of colonialism (Ageron 1984: 585, 589). There certainly is renewed French interest in the Exposition, which is all the more reason to study its past and present place in all aspects of French culture. For example, Didier Daeninckx, a prolific and acclaimed author of detective novels mixing leftist politics with fiction, has published three novels linking the colonial-era story of some Kanak exhibited in Europe during the Exposition with the situation in present-day France, including that of the independence movement in New Caledonia: *Cannibale* (1998), *Le retour d'Ataï* [The Return of Ataï] (2001) and, for children, *L'enfant du zoo* [The Child of the Zoo] (2004). A decade earlier, Erik Orsenna published a novel, *L'exposition coloniale*, titled after the 1931 event (1988: see esp. 333–58).[58] Recently, the French government transformed what was originally called the Musée permanent des colonies [Permanent Museum of the Colonies], built for the 1931 Exposition, into a national museum, the Cité nationale de l'histoire de l'immigration, which opened in 2007.[59] These are striking examples of the continuing importance of the Exposition and its remnants for post-colonial France. Clearly, the event constitutes a memorial site for the French, as do other such exhibitions and related events.

One aspect that has been mostly ignored by critics and historians of such exhibitions, with only a few exceptions,[60] is the extent to which they constitute a *lieu de mémoire* in French *popular* culture, perhaps especially comics and graphic novels. Within and around these graphic representations, one finds three tendencies: the colonial carnivalesque, the commemorative-nostalgic and the critical-historical. The colonial carnivalesque is found already in the first examples, from the nineteenth century, in my corpus of exhibition comics.[61] It is again prevalent in those published in 1931, and also constitutes an aspect of the events in and around the Exposition that – experts have argued – its organizers, led by Maréchal Lyautey, tried to downplay and domesticate when unavoidable, or preferably even eliminate and replace with what they conceived to be a pedagogical, authentic and scientific approach to colonialism.[62] The commemorative-nostalgic approach hews closest to the ideal of the organizers and is found primarily in more recent graphic narratives celebrating the history of the French empire (settlers, army, colonies). It differs from that past ideal insofar as the organizers of the Exposition saw French colonialism as a living, growing project (albeit an endangered one), whereas today's commemorative-nostalgic approach views it as something that was regrettably truncated, or at least as a relatively untroubling component of a lost time and of old artifacts that should be celebrated uncritically. The critical-historical approach toward colonial exhibitions and expeditions is relatively new and rare in French comics, but is shared by the militant novels of Daeninckx and some critical studies, including academic ones. It is both surprising and paradoxical that the three approaches are not necessarily or always mutually exclusive; instead, one or more can coexist, even in a single work, creating unresolved tensions and contradictions.

Early comics, by Saint-Ogan and other cartoonists, that depict colonial exhibitions mostly avoid critiquing the mistreatment of colonized workers at colonial exhibitions. This is mentioned only once, in *Bécassine chez les Turcs* [Bécassine among the Turks] (Caumery and Pinchon 1991), but the artists assign responsibility to an unscrupulous foreign impresario, a Turk named Ernest Pacha, instead of to French organizers, who would in fact be the responsible party in the final analysis.[63] Nor does one find in them a critique of either the fact that all of the colonial exhibitions masked brutal colonialist actions happening elsewhere (Morton 2000: 268–9), or the violent imperialist ideology that permeated the exhibitions themselves: "The violence is everywhere. As much in the look [le regard], the normal, the banal, the good-natured side of these exhibitions, as in the most visible *crimes*" (Bancel et al. 2002: 10, original emphasis; cf. Blanchard et al. 2008). It is therefore dismaying that the current publishers and editors of three of the early comic books analyzed here (*Zig et Puce aux Indes*, *Bécassine chez les Turcs* and *Le mariage de M. Lakonik*) chose to ignore almost completely the violent imperialist ideology of the colonial exhibitions depicted in them. Only in editorial comments by Petitfaux in the Glénat edition of the Zig et Puce series do we find a tepid discussion of the issue. Otherwise, all three implicitly or explicitly promote an uncritical, nostalgic attitude to their colonial stories, through elements as diverse as their old-time material presentation (e.g., cloth bindings on the spine, period-style calligraphy or special end-papers) and editorial comments.[64] One example of a more or less direct intervention by a publisher in the assessment of colonialist comics is a book co-published by Gautier-Languereau, also publisher of the Bécassine books, for the centenary of Bécassine: *Bécassine, une légende du siècle*. Its author, Bernard Lehembre, notes the relative silence in Bécassine about the 1931 Exposition coloniale (2005: 42). He draws the conclusion that Caumery, Pinchon and their series thereby avoided the pitfalls of colonial propaganda, racism and xenophobia, which were rife in other children's periodicals at the time (2005: 50). However, the situation is by no means so simple. Although only one frame relating to the 1931 Exposition was published within the Bécassine comic strip, this did not exhaust the contribution of the character and its creators to the Exposition, or their relationship to it. For example, colonial disguise and blackface surface later in the same story (*Bécassine aux bains de mer*), and may have been inspired by the Exposition (Caumery and Pinchon 1982: 45–7) – that was certainly the case for other comic strips (analyzed below), including one by Raymond de la Nézière, also published in

La semaine de Suzette. I have already shown that Bécassine was part of a colonialist theatrical event for children at the Exposition, which could not have occurred without the agreement of the authors of the strip, one of whom was also its publisher (Caumery, i.e., Maurice Languereau). We have seen that Pinchon personally contributed artwork to this and preceding French colonial exhibitions, and to the colonial propaganda of *Benjamin*, including its special issue for the Exposition. I also analyze below a comic book drawn by Pinchon and first serialized in *Benjamin*, which depicts a human zoo of Africans, much like that found during the 1931 Exposition, as well as on many other occasions.

The two other volumes cited by Lehembre, *Bécassine, son oncle et leurs amis* [Bécassine, her uncle and their friends] and *Les mésaventures de Bécassine* [The Misadventures of Bécassine], raise the issue of internal colonialism at exhibitions, because the former represents Bécassine, her family and friends visiting the 1925 Exposition des arts décoratifs, including the Breton pavilion, whereas the latter shows Bécassine joining a Breton dance troupe at the 1937 Exposition universelle. The two stories represent for us, in a humorous mode, a kind of folkoric, regionalistic integration of Bretons into French national culture, a form of internal colonization (cf. Forsdick 2005a). As Herman Lebovics (1992) shows, this was a strong current within France during this period, which flowed into the traditionalist cultural activism of the Vichy government. It is therefore logical that the larger French empire is not the main focus of these volumes, although it is not completely absent from either. In *Bécassine, son oncle et leurs amis* (Caumery and Pinchon 1926), it appears in the form of advertisements for cocoa and for laundry soap, featuring a black woman (15), in the "architecture exotique des pavillons étrangers et coloniaux" [exotic architecture of the foreign and colonial pavilions] (17), and in a "restaurant hindou" (52–6). In *Les mésaventures de Bécassine* (1986; first ed. 1939), the artists depict representative members of the colonized in Paris for the 1937 exhibition (14, 16). However, one of the most openly hostile representations of the colonized in the Bécassine series occurs later in the volume, in an episode set at a French seaside resort (26–36). There, an Arab, pejoratively nicknamed "Sidi," is a menacing, parasitic figure who is ultimately arrested and expelled. This racist image of Arabs was circulated widely in the French press at the time (Schor 1985: 165–8), and is still with us, both in the republished Bécassine volume and in other, similar media representations produced today.[65]

The analyses of Marie-Anne Couderc (2000, 2005), Alain Tirefort (2001–2) and Alexandra de Lassus (2006) have helped demonstrate the degree to which both the Bécassine series and more generally *La semaine de Suzette*, the periodical where it was published, propagated colonialist and racist notions of white superiority over the colonized, and of the domination of the ethnic majority bourgeoisie over other ethnic groups and social classes in France. The comic strip does so in various complex ways that are mediated via images of the internally colonized Bretons, represented by Bécassine and other characters (cf. Forsdick 2005a). For example, a racialized hierarchy of ethnicity and class is often represented in Bécassine by the relative (lack of) mastery of the French language that the characters from ethnic or racialized groups possess (Couderc 2000: 234). So although the Bécassine series does not include lengthy representations of colonial exhibitions, it certainly does participate in the racist and colonialist ideology of its time. I turn now to a *bande dessinée* by Saint-Ogan that provides an extended representation of the 1931 Exposition and is clearly an expression of colonial racism.

African cannibals at the 1931 Exposition

To a degree, Saint-Ogan's representation of the 1931 Exposition is an example of the colonial carnivalesque and is rooted in the tradition of popular colonial sideshows at fairs and exhibitions (e.g., Schneider 1982; Ageron 1984: 562–4; Morton 2000: 71; cf. Zemon Davis 1975). In *Dimanche-illustré*, where Zig et Puce was serialized, Saint-Ogan helped stir up interest in the Exposition coloniale: he sent his characters to visit it in issues of the periodical published between 29 March 1931 and 20 March 1932. He introduces the theme of the colonial exhibition into *Zig et Puce aux Indes* when his protagonists are trying to escape from a raging Indian elephant.[66] The animal uses its trunk to pick up Zig and hurl him forward across the border into the French territory of Mahé, where he lands in a large jar that a French settler and an Indian workman are preparing to send to the Exposition in Paris. Having been knocked unconscious, Zig is shipped off to France inside the vase, which is eventually delivered to the exhibition grounds at the Bois de Vincennes (Saint-Ogan 1995f:

15–18). At this point, a map reinforces the colony–*métropole*[67] relationship by showing the path that a telegraph sent by Puce takes from Mahé to Paris (19). However, the Indian jar with Zig inside it is not left at the pavilion of the French Indies as it should have been, but rather in an African exhibition space, probably the one for French West Africa, where it is discovered by two black characters.

Historians of French colonial exhibitions have documented and analyzed the French colonial practice of importing members of many different ethnic groups to serve as spectacular live entertainment (Blanchard et al. 1995; Bancel et al. 2002; Blanchard et al. 2008). Comics such as the Tintin and Zig et Puce series did (and do) precisely that: they brought (and bring) exotic, colonized others into the homes of French (Belgian, American...) children – the comic-book collection assembles and displays an array of exoticized ethnic others. Saint-Ogan's two African characters are supposedly primitive counterparts of Zig and Puce: one is short and fat (like Puce), the other tall and slender (like Zig), and the two, although adults, constantly get into trouble, as do the French boys – exemplifying the racist vision of black Africans as "big children" (cf. Dewitte 1995). For a while, the African characters more or less embody the narrative principle of the strip, through their childish projects that repeatedly, but temporarily, disrupt adult European norms. Generally speaking, the strip's playful elements are designed to give it a certain humor and charm, and – along with the picaresque element – propel it forward. However, the implicit equivalence between the two duos is restricted by their governing logics: the reputedly extra-European logic of cannibalism propels the African characters, whereas the initiatives of the French boys are determined by supposedly European logics of capital accumulation (i.e., getting rich) and technological invention.[68] The difference between the two pairs is emphasized by Saint-Ogan's assimilationist narrative about the need to civilize the cannibals. Under French influence, the two Africans have stopped eating human flesh, though they regret that the cafeteria only serves beef and lamb ("Li Fançais gentils, mais défendu manger homme" [Tha Fench nice, but forbidden eat man]). However, even though they joke that it would be nice to eat a human thigh ("[Y]'a bon manger bonne cuisse" [(I)t good eat good thigh]), they remind themselves that they are now civilized, and so must abandon anthropophagy and work for the French: "Non... Non... Nous civilisés... Moi, aller maintenant travailler devant public…" [No… No… We civilized… Me, going now working in front of public] (Saint-Ogan 1995f: 18). However, when the African counterpart of Zig discovers the French boy trying to escape from the jar in the crate, his suppressed cannibal nature reasserts itself, and he shuts Zig back up until he and his friend can cook and eat the boy.

A series of events follows that largely derives its humor from a contrast between African savagery and French civilization (Plate 10). Specific elements reveal a huge gap between these poles, the unfinished state of the civilizing mission, and the necessity of further French colonial activity. The huge mouths and prominent teeth of the Africans emphasize their cannibal nature, whereas their names refer to food products and to their black skin (Kacoco and Radadou; later Cacao and Cocoa). Like most African characters in the strip, they speak pidgin French. Similarly their attempts to pass in French society by putting on European clothes are a source of grotesque humor, because they do not wear shoes (cf. Pierre 1988; Hodeir and Pierre 1991: 94; Met 1996; Berliner 2002: 143–5, 152–5). At the end of the episode, the Africans' cannibalistic desires betray them when they leave the Exposition and ask a local café owner to cook Zig for them. Zig is then released and the Africans imprisoned. The story provides a typically colonialist moral when the American friend and benefactor of Zig and Puce agrees to hire the Africans as domestic servants and save them from being sent back to the colonial exhibition, as long as they suppress their natural penchant for eating human flesh: "Ecoutez, vous m'avez l'air d'être repentants… Je veux bien vous prendre comme domestiques, mais à la première velléité de cannibalisme, je vous donne vos huit jours" [Listen, you seem to me to be repentant… I'm willing to take you in as domestic servants, but at the first sign of cannibalism, I'll give you your week's notice] (29). The two characters immediately don servants' uniforms, still minus the shoes, and proclaim their delight at serving the white boys, exactly illustrating a basic tenet of European colonialism, that darker-skinned, primitive peoples should serve lighter-toned, civilized ones. As is typical with the colonial carnivalesque, here the disruption of European order by the African characters at the Exposition is short-lived, and ultimately serves to reinforce the rigid colonialist system.

In a subsequent volume in the Zig et Puce series, Petitfaux describes the transformation from disruptive, cannibalistic otherness to subservience within the French colonial order (Saint-Ogan 1996a: 47; my emphasis):

> Cacao and Cocoa ([first appeared on] 12 July 1931): they always stick together and count as a single character... These two Blacks, first named Kacoco and Radadou (in the plates of *Dimanche-illustré*), came to Paris for the Exposition coloniale of 1931, and were still cannibals little before then. After a few lingering urges to return to that state, they will mend their ways and end up becoming *very stylish* domestic servants [des domestiques très stylés] for the New York apartment (164 5th Avenue) of Dolly's uncle.

This uncritical synopsis sidesteps the colonialist nature of Saint-Ogan's representation of Africans at the Exposition coloniale. Instead, it draws our attention to the comic's artistic style, specifically the black-and-white pattern of their servant uniforms. Yet Petitfaux neglects to add that this provides a visual contrast to the caricature of African bodies (exaggeratedly large white eyes and teeth, huge lips, very dark skin). An analysis of colonial exhibitions across Western Europe by Jan Nederveen Pieterse (1992: 95) helps make clear what is at stake in the transformation of Cocoa and Cacao: "The peoples on display were the trophies of victory. After the battle was done with, the image of the native warrior, prior to that so threatening and repulsive that it had to be exorcized by means of horror stories and gruesome caricatures, became decorative." Still, despite the domestication and visual transformation of the Africans, when Cocoa and Cacao make a brief appearance at a point much later in the series, we find the titillating suggestion that their savage nature may still be lurking underneath the thin veneer of civilization that they have acquired: one character says "Ce sont Cocoa et Cacao, les anciens anthropophages!" [It's Cocoa and Cacao, the former cannibals!], to which another replies "Hum!... On dit qu'ils le sont encore..." [Hum!... Some say that they still are...] (Saint-Ogan 1999c: 3). In a later volume, Cacao and Cocoa are once again the butt of a cannibal joke.[69] The Exposition coloniale episode is exceptional in Saint-Ogan's series insofar as it is a lengthy representation of colonial difference within metropolitan France itself. Similarly, in order to impress the reality and necessity of empire on the French public, colonial ideologues and statesmen brought in workers from many French colonies to act as a living part of the exhibition, which was a propagandistic spectacle within the imperial capital itself (see, for example, Blanchard et al. 1995; Norindr 1996; Bancel et al. 2002; Berliner 2002: 107–22; Blanchard et al. 2008).

The cartoonist's representation of African workers as cannibals at the Exposition coloniale was part of a popular colonial discourse that was somewhat discouraged by the official organizers of the event, but probably helped to account for the event's enormous popularity among the general public (Hodeir and Pierre 1991: 17; Morton 2000: 3–5, 197–200). For example, "Promenade à travers les cinq continents," an article by Paul-Emile Cadilhac (1931) about a day that he spent at the Exposition, appeared in *L'Exposition coloniale,* a special issue of *L'Illustration.* His grotesque descriptions – of the teeth of an African child, which he compared to those of a young dog, and of African waiters – prefigure his titillating suggestion that cannibals may be lurking somewhere in the West African section of the Exposition, at their own restaurant.

Although Lyautey may have wanted to steer the 1931 Exposition away from the most lurid tendencies of previous colonial exhibitions, they reappear in the official "Bulletin d'informations," published by the Service de la presse of the Commissariat général of the Exposition, in an article entitled "Cannibales authentiques" (issue no. 6, October 1930, pp. 6–7).[70] The anonymous author steers an ambiguous course, until the conclusion, between slyly suggesting that the Pahouins at the Exposition are as authentic as they could be at this point in time, and therefore, by implication, may still be cannibalistic (as the article's title suggests), and, on the other hand, assuring readers that they will not be eaten by the Pahouins at their reconstituted village in Paris. There is a striking echo between these two passages, of journalistic prose (in *L'Illustration*) and of official propaganda (in the *Bulletin*), and the first appearance of Saint-Ogan's cannibal figures: remember that in the comic book they have just left the cafeteria at the Exposition and are regretfully discussing how they may no longer eat human flesh. The passage in the *Bulletin* also prefigures the way in which Petitfaux glosses over Saint-Ogan's representation of cannibalism and praises the transformation of his African characters into the servile creatures of the French boy heroes: the Pahouins at the Exposition may be authentic, but they are very "stylés" and therefore no longer dangerous.

However, Africans were not the only colonized workers in Paris being represented as cannibals during the Exposition coloniale. Kanak, from France's colony of New Caledonia, had also been recruited to work at the Exposition, but then most were sent to the Jardin zoologique d'acclimatation, in the Bois de Boulogne in Paris, where they were put on display as cannibals. From there, some were later sent on to Germany for the same purpose. Certain French individuals who had spent time in New Caledonia were scandalized by the exhibit and protested against it, until the Ministry of Colonies intervened and finally sent them back home, but only just before the Exposition coloniale closed (Hodeir and Pierre 1991: 98–100; Dauphiné 1995, 1998; Daeninckx 1998, 2001; Hodeir 2001; Dauphiné and Bullard 2002).

Hybridity and colonial stereotypes

Bringing colonial and exotic others into the French *métropole* often inspired French cartoonists to depict the French in disguise as their "others" and vice versa, as Saint-Ogan's two duos begin to suggest. One finds a striking example of this role reversal in Petit's *Les mésaventures de M. Bêton* (serialized in 1867–8 and then published in album form, circa 1868). The work features a strong dose of the colonial carnivalesque, integrated with the town–country encounter analyzed by David Kunzle (1990a: 147–74). The Grand Théâtre des Merveilles de la Nature [Grand Theater of the Marvels of Nature], a carnival sideshow at the fête de Montrouge, features (among other characters) two provincial French characters disguised as savages and a male French train conductor as a bearded lady (Figure 4). Including a Turco[71] in the audience permits the unleashing of the colonial carnivalesque as a violent, but temporary, overturning of the bourgeois order: badly startled when the title character is thrown off stage and onto him, the Turco runs amok, causing a riot, killing Parisians and stampeding horses, which pull their carriages and passengers into the Seine at the Pont Royal. The identity-transforming dress of the characters – the provincial French M. Bêton as a savage and the Algerian as a French colonial solder – and the strange but symbolic head/body amalgamation (apparently unnoticed, M. Bêton remains astride the Turco's shoulders throughout his mad rush) help make visible the colonial dichotomy of savage and civilized, overlaying the provincial/Parisian distinction, and their carnivalesque collision and disruption. Here the colonial carnivalesque appears in, and then moves out of, the popular, theatrical space of the fairground

Figure 4   M. Bêton [Mr. Ninny] and *la bien aimée* [the Beloved], two French
provincials from Normandy, perform as savages for a Parisian audience at the
Grand Théâtre des Merveilles de la Nature [Grand Theater of the Marvels of
Nature]. From Léonce Petit (ca. 1868) *Les mésaventures de M. Bêton* (Paris?:
Librairie internationale?), p. 30.

sideshow, temporarily rearranging identities and leaving a swathe of
destruction across the urban landscape.[72] Nonetheless, the general
tone of the comic strip (in this episode and throughout), as fashioned
by the textual and visual narration, is humorous farce.[73]

Sylviane Leprun (1986: esp. 85–94, 154–6, 228–9) has suggested
that, in nineteenth-century France, the rationalized, scientific
order of official colonial exhibitions gradually replaced anarchic,
popular, fairground representations of the colonized, the bizarre
and the monstrous, and that the two incarnated different versions
of modernity.[74] The show in Petit's Grand Théâtre des Merveilles
de la Nature is clearly an example of the earlier, fairground variety,
but another, contemporary comic strip suggests that *bande dessinée*
maintained the popular, more disorderly strain, even when it began
to represent officially organized exhibitions. The encounter with
cultural others as an exotic, disturbing but humorous spectacle
also predominates in "Visite de la famille Cocardeau à l'Exposition
Universelle de 1867," an *image d'Epinal* (one of the ancestors of the
modern comic strip) published by the Pellerin company in Epinal,
in the Vosges region of eastern France. The comics broadsheet,
displayed in Paris at the French National Archives in a 2010
exhibition on "Exotiques expositions" in France and reproduced
in the exhibition catalog (Demeulenaere-Douyère 2010b: 116), is

the earliest example I have seen of a French comic strip set in a formal exhibition: this version, numbered 200, was published for the 1867 exhibition, as its title suggests.[75] A later version, numbered 484, is identical except for its title, from which the date ("de 1867") has been removed, suggesting that it was reissued for one or more subsequent universal exhibitions (e.g., the Parisian ones in 1878, 1889 and/or 1900).[76] In it, an average French bourgeois family visits the exhibition, where they first gaze at modern manufactured goods. Mr. Cocardeau then has a run-in with a "chaise roulante" [rickshaw]. It is at about this point that the strip shifts from a predominant fascination with modern manufactured goods from Europe to focus on the exotic and foreign, a binary focus and historical development typical of universal and colonial exhibitions.[77] After visiting the palace of the Bey of Tunis, Mr. Cocardeau tries to ask an interpreter where the toilets are, but the man speaks only Conchinchinois and slang ("argot"). Not visibly typed as Asian, he may be of French lower-class or criminal background, perhaps suggesting an unsavory origin for French colonials in Indochina. Subsequently, while sitting down for a moment to rest, the family "voit défiler devant elle des Allemands, des Russes, des Espagnols, des Persans, des Chinois, des Indiens, des Mexicains, des Arabes, etc... Venus comme eux pour visiter l'exposition universelle" [sees parading before them, Germans, Russians, Spaniards, Persians, Chinese, Indians, Mexicans, Arabs, etc... Having come, like them, to visit the Universal Exhibition] (Plate 11). Before leaving the exhibition and being robbed by a homegrown pick-pocket on the way out, the family dines on strange food at a Chinese restaurant: "une côtelette de chien à la purée de chenilles... un aileron de vautour piqué de gomme élastique" [a rib of dog in caterpillar sauce... a wing of vulture studded with elastic gum]. Clearly, the virtual consumption of exotic foreigners and the physical consumption of their goods (at the restaurant) played a central part in the exhibition experience, which was sometimes tactile, gustatory or olfactory, but especially visual,[78] at least in the medium of comics. As with Petit's contemporary *Les mésaventures de M. Bêton*, there is reference to French colonialism. Exoticism is not limited to the colonial, insofar as the display of foreigners here puts all of them on more or less the same footing: as visitors to the exhibition they are said to be like the Cocardeau ("Venus *comme eux*"), although the latter nonetheless remain seated, as privileged French voyeurs; and the foreigners in exotic national dress are all presented on an equal footing. Nonetheless, there is a movement from Europeans to more exotic foreign others in the enumeration. Moreover, the reconstructed palace of the Bey of Tunis, a hit at the 1867 exhibition, preceded the 1881 establishment of a French protectorate over Tunisia (Çelik 1992: 61–3, 122–3; Demeulenaere-Douyère 2010b: 126–7; Weiland 2010). Dalenda Larguèche (2004) argues that the exotic representation of Tunisia at the exhibition helped prepare for French colonial domination of the country. The reference in the *image d'Epinal* to a "chaise roulante" may be rooted in growing French influence in Southeast Asia even though the employee pulling it, shown from behind, is not visibly foreign or exotic.

A version of this *image d'Epinal* may have helped inspire "La famille Fenouillard à l'Exposition" (serialized in 1889),[79] by the famous French cartoonist and Sorbonne professor Christophe (Georges Colomb, 1856–1945). He created his strip on the occasion of the universal exhibition for which the Eiffel tower was erected, and made fun of popular interest in the mechanical structure. Here we again find a key feature of the colonial carnivalesque – the temporary transformation of French and colonized identities: Christophe has his petit bourgeois French everyman[80] buy a fez and North African slippers ("babouches") at the Exposition universelle, to replace his top hat and shoes, which he had lost. Immediately, three "sectateurs de Mahomet" [members of Mahomet's sect] take M. Fenouillard to be the "Commandeur des Croyants voyageant incognito" [Commander of the Believers traveling incognito] and bow, which seems pleasing to him (Christophe 1981: 40). Part of the thrill of a trip to the Exposition is apparently the opportunity to try on the identities of one's colonized or otherwise exotic (and credulous) "others." The exercise in self-transformation here confers authority over one's cultural "others."

We find representations of colonial mimicry and masquerade in at least eight other comic strips or books, published in 1931 and at least partially set at the Exposition coloniale, or otherwise related to it or to surrounding events. These fall into two basic categories: the colonized imitating the colonizers, or the colonizers imitating the colonized, although there is often a mix of the two, at least implicitly. The first, published in *La jeunesse illustré*, an eight-page children's weekly composed mostly (6 pp.) of comics, satirizes the common colonial tale of the European become king of a primitive people, found in Christophe's *La famille Fenouillard* (2004 [1893]) and in *En route pour l'Amérique*, the first volume of Zig et Puce (Saint-Ogan 1995a [1927]). In "Marius Galéjade à l'Exposition coloniale" [Marius Galéjade at the Exposition coloniale] (10 May 1931), by S. Pania (Paul d'Espagnat), the name of the title character is symbolic: "Marius" indicates a provenance from southern France and "galéjade" is a Provençal term for a tall tale. The story plays on stereotypes about both the colonized and a regional metropolitan group, the southern French. Marius Galéjade, from Tarascon,[81] arrives in Paris to visit the Durand family, who wish to take Marius to the Exposition coloniale, where "l'explorateur fameux, l'inlassable voyageur" [the famous explorer, the untiring traveler] will tell his Parisian friends all about the colonies. In order to avoid having to confess that his previous bragging about having traveled widely was a fiction, Marius invents another tall tale, about having been to the "Essposition" coloniale the previous day: there, he claims, "une peuplade noire du Centre africain" [a small tribe of blacks from Central Africa], over whom he had once ruled (one of his previous lies), had recognized him – they were there to participate in the Exposition (Plate 12). The Provençal narrator then weaves together a madcap, improbable series of events that involves him being held captive first by the African tribe at the Exposition and then by a Muslim in a mosque there. Returning to the Exposition, Marius claims, would put him at the mercy of his African ex-subjects, irate because he had twice abandoned them: once in central Africa and then at the Exposition. Durand insists nonetheless that Galéjade accompany him, albeit incognito, wearing a false beard previously purchased for Carnaval. However, when the beard accidentally catches fire, Marius's cover is blown: he is obliged by his friend to speak to the Africans at the Exposition, but his "charabia" [mumbo-jumbo] is met by an African's uncomprehending response, providing the punchline to the comic's running joke: "Missié, nous parler français, nous pas comprendre petit nègre!" [Mista, we speaking French, we not understanding little negro!] The carnivalesque transformation of roles extends to Galéjade's very speech, which he has intentionally "negrified" to fool Durand, but which his African interlocutor designates with the colonialist French term used to stereotype attempts by Africans to speak in French.[82] Here again, colonial carnivalesque and disguise (Marius as a sovereign; the Africans as half-acculturated to French norms) destabilize identities only partially and temporarily, and ultimately reinforce the central, standard colonial and national identities. The normative French identity of the Parisian everyman (Durand) is a stable pole against which others are defined as grotesquely different: both Marius Galéjade the Provençal and the half-assimilated black Africans at the Exposition. There is here a grotesque implied niggering of a southern French regional identity,[83] put in parallel with the ridiculous half-assimilation of Africans to the French, figured through linguistic and physical caricature.

The association of the Exposition with masquerading as exotic others even appears in a comic strip whose protagonists are talking animals: "A l'Exposition coloniale: Jeannot-Lapin-dromadaire entre sans payer..." [At the Exposition coloniale: Johnny-Rabbit-dromedary enters without paying...], drawn by Jacques Touchet and published in *Benjamin* (21 May 1931). A human guardian at the entrance to the Exposition prevents Jeannot Lapin and a canine friend from entering, but lets a camel through, because the latter is an *exposant* [participant]. The rabbit then curls up and rides on the back of the dog, disguising them together as a young camel and allowing them to enter, free of charge (Figure 5). Here transforming onself into an exotic other is transferred to the animal realm: mundane "French" animals masquerade as an exotic species from North Africa, allowing them to outwit an authority figure.

The third story, which shares traits with the exhibition episode in *Zig et Puce*, is entitled "Coco, Banania et les poissons volants

Figure 5 Jeannot Lapin and his dog friend, disguised together as a young camel, view the Angkor Wat reconstruction at the 1931 Exposition coloniale in Paris. From Jacques Touchet, "A l'Exposition coloniale: Jeannot-Lapin-dromadaire entre sans payer...," *Benjamin*, no. 80 (21 May 1931), p. 1, frame 9.

Figure 6   Having been carried there by flying fish, black children Coco and Banania arrive at the 1931 Exposition coloniale in Paris to rejoin their parents, who apparently work there. From Henry Caouissin, "Coco, Banania et les poissons volants (Conte de l'exposition coloniale)" [Coco, Banania and the flying fish (Tale of the Exposition coloniale)] *Coeurs vaillants* (31 May 1931), p. 8, frame 8.

(Conte de l'exposition coloniale)" [Coco, Banania and the flying fish (a tale of the Exposition coloniale)] by Henry Caouissin,[84] a cartoonist remembered for his Breton activism and for his implication in collaborationist activities during the Nazi Occupation (Crépin 2001: 111) (Figure 6). The strip was republished in a critical study of colonial iconography (Hodeir, Pierre and Leprun 1993: 137), but originally appeared in the Catholic children's magazine *Coeurs vaillants* (31 May 1931). Like Saint-Ogan's narrative, it shows adult blacks working at the 1931 Exposition coloniale.[85] Its main focus is on their children, who had been left behind in a tropical French colony (perhaps in West Africa or the Antilles), and miss their parents so much that flying fish appear and magically carry them to Paris. Like Cocoa and Cacao in Saint-Ogan's comic, the children speak pidgin French, and their names are derived from terms for food – Coco and Banania – thereby illustrating the economic value of the colonies to France.[86] Their father, with whom they are reunited in an exhibit of thatched huts at the Exposition coloniale, wears a top hat that underlines the incongruity between colonized and colonizer, much as Saint-Ogan's Cocoa and Cacao remain barefoot even when they put on European clothes, and Congolese people wear Western clothes inappropriately in Hergé's *Tintin au Congo*.[87] This comic strip cliché was enacted by colonial performers in their real-life acts at the Exposition. Colonized participants were recruited from among the Western-educated, but when they wore European clothes at the

Exposition they did so in a manner designed to emphasize their non-Western nature: "The organizers went to lengths to prevent assimilated natives from appearing in Western dress, except in carefully controlled circumstances: in those few cases, the point of the display was the inappropriateness of natives in such clothes, 'en travesti'…" (Morton 2000: 112–13; cf. Hodeir and Pierre 1991: 93–5).

My next several examples all involve French characters whom cartoonists depict dressing up as the colonized and darkening their light-colored skin. Taken together, they suggest the extent to which a visit to the 1931 Exposition coloniale stimulated French spectators to imagine themselves not only as colonial explorers for a day, say through the actual purchase and wearing of pith helmets at the Exposition,[88] but also as the colonized. Unsurprisingly, in these representations, masquerading as the colonized does not reveal or critique the violence that colonialism wreaks on the colonized. Instead, it is a temporarily amusing, remunerative or empowering experience, followed by boundary re-establishment. In several pages of "Koko, grand Chef des Becs Rouges," which ran weekly in *Le petit journal illustré*, cartoonist Georges Simon Dharm drew a visit to the Exposition and its consequences for Koko.[89] He is a French orphan boy in the care of his uncle, the fez-wearing Captain Plouf, a retired *zouave* (a French soldier in a colonial unit) living in the countryside near Pontoise, northwest of Paris. The trip to the Exposition itself is perfunctory (a single frame), but its consequences go on for the following five nine-frame pages of the story (31 August–27 September 1931). After Captain Plouf takes his nephew and his servant Cadie (a witless maid much like Bécassine) to the Exposition, the boy and the servant can only dream of "traversées [crossings], voyages, explorations, etc." According to the verbal narrator, "Koko ne vit plus qu'avec un casque colonial ou des plumes rouges sur la tête. Il est tantôt un hardi explorateur, tantôt un grand chef indien, tantôt un roi cambodgien." [Koko now only lives with a colonial hat or red feathers on his head. He is sometimes a brave explorer, sometimes a great Indian chief, sometimes a Cambodian king.] However, the visual narration only shows us Koko wearing a pith helmet, never red feathers. At first Koko has Cadie cart him around in a wheelbarrow, pretending it is a "pousse-pousse" [rickshaw], an anachronistic element in a strip inspired by the 1931 Exposition.[90] However, he soon decides to recruit his village friends to play the role of "sujets nègres qui chanteront sa puissance" [Negro subjects who will sing praises to his power]. He uses shoe-black to get the job done, and is soon sitting on his throne, as a white king surrounded by several French boys dressed up as his "Senegalese and Dahomean subjects," drumming and dancing the belly dance and the "kiri-kiri," as though they were "au fin fond des forêts tropicales" [deep in the heart of tropical forests]. However, the mothers of the boys in blackface soon show up to spoil the show, distributing reprimands right and left, and spanking Koko for having organized it all. In Dharm's story, the Exposition triggers the white colonial fantasy of becoming king of the blacks, found in many comics analyzed here. Although other colonized groups are briefly mentioned, it is black African alterity, represented through blackface minstrelsy and masquerade, that predominates as a seductive but dangerous figure of racial difference and possible colonial domination.

We find a very similar Exposition story in "Un palais nègre" [A negro palace], by Raymond de la Nézière, published on 24 September 1931 on the front cover (6 panels) and page two (3 panels) of *La semaine de Suzette*, the same girl's magazine where Bécassine was serialized: French siblings Claudine and Jean decide to build a "negro palace" on the day after they visit the Exposition.[91] They first put on blackface: "La première chose à faire pour construire un palais nègre, c'est de devenir nègre soi-même: grâce à un bout de bouchon brûlé, la transformation est vite faite. Et, aussitôt, nos deux moricauds se mettent en quête." [The first thing to do to build a Negro palace is to become a Negro oneself: thanks to a bit of burnt cork, the transformation is quickly done. And just as quickly, our two swarthies set out on their quest] (Plate 13). Looking out from behind and across the top of the first two panels, a row of twelve different black African faces and masks stare at the reader, as though they belonged to, or were worn by, characters standing behind the panels and peering over them.[92] These, and three longish poles featuring geometrical patterns, each topped with a stylized carving of a face, constitute a theatrical decor around three outside edges of the comics plate and in the gutter between the two columns of panels. These speechless black characters and visual motifs recall the Exposition's African performers and "l'art nègre" of some African displays there and constitute a striking visual decoration (cf. Nederveen Pieterse 1992: 95). Their unusual presentation – behind, between and around the edges of the panels – also reminds us of the border between the French spectators and the African performers at the Bois de Vincennes.[93] It may be worth recalling here that the French word for comic strip panel and for (African) hut is the same: "*case.*" We could say therefore that the African characters in this strip are peering out from behind the "*cases.*" In fact, the colonized exhibition workers had to be protected from the invasive voyeurism of the French public, for example, through secluded eating and sleeping facilities.[94] Indeed, part of the attraction of the Exposition episode in Zig et Puce is that as readers we become privileged voyeurs of the activities of Africans in their special quarters and of events on the exhibition grounds during night-time hours when access is forbidden to European spectators. In "Un palais nègre," the limit between the two groups is virtually transgressed by the French children, who "become negroes themselves" by applying burnt cork to their faces, necks and hands.

The boundary between fantasy and reality is certainly a permeable one for young children with active imaginations. And almost like the African characters, the children's blackened faces stare out at the reader in the fourth panel. Similarly, their improvised headgear in the sixth frame echoes the curiously eclectic collection of hats worn by the African characters (no two are alike). Moreover, the cartoonist suggests an additional similarity between the blackfaced children and the African characters: "Toute la journée, ils travaillent comme des nègres (c'est bien le cas de le dire), et vers le soir le palais est terminé" [All day, they work like Negroes (what better expression here), and toward evening the palace is done]. This hint at the connection between the Exposition and hard labor by the colonized is undercut by the mischievous smiles of the children and the lack of any external constraint. Although colonial masquerade may involve work, the fulfillment of their fantasy gives pleasure to both the French characters and the young colonial reader-voyeurs observing the little "*nègres*" hard at work.

In addition to partially and virtually masking the African characters and decor behind or around them, the "*cases*" also englobe the reassuringly familiar space of the bourgeois home and garden. The improvised nature of the "negro palace" that the French children are building recalls the facticity of the Africanist buildings at the Exposition coloniale: their hybrid style mixed features invented by French architects with elements copied from African originals (Leprun 1986; Morton 2000). The narrator draws attention to the facticity of the children's construction to highlight their inventiveness (they use a polar-bear skin instead of a panther hide), inspired by the supposedly realistic exhibition buildings. The strip's conclusion simultaneously truncates the fantasy and takes it to a logical conclusion. When the parents return home, they and the family servants dismantle the children's construction and scold them for having disturbed the bourgeois order. They are then "taken away in captivity… to their room." Although the father banishes the colonial carnivalesque, he does so with his tongue firmly in his cheek: "Cela vous apprendra, pillards, conclut Papa, qui, malgré tout, a un peu envie de rire, à voler les chrétiens pour construire vos maisons de sauvages!" [That will teach you, pillagers – concludes Papa, who, in spite of it all, felt a bit like laughing – to steal from the Christians to build your homes of savages!] He, and we the spectators, are allowed the last laugh at the colonial exhibition, at the expense of the hard-working "nègres." Like Kacoco and Radadou (and Koko), Claudine and Jean are forced by a paternal(istic) white figure to abandon the colonial carnivalesque, as the colonial bourgeois order is re-established. Here, as in Zig et Puce, even the spectacle of the colonial clowns being disciplined is meant to amuse the colonial-era child readers, while teaching them a lesson.

The alternate bending and reinforcement of the bourgeois colonial order also provides the narrative motor of my next example, the Pieds-Nickelés at the Exposition coloniale, in an episode drawn by Forton – the anarchistic, bon-vivant creator of the series – less than three years before he died. The Pieds-Nickelés strip, which was eventually drawn and scripted by several artists over the decades, is often celebrated by fans and critics for its working-class and anarchistic spirit (e.g., Francis Lacassin, quoted in Fourment 1987: 209; Gaumer and Moliterni 1994: 500). Its protagonists are three thieving, swindling scoundrels – Croquignol, Ribouldingue and Filochard. Their bizarre names suggest their anti-social traits.[95] Like puppets in a traditional French *guignol* puppet show, the three are constantly getting into trouble and are often beaten up by the police or their would-be victims, but always escape to begin again their single-minded pursuit of ill-gotten gain and the easy life. Upon returning from a voyage to America, they spy the exhibition buildings in the Bois de Vincennes: the reader recognizes the undulating lines of the Angkor pavilion next to the striking conical domes on top of the French West African structure (cf. Morton 2000: 234–69). It is not surprising that the characters view this as a wonderful chance to hoodwink unsuspecting French visitors in search of exoticism. They first stop by the main office ("le commissariat général") to obtain a concession in the sideshow area ("le quartier des attractions") and later, when it begins to bring them more pain than profit (they are beaten up by an angry client), buy out another sideshow from a like-minded huckster who has decided to move on to other things. From the beginning of this episode, the activities of the fictional Pieds-Nickelés resemble in some ways the carnival sideshows of the real-life Fédération Française des Anciens Coloniaux (FFAC) [French Federation of Former Colonials (i.e., colonizers)], which first brought in from "A.E.F. [Afrique équatoriale française] des négresses à plateaux et des pygmées" [A.E.F. (French Equatorial Africa) some Negresses with lip plates and some pygmies] and then the group of Kanak from New Caledonia to the Jardin zoologique d'acclimatation in Paris (Dauphiné 1998: 29; cf. 64, 67, 75, 111). This involved at least three mis-representations: to the New Caledonian recruits – promised better pay and far different (and better) living and working conditions than they received (Dauphiné 1998: 30–6, 63, 81–3); to the colonial administration of mainland France – for example, it was not informed that some of the Kanak were to be exhibited as cannibals in Germany (Dauphiné 1998: 75); and to the spectators, who were presented with a fabricated vision of Kanak "savagery" and customs (Dauphiné 1998: 35, 68–77, 82). Similarly, in quick succession the Pieds-Nickelés dupe the colonial administration, their hiree and the spectators, as they set up and run their first scam. Here Forton re-works the myth of the wild man of Borneo, which associated so-called primitive humans with orangutans (Nederveen Pieterse 1992: 38–44). After having built "une sorte de case faite de bambous, de lianes et de feuilles de palmiers" [a sort of hut made of bamboo, vines and palm-tree leaves], the threesome decides that it would be too expensive to find and bring back the genuine article, and moreover, says Filochard, "je ne suis pas sûr, au fond, qu'il y ait encore des sauvages à Bornéo!" [I'm not sure, deep down, whether there are still any savages in Borneo!] Instead, they trick "un simple clochard" [an ordinary bum] found near the Bois de Vincennes into serving as their savage: all he will have to do all day, they promise, is eat, and for that they will pay him 25 francs. With glue, goat hairs and paint they quickly transform him into "une espèce de gorille d'aspect impressionnant" [a kind of very impressive-looking gorilla].

Forton combines various sorts of colonial masquerade – dressing up his characters as both the colonizers and the colonized, the civilized and the savage. After having transformed the French "clochard" into a man-ape, the three Pieds-Nickelés make themselves up as two dark-skinned, exotic musicians and a colonial explorer, who acts as the carnival barker (Plate 14). Although the cover illustration for the booklet version depicts a ferocious black peeking out of a hut, in the serialized story the attraction was of course the Frenchman made up as a savage. This disconnect between cover image and the story inside already suggests both the power of the stereotype of the black African savage and the swindle that the Pieds-Nickelés engage in: the cover would lead readers to expect a story involving a dangerous African (as in the Zig et Puce Exposition episode), but instead they would find one about a Frenchman made up to look like a savage. The cover and this discrepancy thereby also participate in Forton's satirical manipulation of the Exposition. The "human zoo" is wildly successful, so much so that the "clochard" demands a large portion of the profits, much as the New Caledonians chose to go on strike for better treatment from the colonial entrepreneurs who exploited them (Dauphiné 1998: 113). However, the wild man is outwitted by the three scoundrels, who go so far as to torture him by lighting a fire under the floor of his cage to force him to perform a savage dance, after he has begun a sitdown strike. When the Pieds-Nickelés finally let him out of his cage, after the last spectator has left, the "clochard" runs away, to the delight of the trio. By the time that Forton published these first four pages of his exhibition episode (on 30 July and 6 August 1931), the scandal about the mistreatment of the Kanak had already broken in the French press (beginning 14 May; Dauphiné 1998: 89), so it is entirely possible that the cartoonist was loosely basing this sequence on their story. A crucial difference between the fiction and the actual historical event is that the Kanak were able to attract European support (from religious leaders, colonial settlers, etc.) and thereby successfully exert pressure on the colonial administration to improve their working and living conditions, whereas the lone French "clochard" does not have that option. Another important distinction is that the Pieds-Nickelés are always depicted as sympathetic swindlers, whereas until the Kanak spectacle became a scandal, the FFAC was a respectable and active member of the amorphous group of supporters of French colonialism known as the "parti colonial" [colonial party] (Girardet 1995: 110–19; Dauphiné 1998).

The many and varied ways in which Forton combines colonial clichés with dishonest sideshow techniques to let his Pieds-Nickelés hoodwink the French public throughout the 20-page episode turn the entire Exposition itself into a running joke. Morton (2000: 111) argues that the "physical presence [of colonized natives] in the pavilions was a crucial accessory to the exotic simulacrum, the Exposition." In this episode of les Pieds-Nickelés, the reader sees only one "genuine native" – a Moroccan vendor (of nougat); instead, it is the three French scoundrels (along with the Frenchmen they recruit) who perform as both fake colonized and colonial explorer. After the "clochard" runs off the Pieds-Nickelés engage a street performer to work as their new wild man of Borneo, but he accidentally burns down their stand, and the swindlers themselves are victims of theft during the ensuing confusion.[96] They then dress up in Middle Eastern costumes (complete with a fez), pretend to exhibit tiny pygmies in a dollhouse, sell fake fruit, and steal the clothes and purses that spectators leave in the coatroom before they go in to see the (invisible, because non-existent) pygmies. The Exposition-as-simulacrum is depicted as an elaborate setpiece designed to give French visitors the shake-down – literally, in one scene, where they are rattled so much that their money falls out of their pockets. In another scene, the Pieds-Nickelés combine a sideshow purported to show "Le firmament colonial" with a "Grand jeu de massacre sénégalais" [Grand game of Senegalese massacre]: one French client is duped into poking his head through a hole cut in a curtain, while on the other side of the curtain a second one throws fruit at him (Plate 15). This could suggest that the French colonial world is a dishonest simulacrum and that the participation of Senegalese soldiers in French wars, including the First World War, was a "jeu de massacre" [a shooting gallery] into which the Africans had been coerced or deceitfully lured by French recruiters. Conversely, it might suggest that the white men throwing fruit were like the Senegalese, massacring enemies of France. Both interpretations are plausible and suggest satire: the former more critical of French colonialism and the latter less so.

As I stated earlier, Maréchal Lyautey wished to avoid the "amusement park atmosphere in the colonial sections" of previous exhibitions (Morton 2000: 71; cf. 4–5, 71–4). In his strip, Forton takes the colonial carnivalesque to extreme lengths and inserts a representative of the bourgeois and colonial establishment at which he was thumbing his nose. The cartoonist has an exhibition official sternly intervene twice in the comic strip, shutting down the Pieds-Nickelés' Chinese restaurant business and confiscating their fake identity papers the second time he appears. The trio finally dresses up as Vietnamese ("Annamites") to pull rickshaws seating exhibition visitors, although this ends up involving too much hard labor for their taste and ability, so that their passengers are dumped on the ground or fall into a pond. This part of the episode is completely imaginary, because although the organizers of the Exposition had envisioned including rickshaws, a popular feature of some earlier exhibitions, they finally chose to do without them.[97] So Forton's representation of rickshaws at the Exposition – like cartoons depicting belly dancing there, including one by Saint-Ogan in *Le coup de patte* (30 May 1931) (Figure 7) – was anachronistic, a relic from popular perceptions of past exhibitions (1889 and 1900, in Paris) that persisted in this representation of the 1931 event.[98]

The Exposition episodes in Zig et Puce and the Pieds-Nickelés differ in how they incarnate the colonial carnivalesque. First, Saint-Ogan uses the amusement park for only a page or two, instead situating his colonial carnival mainly in the "serious" colonial exhibitions and thereby temporarily disrupting (in the space of the fiction) the intentions of the exhibition organizers; whereas Forton locates his story in the fairground and the zoo, which come to stand as synechdoches for the entire Exposition. Second, in Saint-Ogan's comic the two African characters mostly take the place of the French ones, but we find the opposite in Forton, where French characters disguise themselves as various colonized groups. Most importantly, in contrast to Saint-Ogan's containment of the colonial carnivalesque through a moralizing colonial conclusion, Forton's protagonists simply leave the Exposition when the risk of being caught and jailed has become too great – they are not jailed (as Saint-Ogan's African characters are, temporarily), do not repent and are not integrated as servants within the bourgeois economic order; instead, they continue their criminal activities outside the Exposition. The critique of the colonial order in this anarchistic comic is limited by the fact that the actions of the Pieds-Nickelés are mainly designed to derive profit from it in a parasitic manner, not to overthrow it. We will see in Chapter 4 that the Pieds-Nickelés profitably dupe Africans when they visit the colonies, just as they fleece the French at the Exposition coloniale in Paris. Indeed, they are shown happily swindling – or themselves

Figure 7 An orientalist fantasy at the 1931 Exposition coloniale in Paris: there was no belly-dancing exhibition there. The image harkens back to the highly popular attraction at previous exhibitions (1889, 1900). The caption reads: "Lovers to the mysterious river, the overexcited to the scenic railway, and the lustful to the oriental dances." From Alain Saint-Ogan, "Les attractions de l'Exposition: Le fleuve à trois remous" [Attractions of the Exposition: the river with three eddies], *Le coup de patte*, no. 3 (30 May 1931), p. 23.

becoming the victims of – virtually any character they meet in the series (cf. Tulard 2008: 61–2, 74). This is the basic principle of the strip – its formulaic mechanism – which readily incorporates and exploits racist caricatures, without adequate critique.[99]

My next example of blackface and the colonial carnivalesque in a colonial-era comic related to the Exposition coloniale is in *Le mariage de M. Lakonik*, a bizarre, picaresque work first published in 1931 by Jean Bruller and recently reissued by the CNBDI (Bruller 2000). Bruller is best known today for *Le silence de la mer*, a celebrated work of prose fiction, originally published in 1942 under the pseudonym of Vercors by the Resistance publisher Editions de Minuit. However, it was as a cartoonist specializing in absurdist humor that he originally became known to the French public. *Le mariage de M. Lakonik* gives a parodic reading of colonial masquerade and the colonial carnivalesque (Bruller 2000: 16–19). In it, M. Lakonik escapes from pursuers by climbing over a wall and taking refuge in a thatched hut surrounded by a tall iron fence. Wild animals (a zebra and a llama) inhabit two other adjacent enclosed areas. In fact, Lakonik is in a kangaroo pen. In order to escape detection, he blackens himself and climbs atop a pedestal, after having removed a statue of a kangaroo hunter from it. When a guardian arrives, Lakonik frightens him away (by yelling and throwing potatoes at him), escapes (followed by the kangaroo) and is subsequently mistaken for a Negro animal trainer by M. Brignochon, director of the Dijon circus. Recent critical histories of the 1931 Exposition coloniale point out that the Vincennes zoo and a large aquarium in the basement of the (then) Musée permanent des colonies were originally created as part of the colonial exhibition,[100] perhaps partially in order to create the illusion that the "human zoo" at the Exposition coloniale was not a zoo at all (Lebovics 2002). The social Darwinian hierarchy of colonialist ideology (Hodeir and Pierre 1991: 96–7; Morton 2000: 119–20, 201, 252) was thereby linked to the sub-human animal world (Hodeir and Pierre 1991: 82–8), much as the bas-relief of the museum associated the colonized with nature and wild animals (Norindr 1996: 29–32). Primitive peoples were seen as closer to the state of nature than Europeans, and so could logically be colonized and then exhibited like other animal species, alongside them. This episode of Bruller's comic is set in the Jardin des plantes in Paris, but partially and playfully reverses the roles of French spectator and colonial worker at the exhibition by briefly putting Lakonik in the kangaroo cage, but without placing a colonial worker in the role of the spectator – instead, it is (only) the reader who occupies that position. The fact that his disguise subsequently convinces another Frenchman (Brignochon) that he really is a black person confirms this reading. Nonetheless, the comic-book episode does not seriously destabilize the colonialist paradigm that it appears to parody, in part because it lacks any overt reference to the Exposition coloniale.

In my final example of the colonial carnivalesque in comics, white French characters trade places with francophone black Africans, but in a way that gives a new twist to the concept of colonial hybridity and masquerade in *bande dessinée*. *Frimousset directeur de jardin zoologique*, by Pinchon and Jaboune, was published in book form in 1933.[101] This work depicts a human zoo run by a young French boy named Frimousset [Rascally Little Face] and three adults with equally silly names – Tante Amélonde, M. Legigot and Mlle Rebidon [Aunt Amélonde, Mr. Muttonleg and Miss Re-belly/Re-oildrum] – who, along with their cat Houpalariquette,[102] are the protagonists of a series of comic books. The drawing style, character types and situations have much in common with other books on which Pinchon collaborated: for example, Frimousset and the tall, thin, bearded M. Legigot resemble the later Gringalou and Professor Cincinnatus of the "Gringalou" series; Tante Amélonde reminds one of Mme de Grand-Air, in the Bécassine series; and the characters repeatedly get themselves into situations that are presented as absurdly funny, sometimes potentially dangerous, but always without any permanent serious consequences for the protagonists. In this case, M. Legigot is persuaded to buy a "Jardin privé des bêtes, célèbre parc d'acclimatation situé près du bois de Montmartre" [Private animal garden, famous acclimatization park situated close to the Montmartre woods] from its owner, M. Delapuce [Mr. Oftheflea]. The fictional zoo is probably based on the Jardin zoologique d'acclimatation located in the Bois de Boulogne, which displayed exotic animals but also colonized peoples, such as the Kanak during the 1931 Exposition coloniale. The story mostly revolves around the efforts of Frimousset and his friends to renovate the dilapidated zoo and attract visitors. As each successive initiative backfires, the new owners experiment with increasingly radical measures. Their final attempt involves signing a one-year contract with "M. Boum, impresario, directeur du 'village nègre Tsé-Tsé'" [Mr. Boum, impresario, director of the 'Tse-tse negro village'] to include Africans in their zoo: "la peuplade des nègres

Tsé-Tsé […] le grand-père, la grand'mère, le père, la mère, quelques oncles et quelques tantes… et une trentaine d'enfants" [the small tribe of Tse-Tse Negroes […] the grandfather, the grandmother, the father, the mother, some uncles and some aunts… and thirty or so children] (Plate 16). Although M. Boum speaks perfect French, he may be based on Carl Hagenbeck (or one of his descendants), the German entrepreneur who did much to establish the tradition of bringing colonized peoples to Europe to put them on display. The Tsé-Tsé are dressed in a grotesque mismatch of Western and African clothes, in ways that we have already seen. For example, the chief wears a grass skirt but also European shoes and socks held up by garters, clearly visible around his calves (not hidden by a pair of pants); he displays a necklace on his bare chest, but has a top hat with feathers; he wears a shirt cuff and cufflink on one otherwise bare arm, and holds a black umbrella in one hand and a chimney sweep's brush in the other (an allusion to the imaginary origins of his blackness). The Tsé-Tsé wreak havoc on the zoo's business by stealing objects from the offices and apartments of Frimousset and his friends, killing and roasting a lion and a monkey, and threatening to eat the children of a visiting nurse. When M. Boum refuses to modify their one-year contract, Frimousset and friends hire a professor to teach them Tsé-Tsé, in order to negotiate directly with the Africans in a last-ditch attempt to save their business. However, when they approach the chief, it turns out that he speaks perfect French, which allows him to make extravagant demands on the owners: "Pour partir, je veux douze chameaux, 1 réveil matin, six lapins mécaniques, 3 moulins à café, 1 kilo de tabac et je veux que tante Amélonde entre dans mon harem comme sultane" [In order to leave I want twelve camels, 1 alarm clock, six mechanical rabbits, 3 coffee mills, 1 kilo of tobacco, and I want Aunt Amélonde to enter my harem as a sultaness] (plate 35). When lengthy further negotiations produce only equally absurd demands, M. Legigot finally has "une idée de génie" [a brilliant idea]: he proposes to hand over ownership of the zoo to the chief, in exchange for an agreement to hire him and his friends for 100 francs per day. The French characters are to work in a white village at the zoo, which allows them to finally enjoy, "sous les yeux du public éberlué, la vie calme et reposante dont ils rêvent depuis si longtemps" [under the eyes of the flabbergasted spectators, the calm and relaxing life that they had dreamed of for so long] (plate 37). The final frame of the story shows Frimousset and friends peacefully engaging in favorite activities as they sit on and around a log in a bucolic setting within one of the zoo's cages: we see, in the background, a covered well and a thatched house; M. Legigot, smoking his pipe, gazes at Tante Amélonde, who is doing some needlework; Mlle Rebidon is feeding some white pigeons; and Frimousset relaxes, eyes closed and a blissful expression on his face. Outside the cage, dozens of Parisian visitors to the zoo gaze in at the exotic rural scene. The conclusion gives a surprising but logical twist to the nightmare that Tante Amélonde had earlier, when M. Legigot announced to her that he had just purchased the zoo: she dreamed that she and her friends were inside an animal cage, while the animals (aardvark, zebra, lion, ostriches, etc.) gazed in at them (plate 7). Even before the book's conclusion, this dream is revealed to be premonitory, insofar as the boundary between the natural world of the animals and the human, cultural world of the French is perturbed: Tante Amélonde does find herself in a lion's cage (plate 23; cf. plate 7); M. Legigot is doused by an elephant while sharing its cage (plate 24; cf. plate 9); and the monkeys escape from their cage, causing the visitors to seek refuge there (plate 30). In the conclusion to *Frimousset directeur de jardin zoologique*, the distinction between savage Africans and civilized French people is disturbed to the point where they trade places and roles. However, as we have seen in the preceding examples of the colonial carnivalesque, the switch is incomplete and therefore fails to radically undermine colonial ideology: the Africans now occupy a subaltern position that Frimousset and his friends did not – the former have now put on the livery of zoo workers (whereas the French protagonists wore their usual street clothes throughout most of the story), and they are still drawn with exaggeratedly large lips and eyes. Moreover, the human zoo's standard representation of savagery from the African hinterland is replaced with a depiction of European rural tranquility – instead of, for example, the savagery of European war. This idealized vision of life in the French countryside, as an exotic attraction for Parisians, also provides a curious echo, almost seventy years later, of the sometimes tense encounter between the country and the city that Léonce Petit had depicted with humor in *Les mésaventures de M. Bêton* (cf. Kunzle 1990a: 152–4). Here too, in the comic book by Pinchon and Jaboune, the figure of the African savage mediates and catalyzes conflicting depictions of European self, as urban or rural, prey to economic responsibilities or carefree, Parisian or provincial.[103]

Exhibition comics and modernity

Patricia A. Morton argues, in *Hybrid Modernities: Architecture and Representation at the 1931 Colonial Exposition, Paris*, that: "[t]he neglected history of colonialism, often omitted from histories of the Euro-American world, is an integral element of modernism. The 1931 Colonial Exposition represents one of those moments in the prehistory of the present [...] through which we can gain insight into modernity" (2000: 8). Surprising though it may seem, analyzing colonial representations in comics from that period may teach us something about modernity, just as the exhibition's architecture and performances do in Morton's study. Comics from 1931 and thereabouts form part of the prehistory of today's visual-verbal depictions of the (ex-)colonized and (former) colonizers in France, whether in advertising, animated cartoons, film, comics, etc. – for example, in comics about multi-ethnic youths in today's *banlieues* (McKinney 2004a), or in *La débauche*, a modern-day fable about the televised spectacle of a "clochard" [bum] in a human zoo at the Jardin des Plantes in Paris, by cartoonist Jacques Tardi and novelist Daniel Pennac (2000). One finds an eerily similar disguise and ironic exhibition in the Pieds-Nickelés story about the Exposition analyzed above. If modernity and postmodernity are, to a large extent, characterized by experiences of dislocation, global migration, cultural hybridity and the new forms of consciousness that these produce (Gilroy 1993; cf. Dayan 1996), then these comics reveal something about the modernization of French society, because they often depict France's colonial others in the heart of the French *métropole* and the transformations of identity that this displacement can provoke and facilitate. The Exposition inspired cartoonists to create representations of colonial hybridity and mimicry, including blackface by white French, and partial assimilation by the colonized.[104] These imaginings were neither unbounded nor untainted by prejudice. On the contrary, they were often extremely conservative, and their most unsettling features – which might disturb the racist (economic, political, and cultural) hierarchy and separation between the French and the peoples they colonized – were quickly contained.

For example, at one point in Saint-Ogan's story about the 1931 Exposition, the African counterpart of Zig meets a white Frenchwoman who tries to convince him to become a vegetarian. At the end of their discussion, she delightedly imagines that she has succeeded in her mission, but the lesson that he takes away is that eating non-human animals is bad, leaving human flesh as the only logical option from his perspective – this adds urgency to the cannibals' project of cooking and eating Zig. In this encounter, cultural miscommunication satirizes conversion narratives, with vegetarianism standing in for other, more mainstream European cultural mores. The meeting's outcome is potentially a pessimistic and anti-colonial one: it could suggest that the hope of converting Africans to European cultural norms is chimerical. However, representing a woman proselytizing for vegetarianism, instead of, say, a missionary preaching Catholicism, neutralizes the implicit critique of colonialism and helps contain the colonial carnivalesque within acceptable limits. The subsequent conversion of the cannibals by a white male capitalist into non-cannibal domestic servants completes the containment.

Saint-Ogan's cannibal tale reminds us that the dislocation of modernity is to a large extent a function of commodification and alienation – of labor, material goods, images and therefore, fundamentally, people – and that the colonial system was a part of an emerging capitalist world market for goods, services and labor (Potts 1990). As Petitfaux (1995: 19) has argued, Saint-Ogan was one of the first French cartoonists to commercialize his comics characters in a wide variety of spin-off products ("produits dérivés"), and with great success. He adapted his comics production to the colonial and capitalist market – not least of all by serializing his comics in various periodicals. He also used his comics and their colonial characters in advertising for other companies and products, including Poulain chocolate,[105] Le Printemps,[106] and Ovomaltine.[107] Throughout his career, he also recycled narrative structures, cartoons and other artistic material in ways that linked colonial ideology and comics as a commodity. For example, he repeatedly published versions of a racist science-fiction story about a confrontation between a technologically advanced white race of beings and a less developed race of black characters,[108] reused cannibal jokes and, we have seen, marketed the Exposition coloniale.

CHAPTER THREE

Colonial Exhibitions in French Comics: A Renewed Tradition

The 1931 Exposition appears to have been unique in French colonial history, in terms of the number of comics produced about it during and after the event. After the peak of large-scale universal and colonial exhibitions in France, the number of comics about them dropped off considerably. This does not mean that traces of exhibitions, and of visits by the colonized to metropolitan France on those occasions, disappeared immediately or completely from comics. For example, one finds mention of the 1900 exhibition in *Les merveilleuses aventures du P'tit Quinquin* [The Marvelous Adventures of Li'l Quinquin], scripted by Marylis, drawn by J.-A. Dupuich and published by Artima (based in Tourcoing, in northern France), probably during the 1950s. The title character, wearing a sailor's outfit, is "un petit gars du Nord qui n'en a pas pourtant le type avec ses cheveux bruns" [a little guy from the North who nonetheless doesn't look like it, with his dark hair]. His name embodies his northern identity: it comes from a famous lullaby, "Le P'tit Quinquin," written in Picard in 1853 by Alexandre Desrousseaux. In the comic book, P'tit Quinquin quickly finds a sidekick, a black boy with a ridiculous name, "Tête de Moineau" [Sparrow Head], who works as a cook on a sea-going ship. The cook is associated with Friday, from Defoe's *Robinson Crusoe*, by the verbal narrator of the comic after the characters have landed on Toutentourédo (i.e., tout entouré d'eau [completely surrounded by water]), an island that initially appears to be uninhabited.[1] When it appears that they may be in Africa, Tête de Moineau's color and heritage are evoked: "Dis donc, Tête de Moineau, tu ne serais pas de la région par hasard?" [Say there, Sparrow Head, you wouldn't be from around here by any chance?] Tête de Moineau emphatically states that he is Parisian, from Montmartre, but does let on that his ancestral origins are more troubling: "'Tout de même, reprend P'tit Quinquin, tes parents ne sont pas nés à Montmartre?' – 'C'est possible, Missié, grand-pé était antropophage à l'exposition de 1900'" ["All the same, replies Lil Quinquin, your parents weren't born in Montmartre?" – "That's possible, Mista, grandpah was cannibul at the exhibition of 1900"] (Plate 17). Tête de Moineau's difference is both linguistic (strangely, he has an African accent) and racial (his cannibal ancestry gives P'tit Quinquin some passing anxiety), though they quickly become close friends. This is the only French comic I have found that represents the *descendant* of a colonized participant in an exhibition. It suggests, and no doubt helped to constitute, a collective memory of how such events had brought colonized others to the French capital itself, and it links that voyage in[2] to an ongoing presence of the colonized in mainland France. It thereby anticipates much more recent developments in French comics, linking colonial exhibitions with cultural diversity in France today.

In this chapter I analyze exhibition comics drawn and published beginning in the 1980s, from an era after most – but not all – French colonies had gained formal independence. This process often brought with it arrested decolonization and a transition to renewed forms of exploitation in the (ex-)colonies, with both local and international aspects. This historical situation has had an impact on the approaches that cartoonists have taken, over the past few decades, toward the colonial past. The ways in which they have used the theme of colonial exhibitions during this period hinge on a variety of other factors too, such as the degree and forms of political engagement, historical awareness and ethnic identification of cartoonists. The symbolic importance of exhibitions means that they have renewed significance for cartoonists interested in colonialism. As huge, propagandistic, didactic displays of colonial power, exhibitions were spectacular events, with both visual and verbal components. Moreover, they deposited large numbers of documents in collections, both public and private, in France and abroad, which means that cartoonists, university researchers and others can readily retrieve materials useful for reconstructing the event. Colonial exhibitions are ideal material for producing a "historical effect" in comics, as well-known events to which cartoonists can anchor their fictions (Fresnault-Deruelle 1979; cf. Barthes 1985).

In addition, the impact of colonial exhibitions on artists at the time was significant, as we have seen. When today's cartoonists look back at colonial exhibitions, they often refer to the visual artists active at and around the events or to their artwork (cartoons, comics, posters) as part of the prehistory of the comics medium. For example, the artist-in-the-text is a recurring motif in these comics, partly due to the self-reflexivity often found in the medium, but also because many cartoonists are aware of the high stakes and complexities of representing colonialism. All of these elements help explain why some cartoonists have chosen to represent colonial exhibitions in comics in recent years. Moreover, claims that organizers made for colonialism at and through exhibitions continue to have relevance for cartoonists – and French society in general – even today: for example, that France's actions were, on balance, motivated by generosity and beneficial to both the colonized and colonizers. They are still echoed, debated and contested by politicians, historians, prose novelists and cartoonists, among others.

My three-part typology of approaches to colonial exhibitions (commemorative-nostalgic, colonial carnivalesque and critical-historical) helps us understand how cartoonists utilize colonial archives, which are increasingly accessible on the web, in critical or historical works on colonialism, in republished facsimile editions of colonial works and elsewhere. Cartoonists who produce colonial nostalgia comics uncritically recycle the ideology, images and language of colonialist documents in order to celebrate colonial leaders, settlers and their achievements. They tend to portray the colonial past as a time of lost innocence and adventure, or of unjustly maligned accomplishments (or all of these). Representing colonial exhibitions is an ideal way of showcasing this vision in comics. By the same token, colonial exhibitions are useful for cartoonists wishing to expose the violence of colonialism and the falseness of its propaganda. Artists can draw contrasts and parallels between the exhibitions in France and the treatment of the colonized both in the *métropole* and in the colonies. Critiques of, and resistance to, colonial exhibitions when they were held have inspired today's cartoonists and helped them to construct alternative, historically informed visions of the era and its representations. I have found multiple examples of both the commemorative-nostalgic and critical-historical approaches. Although the colonial carnivalesque was one of the most prevalent ways in which cartoonists represented colonial exhibitions prior to decolonization, one finds few exhibition comics today in that vein, although there was a resurgence of the colonial carnivalesque in French comics in the 1980s, for example in *Métal aventure* magazine (cf. Smolderen 1984: 63; quoted in Quella-Guyot 1991: 15). I analyze below one example of post-colonial carnivalesque in an exhibition comic.

Recycling colonial propaganda: commemorative nostalgia and critical realism

One finds a commemorative-nostalgic, imperialist vision in *Les bâtisseurs d'empire* [The Builders of Empire] (Saint-Michel and Le Honzec 1994) and its sequel, *Soldats de la liberté* (Saint-Michel and Le Honzec 1995), respectively the middle and last volumes of an "Histoire des troupes de Marine" (i.e., French colonial soldiers, rebaptized "Troupes de marine" during the Algerian War as France was losing formal control of its colonies; Saint-Michel and Le Honzec 1995: 28). *Les bâtisseurs d'empire* ends with a celebration of Lyautey's actions as résident général of Morocco (1912–25), the crushing of the Rif rebellion in Morocco (1921–6), French military interventions in Lebanon, Syria and Turkey (1920–2), and the 1931 Exposition coloniale, directed by Lyautey. The cartoonists' celebration of French military conquests worldwide stands in unintentionally ironic contrast to a proclamation by Lyautey, reproduced in a small frame set against images of the Exposition coloniale: "Coloniser, ce n'était pas uniquement construire des quais ou des voies ferrées, c'était aussi gagner à la douceur humaine les coeurs farouches de la savane et du désert" [Colonizing meant not only building wharves or train tracks, it was also to win over the wild hearts of the savannah and the desert to human kindness] (Saint-Michel and Le Honzec 1994: 44). The celebration of colonial one-ness, evident in this pronouncement and in the cartoonists' repeated figuring of the devotion of colonial soldiers of color to their French officers, rings hollow to this reader.

The following volume, *Soldats de la liberté*, opens with a reproduction of a poster from the 1931 Exposition coloniale, followed immediately by praise for France's civilizing mission in

Southeast Asia and West Africa. This is illustrated by a homage to various French military doctors, whose success in detecting and treating the plague and sleeping sickness is meant to exemplify the humanitarian nature of France's "oeuvre civilisatrice auprès des populations de l'empire" [civilizing mission toward the populations of the empire] (1). The cartoonists perpetuate here a significant propaganda theme of the Exposition coloniale,[3] one designed to deflect attention away from the French massacres and torture that created and maintained imperial control (Benot 2001). The position of the comic book is neo-imperialist for another reason – it celebrates an unbroken continuity between colonial and neo-colonial actions of the French army, specifically through its colonial units: "Aujourd'hui encore, des centaines d'officiers-médecins oeuvrent dans les états issus de nos anciennes colonies qui envoient en formation leurs futurs officiers-médecins en France" [Again today, hundreds of military doctors work in countries that were formerly our colonies, which send their future military doctors to study in France] (Saint-Michel and Le Honzec 1995: 2). In the rest of the book, the cartoonists – the scriptwriter, Saint-Michel, was a trained historian – celebrate forms of French neo-imperialism, including bloody invasions to support pro-French dictators and overthrow democratic and progressive African regimes, although France's activity is always presented by the cartoonists as humanitarian and just.[4]

Recent *bandes dessinées* that refer to colonial exhibitions often do so via reproductions of posters originally created for the exhibitions. Exhibition posters lend an aura of visual and historical authenticity to such works, helping to recreate the atmosphere of a bygone era and produce a "historical effect."[5] For Guy Gauthier (1993: 58) this helps explain why contemporary cartoonists often borrow visual imagery from nineteenth-century publications such as *Tour du monde*. The current meanings and value of the borrowed image depend to a great extent on the cartoonists' view of the colonial events to which the image refers: colonial exhibitions and their posters serve opposite purposes in *Soldats de la liberté* and *Le roi noir n'est pas noir* [The Black King is Not Black] (Logez and Delannoy 2001), which praise and condemn colonialism, respectively (more on the latter work, below). On the other hand, a relatively recent comic set in 1922 presents the Exposition coloniale nationale, in Marseilles, in a manner that does not take sides for or against colonialism in such a clear fashion. Nonetheless, there is a decidedly nostalgic tone around the visit to the exhibition in *Un ange passe* [An Angel Flies Over] (Moncomble and Grand 2001: 43–4): a pregnant young Frenchwoman goes there to visit its papier-mâché reproduction of Angkor Wat to remember two recently deceased dear friends with whom she had visited Cambodia. The publication of a novel by the young woman, *Les ombres d'Angkor*, coincides with the opening of the exhibition. A description of this novel-in-the-text suggests how the cartoonists would like us to view their comic book: "Ce roman est un subtil mélange de mystères, d'aventures et d'exotisme" [This novel is a subtle mix of mysteries, adventures and exoticism] (43). In fact, this *bande dessinée* version of colonial history is as phony as the papier-mâché reproduction of Angkor Wat that the young woman admires. The cartoonists invite us to look back nostalgically on the period as essentially a happy, bygone era when an attractive flapper and two dapper hack writers helped the French army put down a revolt of Cambodian nationalists allied with a European temple robber (28–38). In the end, this too is a way of celebrating colonialism and its mystifying exhibitions.

In two other recent comics, cartoonists reproduce posters from colonial exhibitions within a modern French setting to refer to the colonial roots of contemporary cultural hybridity within France. A poster advertising the 1906 Exposition coloniale in Marseilles is visible on the wall of a Maghrebi-French police officer in the futuristic *A un de ces quatre* [Till One of These Days] (Falba and Di Martino 2001: 24), set in Marseilles in 2082. The reproduction serves as a wink to readers who can recognize the poster. Even though its colors and painterly appearance stand out against the cartoonish style of the frame where it appears, it would be impossible to decipher it without prior knowledge, because most of its lettering is covered by a speech balloon. One finds a more legible critical use of colonial posters in *La voyageuse de petite ceinture* [The Female Traveler on the Little Circle Line] (1985), by Pierre Christin and Annie Goetzinger, set in Paris during the early 1980s. A poster from the 1931 Exposition coloniale hangs in a house that serves as a bordello (37–8). The colonial frame of reference of the poster initiates a critique of neo-colonial exoticism and sexual exploitation that is then developed in the dialogue contained in the speech balloons (39–41). Nonetheless, the over-reliance in this book on degrading clichés about North African immigration (poverty, fragmentation of the family, oppression of Maghrebi-French women, etc.) and the sexualized orientalist voyeurism that pervades the entire work detract from the critique of a neo-colonialist perspective contained in the bordello scene (McKinney 1997b).

Between critique and reproduction of colonial ideology: Ferrandez's *Le centenaire*

The multi-volume "Carnets d'Orient" series, by cartoonist Jacques Ferrandez, constitutes one of the most extensive and complex attempts to revisit the colonial past in recent comics. The fourth volume, *Le centenaire* [The Centennial] (1994b), contains one of the most developed recent treatments of a colonial exhibition in a graphic novel, in this case the Centenaire de l'Algérie française in 1930. Ferrandez was born in Algeria in 1955, during the Algerian War, to a French settler family, but his family moved to Nice in 1956 when he was only a few months old. A remarkable feature of his series lies in the multiple and innovative ways in which he manipulates colonial-era visual and textual sources. He sometimes reproduces these texts directly in his graphic novels, on presentation pages (e.g., at the beginning of a book or a chapter) and then incorporates elements taken from them into his historical saga about a *Pied-Noir* (i.e., French settler) family, partially based on his own family history, but also on historical figures.

There is a revealing mix of approaches to colonial-era documents in the conflicting uses that Ferrandez makes of a poster promoting the Centenaire.[6] He first reproduced it on a full page of *Le centenaire* (1994b: 5), in the middle of a short introductory essay by historian Benjamin Stora, a well-known specialist in Algerian history and himself a Jew from Algeria. The historian strongly criticizes the colonial exhibition, in part because its organizers erased and minimized the violence of colonization from their celebratory representations of the French presence in Algeria. *Le centenaire* attempts to supply the missing critique of colonial violence and partially succeeds. To that extent, the reproduced exhibition poster and the colonial ideology that it transmits through ethnological and economic visual references are implicitly the object of Ferrandez's critique. Yet in *Le cimetière des princesses* (1995: 3), the following volume in the series, we find an Algerian character whom we had first seen in the poster. In this case, Ferrandez uses the ethnological reference of the poster as visual documentation. This gets to the heart of colonial exhibition as "human zoo": the representations of colonized groups that served as a spectacle for the French were supposedly based on sound ethnographic documentation, but were in fact shot through with colonialist assumptions (Bancel et al. 2002; Blanchard et al. 2008). To use them in a realistic, documentary fashion, as Ferrandez does the second time, without critiquing their colonial ideology risks simply perpetuating the exoticizing of colonial others.

Ferrandez loosely based much of his portrayal of the Centenaire on material that he borrowed from *Le livre d'or du Centenaire de l'Algérie française* [The Visitor's Book of the Centennial of French Algeria] – an almost 600-page document illustrated with many photographs, recently reissued in a facsimile edition (2003; first ed. 1930) by Gandini, a publisher in Nice specializing in colonial nostalgia publications about French Algeria. The contradictory ways in which Ferrandez has integrated material from *Le livre d'or* into his graphic novel reveal the extent to which his *bandes dessinées*, as well as many other publications about Algeria, are caught in the contradictions between a critique of colonialism and an attempt to memorialize family and ethnic history. This is evident in the main character, Paul, modeled on Ferrandez's grandfather, but also on Albert Camus, especially his journalistic period of the 1930s when he published articles critical of French injustices toward the colonized. Paul, now a newspaper reporter working for *Les nouvelles illustrées* [The Illustrated News] in mainland France, has been sent back home to Algeria to cover the Centenaire in a series of articles. The book narrates Paul's quest for his roots, which ultimately leads him to southern Algeria, where he meets Capitaine Broussaud, who long ago retired from the French army and now lives like a hermit. Like French Algeria, Broussaud turns one hundred years old in 1930, but the former officer is highly critical of the official celebration: "Ces fêtes sont une insulte aux indigènes!... On commémore leur défaite, leur humiliation et on a l'arrogance ou l'inconscience de les associer aux cérémonies pour qu'ils célèbrent leur vainqueur!" [These festive celebrations are an insult to the natives!... One commemorates their defeat, their humiliation and one arrogantly or oblivously incorporates them into the ceremonies so that they celebrate those who vanquished them!] (56). For Paul, whose return to Algeria has begun to open his eyes to the racism and exploitation that the French inflict on the Algerians, Broussaud represents the best aspects of French colonialism.

Here again, the theme of disguise occurs in the context of a colonial exhibition, but for purposes very different from what we saw earlier, for example in the case of the Pieds-Nickelés or of "Un palais nègre." Broussaud dresses in Algerian clothes, lives in a former marabout (the dwelling of a Muslim holy man in North Africa) that is furnished with poofs and a carpet, and is said by some to be a practicing Muslim (53–8). Like Paul, Broussaud in *Le centenaire* is clearly based in part on a historical figure, but a different one – the French painter Etienne Dinet.[7] By the end of his life Dinet had converted to Islam, taken the Muslim name Nasr'Edine and had made the pilgrimage to Mecca. He had added the painting of kitschy religious illustrations for pious works on Islam to his normal register of racy orientalist nudes of Algerian women and girls and a range of ethnographic paintings of scenes from Algerian society. He was also very critical of the manner in which the Centenaire was being organized, much in the vein of the quote from Broussaud in *Le centenaire*, above. Ferrandez illustrates the marginalization of this kind of trans-cultural identification with the colonized during the Centenaire by first making Broussaud have a stroke ("une attaque de paralysie") that deprives him of speech. He then introduces another journalist character into his narrative: a photographer who works for the same newspaper as Paul but shares none of his scruples or reservations. The photographer brings the now physically – and perhaps mentally – diminished Broussaud to Algiers, dresses him in a uniform from the nineteenth century and photographs him standing next to the French president Gaston Doumergue during the latter's visit to Algeria for the Centenaire (Plate 18).[8] Paradoxically, dressing up Broussaud as an officer of the French Armée de l'Afrique becomes a stigmatized form of colonial masquerade, because it masks the critique of colonialism that Broussaud had expressed to Paul before his attack.

Ferrandez's critical uses of colonial cross-dressing include an episode involving an Algerian teacher and war veteran who defends a shoe-shine boy. The latter has just been victimized by two Frenchmen (one runs off without paying for a shine, and the other trips the boy when he tries to pursue his client). This is one of several significant rewritings by Ferrandez, in "Carnets d'Orient," of scenes from Hergé's Tintin series, which is an important inspiration for Ferrandez's drawing style too. The scene – to which those who defend Hergé from accusations of racism often point – involves two *métis* [mixed-race] South Americans who trip up an Indian orange-seller.[9] Tintin dares to defend the boy against the bullying men, and is recognized and rewarded for this by an Indian onlooker. In Ferrandez's rewriting, the Algerian *évolué* takes the place of Tintin, whereas Paul – otherwise the most Tintin-like character in this volume (in physical appearance and profession) – provides the reader with a critical perspective on the scene, but does not intervene in favor of either the boy or the Algerian teacher, who is publicly humiliated by the second French bully (the one who had tripped the shoe-shine boy) with racist epithets and accusations. The bully's tirade – with its manichean division between the native and colonizer quarters in the colonial city, and its suggestion of colonial male rivalry for women, and even rape – recalls an oft-quoted passage in Frantz Fanon's *Les damnés de la terre* [The Wretched of the Earth] (2002: 43). It also clearly illustrates the limits of assimilation by the colonized into the colonizing society. This is precisely one of the criticisms of the Centenaire: that it celebrated a false union and masked the fact that French settlers persisted in maintaining institutional barriers to assimilation, to marginalize and deprive even the most Francophile Algerians of equal rights (Ageron 1979: 409–11; Benjamin 2003: 250–1)

Despite his important critiques of French colonialism, Ferrandez saves his strongest critique of colonial representation for photography, in the way it denatures a French critic of colonialism (Broussaud); by contrast, he avoids making a similar critique of how colonial photographic studios represented the colonized in Algeria. Ferrandez incorporates elements from postcard photos of Algerian shoe-shine boys and erotic photographs of Algerian women in ways that are sympathetic to the prostitutes and the boys who served as models, but provides no critique of the colonial practices and ideology behind these *visual* representations from which he borrowed (12, 17, 34–6).[10]

Post-colonial carnivalesque

A counter-cultural example of exhibitions in comics was published in a 1983 issue of *Viper*, an alternative comics magazine published by Sinsemilla éditions. Given the publisher's name, it is not surprising that many of its stories celebrate the recreational consumption of various illicit drugs. "L'expo," by Gérard Santi, the magazine's publisher, and Larbi Mechkour (Larbi and Santi 1983: 54–5), a Maghrebi-French cartoonist, appears in a special issue whose theme is an imaginary Exposition universelle of 1989. Although not clearly stated, it is obvious that the entire issue was designed in part as an irreverent preview of the upcoming bicentennial celebration of the French Revolution and of the plan (1981–3), eventually aborted, to have an Exposition universelle in Paris in 1989, on the centennial anniversary of the 1889 Paris exhibition (Ory 1989: 144), for which Christophe had launched his "Famille Fenouillard" series.[11] The strip by Mechkour and Santi takes us full-circle in our examination of exhibitions, back to the national and ethnic stereotypes of Saint-Ogan and Forton, because it includes caricatures such as Indian fakirs with a boa and a sacred cow, a black African as a savage and a Vietnamese person with protruding front teeth, a huge grin and slits for eyes. Although these are offensive stereotypes (cf. Lionnet 1995), there are significant differences between Saint-Ogan's colonial exhibition and the post-colonial one imagined by Mechkour and Santi. For starters, the exhibition is held "somewhere in Belleville City," which refers to Belleville *tout court*, the neighborhood of Paris where ethnic mixing so often occurs in both French comics and prose fiction. The protagonist, named Slimane, is a rat, which clearly alludes to a colonial-era French racist epithet for North African Arabs and Berbers ("raton" [little rat]), as well as reminding us of comic-book characters such as Mickey Mouse and his own genealogy in American minstrelsy (Willis 1991: 108–32).

However, the fact that one of the cartoonists is himself Maghrebi-French suggests that we may read this as second-degree humor that neutralizes colonial stereotypes through parody. Moreover, the cartoonists make fun of the Franco-French: for example, Jacques Chirac, then the right-wing mayor of Paris, complains vociferously at the gate because he has been asked to pay to enter the exhibition; by contrast Slimane grumbles to himself about the high entrance fee, but only after having forked over the sum without protesting to the gatekeeper. Here, equality in the French national slogan – "liberté, égalité, fraternité" [liberty, equality, fraternity] – finally applies to all. Further on, a Frenchman with a beret swears as he struggles to remain atop a pole bearing the French banner, erected above the stands of Tunisia, Vietnam and Algeria, suggesting French nationalist frustration at failed colonial rule abroad and current related multi-ethnic diversity in France (Plate 19). A forlorn African savage lives in a doghouse and eats leftover food tossed down to him by a swinish white South African, whose colonial helmet is in view, in a setting that evokes imperial Roman decadence. The American exhibition stand is a McDonalds restaurant that sells only highly destructive weapons, which suggests predatory capitalism and clearly refers to Cold War neo-imperialism. The cultural hybridity of Great Britain after Indian independence is alluded to in a parody of the *Sgt. Pepper* record album cover, with two of the Beatles appearing as Indians and one as a punk rocker. Slimane walks past these and other stands, oblivious to them because he is concentrating on trying to make some money by selling Moroccan hashish. Although the hapless, small-time drug dealer never succeeds in making a transaction, he takes us on a deconstructive tour of national and ethnic stereotypes that succeeds where Saint-Ogan failed. Cultural differentiation linked to colonial history is again situated in an exhibition in the heart of Paris, but in such a way as to satirize stereotypes created by the colonizers about both themselves and the colonized. Moreover, the colonial relation itself, in various forms, is the object of implicit political critique: the French colonization of Algeria, Tunisia and Vietnam, but also the Israeli-Palestinian conflict, apartheid in South Africa, and violent global expansionism by the United States.

Tuan's way

Le chemin de Tuan (2005), by Clément Baloup (script) and Mathieu Jiro (art), is both a remarkable work of comic-book art and exemplary of several trends in critical-historical treatment of colonial exhibitions in comics – and, more generally, of the return to colonialism in French comics today. It was prefaced by Pascal Blanchard, a French historian who has contributed much to the re-evaluation of colonial exhibitions, and is the author or editor of numerous works on colonial imagery and post-colonialism. Baloup is a graduate of the program for cartoonists of the Fine Arts school in Angoulême. He is also of mixed, French and Vietnamese, parentage, so it is not surprising that he has incorporated Vietnamese themes into several of his works. The preface by Blanchard, and the cartoonists' printed note of thanks to the historian, indicate that the graphic novel by Baloup and Jiro was partly inspired by the work of the historian. Indeed, one of the characters, a black man named Placide, describes the abject exhibit in which he was a featured attraction as a "zoo humain" (Plate 20). The expression recalls the title of a historical work that Blanchard co-edited, *Les zoos humains* (Bancel et al. 2002; Blanchard et al. 2008), and a documentary film too. Moreover, certain elements in *Le chemin de Tuan* appear to have been borrowed from a book that Blanchard co-edited with Eric Deroo (2004): *Le Paris Asie: 150 ans de présence de la Chine, de l'Indochine, du Japon... dans la capitale*. Like Nguyên Tât Thành (a.k.a. Nguyên Ái Quôc, later known as Hô Chi Minh), Hai, one of the characters of Baloup and Jiro, is a "retoucheur-photographe à Paris" [photograph-touch-up artist in Paris] (Blanchard and Deroo 2004: 109; Baloup and Jiro 2005: 29–32, 93, 120). He also wears the same kind of hat ("un chapeau melon" [a bowler hat]) as the future Hô Chi Minh does in a photograph taken on the Parisian Pont Alexandre III in 1921, and his face resembles that of the real-life Vietnamese revolutionary leader. Moreover, of all the characters in the book, Hai is the most closely allied with the Communists (Baloup and Jiro 2005: 89–93), just as Nguyên Tât Thành was the most militantly Communist among the group of Vietnamese activists with whom he collaborated in Paris (Blanchard and Deroo 2004: 95, 109). The dream of Hai is to attend the Université des travailleurs d'Orient in Moscow (Baloup and Jiro 2005: 92–3), much as Nguyên Tât Thành was sent by the Communist International to the Université des travailleurs de l'Orient (Blanchard and Deroo 2004: 109). Hai belongs to a multi-ethnic activist group named L'union des parias [The Union of Pariahs], which publishes a newspaper entitled *Le cri indigène* [The Native Cry] (Baloup and Jiro 2005: 53, 56, 88–9, 121). This is clearly based on the activities of Nguyên Tât Thành, who wrote articles under the name Nguyên Ái Quôc for *Le paria: Tribune du prolétariat colonial* [The Pariah: Tribune of the Colonial Proletariat], published by L'Union intercoloniale of the Parti communiste français (PCF).[12] The fictional characters discuss whether to continue publishing articles about France's Rif War in Morocco (Baloup and Jiro 2005: 32–3, 58); similarly, a front page of *Le paria* (issue of June–July 1925), reproduced in *Le Paris Asie*, is all about the Rif War (Blanchard and Deroo 2004: 95).

However, the graphic novel is by no means a political hagiography of the Vietnamese revolutionary leader. The depiction of his fictional double, Hai, is certainly not unequivocally positive: he is boastful and unfairly criticizes his fellow members of L'union des parias (Baloup and Jiro 2005: 40–1), he appears ready to kill a recently arrived Vietnamese man (Tuan) as a potential spy (50–1), but later proves gullible and initially refuses to believe that Tuan has indeed become a spy for the French police, despite credible evidence to that effect (82–4, 104). Instead, the title of the graphic novel, *Le chemin de Tuan* [Tuan's Way], suggests the nature of the work – it is a *roman d'apprentissage* [novel of apprenticeship] about assimilation into French colonial society in the capital city. It focuses on the various different strategies chosen by the characters, ranging from the political radicalism of Hai to identitarian reflections on blackness by a character named Mounir – who leaves L'union des parias for La défense nègre [The Negro Defense] (87–90) – to the defense of colonial modernization in Indochina by Tuan (91–3). The theme of representation – in the two main senses of the word – suggests that here, too, the cartoonists are interested in both political (self-) representation and in the ways in which colonizers and colonized perceived and represented themselves and others, through word and image. Self-representation through political activism (*Le cri indigène*, public demonstrations) is problematic insofar as it can bring manipulation by the PCF, whose interests may diverge from those of the colonized, and by the police through informers. It also brings an attack by a far-right group of Frenchmen and repression from the French authorities (the seizure of *Le cri indigène*; a police raid, jail and beatings; dissolution of L'union des parias). Its effectiveness is not obvious either, because the colonized activists cannot agree on common goals and methods, and the French police subjects them to tight surveillance (cf. Norindr 1996: 34–51).

The themes of artistic representation of the colonized and contact between the French and exoticized others is similarly fraught with ambivalence: the police informer who handles Tuan (and is ultimately killed by him; 109) sings "J'ai deux amours, mon pays et Paris" [I have two loves, my country and Paris] (42–3), but this allusion to the film song sung by African-American performer Josephine Baker reminds us of both the possibilities and the limits of colonial exoticism and interracial love between colonizer and colonized (Sherzer 1996: 231), just as a sexual encounter between Hai and a Frenchwoman is warped by the weight of colonial stereotypes about French Indochina – lacquer, tigers, coolies and savages (65–73).

Similarly, Placide's participation in a human zoo allows him to travel to France, but reinforces French colonial stereotypes about so-called African savages (77–8). Moreover, he explains that the three years he spent pretending to be a cannibal produced mental barriers in his own mind too (Plate 20). A Frenchman who had worked at the 1922 Exposition coloniale in Marseilles, which included a section on French Indochina, strikes up a conversation with the newly arrived Tuan, just off the boat in Marseilles; however, we soon learn that he has accosted the young Vietnamese man in order to steal his money (22–4). And Mounir enjoys reading the French magazine *L'intrépide*, but upon closer inspection we realize that his is an alienated form of humor: he is laughing at a colonialist strip that pokes fun at a black volunteer for serving in the Great War (87–8). All of these examples, and especially the last three, demonstrate that the cartoonists are well aware that the representations of colonized others in French popular culture have a problematic genealogy. Drawing attention to this genealogy is a meta-representational strategy that encourages readers to interrogate today's images of colonial and exotic others in French popular culture, including comics. This is precisely the opposite path to the one followed by Petitfaux, for example: as editor of Zig et Puce, he effaced and tried to downplay the violent historical background and the racism of the colonialist representations of blacks, Arabs and other groups in Saint-Ogan's comics.

Colonial ideology and practice: connecting a human zoo to a bloody colonial expedition

My next example of the critical-historical approach to colonial exhibitions in comics – *Le roi noir n'est pas noir* by Frédéric Logez and Pierre-Alban Delannoy (2001) – deserves extensive analysis because of its combined artistic and political value. It constitutes a powerful anti-imperialist intervention in the ongoing debate over the nature of French forays on the African continent. Its version of colonial history contrasts radically with that of *Les bâtisseurs d'empire* (Saint-Michel and Le Honzec 1994), which includes several pages about the same historical events. Before delving into the graphic novel itself, I must provide some background on the important historical event that it recounts. Historians critical of French colonialism have convincingly argued that it was a system ultimately based on terror, bloodshed and torture.[13] The most spectacular examples of colonial brutality are the lynchings and massacres of colonized peoples, such as those analyzed by the late Yves Benot in *Massacres coloniaux, 1944–50: La IVe république et la mise au pas des colonies françaises* (2001; cf. Forsdick 2007). One infamous series of colonial massacres was carried out in 1898–9 by the Mission Afrique Centrale, first led by officers Paul Voulet and Julien Chanoine, whose task was to secure control of Lake Chad, an important natural resource, and the areas around it.[14] This undertaking was imbued with urgency because of rival imperialist designs on the region, especially British but also German and Ottoman. When complaints about the scorched earth policy of the Mission filtered back to Paris, the government acted to remove the leaders, who retaliated by declaring themselves independent of French authority and, on 14 July 1899, killing the principal French emissary sent to relieve them of their command (Colonel Arsène Klobb) and wounding the other (Lieutenant Octave Meynier). Chanoine and Voulet were said to have been killed a short time thereafter by their own African soldiers, although French colonial officer Robert Delavignette is said to have discovered later that their tombs were empty, leading to speculation that they had not been killed and instead had been allowed to live quietly in Africa (Ahounou 2001: 148), although this has been dismissed by at least one French historian (Mathieu 1995: 159). The Mission ultimately continued on to its original destination and thereby played a highly successful role in assuring French control over the region. Two of the officers who led the expedition after the demise of Voulet and Chanoine, Lieutenants Joalland (part of the original group) and Meynier, subsequently became generals. Some historians of French colonialism (e.g., Mathieu 1995: 245–8) have argued that despite the anti-colonial outcry and parliamentary debate about the torture and murder perpetrated by the column, this kind of conduct by French colonial officers was common and generally very well tolerated by French governmental authorities – indeed, Voulet and Chanoine had been highly praised for an earlier conquest of the Mossi region in which they had used the same methods (Mathieu 1995: 37–45). Moreover, despite the fact that Joalland had been a party to the atrocities committed by Voulet and Chanoine, and committed similar ones after becoming head of the Mission, he was never punished (Mathieu 1995: 239–41). One explanation, given by historian Muriel Mathieu (1995: 243–7), for the government's decision to single out Voulet and Chanoine for investigation was the governmental crisis created by external tension from rivalry between the imperialist powers France and Britain, which came to a head in the Fashoda incident (19 September 1898), and by internal tension from the Dreyfus Affair.[15]

Several historians, including an African, have analyzed and debated the exemplary case of Voulet and Chanoine (Mathieu 1995; M'Bokolo 1999; Ahounou 2001; Pierre 2001). This story reached the pages of the French newspaper *Le Monde*, which ran two articles analyzing the significance of the Mission Afrique Centrale in the 27 September 1999 issue (Guyotat 1999; M'Bokolo 1999). There it was described by historian Elikia M'Bokolo and by journalists as only one of the most notorious examples of violence by a French colonial system based on terrorizing Africans. Subsequently, the grandson of General Meynier wrote a letter to the editor, defending the memory of his grandfather (Sylvander 1999). A second letter to the editor was printed in response to the discussion of Voulet and Chanoine, this time from a retired history teacher (born in Senegal to colonialists), who defended France's civilizing mission in Africa by citing Senghor, Eboué and Houphouët-Boigny as examples of French success, and argued that brutal methods do not constitute a system of terror (Filliol 1999). A few years earlier G. Tourot – the son of Maréchal des logis Tourot, one of the NCOs of the Voulet and Chanoine expedition – had self-published "*La griffe du destin* [The Mark of Destiny], La Pensée universelle, Paris 1993, whose principal goal was to rehabilitate the memory of his father and of his companions in misfortune, victims of the *regrettable circumstances* that surrounded the Mission and its tragic destiny" (Mathieu 1995: 6; original emphasis).[16]

Moreover, across the last quarter century, the Voulet and Chanoine expedition has been rediscovered and recounted in prose by Jacques-Francis Rolland (*Le grand capitaine*, 1976), Abdoulaye Mamani (*Sarraounia: Le drame de la reine magicienne*, 1980) and Yves Laurent and Serge Moati (*Capitaines des ténèbres*, 2006); in film by Med Hondo (*Sarraounia*, 1986),[17] Laurent and Moati (*Capitaines des ténèbres*, 2004) and Manuel Gasquet (*Blancs de mémoire*, 2004); as well as in the graphic narratives *Les bâtisseurs d'empire* (Saint-Michel and Le Honzec 1994) and, much more extensively and critically, *Le roi noir n'est pas noir* (Logez and Delannoy 2001).[18] A brief comparison of two works of historical prose fiction, one by a

French author and the other by an African, shows contrasting visions of colonial history that provide a useful context for my subsequent analysis of *Le roi noir n'est pas noir*, which I will also compare briefly to *Les bâtisseurs d'empire*. In his carefully researched historical novel, *Le grand capitaine*, Rolland strives to illustrate the single-minded determination of Voulet, seconded by Chanoine, to conquer central Africa. Rolland's novel effectively debunks the colonial myth that Voulet's rebellion against French authority was due to a fit of madness ("la soudanite") that might have struck any unfortunate European in insalubrious African conditions (here, the Sudan), as in *Heart of Darkness* by Joseph Conrad and *Voyage au bout de la nuit* by Céline.[19] The insanity plea, quickly made by supporters of Voulet in the French parliament and elsewhere, is still invoked today. The first part of Rolland's account is titled "La sorcière" (chapters 1–7, pp. 9–51), yet only the first few pages (11–25) recount the confrontation between the French forces and those of Sarraounia, an African queen and "sorcière" (a sorceress or priestess in a traditional African religion), who also resisted Muslim expansion in the region. It is true that Rolland frames this difficult combat as a turning point for the French military expedition: he presents it as Voulet's motivation for cutting off communication with Paris, as a prelude to illegally crossing the border established with the English government. His superiors had expressly forbid this, even though the column may well have needed to take the shortcut to reach its destination, Lake Chad. By contrast, Mamani constructs *Sarraounia: Le drame de la reine magicienne* entirely around the conflict with Sarraounia's forces, which he suggests is what ultimately led to the downfall of the expedition's leaders. The difference in historical vision between the two novels is especially apparent in narrative focalization and the allocation of novelistic space: *Le grand capitaine* focuses exclusively on the viewpoints of the French and their African soldiers, essentially relegating African rulers and their people to the role of victims of French colonial violence. On the other hand, by imagining the thought processes and depicting the active resistance of Sarraounia and other African leaders to the French, Mamani constructs the former as characters on an equal footing with the opposing French officers, or as more important than them.

My lengthy detour demonstrates that cartoonists Saint-Michel and Le Honzec, and subsequently Logez and Delannoy, chose to engage in an important, wide-ranging debate within France and Africa about the nature and impact of colonialism and imperialism. *Le roi noir n'est pas noir* provides a welcome antidote to the neo-imperialist propaganda of *Les bâtisseurs d'empire* and to the disturbing colonialist nostalgia in comics exemplified by the uncritical editing and republishing of Zig et Puce. *Le roi noir n'est pas noir* is a graphic novel that uses an experimental, black-and-white visual style and multiple narrators to convey a radically anti-colonial perspective and dialogize competing African and French visions of colonialism. Its prologue represents the display of Africans ("Nubiens") in the Jardin zoologique d'acclimatation in the Bois de Boulogne, Paris, in 1883, much like the 1931 display of Kanak.[20] We have already seen similar human zoos in several comics, including *Attractions sensationnelles*, *Frimousset: Directeur de jardin zoologique* and *Le chemin de Tuan*. Images of Africans in cages adjacent to ones containing monkeys illustrate a conversation between a French boy, Ernest Ratillon, and his uncle, who describes the caged people as animals and savages. This dehumanizing spectacle conforms to the fragmentary evidence about how French visitors to the Jardin zoologique d'acclimatation actually envisioned colonized people exhibited there.[21] Yet visually it is the Parisian visitors who are most dehumanized in the graphic novel, because they are drawn as clothed skeletons, suggesting a *danse macabre*. Fifteen years later, in a letter mailed from Africa to his wife in France, Ratillon remembers this outing as a personal turning point, which had oriented him toward a career as a colonial soldier, much as Minister of Colonies Paul Reynaud hoped that the 1931 Exposition coloniale would inspire French youths to play a direct role in colonization. Now a participant in the bloody French military mission to Chad (Mission Afrique Centrale) led by Voulet and Chanoine, Ratillon bitterly regrets his first colonial encounter in the Jardin zoologique d'acclimatation in Paris at the impressionable age of ten.[22] The terrible personal legacy that the visit to the exhibition holds for Ratillon is suggested by a ghastly image of Voulet and Chanoine leading a column of French soldiers, African auxiliary troops and porters as clothed and armed skeletons traveling on horseback and on foot – accompanied by a vulture and a hyena – and bearing the French tricolor flag with a skull emblazoned on it.

Through such imagery *Le roi noir n'est pas noir* represents French colonialism as the bloody horror that it has been to a considerable degree, from the perspective of its victims.[23] The cartoonists' historical fiction connects the propaganda and popular culture of empire (the public exhibition of Africans in Paris – a mass medium of the time) with the ruthless exercise of military power to which they were closely wedded. Through the use of multiple (African and French) narrators, and literary-visual symbolism mixed with historical fact, it offers to the reader an imagined dialogical relationship between various participants, victims and observers of the Voulet and Chanoine expedition. With the words of Ekélé Okolo, an African seer, it also connects the earlier colonial devastation with African immigration to France today: "Voici le destin maudit de ceux d'Afrique promis aux cheminements incessants de l'exil, des voyages sans espoir, de la déportation, de l'esclavage, de l'immigration" [Here is the accursed destiny of those from Africa promised to the incessant wanderings of exile, hopeless voyages, deportation, slavery, immigration]. This goes against the grain of the dominant discourse in France, which denies a connection between the colonial past and the neo-colonial present. Logez and Delannoy rework the colonial myth of Voulet's Africa-induced madness into two "rêves de l'absinthe" [dreams of absinth], which weave together anti-African racism, antisemitism and anti-British rivalry. By placing these delirious rantings before Voulet embarks on his trans-African march, the cartoonists suggest that his rebellion against French authority was due not to the physical hardships of the trek, but rather to a drunken thirst for the blood-soaked rewards of imperialist conquest: power, precious raw materials, military glory and ascendancy over European rivals.

In the graphic novel's representation of the Mission, the combat against Sarraounia plays an important role, as it did in the prose novels. Here too, the threat that Sarraounia poses to French hegemonic power over the resource-rich region is symbolized by her recourse to rudimentary biological-chemical warfare: she possesses a recipe for a poison for arrows concocted from the venom of serpents and marinated in a plant compost. The victims of the poisoned arrows become insane and die. Logez and Delannoy do not make the conflict with Sarrounia the point of departure of their narrative, as is the case in *Le grand capitaine*, nor do they situate it as the focal endpoint of their text, as Mamani did in *Sarraounia: Le drame de la reine magicienne*. Instead it appears within the central chapter, where some of the worst atrocities are committed and the Minister of the Colonies decides to have Voulet and Chanoine arrested by Klobb. A chapter subtitle – "où l'on découvre à quoi sert le canon de Joalland" [where one discovers the purpose of Joalland's cannon]

– helps suggest that the episode serves to impress on the African soldiers in the French army, who are about to mutiny, the superiority of French weaponry, and likewise to strike fear into other African leaders who might be tempted to resist French imperial design. The polyphonic narrative includes a portion of "Le palabre d'Ekélé Okolo" [the palaver of Ekélé Okolo], inserted between the French attack and a journal entry by Ernest Ratillon that refers to its horrific result ("10 avril 1899. Nous quittons Lougou sous des nuées de mouches attirées par les cadavres." [10 April 1899. We leave Lougou under clouds of flies drawn here by the dead bodies.]) In the verbal narration of the intercalated palaver, Okolo provides a voice-over description of the power of Sarraounia. His words are set against and above a series of geometrical patterns (e.g., from African cloth), which provide the background for silhouettes of spears and African warriors. Together, the words and images represent African resistance and cultural accomplishments. This is a very different use of African artistic patterns from what we saw earlier in "Un palais nègre."

Although Saint-Ogan made fun of certain French stereotypes and used the colonial relationship as a source of humor, these were never the object of a political critique. On the contrary, his story about the 1931 Exposition coloniale, for example, ultimately supports the Western civilizing mission. The existence of sharp critiques of colonialism made by the Communists and the Surrealists during the time when Saint-Ogan was publishing apparently never led him to seriously question the colonialist and imperialist aspects of his own art work – instead, he mocked those critiques in the parody of *L'Humanité*. By contrast, *Le roi noir n'est pas noir* stands the civilizing mission on its head. Instead of Saint-Ogan's grotesque containment narrative of how African cannibals at the exhibition are transformed into the domestic servants of French visitors and their American sponsor, Logez and Delannoy suggest that a visit to a colonial exhibition can transform the European spectator into cannibalistic walking dead who prey, vulture-like, on Africans.

Standing in stark contrast to *Le roi noir n'est pas noir*, *Les bâtisseurs d'empire* (Saint-Michel and Le Honzec 1994: 26) suggests that "Voulet et Chanoine sont devenus dingues" [Voulet and Chanoine went bonkers] (cf. Wolgensinger 2002: 47–8), thereby side-stepping the fact that similar massacres, wanton killing and other forms of violence (rape, burning of civilians' homes, etc.) were frequent throughout the other French colonial conquests depicted – but without the damning evidence – in "Histoire des troupes de Marine." Instead, the cartoonists uncritically support the standard colonialist justifications for French imperialist expansion: that it was primarily motivated by the desire to eliminate slavery (22, 28) and piracy (3–5), to punish local warlords who broke legitimate colonial treaties (7), to avenge unprovoked attacks on the French army and massacres of its nationals (4, 9–16, 20, 35); that it was a liberating (22) and pacifying (not a subjugating) force (21, 33, 35); that it constituted a legitimate attempt to defend France's glory and its rights to expansion against rival imperialist European nations such as Great Britain (1, 15, 25), Germany (20) and Belgium (22); and so on. The courage of the French and their colonial soldiers, and the treachery and cowardice of their native opponents, are constant themes in the cartoonists' "Histoire des troupes de Marine."

Conclusion: the reappearance of exhibition comics

The fact that several of the works analyzed here were either first published between the early 1980s and now, or else are recently reissued colonial-era publications, gives my investigation of the exhibition theme heightened relevance today. It also raises interesting questions, such as to what extent, why and how there has been a resurgence of comics with colonial-era themes, specifically ones that thematize the colonial exhibition: can this be attributed to a return of the colonial repressed from a collective unconscious, or do other explanatory paradigms make more sense? I prefer the latter.[24] For example, it is important to recognize the significance of comics fans, booksellers, critics, magazines and publishers in the retrieval and return of colonial-era themes and events. Comics collectors and booksellers who trade in old comics help create a speculative market for colonial-era works, including on the web. In turn, this and other market pressures and incentives encourage comics publishers and copyright holders to reissue colonial-era comics, often in facsimile or other special editions. Bécassine books have remained in print more or less continuously since the colonial era; however, the old-time aspect of the series was re-emphasized from 1968, for example through the reintroduction of cloth binding on the spine and a matte cover (cf. Béra, Denni and Mellot 2006: 107). The physical appearance of Zig et Puce, Bécassine and other colonial-era series and collections of works – such as "Patrimoine BD" [Comics Heritage], issued by Glénat – is now very similar. The CNBDI reissued *Le mariage de M. Lakonik* in its series "La bibliothèque du 9e art" [The library of the 9th Art]. I have already referred to the roles of comics editor and critic Petitfaux, and of comics publishers Futuropolis and then Glénat, in the republication of Zig et Puce, with its Exposition episode. These constitute approaches to the comics heritage ("le patrimoine de la bande dessinée"; Beaty 2008) that are problematic from an anti-colonialist perspective, because editors and publishers fail to adequately foreground and contextualize the racist and colonialist aspects of reissued works.

Comics magazines have constituted another important agent in the return of colonial exhibitions and related events. One important representative of this trend was *Métal aventure*, a short-lived magazine that was an offshoot of *Métal hurlant* [*Heavy Metal*]. *Métal aventure* published comics, photographs and illustrated articles that re-evaluated and recycled colonial material. Its focus on "adventure" helps explain why it devoted so much space to relics of the colonial era, when French colonies were widely depicted in comics, prose fiction, film and news magazines as a space where boundless adventure was available to white men and boys (and, much less often, women and girls). The second issue, published in November 1983, featured a special section on "Nostalgie coloniale" and a cover illustration by French cartoonist Yves Chaland in his typical *ligne claire* retro style: fierce African warriors who could be the comics descendants of Saint-Ogan's cannibals lurk outside the house of a white Catholic, probably Belgian, family from the 1950s, busy opening Christmas presents with an African theme (a leopard-skin dress for the mother, an African warrior disguise for the boy, and a tie with palm trees painted on it for the father). A significant difference between the African cannibals of Saint-Ogan in 1931 and those of Chaland in 1983 is that we have moved from modernism to postmodernism, which is often characterized by pastiche (Miller 2007: 142). The drawing sets the tone of postmodern, ironic nostalgia that permeates this issue, which is a veritable compendium of colonial material and includes journalistic descriptions of important colonial events, including the 1931 Exposition coloniale (39) and the bloody massacre of Voulet and Chanoine (30–2). *Métal aventure* is a concentrated sampler of a 1980s trend diffused throughout popular culture, including comics: the rediscovery of the colonial era, which involved unearthing, dusting off and rehabilitating a great many colonial clichés, often in an ironic mode. Jean-Luc Fromental (p. 3), the editor of the magazine, justified the return to colonial adventure: "Colonies sans honte et sans reproche. Notre génération n'a rien à expier, rien à regretter que le souvenir d'un souvenir, truqué, menteur et fascinant." [Colonies without shame and without reproach. Our generation has nothing to expiate, nothing to regret, apart from the memory of a memory, faked, lying and fascinating.] Now freed from, or absolved of, any guilt, regret or responsibility – claims Fromental – a new generation of cartoonists, journalists and readers can play freely with colonialist identities again, much as one tries on a set of colonial clothing that one has inherited or rediscovered: indeed, a page of this issue has three photographs, supposedly taken in the Royal Colonial Museum in Belgium (Tervuren), with models demonstrating colonial attire for upcoming New Year's Eve celebrations ("Cet hiver le look tropical est de rigueur pour les réveillons de fin d'année" [This winter the tropical look is indispensable for New Year's parties], p. 40). This issue of *Métal aventure* is a significant example – and by no means an isolated one – of how, in the early 1980s, there was a renewed interest within popular culture – including in and around the comics industry – in (neo-)colonial-era stories, iconography and comics.

Indeed, we have seen that there are several new comics and graphic novels that thematize or allude to colonial exhibitions (Appendix 2). In post-1962 comics, references to French colonial exhibitions began in the 1980s, continued in the 1990s, but have picked up especially since 2000: at least nine new comics stories (as series or individual volumes) referring to, or depicting, colonial exhibitions were published from 2001–9. This was a greater number than I found for the entirety of the preceding seventeen years, beginning with "L'expo" in 1983. So there has clearly been a growing interest in colonial exhibitions in recent years, but in which of these events are cartoonists most interested? Returning to the issues raised by Ageron about the degree to which the Exposition coloniale of 1931 is a memorial site for the French, we can see that comics provide us with some relevant information. Counting both colonial-era and recent comics in my sample, there are far more stories (twelve) that clearly depict or allude to the 1931 Exposition than to any other exhibition. Second in number of appearances are the Exposition universelle of 1900 and the Centenaire de l'Algérie, with four comics each. On the other hand, if one counts only the post-1962 comics in my corpus, one finds an equal number of comics stories (three each) that represent or refer to the Centenaire de l'Algérie, the 1931 exhibition in Paris, colonial exhibitions in Marseilles (1906, 1922), and (other) human zoos at the Paris Jardin d'acclimatation or elsewhere. This suggests that although the 1931 Exposition coloniale is indeed a *lieu de mémoire* in French comics, other colonial exhibitions are important too.

So why has the theme of colonial exhibitions re-entered the market in new stories and in these ways? There are several factors. Of course the circulation, selling and republication of colonial-era comics about such events have probably helped reintroduce the theme to cartoonists in recent decades. In the 1990s, one finds depictions of colonial exhibitions in a graphic novel that both celebrates and critiques the actions of French colonizers in Algeria (*Le centenaire*) and in an entirely uncritical homage to the French colonial army (two volumes by Saint-Michel and Le Honzec). The latter, especially, is representative of a neo-imperialist rehabilitation of French colonialism that has been very visible among the most conservative and retrograde institutions, individuals and groups in French society, including the resurgent French far right, represented by Jean-Marie Le Pen and his political party, the Front National (now headed by Marine Le Pen). However, individuals and groups across most of the political spectrum have indulged in colonial nostalgia and imperialist rehabilitation at one time or another over recent decades.[25] More critical forms of exoticism can also play a role in the return to the colonial exhibition and colonial history in general (cf. Forsdick 2002, 2005b): for example, historian Pascal Blanchard has spoken of two cartoonists' "double passion for Asia – one [Jiro] with a fascination for the culture of the Far East and the other [Baloup] in a historical filiation, with a father of Vietnamese background" (in Baloup and Jiro 2005: 11).

Another explanation, also reflected in Blanchard's statement, is the arrival on the comics publishing scene of artists with a direct family connection to colonial history and its links to multi-ethnic France today. The renewed interest in colonial exhibitions beginning in the early 1980s is therefore related to the increased visibility and activities of those ethnic minority groups living in France that originated in former French colonies (Indochina, North and sub-Saharan Africa, etc.) and participated in colonial exhibitions, and of colonial settler groups (e.g., from North Africa or New Caledonia). Of the cartoonists who have published exhibition stories over the last few decades, at least six have this kind of personal link: Mechkour (Franco-Algerian), Baloup (of French and Vietnamese parentage), Bernard Berger and JAR (*Caldoche*, i.e., of New Caledonian colonizer heritage), Joyaux-Brédy (*Pied-Noir*) and Ferrandez (born in Algiers to a French settler family and raised in southern France). There are related connections between exhibition comics and various forms of activism by cartoonists. For example, Joyaux-Brédy was inducted into the prestigious French Légion d'honneur for having created a branch, in Aix-en-Provence, of the Cercle Algérianiste, an association that promotes a colonialist perspective on French Algeria.[26] The comic-book series that she scripted to defend French Algeria, including its Centenaire de l'Algérie française, was published, and is distributed, by her organization.[27] Mechkour helped produce artistic material (posters, comics, etc.) that depicted or promoted ethnic minority activist initiatives of the early 1980s, which correlates with the lampooning of French racism in his parodic, post-colonial exhibition comic. Ferrandez contributed artwork to a collective volume that condemns a French police massacre of peaceful Algerian protestors on 17 October 1961, during the Algerian War – he also (partially) critiques colonialist ideology in his book dedicated to the Centenaire de l'Algérie française (1994b). Christin was active in anti-colonialist movements, although he has no ethnic connection to the colonies – he too is therefore closely attuned to the colonial roots of *métissage*, exoticism and racist exploitation in France's multi-ethnic society of today (Christin and Goetzinger 1996). Despite their important political divergences and different ethnic backgrounds, all of these artists share a goal of disseminating their artistic and historical vision of the colonial era. Cartoonists with an interest in regional French identity and its connections to colonial history depict the historical antecedents of post-colonial ethnic diversity there (e.g., Falba and Di Martino, as well as Baloup and Jiro, all on Marseilles).[28]

Nonetheless, almost all of the comics and graphic novels that thematize colonial exhibitions were scripted and drawn by either ethnic mainstream cartoonists or cartoonists from settler groups; only Mechkour and Baloup (of mixed heritage) are from post-colonial ethnic minorities. Moreover, as we have seen, Mechkour's references are to French colonialism in the framework of a future exhibition (1989) more than twenty-five years after Algeria gained formal independence, not to a past one. So although the theme of colonial exhibitions is related to the emergence in France of ethnic minorities of color with historical roots in French colonialism, cartoonists from those groups have not generally chosen this theme. This may be because the representations of their ethnic forebears at these events were generally marked by colonial exoticism and abjection (cannibals, savages, poorly assimilated, primitive, etc.). Indeed, this may be part of the reason why Berger and JAR (2001) did not depict the 1931 exhibition of Kanak, but instead showed the New Caledonian exhibition building and its Kanak artifacts from the Exposition universelle of 1900.[29] To have restaged the racist display of Kanak in Paris could have been a divisive gesture, which might have spoiled the vision of trans-ethnic unity among New Caledonians that the cartoonists promote in their four-volume series (Macdonald 2008).[30] Although Baloup and Jiro (2005) mention three examples of colonial exhibitions in *Le chemin de Tuan*, they do not actually depict Vietnamese at the colonial exhibitions in Marseilles (1922) or Paris (1931), preferring instead to focus on the anti-colonialist activism of Vietnamese and other colonial groups in Paris during the intervening period. Still, they do visually depict and verbally narrate the abject display of a black African as a cannibal in France (77–8).

The professional interest of certain individuals and groups in representations of the colonial period also helps explain the reappearance of colonial exhibitions in comics: for example, Saint-Michel, who scripted two of the comics analyzed above, was a historian by training, Christin is a professor of journalism and Delannoy is a professor of visual semiotics, who has published a study of Art Spiegelman's *Maus*. Two of the graphic novels analyzed in this chapter were prefaced by prominent French historians of colonialism and post-colonial culture: *Le centenaire*, introduced by Stora, a historian of Algeria; and *Le chemin de Tuan*, presented by Blanchard, a specialist on colonial history and "human zoos," and a member of the ACHAC group. The authors of these comics read, and were inspired by, the research of these and other historians and critics. It is clear that the two following comics also have connections to professional historical research such as that published by ACHAC. In *Le diable amoureux et autres films jamais tournés par Méliès*, which uses fantasy to recreate Paris from 1900 to the late 1920s, the cartoonists begin a short story, entitled "Un fantôme sur la lune," at the foot of the Eiffel tower (Vehlmann and Duchazeau 2009: 27). As Georges Méliès and his wife observe the "village nègre" [Negro village] of the 1900 Exposition universelle, he imagines a film that he could make, with himself in blackface, performing a dance like the Africans they are watching (cf. Bergougniou, Clignet and David 2001: 78–80; Hale 2008: 32–9). His wife, shocked by the spectacle, calls it a "zoo humain," a concept spread by a published historical study (*Zoos humains*, Bancel et al. 2002; cf. Blanchard et al. 2008), a documentary film and numerous articles in the press and scholarly journals. A bystander, perhaps an organizer, curtly corrects her: "On dit 'spectacle ethnologique,' Madame" [We say "ethnological spectacle," Madam]. The rest of the story is a fantastic fable, recounted by a medium (Mage Raimondo), that turns on its head the animalization of Africans by the French: a human is captured by anthropomorphized rats, who have taken over a neighborhood of Paris. After vivisecting him, they display him in a cage so that high-society rats, dressed like Parisian bourgeois, can observe him and, paradoxically, comment on his bestiality and backwardness, parodying French social Darwinism and racism. A female rat, dressed like a Parisian, defends his humanity, exactly as Méliès's wife had done at the Exposition. The specter of (African? French?) cannibalism, and of revenge for racist or trans-species mistreatment, is introduced obliquely in the conclusion, through an ironic reference to the consumption of rats by Parisians during the Prussian siege of 1870–1.

Zoo humain is also the title of the second volume in the "Kia Ora" comics series (Jouvray, Ollagnier and Effa 2008), whose characters are displayed at the Jardin d'acclimatation in Paris around 1910, and elsewhere. There, as in "Un fantôme sur la lune," the cartoonists point to the collusion between colonial ethnology and racist popular spectacle: they show ethnologists at work, measuring, denuding and photographing colonial subjects in order to classify them racially (Jouvray, Ollagnier and Effa 2008: 32–3). Curiously, the main focus in this French-language series is on the Maoris, a group colonized by the British, not the French or the Belgians. This probably has something to do with the fascination in France today for the Maori dance that the New Zealand national rugby team performs at matches to impress the public and rival teams – the initial engagement of the Maori actors is for them to perform precisely this type of dance. However, the series does try hard to present colonial history and human zoos in a critical light to today's youth, by humanizing a colonized group and connecting their exhibition with other forms of human teratology (e.g., people shown as freaks at Coney Island in New York). In the absence of much historical evidence about how the colonized at exhibitions actually felt about these events, or what they thought about them (L'Estoile 2008), the cartoonists imagine what they might have felt and ascribe agency to them: the fiction presents their reasons for agreeing to participate in an exhibition; the subsequent anger of some indigenous actors when conditions become too demeaning; a resulting organized work stoppage; and the desire of others to continue performing nonetheless. The limited historical documentation that is available suggests that the reactions and perceptions of participants in such events were both complex and diverse: although they protested strongly against the conditions to which they were subjected, when it was time to return home some preferred to remain in Europe for a time (Dauphiné 1998: 81–118, 126–7; Bergougniou, Clignet and David 2001; L'Estoile 2008). It is worth remembering that despite the oppressive conditions for the colonized that often prevailed in metropolitan France, colonial repression and exploitation could be far harsher in the colonies themselves. Still, "unruly natives" in the *métropole* could be quickly expelled, if police surveillance detected their anti-colonial activities (e.g., Stora 1989; Norindr 1996: 33–51).

Another recent work, *La décolonisation*, volume three of a *Petite histoire des colonies françaises*, by Grégory Jarry and Otto T. (2009), parodies both the 1931 Exposition coloniale and the counter-Exposition (by the Surrealists and Communists), as part of the artists' satirical representation of the colonial epic story of France. Much of the sardonic humor of the series comes from a disjunct between visual and verbal narration. For example, the narrator of the first three volumes is de Gaulle, or rather "l'image du général de Gaulle, reconstituée à partir des archives de l'époque" [the image of General de Gaulle, reconstructed from period archives], as he himself proclaims in the introduction to the first volume (Jarry and Otto T. 2006: n.p.), but he is represented as a stick figure and so is by no means an archival reconstitution, at least in visual terms. In the first of three pages that recount first the Exposition and then the counter-Exposition, the artists represent the Exposition as an advertising extravaganza dedicated to (mostly food) products commonly associated with blacks and with sub-Saharan Africa in colonial times: the chocolate-flavored Banania breakfast food; Menier (French), Nestlé (Swiss), Poulain (French) and Van Houten (Dutch) brands of chocolate; and shoe polish (Plate 21). The artists also represent figures associated with such products, with the Exposition and, more generally, with French colonial representations of black Africa: a drawing of a Senegalese rifleman appears on the Banania building, because that remains the company's best-known advertising icon, still used in various forms today;[31] and there is a statue of Josephine Baker, the African-American singer and actress, recognizable here by the pose and the banana skirt that she famously wore.[32] No indigenous actors are visible at the scene; instead, white men get drunk on Kronembourg [*sic*] beer, while white women and children, eating cotton candy, visit the exhibitions. This parodic image of the event represents it as an orgy of oral consumption and colonial advertising. It is preceded by a recounting of the bloody Kongo-Wara war, in Oubangui-Chari (in French Equatorial Africa), where French colonial forces brutally repressed an African revolt. The textual narrator's transition suggests the depth of colonial cynicism that could produce an event such as the Exposition: "La révolte écrasée, nous décidâmes de faire table rase du passé en organisant une merveilleuse opération de communication: l'Exposition coloniale internationale de 1931" [The revolt having been crushed, we decided to make a clean sweep of the past, by organizing a marvelous communications operation: the Exposition coloniale internationale of 1931]. The following page parodies the colonialist representation, at and around the Exposition, of the savage virility of Kanak men from New Caledonia by depicting a Kanak man pulling up his grass skirt and showing his genitals to European children who pass by, frightening them and getting one into trouble with his father by accusing the boy of peeping. The following page constitutes the only representation of the counter-Exposition that I am aware of in comics. It lampoons the very low attendance at the event, which all recent historical accounts underline (Plate 22). The thrust of the book (and the series) is nonetheless clearly anti-colonial, which renders this gentle joke about the relative failure of the counter-Exposition very different from Saint-Ogan's contribution to the parody of *L'Humanité* in *Le coup de patte*. At the end of the volume, the cartoonists list the various films and books, including several by prominent historians of French colonialism, that they consulted to produce their critical view of France's colonial epic story.[33]

In fact, all of the recent historical comics in Appendix 2 rely at least to some extent on learned publications by historians of French colonialism, and some artists go to impressive lengths in their search for accurate historical material and authentic visual documents on which they base their fictions in fascinating ways. The recent historical research on colonial exhibitions has undoubtedly stimulated the interest of cartoonists in these events. Therefore, several of the recent comics thematizing exhibitions exemplify a trend found also in other comics about the colonial period: an alignment with developments in scholarly research, publication and intervention in public debates over how to view colonial history and treat post-colonial minorities.

CHAPTER FOUR

French Trans-African Expeditions in Comics

Colonial expeditions

... and Mr. Citroën, for his part, throws his civilizing 'caterpillar' across the Sahara... [which will] consolidate the position of the colonial sharks. (Nguyên Ái Quôc)[1]

The French colors shiver under the warm southern breeze. The nostalgia of the fifes mixes with the vibrant salutation of the bugles, and off we go towards the great adventure. (Haardt and Audouin-Dubreuil 1971: 17)[2]

In two comic books in which the characters Zig, Puce and Alfred travel across Africa and meet its colonized inhabitants, celebrated cartoonist Alain Saint-Ogan borrowed directly from one or more in a series of colonial-era automobile expeditions. These were called "traversées" [crossings], "raids" – a military term[3] – or "croisières" [cruises], of which the most famous were "La croisière noire," across Africa (28 October 1924–26 June 1925), and "La croisière jaune," across Asia (4 April 1931–12 February 1932).[4] The term "cruise" suggests an oceanic voyage, as Croisière noire directors Georges-Marie Haardt and Louis Audouin-Dubreuil (1971: 33) explain in their published account of the expedition (cf. Wolgensinger 2002: 205). In his preface to the account of an earlier trans-Saharan Citroën trip (17 December 1922–6 March 1923), which preceded the Croisière noire, André Citroën plainly described the colonialist, national – both military and economic – motivations behind "[t]he Citroën Raid: The First Automobile Crossing of the Sahara, from Touggourt to Timbuktu, by way of Atlantis" (Haardt and Audouin-Dubreuil 1923: 8–9). The dream of Citroën, as a French industrial capitalist, was to have his automobiles profitably connect French colonies in Africa, thereby replacing trans-Saharan African camel caravans.[5] The best-publicized crossing of Africa was the Croisière noire, undertaken in half-track, caterpillar vehicles [*autochenilles*] by the Citroën company, which collaborated with the French government and army and other European colonial authorities (Belgian and British).[6] The tight colonial collaboration between industrial and government sponsors is illustrated by the fact that, at the request of French president Gaston Doumergue, the original itinerary was modified to include Madagascar so as to symbolically link the island with France's other African colonies (Haardt and Audouin-Dubrueil 1971: 9; cf. Deschamps 1999: 79; Wolgensinger 2002: 200–1).[7]

Beyond the primary aims of commercial expansion and empire-building, automobile raids could include virile colonial rest and relaxation: the Croisière noire certainly mapped a route across the Sahara, symbolically linking France's North African colonies to its West African ones, and then across to Madagascar, but progress across the continent was interspersed with hunting expeditions. The Croisière noire was also an imperialist extravaganza, documented in books, magazines, photographs, film, drawings, paintings and museum exhibitions, which recorded meetings between the directors of the expedition and compliant African leaders, but also depicted naked African women, the technological taming of nature by the white man, and the wild game slaughtered along the way.[8] It was a distant, commercial, twentieth-century echo of Napoleon's invasion of Egypt in 1798, the French capture of Algiers in 1830 and many subsequent imperialist incursions, in the sense that, although not a military invasion or conquest, the Croisière noire did include military, scientific and ethnographic components, as had those earlier imperialist expeditions. Audouin-Dubreuil and Commandant Bettembourg (another participant in the Croisière noire) had both participated, as officers, in a French army expedition in the Sahara in 1919 (see Citroën, in Haardt and Audouin-Dubreuil 1923: 10–11). Aircraft machine guns were mounted on some or all of the half-tracks during the first Citroën trans-Saharan expedition, for defense against hostile Africans (Citroën in Haardt and Audouin-Dubreuil 1923: 16–18; Deschamps 1999: 64, 74, 77), and some Croisière noire vehicles carried mounted machine guns too.[9] The expedition collected information about African regions crossed, and brought back specimens of plants and animals found there. And it relied on, recapitulated and added to colonial ethnography and ethnology about the colonized, through post-voyage accounts and the many African artifacts brought back to France and exhibited there. For example, its organizers excitedly describe the Mangbetou people in colonialist terms that evoke an evolution from cannibal to civilized and recall European infatuation with "art nègre": their artistic achievements "bear witness to a sense of harmony of lines and of composition that it is troubling to discover among natives who were still cannibals a few years ago" (Haardt and Audouin-Dubreuil 1971: 258).[10] *La croisière noire*, their written account, is a compendium of colonialist and imperialist myths and commonplaces,[11] many of which have been recycled, rarely in a critical fashion, in French and Belgian comics over the last thirty years: for example, repeated references to African cannibalism (e.g., Haardt and Audouin-Dubreuil 1971: 118–28, 132, 200, 210, 222, 228);[12] Robinson Crusoe and conquest as a quest for paradise (90–1);[13] an erotic fascination with Algerian Ouled-Naïl women, reputed to prostitute themselves in order to accumulate a dowry (23–4, 27, 222);[14] a description of a West African woman as a *Vénus noire* [black Venus] (48–9) or Eve after the fall (282);[15] a fascination with the harem (53–6);[16] the self-justifying claim that French and European imperialism were the legitimate heirs of the Roman Empire (49–50, 92, 130–1, 214, 300);[17] the depiction of Africans, including Senegalese riflemen (black colonial auxiliary soldiers), as big children (16, 239);[18] the Arabian Nights as an interpretive paradigm for understanding Arabo-Muslim Africans (24, 43, 46, 160);[19] rebel African secret societies of leopard-men or panther-men (121–4);[20] *femmes à plateaux* [women wearing large lip plugs] (105–8);[21] Stanley – and, by extension, any white man imbued with his aura – as a "boula-matari" [breaker of rocks], and as such, greatly admired by the Congolese (197–9, 234, 238, 355);[22] Africans (pygmies) as monkey-like (225–34); the slow evolution of African societies toward the supposedly much higher stage of European civilization (302–3); and colonial exhibitions as suppliers of accurate cultural information about the colonized (108).

Zig, Puce et Furette: Saint-Ogan and the Croisière noire

The Citroën expeditions and other European trans-African road trips inspired several cartoonists to create French-language comic strips and books, published from 1923 through at least 2006 (Appendix 3). These comics generally feature a half-track or caterpillar vehicle similar to the ones used in the Citroën road trips. Here, as in Chapter 2, I begin by analyzing comics by Saint-Ogan, for several reasons: he and his comics occupy an important place in the canon of French comics; his depictions of colonial expeditions were some of the earliest in comics and have been republished at least twice since most French colonies gained formal independence; and one episode of Zig et Puce (*Zig, Puce et Furette*) retains essential features of the Croisière noire, and is quite long. Saint-Ogan first refers to half-tracks in Africa in volume two of the meandering, picaresque adventures of his young French protagonists, when Zig and Puce, with their pet penguin, Alfred, and American girlfriend, Dolly, encounter a gang of French bandits and kidnappers, and their African assistants, in Senegal (1995b: 18–19; serialized 1927–8; first book edition, 1928). The children try to escape in the bandits' half-track, but the brigands immediately foil their getaway by causing their vehicle to explode. The first mention of an organized trans-African crossing in half-tracks occurs in the fourth volume, *Zig et Puce à New York* [Zig and Puce in New York] (Saint-Ogan 1995d; serialized 1928–30; first book edition 1930). When a skittish camel runs off, leaving Zig, Puce and Alfred stranded in the Sahara, they befriend a lion (an adaptation of one of Aesop's fables) and must pacify Africans afraid of the beast, before being rescued by a caravan of half-track vehicles which takes them to Pretoria (32–40). As did the French leaders of the Croisière noire, Zig and Puce capture wild game (the lion), assert their dominance over the Africans they meet and cross the desert by half-track, thereby echoing Citroën's claim (in Haardt and Audouin-Dubreuil 1923: 8–9) about the superiority of the car over the camel for crossing the Sahara, that is to say, of new Western over traditional African technologies of transportation.

Saint-Ogan later returned to the colonial motif of a motorized trans-African voyage, greatly reworking and extending it. Beginning in 1932, he serialized a lengthy episode, subsequently published in book form as *Zig, Puce et Furette*, in which Zig and Puce cross Africa again, but as drivers of an expedition clearly based on the Croisière noire (Saint-Ogan 1996a).[23] The boys undertake the journey to help rebuild the fortune of their American benefactor by generating publicity for "Furette," an amphibious vehicle produced by his automobile factory. The narrative tension comes from attempts by the boys to overcome three types of setbacks: their initial unfamiliarity with the vehicle; mechanical malfunctions of the prototype; and perfidious attempts by a rival car manufacturer to sabotage the expedition, which echoes the genuine rivalry between Renault and Citroën.[24] Saint-Ogan reduced the multiple colonial goals of the real-life *Croisière noire* to the commercial aspect. He also inverted the itinerary's direction, perhaps to more plausibly have his characters finish their expedition by arriving in New York, triumphantly meeting their sponsor and visiting the American vehicle factory (19), much as Charles Lindbergh visited the Citroën factory in Paris after his transoceanic flight in May 1927 (Wolgensinger 1996: 52–4). Sponsorship of the expedition by an American company instead of a French one makes its connection to French imperialist propaganda and commercial publicity less obvious or direct.[25] However, the real-life French original is still implicitly present in the national identity of the boys and in their African itinerary: Port Saïd (Saint-Ogan 1996a: 18), the northern gateway to the Suez Canal (a key imperialist project), and then through the Somali coastal region, Madagascar, the Congo, Oubangui, Upper Volta (now Burkina Faso) and Mauritania (19) – in reverse order, this corresponds closely to the route taken by the *Croisière noire* across France's colonies (Plate 23).

The French boys, their bird and their car, a symbol of Western technological progress, are wildly acclaimed by the local inhabitants, just as in the visual and written documents produced by the organizers of the *Croisière noire* and by the French news media. On the other hand, when the boys drive across Madagascar, they surprise the island's inhabitants, which helps to translate one aspect of colonial ideology. In "L'imaginaire colonial dans la bande dessinée," Yann Holo (1993a: 75) argues that in this episode of *Zig et Puce* one finds both a "documentary desire" and a "colonial discourse [...] opposing the tradition of portage to the modernity of the automobile": the car driven by Zig and Puce is contrasted to the colonial "chaise à porteurs" [sedan chair].[26] The victory of Western technical know-how and perseverance is also represented by an image of Furette wearing a laurel wreath (19), recalling the imperialist claim that France had inherited Rome's mantle of empire, as Haardt and Audouin-Dubreuil stated (1971: e.g., 130).

Tintin in the Congo: early traces of the Croisière noire in comics?

Several other comics created by French cartoonists and published in France were inspired directly or indirectly by trans-African colonial road expeditions, especially the Croisière noire. There is also *Tintin au Congo*, by Belgian cartoonist Hergé and set mostly in the Belgian Congo. It is important as an early, and still influential (though now controversial), model of a trans-African crossing and as a prime example of how Africa has been depicted in French-language comics – we will see, for example, that the most recent comic inspired by the Croisière noire parodies Hergé's seminal colonialist story. Hergé may have partially modeled his story on French trans-African expeditions such as the Croisière noire – although Tintin travels by ship[27] to Matadi (via Boma) in the Belgian Congo, he there acquires a battered car described by the salesman as a "modèle transsaharien excellent," in order to continue his journey to the interior of the country (Hergé 1973: 184, 197, 201).[28] Alison Murray Levine (2005: 87, 92), a historian who has studied the Croisière noire, has plausibly suggested that *Tintin au Congo* was indeed inspired by that event (cf. Deschamps 1999: 165). Hergé – with his parents and his (then) girlfriend Germaine Kieckens – is said to have visited the Exposition coloniale in Paris, in May 1931 (it may have been on this trip that he met Saint-Ogan).[29] The Exposition included an exhibition dedicated to the Croisière noire,[30] but serial publication of *Tintin au Congo* (5 June 1930–18 June 1931) was almost complete before the Exposition officially opened (on 6 May 1931), so if the artist did draw inspiration for his story from the Croisière noire it must have been earlier, via other sources. In fact, media coverage and Citroën publicity related to the Croisière noire, including a documentary film about the event, had already circulated widely,[31] and had reached into popular culture and children's literature, for example in André Hellé's illustrated storybook *Le tour du monde en 80 pages* [Around the World in 80 Pages] (1927: n.p.), or through a two-volume adaptation by Henri Pellier (1928a, 1928b) of the prose account of the expedition published by Haardt and Audouin-Dubreuil the preceding year. Pellier's version, *Avec la Croisière noire* [With the Croisière noire], appeared in "Les livres roses pour la jeunesse," a series of illustrated children's stories distributed by Librairie Larousse (Plate 24). In it, a girl and a boy (Marcelle and André) actively participate in the expedition, offering a child's perspective on the event.[32]

Hergé's story certainly shares many features with the Croisière noire: Tintin uses a movie camera to film Africa and its animals, much as film director Léon Poirier did (Levine 2005: 87; Hergé 1973: 201, 226–7, 278–87) – indeed, Levine (2009: 190) notes that Tintin's movie camera "exactly resembles that of Poirier and Specht" from the Citroën extravaganza; although the Croisière noire passed mainly through French colonies, it included a lengthy segment in the Belgian Congo (Haardt and Audouin-Dubreuil 1971: 209–93); the theme of world-wide reporting about a trans-African trip is prominent in the Tintin story (Hergé 1973: 184, 197, 200–1, 268, 272–3, 275, 289–91), recalling the enormous publicity surrounding the Croisière noire; Tintin meets pygmies (Hergé 1973: 266–9) – an encounter with them was a highlight of the Croisière noire (Haardt and Audouin-Dubreuil 1971: 225–34); Tintin is carried in a "tippoy" [carrying hammock or seat] or "chaise à porteurs" [sedan chair] (Hergé 1973: 276–7) – an almost identical one was used on the Croisière noire (1971: 159–62; plate between pp. 104–5 in Haardt and Audouin-Dubreuil 1927a);[33] the principal African antagonist of Tintin is an "homme-panthère" [panther-man] (Hergé 1973: 236–9), whose secret society is described by Haardt and Audouin-Dubreuil (1971: 121–4);[34] they discuss and use the term "boula-matari," the supposed nickname of Stanley (1971: 197–9, 234, 238, 355), which is used to refer to Tintin too (Hergé 1973: 293);[35] and, as many Hergé experts have noted,[36] and as Hergé himself acknowledged (in Sadoul 2000: 123), big-game hunting by Tintin turns into a massacre (Hergé 1973: 208–11, 250–5, 280–8) – much as Haardt, Audouin-Dubreuil and their companions shot many wild animals during their trip across Africa (1971: 141–87, 245–84; Deschamps 1999: 150–5; cf. Met 1996).

I have not found confirmation that Hergé was familiar with the historical event in recent publications about him. However, Huibrecht Van Opstal (2006), who published an authoritative work on Tintin and Hergé (Van Opstal 1998), stated that, although he could not confirm whether the Croisière noire was a source of information for Hergé, if the event had been widely publicized (as was indeed the case), Hergé had probably heard of it. There are no half-tracks or caterpillar vehicles in *Tintin au Congo*, whereas their appearance in French comics typically indicates that the Croisière noire or other

Citroën expeditions inspired them. Still, the reference to a "transsaharien" automobile is a wink at trans-African expeditions such as those sponsored by Citroën or Renault.[37] Tintin's dog companion, Milou ("Snowy" in the English translations), may also have been modeled after Flossie, the mascot of the first trans-Saharan half-track expedition that Haardt and Audouin-Dubreuil directed together, in 1922–3 (Haardt and Audouin-Dubreuil 1923: 35, 95, photo between pp. 48–9; Deschamps 1999: 66, 73, 85; Wolgensinger 2002: 80).

Automobile expeditions keep on rolling through colonial-era French comics: cars and camels, troops and Touaregs

"Tintin au Congo," which was serialized earlier than most of the other comics in my corpus (see Appendix 3), could have influenced their creators, although the reference to a trans-African expedition in *Zig et Puce à New York* predates the Tintin story, and Saint-Ogan's work was itself an early model for Hergé's comics (Groensteen 1996a; Sadoul 2000: 123). On the other hand, at least three cartoonists – Louis Forton, Jean Bruller and Saint-Ogan – may have drawn their inspiration for expedition comics from the Paris Exposition coloniale of 1931 (and may have influenced each other), because they all created an exhibition episode during or after the Exposition and followed that with an expedition episode. The Citroën exhibit on the Croisière noire at the Paris Exposition (near the entrance), and commemorative material there on related trans-African colonial expeditions, could easily have inspired these three cartoonists. Moreover, trans-African road trips were organized in conjuction with both the Centenaire de l'Algérie, in 1930, and the Exposition coloniale internationale, in 1931.[38] These factors may explain why expedition episodes in comics by the three artists appeared after the Exposition instead of earlier, closer to the time of the Croisière noire (1924–5).[39] In any case, their twin exhibition–expedition sequences remind us that the organizers of the Exposition hoped that a visit to it would inspire children and others to travel to the colonies. This connection is latent in the three comics – a narrative sequence, rather than an obvious causal logic, connects the two events, although Forton's Pieds-Nickelés characters do refer to the Exposition during the expedition episode. Moreover, the African adventures that the three comics offer children deviate significantly from the colonial ideal of the Exposition organizers.

Je reviens à moi, au milieu d'un bruit de chaînes infernal.
J'ouvris les yeux: le drapeau de la France! C'était la mission
Haardt-Audoin-Dubreuil. J'étais sauvé.

Figure 8   A mechanical ending to a misogynist parody of an orientalist tale: the first trans-Saharan Citroën expedition saves a Frenchman after his erotic fantasy disappears like a mirage. Jean Routier, "Elle??...," *Automobilia*, no. 136 (15 January 1923), p. 29, frame 8.

I have located six examples of pre-1962 comics that depict trans-African journeys in French comics and appear to be inspired by the Croisière noire or similar expeditions (including the two expedition episodes in Zig et Puce, analyzed above; see Appendix 2). Here, as for colonial exhibitions in pre-1962 French comics (see Chapter 2), the main mode of depiction is the colonial carnivalesque, used in varying ways. In these colonial-era comics, although the carnivalesque can be used to mock colonialist projects and pretensions, it does not entail a radical, politicized critique: it may reverse the colonial hierarchy, but only for a limited time. "Elle??...," a two-page comic that appeared in the magazine *Automobilia* (15 January 1923, pp. 28–9), explicitly refers to the first expedition by Haardt and Audouin-Dubreuil, across the Sahara desert, 17 December 1922–6 March 1923 (Figure 8).[40] The narrative, by Jean Routier, is a misogynist parody of an orientalist tale:[41] the French narrator-protagonist crosses the Sahara in search of "Elle," finds her in an isolated Saharan castle (guarded by Touaregs) and sees that she is old and ugly.[42] He then flees into the desert, almost perishes of heat and thirst, but is rescued by Haardt and Audouin-Dubreuil in their half-track in the nick of time.[43] We have already seen the theme of a colonial expedition saving a French person lost in the desert in *Zig et Puce à New York*.[44] It is related both to the myth of the providential explorer (e.g., Stanley arriving to "save" Livingstone) and the depiction of the Sahara desert as an inhospitable place for Westerners, inhabited mostly by fierce nomads and their camels but conquerable by Western technology. The Croisière noire certainly harnessed, and contributed to, this colonialist imagery. Many expeditionary comics, even recent ones, replay the colonial rescue motif.

Bruller's *Le mariage de M. Lakonik* [The Marriage of Mr. Lakonik] reworks these colonial commonplaces in a carnivalesque manner. His book was first published in 1931, the year of the Exposition coloniale. Its protagonist, M. Lakonik, is a hapless, low-level French bureaucrat who makes a bizarre voyage across the globe, during which he is transported by white explorers driving a half-track from Tunis to Lake Chad (Bruller 2000: 33–4). Bruller transparently spoofs Citroën's trans-Saharan crossings and their famous leaders (Plate 25). His fictional expedition, consisting of two Frenchmen – one tall and thin, like Haardt, and a shorter one, like Audouin-Dubreuil – driving a large *autochenille*, is named "Mission John Citron. Traversée du Sahara Tunis-Lac Tchad" (Bruller 2000: 34). Although the Croisière noire is never mentioned by name, it is alluded to through the fictional expedition's title, including its pun: John Citron. When the first name is pronounced with a French accent, the full name sounds like "jaune citron" [lemon yellow]. A Citroën car, model 5CV type C, mass-produced from 1922, was often painted yellow and consequently nicknamed "la petite citron" – "citron" is sometimes used to refer to other Citroën cars too.[45] The fictional title also recalls the names of Citroën expeditions and the books that Haardt and Audouin-Dubreuil published about them, for example, *Le raid Citroën: La première traversée du Sahara en automobile: De Touggourt à Tombouctou par l'Atlantide* (1923); "L'expédition Citroën Centre-Afrique" was the official name of the Croisière noire; both expeditions were also referred to as "missions"; and reaching Lake Chad was the first major objective of the Croisière noire (Haardt and Audouin Dubreuil 1971: 62–3).[46]

The fictional doubles of Haardt and Audouin-Dubreuil abandon Lakonik in the middle of the Sahara desert, because when he requests to be taken to Bizerte, where he hopes to board a boat for France, and not continue on to Chad, they think that sunstroke [un coup de soleil] has driven him mad (a common colonial motif, as we saw above) and are unwilling to change course. Here, Bruller inverts the theme of rescue by a providential explorer in a carnivalesque manner: instead of first getting lost in the Sahara and then being saved by the colonial expedition (as in "Elle??..."), Lakonik joins the expedition by mistake and is subsequently abandoned by it in the desert. Lakonik and his fiancée next encounter plundering, murderous North Africans and then gullible black cannibals (34–8), much like those in volume one of *Zig et Puce* (see above, Chapter 1). However, Bruller's representation of North Africans in *Le mariage de M. Lakonik* differs significantly from the one in *Zig et Puce: En route pour l'Amérique* (serialized 1925–7). In Saint-Ogan's volume (1995a: 10), created around the time of the Rif War, there was an explicitly political dimension to the initial portrayal of North Africans: Zig and Puce cry out "les Rifains!" when they are captured and later, "Vive la France!" when, after having escaped, they are surrounded by French soldiers whom they first mistake for Moroccans.[47] By contrast, *Le mariage de M. Lakonik* was drawn later, after the Europeans had defeated the Moroccan resistance. In Bruller's comic, although North African characters take M. Lakonik captive, their violence is directed mainly against one another, and is pushed to absurd lengths for humorous effect.

Images of raiding nomads are widespread in colonial-era French and Belgian comics set in North Africa, most memorably in Hergé's *Le crabe aux pinces d'or* [The Crab with the Golden Claws] (Hergé 1980: 306–13; first edition, 1940), where colonial troops save the European protagonists (Tintin, Captain Haddock and Snowy) from a group of "pillards Berabers" [pillaging Berbers].[48] Like Hergé's *Le crabe aux pinces d'or* and many other volumes in the Tintin series (Van Opstal 1998: 29, 129–31), *L'idole aux yeux d'émeraude* [The Idol with Emerald Eyes], by Frédéric-Antonin Breysse (1995), was serialized (1948–9) in France in the Catholic children's magazine *Coeurs vaillants*. And like Hergé, Breysse shows European characters first attacked by Berber brigands in the Sahara, but later saved by French and North African colonial soldiers, riding camels (13–24). However, in Breysse's story the French civilians use a caterpillar vehicle ("une chenillette") and trailer to take them and their equipment to scientifically observe an eclipse of the sun. Here the story revolves around an imperialist encounter between French scientific, technical prowess – backed up by military power – and superstitious, savage Africans.[49] The *autochenille* or *chenillette* is a fetishized symbol of French technological superiority in comics, much as Citroën and his engineers considered it to be in reality. The unacknowledged irony in both *Le crabe aux pinces d'or* and *L'idole aux yeux d'émeraude* is that the Europeans are rescued thanks to camels, after technologically advanced means of transport have failed (respectively an airplane, a caterpillar vehicle and a helicopter), whereas Citroën had boasted that he would replace beast with machine. In all of these comics, except for the early *Zig et Puce: En route pour l'Amérique!*, representations of lawless North Africans depoliticize the armed activities of the colonized by transforming them into ordinary criminals (pillaging and kidnapping). In fact, the European image of the nomadic North African raider as a common criminal masked popular resistance to French colonialism. In colonial texts such as *La croisière noire*, these attacks were represented as an obstacle to European technological progress and pacification of the region. For example, Haardt and Audouin-Dubreuil explain the need to keep guard over the expedition at night in the Sahara desert: "because close to some wells one must be on guard against Moroccan raids [rezzou]" (1971: 20). A similar reason was given for the last-minute cancellation of another trans-Saharan voyage sponsored by Citroën (2–4; cf. Murray 2000).

"Life is beautiful," when you rule: Ribouldingue replaces the Minister of Colonies

Forton used the colonial carnivalesque in a Pieds-Nickelés episode apparently inspired by the Croisière noire, much as he had done in the earlier sequence about the 1931 Exposition coloniale (see Chapter 2). In *La vie est belle* [Life is Beautiful], one of the Pieds-Nickelés – Ribouldingue – pretends to be the Minister of Colonies, as the narrator reminds readers (Forton 1949: 45; first ed. 1933):[50]

> On sait que le ministre français des Colonies, frappé de sa ressemblance avec Ribouldingue, avait offert à celui-ci de le remplacer dans un voyage officiel pour lequel il ne se sentait aucun goût. Ribouldingue avait donc encore en sa possession les papiers du Ministre, y compris les passeports et sa photographie.

[We remember that the French Minister of the Colonies, struck by his resemblance with Ribouldingue, had suggested that he [Ribouldingue] replace him [the Minister] on an official trip that he had no wish to undertake. Ribouldingue therefore still had in his possession the papers of the Minister, including the passports and his photograph.]

The booklet version of the serialized story typically begins *in media res,* when the trio arrives at the outskirts of Bangui, capital of the French colony of Oubangui-Chari (now the République Centrafricaine; cf. Haardt and Audouin-Dubreuil 1971: 84–96). They are driving a caterpillar vehicle (an *autochenille,* but not a half-track here) put at their disposal at the end of the previous volume by the Négus, King of Abyssinia, whom they had visited on an official trip, replacing the real French Minister of Colonies and his aides (Forton 1935b: 63–4; first ed. 1933).

In Bangui, the Pieds-Nickelés quickly fool an African colonial policeman and then the French governor into thinking that they are the Minister and his assistants (3) (Plate 26). As in *Tintin au Congo* and the real-life Croisière noire, their visit to sub-Saharan Africa includes big-game hunting, here for a panther and ostriches (5–8). However, the Pieds-Nickelés are, as usual, most interested in eating and drinking at the expense of others and, especially, in getting rich quickly and illicitly. They therefore initiate a series of schemes to fleece the Africans, much as the comic's Exposition episode involved defrauding French visitors. The Pieds-Nickelés series thereby establishes a perverse form of equality: colonizers and colonized are both susceptible to becoming the victims of the Pieds-Nickelés (cf. Tulard 2008: 61–2, 74; Dufay 2008). The reverse is also true – even among the Africans, exceptional individuals are capable of outwitting the Pieds-Nickelés on occasion, as Croquignol reminds readers (Forton 1949: 3): at the end of the previous volume, *Les Pieds-Nickelés ont le filon* [The Slackers Strike It Rich], the Pieds-Nickelés had been swindled by an African guide during an elephant-hunting expedition. Croquignol suggests that the African must have learned his tricks at the Parisian Exposition. Is Forton implying here, and in the Exposition episode (see Chapter 2), that the official Parisian event was primarily designed to defraud the French public? After all, the official events constituted an enormous spectacle in a theater-like decor, and there were sideshows too. Or is he simply implying that the Exposition provided the occasion for the Pieds-Nickelés and similar marginal figures, even colonized Africans, to engage in fraud? We might also read the comment by Croquignol as an indirect critique of the civilizing mission, via a reference to the notion of the noble savage: Africans, originally innocent, are corrupted by contact with French colonialism. Of course according to the prevailing logic in Forton's Pieds-Nickelés, knowing how to cheat others is a good skill to have.

Despite this possible critique of the colonial system, the language and rules governing the strip here are profoundly colonialist in important respects. When the Pieds-Nickelés arrive at "un important centre indigène" [a sizeable native center], Ribouldingue, as the (fake) Minister of Colonies, calls a meeting of the local Africans and the French governor to give a speech. He promises to spread French ideals of liberty, equality and fraternity by, paradoxically, beating and shutting away anyone who perturbs the government (i.e., himself and his friends) with an "observation, réclamation ou interruption" [observation, request or interruption] (9). He then establishes an equally dubious form of democracy: "Tout d'abord, nous déclarons ouvert un nouveau scrutin. Dès aujourd'hui chaque village nègre sera représenté par un ou plusieurs députés indigènes. De plus, les femmes voteront." [First of all, we declare another election open. Beginning today each Negro village will be represented by one or several native deputies. Moreover, women will vote.] Ostensibly to get around the problem of widespread illiteracy, the Pieds-Nickelés have the Africans bring a fruit to cast their votes, with each type of fruit (banana, coconut) representing a different candidate. The fake Minister of Colonies and his friends, who run the election, thereby receive a large quantity of fruit, which they later sell back to the Africans, pocketing, of course, the resulting windfall profit (10–11). This tongue-in-cheek depiction of the so-called French civilizing mission hits close to the truth indeed, but changes nothing for the Africans – it is a striking example of the colonial carnivalesque.

In the same first meeting, Ribouldingue also promises to end the onerous system of forced labor that France long imposed on colonized subjects in West Africa and elsewhere (Ruedy 1992: 89; Aldrich 1996: 219–24): "Nous décrétons également que les heures de travail seront ainsi réglementées: journée de deux heures. Un jour de travail par semaine, le dimanche. Repos forcé et obligatoire les autres jours." [We also decree that working hours will be regulated as follows: a two-hour day. One day of work per week, on Sunday. Forced and mandatory rest on the other days] (9). The measure is vigorously applauded by the Africans and protested only by the French governor, whom Ribouldingue immediately fires (10). However, the Pieds-Nickelés turn the newly elected village delegates into their work foremen and charge them with extracting from their electorate the unpaid labor that the French trio had apparently abolished at the meeting (11). Complaints by the laborers are dismissed by the French trio with some sophistry about unpaid work being a form of pleasure, so that it can be neither salaried nor counted as part of the two-hour work week. This unpaid labor provides the Pieds-Nickelés with a colonial "comptoir" [trading post], erected by the Africans, where the French can sell the fruit they had received in the election, as well as several other products, all obtained through various forms of local market manipulation, fraud and repression (unpaid, hard labor by prisoners, etc.).

At one point in *La vie est belle* Croquignol reminds his henchmen why they are in Africa (Forton 1949: 17): "Il ne faut pas oublier que nous sommes ici en mission spéciale pour réformer la colonie et développer la race nègre" [We must not forget that we are here on a special mission to reform the colony and develop the Negro race]. One must of course read this as an ironic jab by Forton at France's self-appointed civilizing mission in Africa. But readers familiar with the Pieds-Nickelés cannot be surprised that each technological innovation that they introduce – radios (11–12), water pumps (13), trains (19–22) and cinema (25–6) – entails swindling the Africans: the radios are wired as an intercom, through which Croquignol rigs the local banana market by broadcasting false forecasts; the pumps are not hooked up to a water distribution system; the Africans build the railroad and the train (out of wood), and pay for tickets, but then must propel the machine forward themselves by pedaling; and an errant lion jumps through the cinema screen and frightens off the spectators. Forton (31) paints the Africans as extremely naive, to the point that Ribouldingue even feels a passing twinge of remorse as the Pieds-Nickelés ride off in their *autochenille*, leaving their now destitute victims behind, because they had let themselves be fleeced so easily. This naïveté derives from the common French image of black Africans as big children (e.g., Haardt and Audouin-Dubreuil 1971: 16, 239) and perhaps, further back, from the Enlightenment image of the noble savage. By contrast, the French victims of the Pieds-Nickelés at the Exposition coloniale are generally far quicker to realize that they are being hoodwinked by scoundrels and then to protest more vigorously and effectively. Forton can also present the Pieds-Nickelés as able to repeatedly swindle the same group of Africans (by contrast with the constant turnover in French victims at the Exposition), through some fourteen or so different schemes, because Ribouldingue pretends to be the French Minister of Colonies, which makes the Africans his subjects.

The pleasure for the juvenile French colonial reader of this expedition comic must have derived, to a large extent, precisely from both the inventiveness of the money-making schemes and from the extreme gullibility of the Africans. It certainly also comes from the temporary contesting of authority and reversal of roles (Gaumer and Moliterni 1994: 500; cf. Tulard 2008): when women get the vote, some men protest but are silenced by "de solides amazones qui, la matraque au poing, firent instantanément la place nette de perturbateurs" [solid Amazons who, billyclub in fist, immediately cleared out the trouble-makers] (Forton 1949: 9); and the criminal Pieds-Nickelés temporarily take the place of the legitimate French colonial authorities, allowing them to receive all the attendant privileges. "Life is beautiful" for them, as it had been for the French governor in Bangui, who was resting in his hamac when the Pieds-Nickelés arrived (3). True, the Pieds-Nickelés do sometimes end up as the butt of the joke, for example, during their big-game hunting (5–7) – this too is designed to provide (a sadistic) pleasure for the young reader.

There is also the colonial pleasure of seeing exotic African animals and the visually caricatured Africans, with their strange clothing. Probably the strangest image of Africans for the reader comes early in the booklet, when three "femmes à plateaux" use their large lip plates as serving platters for the *apéritif* that they offer the Pieds-Nickelés at the governor's palace in Bangui – this is an obvious visual pun referring to these two meanings of "plateau" in French.[51] After several drinks, Ribouldingue feels so good that he elevates the French governor to the rank of "commandeur" in the Légion d'honneur and inducts the African women into it as "chevalières" [knights]. This, in turn, delights the African women (Figure 9) (Forton 1949: 4; my emphasis):

> Les négresses, enthousiasmées, demandèrent à *manifester leur contentement en esquissant un pas de danse* en l'honneur des hôtes du lieu. Ce fut un spectacle des plus charmants. Avec des grâces de *pélicans*, ces dames se mirent à se trémousser en heurtant l'un

que je suis. J'aime mieux un bon verre d'apéritif qu'un discours politique. Et puis on peut le redoubler, tandis qu'un discours, on ne tient pas à remettre ça. Alors, voilà. Je déclare que tu es le plus adroit des gouverneurs. Aussi, en vertu des pouvoirs qui me sont conférés, je te fais commandeur de la Légion d'honneur! Filo! Passe-moi la cravate, qu'on le décore. Attends, pendant qu'on y est, on va décorer aussi les négresses. Mesdemoiselles, en vertu... etc... etc... je vous fais chevalières! Et je vous dispense de m'embrasser. Avec des gouffres pareils, j'aurais trop peur d'avoir le vertige! » Les négresses, enthousiasmées, demandèrent à manifester leur contentement en esquissant un pas de danse en l'honneur des hôtes du lieu. Ce fut

Figure 9   African "femmes à plateaux" [lip-plate women] characters are used to produce a sexualized spectacle of the colonial grotesque. From Louis Forton, *Les nouvelles aventures des Pieds-Nickelés*, vol. 10: *La vie est belle* (Paris: Société parisienne d'édition, 1949 [1st ed. 1933]), p. 4, frame 3.

contre l'autre *les plateaux de bois qui déformaient* leurs lèvres et qui rendaient ainsi *comme un singulier bruit de castagnettes.* A la bonne heure! fit Croquignol. C'est ce qui s'appelle *claquer du bec!*[52] – Et encore! reprit le gouverneur. Ça, c'est rien. *Faut les voir quand elles n'ont pas déjeuné depuis trois jours.*

[The enthusiastic Negresses asked to *show their contentment by beginning a dance* to honor the guests of the place. It was one of the most charming spectacles. With the grace of *pelicans*, these ladies started to shake it, while knocking, one against the other, *the wooden plates that deformed* their lips and thereby giving off *something like a peculiar noise of castanets.* Well done! said Croquignol. That's what I call *banging your beak!* – Hold on! replied the governor. That's nothing. *You should see them when they haven't eaten for three days.*]

There are striking similarities between this passage in the comic book and the following excerpt from the published account by Haardt and Audouin-Dubreuil of their encounter with some "femmes à plateaux" in Chad – then the French colony just north of Oubangui-Chari (1971: 106–8; my emphasis):

Les plateaux des Sara-Djingé *sont en bois* et mesurent jusqu'à vingt-quatre centimètres de diamètre. On dirait *le bec monstrueux de quelque pélican* d'Apocalypse. [...]

Lorsque les femmes, en file indienne, transportent sur leurs têtes de lourds fardeaux, *elles rythment leur pas au son de ces castagnettes* macabres.

Boire et manger sont, on le conçoit, des manoeuvres difficiles, d'autant que le frottement des plateaux sur les gencives fait rapidement tomber les dents des malheureuses, obligées alors de se nourrir avec des boulettes de pâte de mil fermentée. [...]

Mais les femmes Sara-Djingé ne sont pas de mauvaise humeur; [...] enfin elles *dansent, donc elles sont heureuses...*

[*The plates of the Sara-Djingé are of wood* and measure up to twenty-four centimeters in diameter. One would say *the monstrous beak of some pelican* from the Apocalypse. [...]

When the women, in single file, carry heavy loads on their heads, *they walk to the beat of these* macabre *castanets.*

Drinking and eating are, as one can imagine, difficult maneuvers, especially since the rubbing of the plates on the gums quickly makes the teeth of the poor women fall out, obliging them then to feed themselves with little balls of fermented millet paste. [...]

But the Sara-Djingé women are not bad-humoured; [...] in any case they *dance, so they are happy...*]

Despite the difference in tone (humor versus horror) and genre (comic-book fiction and documentary travelogue), the stories here share imagery and participate in the construction of a teratology about Africans (cf. Bogdan 1994; Sharpley-Whiting 1999: 16–31; Thode-Arora 2002: 84). The passage in Forton combines references to the monstrous with suggestions of the *Vénus noire* (see below): the spectacle that the three African women provide for the Pieds-Nickelés and the reader is "one of the most charming"; and "[w]ith the grace of pelicans, these ladies started to shake it." Ribouldingue even suggests that they might wish to kiss him, but quickly banishes this disturbing possibility: "Et je vous dispense de m'embrasser. Avec des gouffres pareils, j'aurais trop peur d'avoir le vertige!" [And I exempt you from kissing me. With chasms like that, I would be too afraid of getting dizzy!] (Forton 1949: 4).

The presence of the colonial carnivalesque is made explicit through a reference to circus acts, as the governor continues (4):

Ainsi, messieurs, vous pouvez voir qu'il n'y pas ici de quoi s'ennuyer et que le pays ne manque pas d'attractions! Tenez! Nous sommes justement en possession actuellement d'un assez curieux phénomène, connu dans les foires sous le nom d'homme-serpent et que je me propose de vendre à Barnum au profit du Trésor public!

[Therefore, sirs, you can see that there is no getting bored here and that the country isn't lacking in attractions! Here you go! We do in fact now have in our possession a rather curious phenomenon, known in fairs as a man-snake and which I plan to sell to Barnum for the benefit of the Treasury!]

This passage of cruel visual-verbal humor, which refers explicitly to circus shows (Barnum), closely resembles one from *Tintin au Congo*: here, the python has swallowed an African, who makes the snake dance by wiggling; in Hergé's story, it is Tintin's dog Snowy that has been swallowed and causes the reptile to move involuntarily (Hergé 1973: 243–5). The depiction of "lip-plate women" and of fairground or circus attractions in *La vie est belle* may also remind the reader of the fact mentioned earlier (see Chapter 2) that the Fédération Française des Anciens Coloniaux (FFAC) brought "négresses à plateaux" (and pygmies) to Paris as a money-making act, before recruiting the Kanak for an appearance during the Exposition coloniale (Dauphiné 1998: 29; cf. Hale 2002: 317). The colonial carnivalesque is a common element in Croisière noire material, Forton's comic and the FFAC's activities, in the sense that all involved exhibiting African women and men as a spectacular, monstrous, fairground-type sideshow, whose grotesque elements were designed to titillate the French reading and viewing public. Although the similarities between the texts concerning the "lip-plate women" do not provide absolutely conclusive proof that Forton had read the book by the leaders of the Croisière noire, or had seen the documentary by Poirier about the Citroën trip, this is a strong possibility. Moreover, the conversation between the Pieds-Nickelés and the French governor recalls many discussions between Haardt, Audouin-Dubreuil and European colonial administrators of the African regions that they crossed, including chats about the bizarre (to the French) customs of the exotic ethnic groups that they observed during their voyage – these are recreated for readers of *La croisière noire: Expédition Citroën Centre-Afrique* (1971).

The Croisière noire in post-1962 comics: renovating, rescripting, replicating

After most French colonies gained formal independence, the Croisière noire did not completely disappear as a theme in comics, although here – as with colonial exhibitions in comics – there appears to have been a break in continuity and then a return to the event. The

Citroën car company itself may deserve part of the credit for the event's resurgence. It commissioned cartoonist and illustrator René Follet to create paintings depicting the Croisière noire, which were used in a 16-page, full-color brochure that the company published about the expedition in 1974 (*La Croisière noire: Edition spéciale*). About twenty years later, Follet drew a two-volume comic-book history of the company, which included a celebration of the Croisière noire (see below). In 1975, to celebrate the fiftieth anniversary of the Croisière noire, *Okapi*, a Catholic children's magazine, published a special insert about Citroën, which included 17 photos of Citroën expeditions, mostly the Croisière noire. In 2004, the same magazine published a 12-page comic recounting the Croisière noire (Dieter and Malès 2004).

Producing a genealogy of colonial themes in comics involves asking how colonial elements are transmitted and modified. Today this process happens in part through the redistribution of materials from the colonial archive, made accessible again by historians and others; through debates between different individuals and groups with links to the colonial era; and through the transformation of France through post-colonial immigration. However, one might ask, for example, whether recent comics about Western trans-African expeditions are connected through amorphous, indirect links or via more clearly traceable and direct continuities to colonial expeditions of the 1920s and 1930s and the comics that they inspired between 1923 and 1962 (cf. Henry 1997). There are at least three main ways in which cartoonists have reworked the colonial theme of vehicular, trans-African expeditions: renovating, rescripting and replicating. All involve forms of intertextuality, intericonography and the transmission of historical models for representing relations between France and the rest of the world (especially Africa) in visual-textual narrative.

At least one cartoonist has renovated a colonial-era expedition comic, modifying it in significant ways. The Belgian cartoonist Greg (1931–99) created a renovated version of Saint-Ogan's series – he attempted to update the Zig et Puce stories by making both their visual appearance (e.g., drawing style) and themes more contemporary and relevant to his readers. He produced three short stories and six book-length ones (1963–9), which have been republished by Glénat in conjunction with their reissue of Saint-Ogan's original series. As Petitfaux (in Saint-Ogan 1995f: 55) points out, Greg partially recycled Saint-Ogan's already published stories. He reworked the colonial expedition story from *Zig et Puce aux Indes* in *Le prototype zéro zéro* (Greg 1995b; serialized 1964, first ed. 1967), but replaced the expedition across Africa with a version of the Robinson Crusoe story of island castaways, thereby substituting an older, English colonialist narrative for the more recent French one of the Croisière noire (see also Robinson Crusoe in *Les Pieds-Nickelés et le raid Paris-Tombouctou*, analyzed below). Moreover, he exchanged a gorilla for the character Friday, thereby eliminating any contact with non-European peoples. The result is a story divested of some of the more historically specific and offensively racist aspects found in *Zig, Puce et Furette*, although the substitution of a gorilla for Friday is suspect, given the long colonialist association, including in comics,[53] between various indigenous groups and monkeys or gorillas.[54]

Other cartoonists have rescripted the theme of the Croisière noire in very deliberate ways, basing their comics on documents (texts and photos) produced by the French expedition members, as well as on recent works, such as books about the Croisière noire and about the trans-Saharan Citroën expedition that preceded it, written by Ariane Audouin-Dubreuil (2004; 2008), daughter of Louis Audouin-Dubreuil. The third way that cartoonists have returned to the theme of these *expeditions* is not (yet) found in recent comics about colonial *exhibitions*: comics have been inspired by the Paris–Dakar race, a sporting event first held in 1978, that partially replicated the earlier, colonial-era, trans-African vehicular expeditions. The potential connection between the two generations of road trips is explicitly made by the title and content of a book by participants in, and reporters on, the Paris–Dakar: *Les raids: De la Croisière noire au rallye Paris–Alger–Dakar* [The Raids: From the Croisière noire to the Paris–Algiers–Dakar rally] (Sabatès, Beaudet and Cortanze n.d.; cf. Wolgensinger 1974). In turn, comics about the Paris–Dakar replicate earlier representations of the Croisière noire and other trans-African expeditions in French comics of the 1920s–40s, even though there is not necessarily a direct connection between the two sets of comics. Their creators were all inspired by current events (their comics were, or are, in the spirit of the times), as opposed to colonial nostalgia comics, whose authors return to, and rescript, events from a (relatively) distant past.

Nostalgically rescripting colonial expeditions: "L'oublié de la Croisière noire"

Another comic strip clearly calls attention to its historical antecedent, the Croisière noire, beginning with its title: "L'oublié de la Croisière noire, une aventure de Ric Brio" [The forgotten man from the Croisière noire, a Ric Brio adventure], by Armand and Bergouze. The strip was first published in the magazine *Métal aventure* in 1985, then republished the following year by Futuropolis in a small-format book, *Ric Brio* (Armand and Bergouze 1986), that collected together three stories. It exemplifies the tendency among many French and Belgian cartoonists to return to colonial history for inspiration, beginning in the early 1980s. Set in 1984, "L'oublié de la Croisière noire" uses a flashback narrative device to retell the story of the Croisière noire. In the frame narrative, Ric Brio, a fictional reporter for *Métal aventure*, and his friend Gazin fly to Africa in search of an old half-track vehicle about which they have received a tip. They discover it, but are soon surrounded by boys and attractive young women, all of them French-speaking Africans. They turn out to be the offspring of Lucien Trougnard, an apprentice mechanic at Citroën, who – according to the cartoonists' fiction – followed the Croisière noire caravan in a ninth half-track, without the knowledge or permission of André Citroën or the leaders of the expedition. When he arrived in sight of Mount Kilimanjaro, Trougnard fell ill to the point of delirium and was rescued and nursed back to health by an African family, including Odoma, a ravishing young woman (Figure 10). At this point, the French apprentice, already fascinated with Africa, fell for the charms of the African beauty:

> Une reine, les gars. Vous auriez hésité, vous, entre les greluches de Belleville et la reine de Saba? J'étais plus Lucien l'apprenti, je devenais d'un coup le père Salomon. On s'est marié, enfin, suivant leurs coutumes...
>
> C'est comme ça que je vis ici depuis soixante ans. Odoma e[s]t morte il y a dix ans, mais j'ai une sacrée famille pour m'entourer... Alors, vous allez faire un bel article qui m'amènera plein d'emmerdes et de casse-pieds?
>
> [A queen, guys. Would you have hesitated between the bimbos of Belleville and the Queen of Sheba? I wasn't Lucien the apprentice any more, all of a sudden I was turning into daddy Solomon. We got married, at least, according to their customs...

Figure 10 Nostalgically recreating the black Venus in a mid-1980s return to the Croisière noire. From Jacques Armand [Jean-Jacques Martin] (art) and Philippe Bernalin (script), "Une aventure de Ric Brio: L'oublié de la Croisière noire," *Métal aventure*, no. 9 (1985), p. 46.

So that's how I've been living here for sixty years. Odoma died ten years ago, but I have quite the family to support me... So you're going to write a fine article that's going to bring me a shitload of trouble and ball-breakers?]

Ric Brio accedes to Trougnard's request for privacy and throws out his notes as he flies away. Of course, the flip side to the fictional request for privacy by the comic book character is the cartoonists' choice to resurrect and rescript part of France's colonial history in a peculiarly revealing way. Armand and Bergouze carefully based the drawings of their strip on images from the Croisière noire. For example, the strip reproduces the emblems assigned to the half-tracks (Haardt and Audouin-Dubreuil 1971: 7–8). The comic-strip depiction of a half-track vehicle in a tree cluster appears to be based on an image from the front cover of an early edition of *La Croisière noire*.[55] The cartoonists also copied a photograph of Haardt and Audouin-Dubrueil beside hippopotami they had killed (Haardt and Audouin-Dubreuil 1927a: plate between pp. 120–1) and apparently reworked one of Citröen standing beside a map of the itinerary of the first trans-Saharan Citroën expedition (Wolgensinger 1996: 58). Many other elements in the comic come straight from *La Croisière noire*, including the given name (Clovis) of one of the mechanics (Haardt and Audouin-Dubreuil 1971: 7–8; Audouin-Dubreuil 2004: 202).

Another kind of fidelity to the original colonial script created by the leaders of the expedition lies in the way the cartoonists view colonial history: like many stories published in *Métal aventure*, "L'oublié de la Croisière noire" presents colonialism as a wonderful adventure, as did colonial-era comics, including *Zig, Puce et Furette*. Indeed, two French anthropologists have singled out the Croisière noire and its sequel, the Croisière jaune, as significant examples of the colonial adventure – of colonialism experienced by Europeans as an adventure – during the first part of the twentieth century (Le Breton 1996: 63–5; Michel 1996: 124).[56] Through Trougnard's account, the cartoonists present André Citroën as a visionary whose grandiose plans for encouraging, and capitalizing on, European tourism in the French-occupied Sahara were admirable, and failed only because they were ahead of their time. The strip helps rehabilitate French colonialism as a glorious national epic, which is – for example – how the leaders of the Croisière noire described the earlier French conquest of Chad and West Africa ("quelle magnifique page d'épopée!" [what a magnificent epic page!]; Haardt and Audouin-Dubreuil 1971: 69), which had made their own exploit possible. In this, they are joined by key French political figures today, and by at least one descendant of the Croisière noire leaders.[57] Genuflexion to a pantheon of the great men of colonialism was originally a colonial-era gesture. For example, Haardt and Audouin-Dubreuil paid homage to their more or less well-known imperialist predecessors, including Charles de Foucauld (Haardt and Audouin-Dubreuil 1971: 24, 69), Colonel Leboeuf and Lieutenant Châtenay (25), Generals Laperrine (25, 69), Gouraud (58) and Faidherbe (69), Savorgnan de Brazza (69) and many others (69–73). A key difference between the colonial adventure in the Zig et Puce series and in "L'oublié de la Croisière noire" is that it is located in the past for Armand and Bergouze: it can only be experienced vicariously, as a half-forgotten story told by the last members of a vanishing generation. From their vantage point in the 1980s, the cartoonists represent colonial history nostalgically: although Ric Brio and Gazin gaze longingly at Trougnard's French-African (grand)daughters, they do not permanently go native to relive an erotic and exotic African idyll, as Trougnard had done with Odoma. Nor can they participate directly in the Croisière noire, but only second-hand, by hearing Trougnard finally tell his version of the expedition's story. Similarly, the reader of the comic is invited to participate vicariously, though at even greater remove, in this comic-strip memorial to the colonial adventure: he or she reads the cartoonists' fictionalized reworking of the written and visual account that Haardt and Audoin-Dubrueil had already presented in *La Croisière noire*.

Another key difference between most older and more recent versions of the expedition in comics is exemplified by the fact that Armand and Bergouze injected a salacious element into their story, aimed at an adolescent and adult readership and published after counter-cultural comics had opened up the French comics market to eroticism and even pornography. They included visual and verbal references to the erotic aspect of the Croisière noire and similar expeditions, which Saint-Ogan and Bruller had avoided mentioning in their comics, which were aimed at children. In this, Armand and Bergouze again hew closely to documents left by the expedition's leaders and other participants. The cartoonist's visual depiction of (half-)naked African women, including Odoma, is based on the photographs of Nobosodrou, a Mangbetou woman, in *La Croisière noire* (1927a: plate between pp. 182–3), and the references to "la reine de Saba" and "père Salomon" by the fictional Trougnard (quoted above) are derived from *La Croisière noire* (Haardt and Audoin-Dubreuil 1971: 259): "Here is the beautiful Ourou, with a copper tone, an enigmatic air, whose voluptuous saunter recalls the passage of great courtesans, and here also is Nobosodrou, whose disdainful pout and haughty pose are worthy of a queen of Sheba." It is worth noting that the photograph of Nobosodrou that appeared in the original Plon edition of *La Croisière noire* emphasizes her beauty – the "other" as seductive: she is shown in profile from the chest up, displaying the elongation of her head, her distinctive hairdo and her naked breasts (Haardt and Audouin-Dubreuil 1927a: plate between pp. 182–3). Another photo of Nobosodrou, reproduced elsewhere, shows her from the front (Deschamps 1999: 147). In it her eyes look strangely displaced, which may be a result, at least in part, of the head elongation to which she was subjected as a child. Including a frontal image in *La Croisière noire* could have moved her representation away from the seductive and toward the freakish: more like the "lip-plate women" than the queen of Sheba.[58] We have already seen a similar tension between seductive and grotesque depictions of

African women in Forton's treatment of the "femmes à plateaux" in *La vie est belle*.

The subsequent passage in *La Croisière noire* describes two instances in which the Europeans envisioned and rejected the idea of marrying, or having sex with, an African woman or girl (1971: 266, 268–9): the suggestion of marriage between Léon Poirier, the cinematographer of the expedition, and Neginga, a Mangbetou woman;[59] and the offer by Ekibondo, chief of the Mangbetou, to Poirier of his favorite daughter as a sexual present. Faithful to the imagery and text of *La Croisière noire*, the cartoonists reiterated or renewed colonial iconography; for example, colonial-era illustrators had used the side profile photograph of Nobosodrou as their model for a drawing published on the cover of a catalog for an exhibition of artifacts and trophies taken from the Croisière noire, and as an advertisement for cigarettes.[60] It appears that the trade in African women associated with such expeditions was not limited to their commodified images or to titillating prose narratives about them. Here is an account, from a book by a former employee of Citroën, of an episode from the company's aborted project for developing European tourism in the desert, which had been intended as a commercial outgrowth of the first trans-Saharan expedition (cf. Deschamps 1999: 50–1, 229):

> The arrival on the Niger of a bunch of well-paid Frenchmen, a bit reckless and persuaded that they were out to conquer the world, had a comic consequence that needs to be told:
>
> At the native rate, one could then buy a black wife from her parents for a few dozen francs.
>
> The Europeans, with full wallets, pushed up the going rates to dizzying heights in a few weeks. They dealt in quantity, and the locals [i.e., bachelor men] wishing to wed cast a very hostile eye on this increase, of which they were the victims.
>
> After their departure, there must have been crashes, just like on Wall Street.
>
> And all that happened a few weeks before the inauguration [of the Compagnie de transport transaharienne Citroën]. (Rocherand 1979: 113; first ed. 1938)

The publication of "L'oublié de la Croisière noire," first in *Métal aventure* (1985) and then by Futuropolis (1986), coincides with the beginning of the first complete republication of the Zig et Puce series, also by Futuropolis (from 1986). This is not a complete coincidence, if only because during this period two parallel trends within comics had important commonalities: a return to the origins of French and Belgian comics; and a revisiting of colonial themes, texts and imagery, including from colonial-era comics, as sources of inspiration for exotic adventure fantasies in comics and elsewhere. In "L'oublié de la Croisière noire," Armand and Bergouze may have also been rewriting another colonial-era comic, one that was probably inspired in part by the Croisière jaune: *Jean Valhardi et les êtres de la forêt* [Jean Valhardi and the Forest Beings], by Belgian cartoonists Eddy [Edouard] Paape (art) and Yvan Delporte (script). The Valhardi story, serialized in *Spirou* magazine in 1950, was republished in book form in 1987, after "L'oublié de la Croisière noire" had already appeared in print, so if Armand and Bergouze's story was inspired by the earlier comic, it must have been via the serial version.[61] The book publication of the Valhardi story was part of the return to the (colonial) origins of French and Belgian comics in the 1980s: it is advertised on the front cover as "Spécial âge d'or 1950" and as a "classique Dupuis" book, and includes both an afterword by Thierry Martens and a preface by the scriptwriter, who begs indulgence for his script – "It was a long time ago, and the world was more simplistic [simplet] than today" (Paape and Delporte 1987: 3). We may read this as an implicit acknowledgement of the colonialist ideology that structures the story. Delporte also situates his story geographically and mentions one of its inspirations: a story he had read about "'the most primitive tribe in the world,' the Phi-Tong-Louang." This group has been the object of anthropological study from colonial times to the present, and the *bande dessinée* foregrounds this: Professor Bols, from Leiden University, is intent on studying this ethnic group (renamed the Vat-Fenh-Ling), but is stymied by a trio of thieves, led by a white woman, bent on melting and stealing the gold objects found in ancient stone temples hidden in the forest. To do so, they have enslaved the strong but simian and childlike Vat-Fenh-Ling (cf. Delisle 2008: 58). The thieves have an *autochenille*, which Jean Valhardi (an insurance detective and the eponymous hero of the series), his friend Jacquot and the professor use to escape, after having defeated the thieves and having helped to liberate the Vat-Fenh-Ling, thereby replaying the colonial rescue theme – here good whites liberate backwards, vulnerable natives from bad whites (cf. Halen 1993a: 163–5; 1993b). The geographical setting of the story and the prominence of the half-track vehicle suggest that the Croisière jaune might have served as an inspiration for Paape and Delporte. Although the Valhardi story is set not in Africa but in Southeast Asia – in the highlands where colonial-era Tonkin, Laos and Siam meet – some key elements suggest that Armand and Bergouze may have used it as a basis for their "L'oublié de la Croisière noire": both stories involve a half-track voyage in the jungle, where white explorers encounter "savage" native peoples who turn out to be sympathetic; and upon leaving this group, one of the investigators (Professor Bols; Ric Brio) chooses to tear up his notes and throw them out of a vehicle, to protect the privacy of those whom they have discovered. Among the notable differences is the transformation of the erotic theme between the 1950s and the mid-1980s: in the Valhardi story, the suppressed erotic rapport is between the handsome blonde protagonist and the white, blonde *femme fatale*, the "Capitaine" of the temple thieves; whereas the openly erotic relationship in "L'oublié de la Croisière noire" is between Lucien Trougnard and the sexy African woman, Odoma.

The return to the colonial past in French comics during the 1980s was triggered in part by civil rights activism and cultural activities of ethnic minorities from (former) French colonies, especially those of North and West Africa, and by the rise of the French far right, which peddled colonial nostalgia and hate speech targeting post-colonial minorities in France. Nostalgia for certain aspects of the colonial era can also take forms that are far less brutal for (formerly) colonized groups. Cartoonists such as Jacques Ferrandez – of Pied-Noir, Catholic background (see Chapter 3) – and Joann Sfar, a French Jew, have created works depicting colonial-era Algeria and its diverse but divided communities of Jews, Christians and Muslims. As we will now see, a comic book by Sfar even engages, a bit surprisingly, with the colonial heritage of the Croisière noire.

Rescripting the Croisière noire with critical nostalgia: *Jérusalem d'Afrique*

Critical nostalgia is a paradoxical term, but it may come closest to describing the historical and artistic approach of Joann Sfar in the fifth volume of his internationally acclaimed series "Le chat du rabbin," translated into English and published by Pantheon as *The Rabbi's Cat* (in two volumes; 2005b, 2008).[62] In *Jérusalem d'Afrique* (2006), Sfar chose to research and rework the Croisière noire as deliberately and self-consciously as Armand and Bergouze had, but somewhat more critically.[63] As he re-evaluates this part of the colonial inheritance of French culture and comics, he confronts the processes of stereotyping and othering. His rescripting of this event is surprising because up until this point his series had focused mostly on the Jewish community in Algeria and, to some extent, in mainland France during the interwar period.[64] It is true that a nostalgic vein runs throughout Sfar's series, especially in his fictional memorializing of the Algerian Jewish community before Algerian independence in 1962, when it departed and dispersed.

He inserts his rescripting of the Croisière noire into this framework, fundamentally transforming the trans-African expedition – it becomes a search for the "Jerusalem of Africa." The voyage is suggested by an unnamed, young and handsome Russian Jewish painter, who had succeeded in escaping from Communist Russia.[65] The trans-African trip is financed by Vastenov, a wealthy former officer in the Czar's army now exiled in Algiers, along with his wife. Other members of the expedition include the rabbi (Abraham Sfar) and his cat, but also Mohammed Sfar, a good friend and distant cousin, who is a Muslim cheikh and an itinerant musician. As Armand and Bergouze did in "L'oublié de la Croisière noire," Sfar makes intertextual and intericonographic references to the Citroën expedition within his fiction. He also provides a bibliography of selected works consulted during the story's creation (4), as do several other historical *bandes dessinées* about colonialism. In *Jérusalem d'Afrique*, the rabbi and his fellow travelers felicitiously obtain an *autochenille* from the Croisière noire (43). This may remind us of both the second-hand "modèle transsaharien excellent" used by Tintin in the Congo, and the ninth *autochenille* imagined by Armand and Bergouze: all three examples foreground a self-conscious borrowing from external reality, and rescript a historical event within fiction, displacing it instead of simply duplicating it – this technique provides fictional elbow-room and is often used today by cartoonists redrawing French colonial and imperialist history.[66]

The self-conscious interplay between history and fiction continues when Abraham reads to his travel companions from a book that his cat – who has magically gained the power of speech (an ability that may remind us of Tintin's dog, Snowy) – describes in its role as textual or verbal narrator: "Pour se documenter sur l'Afrique, mon maître dispose d'une édition populaire des notes de la croisière

Citroën. Durant notre périple, il nous raconte les anecdotes des compagnons d'Audouin-Dubreuil." [My master has a popular edition of the Citroën Croisière notes, as documentation on Africa. During our long and complicated journey, he recounts the anecdotes of the companions of Audouin-Dubreuil] (63). The stories that Abraham tells include a cruel missionary joke about an African man who kills two of his three wives to conform to the Catholic directive that he have only one (Sfar 2006: 63; cf. Deschamps 1999: 175); and warnings that they should watch out for African cannibals (Sfar 2006: 63; cf. Haardt and Audouin-Dubreuil 1971: 118–28, 132, 200); and for Touaregs too, "parce que c'est les pirates du désert" [because they are the pirates of the desert] (Sfar 2006: 64; cf. Haardt and Audoin-Dubreuil 1971: 20, 138). However, Mohammed dismisses the Africanist clichés that Abraham reads to him: "Ecoute! Tes Citroën auraient écrit le même compte-rendu sur les Juifs, tu dirais qu'ils n'ont rien compris." [Listen! If your Citroëns had written the same report about the Jews, you would say that they had understood nothing] (Sfar 2006: 63). Mohammed tells Abraham to formulate his opinions from his own knowledge, obtained empirically, instead of relying on the travelogue by Haardt and Audouin-Dubreuil (Sfar 2006: 64), which is a compendium of colonialist clichés and references to, and quotations from, earlier colonial texts, which serve as "antecedent authority" (Said 1994a: 176).[67] The rabbi eventually stops filtering his travel perceptions through the guidebook and concentrates instead on what he can learn directly from the trip. However, this leaves the reader of the comic book with a paradox: the trans-African expedition of *Jérusalem d'Afrique* (41–84) is indelibly marked throughout by Joann Sfar's reading of the textual traces left by others in and around the Croisière noire. True, the cartoonist modifies them significantly when he imports them into his fiction, thereby providing a counter-model to the literalist re-reading that Abraham made of the Croisière noire book.

Sfar's characters generally follow the itinerary of the Croisière noire and encounter some of the same individuals, ethnic groups and scenery. For example, they travel across the Sahara desert, including the Tanezrouft region (Sfar 2006: 48; Haardt and Audouin-Dubreuil 1971: 24–36), spending time with Touaregs on the way (Sfar 2006: 64; Haardt and Audouin-Dubreuil 1971: 33–6, 42–3, 49–50). This encounter turns into an exchange of musical knowledge with Mohammed (who plays the oud [lute]) and Abraham (who drums), and is the turning point where the rabbi abandons his reading of *La Croisière noire* by Haardt and Audouin-Dubreuil: he realizes that Mohammed had been right – the Touaregs are not generally "les pirates du désert" (Sfar 2006: 64). As we have seen, the image of Berber or Touareg pillagers is a recurring colonial cliché found in Haardt and Audouin-Dubreuil (1971: 20), colonial-era comics – such as Hergé's *Le crabe aux pinces d'or* and *L'idole aux yeux d'émeraude* by Breysse – and new French comics that recapitulate colonialist discourse.[68] Sfar also transforms a harem scene from Haardt and Audouin-Dubreuil, though less radically so. When his characters meet a sultan in Maradi, Niger, the Russian painter wishes to visit his harem, but cannot (Sfar 2006: 65; Haardt and Audouin-Dubreuil 1971: 51–6; cf. Wolgensinger 2002: 212–13). The Croisière noire's leaders, hoping to obtain titillating film footage, had been allowed into the harem, but could only convince the sultan to unveil one of his wives (Haardt and Audouin-Dubreuil 1971: 56). In Sfar's version the fantasy of entering the harem to view its hidden women is evoked in part through a sexual joke that foregrounds the lurid animal interests of the European (would-be) voyeurs: after the departure, the rabbi's cat reports that *he* had been able to visit the harem, but that there were "[t]rop d'humaines, pas assez de chattes" [(t)oo many female humans, not enough pussies] (Sfar 2006: 65.6).[69]

Sfar does not jettison the feminized and eroticized vision of Africa transmitted by the Croisière noire; instead, he modifies it in interesting ways. One of the most striking borrowings that Sfar made from the Croisière noire is the fantasy of the "Vénus noire aux formes parfaites" [Black Venus with perfect shapes] (Haardt and Audouin-Dubreuil 1971: 48) to which the leaders of the Croisière noire return repeatedly in their account (cf. Savarese 1995; Berliner 2002: 189–204). We have already seen that the mixed, African and European, colonial couple is evoked elsewhere in Croisière noire comics, either as grotesque (Ribouldingue and the "lip-plate women" in Forton's *La vie est belle*), or as an erotic-exotic dream come true (in Armand and Bergouze's "L'oublié de la Croisière noire"). In *Jérusalem d'Afrique* the Russian painter – a reworking of the colonial adventurer figure (Sfar 2006: 70; cf. Miller 2004) – falls in love with an unnamed black barmaid, who joins the expedition in sub-Saharan Africa. However, Sfar chose not to have a Mangbetou woman incarnate the *Vénus noire*, although he did include one in the bar, talking with two white men – her distinctive hairstyle is recognizable (68.4).[70] By contrast with Haardt and Audouin-Dubreuil, who suggest that they avoided having sex with African women whom they met along their route (see above), the Russian man and the African woman in Sfar's *bande dessinée* immediately make love (70, 72), she becomes pregnant, and they ask the rabbi to marry them (74–5). Much as Mohammed had encouraged Abraham to abandon the ready-made colonialist vision of the Croisière noire book, the African woman confronts her Russian lover when he asks her about the "femmes à plateaux": "Pourquoi elles lèvres comme ça?" [Why they lips like that?] (Sfar 2006: 73; cf. Haardt and Audouin-Dubreuil 1971: 105–8). She teases him: "C'est grand, l'Afrique; et ici je ne connais pas plus que toi. Je ne trouve pas qu'ils me ressemblent, ici. C'est comme si je te demandais de m'expliquer la Hollande sous prétexte que tu es blanc." [Africa's big; and here I don't know any more than you do. I don't think they resemble me here. It's as though I asked you to explain Holland to me, just because you're white.] On the preceding page, Sfar similarly flips a colonialist cliché on its head, by comparing the difference in two characters' ability to speak French (72): the Russian says, "Pas rire! Difficile pour moi parler français!" [Not laugh! Difficult for me speak French!]; to which his lover replies, "Je rigole parce que les autres Blancs aussi me parlent comme ça. Mais toi tu ne le fais pas exprès." [I'm laughing because the other whites talk to me like that too. But you don't do it on purpose.] Associating pidgin French with colonized speakers is of course a common feature of colonial texts (e.g., Haardt and Audouin-Dubreuil 1971: 135), including comics, where it generally serves as a marker of French superiority and (only) partial assimilation by the colonized (cf. Siblot 1991; cf. Coquery-Vidrovitch 2003: 173).

Sfar reverses colonial codes of representation in another passage, where he parodies Hergé's *Tintin au Congo*. Sfar's characters encounter Tintin, Snowy and their car (but not Tintin's African sidekick, Coco) in the Belgian Congo, appropriately enough (67), where Tintin is hunting, indiscriminately, as the cat tells us: "Il tire sur tous les animaux qu'il croise" [He shoots at all the animals he runs into]. This is visually juxtaposed with the attitude of Sfar's own characters toward African animals, on the facing page, where they observe animals peacefully instead of killing them – water buffalo, giraffes and hippopotami (66).[71] The two hippopotami, peacefully grinning in the sunset, cannot fail to remind us of the photograph in *La Croisière noire* of their real-life models, dead and upside down, with Haardt and Audouin-Dubreuil standing victoriously over them (1927a: plate between pp. 120–1) – an image copied in "L'oublié de la Croisière noire" (Armand and Bergouze 1986: n.p.).[72] Although Sfar's talking cat may owe something to Hergé's Snowy (who conversed with Tintin in the early stories of the series), *Jérusalem d'Afrique* differentiates the two, again through a critique of colonialist attitudes toward language: the white dog from Europe tells the gray cat from Africa, "Toi y en a pas griffer moi!" [You not scratching me!]; to which the narrating cat responds by telling us that "[s]on chien est stupide" [(h)is dog is stupid] (67). Sfar's version of Tintin understandably bothers his main characters because he is verbose, patronizing to them and brutal to wild animals, but in this parody the cartoonist also distances his own work from a dismissive attitude toward comics (Tintin says they are easy to read, even for his African interlocutors), seen as a lower, commercialized art form – a view that Hergé himself seems to have shared to a degree (Sadoul 2000: 44–6, 94–5). By contrast, the defense of comics as a legitimate means of artistic expression is generally shared by the new wave of European cartoonists, to which Sfar belongs (Beaty 2007).

Despite generally adhering to the itinerary of the Croisière noire,[73] Sfar radically deviates from it at the beginning and end of his fictional road trip. First, his characters set out from the Jewish ghetto of Algiers. In the Sahara desert, instead of paying colonial homage to Charles de Foucauld – as Haardt and Audouin-Dubreuil did on the Croisière noire, visiting his hermitage (1971: 24; cf. 69) and on their previous expedition, paying their solemn respects at his tomb and that of General Laperrine at Tamanrasset (1923: 263–89; 1971: 69) – Abraham and Mohammed pay homage instead to their common ancestor (Sfar 2006: 41–3, 62), whose Saharan tomb they visit each year (Sfar 2003: 36–41). Sfar also diverges from the Croisière noire at his endpoint: instead of sending his characters from Uganda to Mozambique, they travel to Eritrea to visit the black Jewish community there. From there, they continue their search for an African Jerusalem. Through this, Sfar reworks diasporic Jewish stories of a return to the promised land with a recurring Africanist trope: the voyage to a hidden paradise, an El Dorado or a lost world, evoked by Haardt and Audouin-Dubreuil in their written account of their first joint trans-Saharan voyage,

Le raid Citroën: La première traversée du Sahara en automobile, de Touggourt à Tombouctou par l'Atlantide (1923; my emphasis).[74] Sfar's utopian voyage also reminds one of the longed-for return of the children of other emigrants and exiles to an ancestral homeland (Ainsa 1982), in this case a return to Algeria by French descendants of Algerian Jews.

Sfar's mixed couple and the rabbi's cat finally reach the African Jerusalem and finds a "cité impossible," peopled by black giants unencumbered by the heavy inheritance of slavery or diasporic exile, as the cat tells us (80): "Des Noirs que personne n'a jamais réduits en esclavage. Des juifs qui n'ont jamais quitté la terre de leurs ancêtres. Des gens heureux, équilibrés, bien dans leur peau." [Blacks whom no one has ever turned into slaves. Jews who have never left the land of their ancestors. People who are happy, stable and at ease] – although the images of the unsmiling Jewish giants partially contradict this textual description. To their chagrin, the mixed couple discovers that the black Jews who inhabit the promised land reject them: the Russian man because he is white (they believe that all Jews are black), and the African woman because she is not a Jew (82). As often happens in utopian journeys, the characters are expelled from paradise. They have no choice but to return to Mohammed and Abraham who, too exhausted to go further, had been awaiting the return of the lovers and the cat. The volume ends with the mixed couple sitting together naked, observed by the cat, and wondering aloud whether to reveal the city's existence to the two older men. The painter gives an artist's response – "Raconter les choses comme elles sont, c'est pas mon travail" [Telling things the way they are, that's not my job] – suggesting that he will not tell his elders what the trio had seen. Although this pirouette may be a fitting conclusion for a work of fiction, it seems to contradict a basic tenet of a fictional journey designed, to a considerable extent, to contradict some of the most widely disseminated colonial-era myths about Africa. It also raises the question of whether the benefits of rescripting Croisière noire imagery and stories today in a best-selling *bande dessinée* series – and a movie – outweigh the risks of recirculating them, if one's goal is to move beyond colonial myths.

A similar question arises about Sfar's decision to depict a group of Arab Muslims as sanguinary religious fanatics at the outset of his characters' journey (2006: 48–62). The Arabs end up killing Vastenov, after he has killed the group's religious counselor in a duel. Before that, the imam had tried to prevent the Russian painter from making a portrait of his prince (51–2). The cartoonist may have based this section on an episode in *La Croisière noire*, but only very loosely, because Haardt and Audouin-Dubreuil describe (1971: 22–4), albeit in orientalizing terms, an uneventful banquet with the local *caïd* at the oasis town of Beni-Abbès. It is true that Sfar's book also features an enlightened Muslim character (Mohammed Sfar), a Jewish kabbalist who makes similar objections to the visual representation of human faces (32–5) and a violent European (Vastenov). This creates "un effet de *balance idéologique*" [an *ideological scales* effect] (Halen 1993b: 368; his emphasis) which exists in other Belgian and French comics about Africa produced since (most) of the colonies gained formal independence: attempts to mediate between conflicting colonial and post-independence visions. However, the primary inspiration for this episode in *Jérusalem d'Afrique* appears to be "l'affaire des caricatures de Mahomet" – the publication of images of the prophet Mohammed, and related caricatures, in Denmark and elsewhere, including in the French satirical weekly *Charlie Hebdo*, where Sfar has published. Sfar finished his book on 1 June 2006, after the controversy had broken out. His work intervenes in that debate, but at the price of once again depicting (some) Muslims as intolerant and violent religious fanatics. There are of course many such people from other religious faiths: in the preceding volume, for example, Sfar depicts the antisemitic, hate-mongering Abbé Lambert (Sfar 2005a: 40–5; cf. Stora 2004: 67–8).

Sfar has also adapted into comics a work that remains one of the most widely read French colonial narratives throughout the world: Antoine de Saint-Exupéry's *Le petit prince* [The Little Prince] (1992; first ed. 1946), set in the Sahara of colonial Africa, and from which the North Africans themselves are strangely absent.[75] Moreover, the cartoonist has named the film production company that he founded with Antoine Delesvaux and Clément Oubrerie, the artist known for drawing the "Aya of Yopougon" series (set mostly in late-1970s Ivory Coast), "Autochenille production."[76] The company logo depicts an animal – a black cat? – driving a half-track. Taken together, this material suggests a considerable nostalgic investment by Sfar in French colonial narratives. Precisely how critical his nostalgia is of the colonialist aspects of these narratives is a matter that deserves further investigation and debate.

Replicating the colonial expeditions: the Paris–Dakar in comics

The tradition of representing colonial expeditions in comics also continues through *bande dessinée* stories about the Paris–Dakar race, insofar as it is a modern replication of the Croisière noire and related expeditions. Like those earlier events, the Paris–Dakar dramatizes for French audiences the ways in which Western drivers and their motor vehicles overcome natural obstacles on an adventurous journey through African wilderness (i.e., Western technology triumphs over African nature). Here, as in Saint-Ogan's *Zig et Puce aux Indes* and Greg's *Le prototype zéro zéro*, one finds the theme of competition between rival automobile manufacturers, which dates back to the function of the Croisière noire as an advertising campaign for Citroën in its struggle with Renault (and other companies) for control of the automotive market. *Les Pieds-Nickelés et le raid Paris–Tombouctou* (Pellos 1990), drawn by René Pellos and scripted by Jean-Paul Tibéri, spoofs the advertising aspect. The *bande dessinée* was first published in book form in 1981, soon after the Paris–Dakar was launched in 1978. In it, Croquignol, Ribouldingue and Filochard put on a sea-and-road race as a publicity stunt for Renato Lasauce, a manufacturer of pasta products. Jean Tulard (2008: 70; cf. 62) argues that when Pellos took over Forton's anarchistic strip he ruined it: "These are new Robin Hoods. Whereas Forton sent packing both rich and poor, healthy and sick, colonizers and colonized, the tone [here] becomes somewhat moralizing." However, the cartoonists certainly managed to fill this *bande dessinée* with a full complement of colonial clichés that would have been perfectly at home in Forton's vision of Africa: a mention of Robinson Crusoe (71); bare-breasted, dancing African (71) and Tahitian (77) women; black cannibals cooking white men (58, 61, 75); wild animals (61, 75); and raiding Touaregs, who capture the protagonists (78–84). A significant difference between this and earlier, pre-1962 texts is that the main target of the rebellious Touaregs is no longer the European travelers (temporarily held as hostages), but instead the Malian government.

In *Quatre x Quatre* the cartoonist Marc Wasterlain (1986: 32) describes the same road race in terms that recall the hype of the Croisière noire and similar motorized colonial expeditions: "Le Paris–Alger–Dakar est une course folle contre les éléments, le temps (20 jours) et l'espace (14.000 km)" [The Paris–Algiers–Dakar is a wild race against the natural elements, time (20 days) and space (14,000 km)]. In the comic, the race passes through six African countries colonized by France (Algeria, Mali, Niger, Upper Volta, Ivory Coast and Senegal). As in the colonial-era comics already studied, the difficult crossing of the Sahara desert receives considerable attention (Wasterlain 1986: 32–43) and includes the obligatory encounter with camel-riding nomads for local color (36). Here they are not the pillaging raiders of Saint-Ogan, Bruller, Hergé or Breysse, but instead simply the butt of a joke, when a press vehicle carrying Jeannette Pointu, the protagonist, charges through an encampment at break-neck speed. No one is hurt in the fictional encounter, but in reality there have been numerous African victims hit by race vehicles. The artist appears more concerned with Europeans who have died in race-related accidents: he dedicated the book to Daniel Balavoine, a French pop singer who died in a plane crash while on a humanitarian mission to Africa made in conjunction with the race. Toward the end of the story there are two brief references to humanitarian aid to African victims of drought and childhood disease (44, 47). The authors of *La Croisière noire* also similarly justified the colonial enterprise, of which they were a part, through reference to humanitarian activities (1971: 212), despite the fact that their trip must have been costly in terms of African suffering: for example, they state that the Belgians forced 40,000 Congolese to build a 700-kilometer road through the jungle for the Croisière noire (197), and an African is beaten for having stolen from them (325–6). Moreover, Wasterlain's comic never fundamentally questions the neo-colonial aspects of the Paris–Dakar, nor the idea of the trans-African expedition as a European adventure.

My final example of a comic book that depicts trans-African road races is "Les autos de l'aventure" (Follet and Royère 1996, 1998), a hagiographic, two-volume history of the Citroën car company. In *La passion des défis* [The Passion for Challenges], the first volume, Follet and Jean-Claude de la Royère devote several pages to each of Citroën's color-coded Croisières, as well as the first trans-Saharan expedition of Haardt and Audouin-Dubreuil (see Appendix 3). The pages about the Croisière noire focus on the erotic aspects of the Mangbetou episode (Follet and Royère 1996: 19–20). Here, as in other reworkings of the Croisière noire analyzed by Levine, the function of the Croisière noire "as a way of furthering French colonial domination of Africa has been virtually written out of its memory"

(Levine 2005: 94). Instead, Follet and Royère recreate the Croisière noire story as a grand adventure of technological prowess and grandiose marketing. The second volume maintains this perspective in its depiction of many other road races in which Citroën vehicles participated, including the Paris–Dakar. This type of narrative can be costly, as historians have pointed out (Levine 2005: 93):

> Indeed, automobile rallies such as the Paris–Dakar continue to exploit the image of Africa as a virgin continent where the ultimate limits of man and machine can be tested. The historian Maurice Guimendego finds this deeply problematic, arguing that clichés and stereotypes continue to be perpetrated because visitors, and the media, take an intense but fleeting interest in the continent while remaining studiously indifferent to the fact that its internal troubles are tearing it apart.

Of course these troubles are not just internal, in the sense that they are in part the product of decades of European colonial domination and of the continuing exploitation of Africa by more powerful nations and by rich, multinational corporations based elsewhere.

Conclusion

I have found fewer comics clearly related to the colonial expeditions than to the exhibitions. Still, I have reconstructed a relatively extended genealogy for them, reaching from 1923 to the present. Some of the same artists and works are involved here as with colonial exhibitions (Saint-Ogan's Zig et Puce, Bruller's *Le mariage de M. Lakonik*, Forton's Pieds-Nickelés), and similar questions about colonial representation arise. For example, there is the recent republication of colonial-era comics, in various forms: "Elle??..." reprinted in a celebratory book about Citroën; the Zig et Puce series, republished by Futuropolis and Glénat; *Le mariage de M. Lakonik*, edited by Thierry Groensteen and republished by the CNBDI; *L'idole aux yeux d'émeraude*, reissued by Les éditions du Triomphe for the first time in book format. Publishers and editors justify this activity as the rediscovery of classic comic books. It involves the veneration of a bygone era, an important figure of French industry (Citroën) or great cartoonists of the past. The construction of a French national canon of comics is again clearly behind the republication of the works by Saint-Ogan and Bruller. Another similarity between comics related to colonial expeditions and colonial exhibitions is the reappearance of the colonial theme in the 1980s, notably in the magazine *Métal aventure*. We have seen that the most interesting reworking of the Croisière noire in comics is also the latest one, Joann Sfar's *Jérusalem d'Afrique*. It is an example of how one French cartoonist has finally trained a critical eye on at least some aspects of a project of imperialist domination and colonial exploitation – the Croisière noire – that has been mythologized from the beginning.

CONCLUSION

The Rotting Corpse
of Colonial Representation
and its Eerie Aura

Throughout this study, I have shown how implicated cartoonists were in colonial culture before 1962: for example, both the contributions that Alain Saint-Ogan, Joseph-Porphyre Pinchon and Raymond de la Nézière made to official colonialist propaganda, and the colonialist and imperialist aspects of their comics. One might well ask what is remarkable about this, given the fact that these values and representations were well within the mainstream of French society and culture at the time. One answer, given by African-American cartoonist, novelist and professor Charles Johnson (in Strömberg 2003, 2010), is that it represents a failure of artistic imagination, of the ability to imagine the situation of others (see Chapter 1). Another answer is that a minority of artists and authors did think differently, so some alternatives, including anti-colonialist ones, were possible (see Chapter 2). In any case, this area of comics deserves a full and public airing and critical debate, because it remains an important part of the heritage of French comics and culture.

Although there is still a great deal of uncritical regurgitation of colonial and imperialist ideology in contemporary French-language comics, we have seen that there are also cartoonists who are reworking the French colonial and imperialist inheritance in ways that are – in the best cases – at once artistically, historically and politically provocative. I conclude my study with a look at another such work, this time drawn by Yvan Alagbé, a cartoonist who first co-directed the avant-garde comics publishing house Amok, and then Frémok (Jennequin 1996; Bellefroid 2005: 64–77; Beaty 2007). Alagbé's experimental *Nègres jaunes* [Yellow Negroes] (1995), about post-colonial immigration and the aftermath of the Algerian War, has drawn some well-deserved critical attention (Groensteen 1996b; McKinney 1997b: 178; Beaty 2007: 97; Frey 2008b). Alagbé was born in Paris in 1971 to a French mother and a father from Benin. Here I analyze a short story that he drew, which self-consciously thematizes the colonial heritage but in ways strikingly different from the comic books by Hergé and Saint-Ogan that I analyzed in my Introduction. Interestingly, as with the legacy of those two founding fathers of French-language comics, both Nazi-era Europe and the colonial past are key elements of the heritage evoked in "Le deuil" [The Mourning], a 14-page comic by Alagbé and Eléonore Stein (1997).[1] In it Claire, a character who also appears in the remarkable *Nègres jaunes*, returns to her paternal grandparents' home in the Creuse region to attend their wake and funeral, despite having been estranged from them and from her racist father for years. While there, she digs up (*elle creuse*) the colonial past of her grandparents, especially her grandfather, and renegotiates her relationship to them in light of what she finds in the family's own archive of colonial representations: a photo album containing pictures that her grandfather had taken while living and working in Dakar. There, Claire and her cousins find photos of half-naked African women, including an image of three who are holding up their blouses and exposing their breasts for the photographer (Alagbé and Stein 1997: 29) (Figure 11). The sight of her grandfather's African photographs – an individual version of the mass-produced colonial postcards used by Ferrandez and many other French cartoonists today – leads Claire to reflect on her relationship to her grandfather: "Je suis une petite-fille de colon. Je suis la petite fille d'un colon qui demandait aux Africaines de montrer leurs seins pour la photo. Que leur demandait-il d'autre?" [I am the granddaughter of a colonizer. I am the granddaughter of a colonizer who asked African women to show their breasts for the photo. What else did he ask of them?] (30). A chain of memories is unleashed in Claire, which leads her to connect her present love for a black African man with her childhood memories of watching Arab and West African men laughing, talking and playing/gambling (*jouer*) in the streets of the Barbès neighborhood of Paris, where her grandparents ran a bordello for Arab men.

The conclusions drawn by Claire are provocative, as are the implied parallels made by the cartoonists: (1) between the grandfather's erotic interest in African women and the granddaughter's love for an immigrant African man; and (2) between the grandfather's

Figure 11 Confronting the colonial past, as an inheritance of the white male colonizer's erotic fascination with colonized black African women. From Yvan Alagbé (art) and Eléonore Stein (script), "Le deuil," *Le cheval sans tête*, vol. 4: *Un héritage* (November 1997), p. 29, frames 1–4.

photographs and the comic's frames containing images of Claire's naked body touched by her African lover. The comic thereby locates the roots of post-colonial eroticism in colonial eroticism, and posits a reconciliation of Claire with her grandparents, despite her rejection of the racist intolerance and exploitation that her grandfather represents: "Je me rappelle la gifle que m'a donnée Pépé le jour où j'ai dit que je me marierai avec un Noir. J'avais cinq ans, mais il savait que j'étais sérieuse. Il savait que je n'aurai, comme ma mère, aucun respect pour son ordre et ses valeurs." [I remember the slap that Pappy gave me the day when I said that I would marry a black. I was five years old, but he knew that I was serious. He knew that I would not, like my mother, have any respect for his order and his values] (30). Yet now Claire blesses her dead grandparents and paradoxically proclaims her resemblance to them, while she also projects a future that probably would have horrified them: she envisions the day that she, her African lover and their children will come and play on the grandparents' land. This is a new kind of community, both lived and imagined (Anderson 1991), one that transforms the colonial inheritance of the past, not into an ethnically restrictive genealogy of the nation (Balibar and Wallerstein 1991), but instead into a new "droit de cité" [right to freedom in the city] open to formerly colonized peoples (Balibar 1998; cf. Hargreaves and McKinney 1997).

Alagbé and Stein's graphic narrative suggests that the colonial inheritance includes visual representations (colonial photographs, orientalist paintings, colonial-era comics, etc.) and personal memories, but also colonial racism (Claire's father has inherited his parents' hatred of Arabs) and material wealth, represented here by the business the grandparents had bought for Claire's father with their ill-gotten money, as well as by the house in the Creuse and apartments in Paris which the grandparents possessed "after the war." This may refer either to the Algerian War – which is mentioned in a short preface[2] – or to the Second World War, also evoked there.[3] Two parallels are thereby implicitly established: (1) between, on the one hand, the expropriation of French Jews by Christians, French companies and the French Vichy government and, on the other hand, France's exploitation of colonized Africans; and (2) between the French government's responsibility for returning property to Jews dispossessed during Second World War and to their descendants, and restitution to be made to Africans (both in Africa and as immigrants in France) who have been exploited by French (neo-)colonizers – the free use and sharing of the grandparents' land by Claire, her African lover and their future children would be another instance of belated justice.[4]

Like the grandparents' decomposing bodies, which appear eerily alive to Claire when she gazes at them (22), colonialism's visual representations can take on an uncanny life of their own, especially when they are examined through the prism of what Renato Rosaldo (1989) termed "imperialist nostalgia." Alagbé and Stein carefully frame their representations of this colonial voyeurism in ways that echo what Bal (1996: 220) proposed at the end of her reading of Alloula (1986; cf. 1981, 2001) and of other critical works that re-enact the colonialist gestures of the images that they expose. In Alagbé and Stein's "Le deuil," the images of African women are not passed off as unproblematically "erotic," and it is the viewing subjects that are thematized (the grandfather, Claire and her cousins, and implicitly the readers of the comic book) along with the act of looking at (semi-)naked bodies of colonized African women. Moreover, the images are inserted into a critical narrative that provokes reflection on their meaning, so that we are not seduced by their cadaverous aura (it is not the original object of the gaze – the African women – that is cadaverous, but the colonialist gaze, its deformations and its commodification). Finally, "the look of the [ex-]colonized [that is] cast upon the [ex-]colonizer" is critically exposed by the cartoonists in two ways: (1) through a zoom in on two of the women in the photograph, which allows the artists to underline the women's resistant, unhappy facial expressions – the defiant look of one and the downcast look of the other (cf. Berliner 2002: 136–8); and (2) in a subsequent shot/reverse-shot sequence, where we are offered the position of Claire's African lover, who looks at and caresses her body – we may then contrast this short sequence with the dead grandfather's gaze, preserved in his photograph, and the distance separating him, and us, from the African women in it. In "Le deuil," colonial representation and history constitute an inheritance ("un héritage") borne, wittingly or not, by former colonial settlers and their descendants, now living in France.

Post-colonial, ethnic minority cartoonists who have returned to the history of French colonialism and imperialism in their comics, as well as cartoonists from other groups who are sympathetic to anti-colonialism and the viewpoint of the (formerly) colonized, have made significant progress toward reconfiguring comics production. I have shown throughout this volume that colonialism and imperialism left an imprint on French comics, generally in the form of unsavory imagery and colonialist narratives. There are, of course, still both republished and brand new works that perpetuate the tradition of colonialist ideology and imagery, so there is much that remains to be done to reconfigure the field of comics. There are also vast areas of colonial history and anti-colonial struggle that have not yet been represented in *bande dessinée*. Similarly, there still remains much to be studied about how French comics are connected with colonialism and imperialism. The present volume simply represents one step in an ongoing critical process.

Notes

Introduction

1 Dominique Petitfaux gives Saint-Ogan's full name as Alain Marie Joseph Paul Louis Fernand Denis Lefèvre Saint-Ogan (in Saint-Ogan 1995a: 45).

2 All my information for serial and first edition publication of Saint-Ogan's comics comes from Petitfaux's bibliography, in Saint Ogan, *Zig et Puce aux Indes* (1995f: 59–61).

3 Throughout this volume I use "Zig et Puce" to refer to the series of comic books, and "Zig and Puce" for the protagonists.

4 On France's earlier economic and colonial presence in India, see Haudrère (1995a, 1995b). On the connections between the triangular slave trade and trade with the "East Indies," see those sources and also Célimène and Legris (2002).

5 On French colonial "comptoirs" in India, and Franco-British rivalry there, see Le Tréguilly and Morazé (1995) and Haudrère (1995a, 1995b).

6 De Boigne eventually became the military advisor of Marathe leader Sindhia (Le Tréguilly 1995: 56). L. Russel, a French *capitaine de hussards* – like Saint-Ogan's fictional Onésime Puce, but from an earlier era – was sent to Mysore by the French army in 1769, as part of a secret military mission, to assist the Indian leader Hyder Ali against English military and mercantile forces in the region, specifically the East India Company (Lafont 2001).

7 Egypt was under British control at the time, but French colonial influence through cultural avenues (newspapers, schools, missions) also existed, as Robert Solé (1997) has argued.

8 The name Onésime Puce may also remind us of the French geographer Onésime Reclus (1837–1916), generally cited as the inventor of the term "francophonie," who championed French imperialist and colonial expansion.

9 All told, France ruled five Indian cities as *comptoirs* until 1954: Pondichéry, Karikal, Yanaon, Mahé and Chandernagor. It also had enclaves in nine other locations in India.

10 Groensteen (1996a: 16) also points out a narrative transfer from *Zig et Puce aux Indes* to *Le trésor de Rackham le rouge* [Red Rackham's Treasure].

11 All translations from the French throughout this volume are mine, unless otherwise indicated.

12 On this, see for example Nederveen Pieterse (1992), Met (1996) and Pigeon (1996). Fabrice Leroy kindly brought the article by Philippe Met to my attention.

13 This calls into question the primacy of war over commerce that Apostolidès (1984: 252) finds in Hadoque. In their commentary on this passage in the first serialized version of Hergé's "Le secret de la licorne," Daniel Couvreur and Frédéric Soumois do not discuss the issue of slavery (in Hergé 2006: 38–9; cf. Hergé 2007).

14 On Hergé's models for this ship, see Farr (2001: 111) and Peeters (2004: 75–6).

15 "Colbert then [in 1670] officially encouraged the director of the West India Company to foster the production of sugar cane in the French Caribbean" (Pétré-Grenouilleau 1998: 27). Pétré-Grouilleau also notes that "Sugar production here [in the western part of Saint-Domingue] begins its expansion around 1700." This was part of a transition from a French Caribbean economy based substantially on indentured European labor to one relying massively on African slaves (Pétré-Grenouilleau 1998: 28–30, 35–8; Frostin 1972). Although the sugar economy and associated slave trade in the French Caribbean were essentially built in the eighteenth century, importing African slaves to the French West Indies had already begun in the seventeenth century (Law 1994; Pétré-Grenouilleau 1998: 38–40), when Hadoque's story is set. According to Gough (1998: 88): French Caribbean "planters [...] distilled their wine to make what they called rhum, tafia, or guildive [...] To protect distillers in France from having to compete with a beverage made cheaply from the waste products of sugar refining, exportation of rum to France was banned by a royal decree of 24 January 1713"; cf. Ferré (1985).

16 Although Apostolidès (1984: 150) helpfully points out some links between Hergé's fiction and the history that it reworks, he completely ignores the essential fact of slavery, in both the trans-Atlantic slave trade and economic production in the Caribbean: "Four years after this gift, in 1698, the king sends his lieutenant to pick up a cargo ('There was mostly rum,' Haddock specifies), at Saint-Domingue island, that the Treaty of Ryswick, one year earlier, had recognized *de facto* as a French possession. Two days after having left Haiti behind, the Unicorn vessel (an emblematic animal, associated with the royal image) is chased by pirates." The Code Noir governing slavery was promulgated in 1685 and applied to African slaves on French islands in the Caribbean.

17   On Hergé's models for Red Rackham, see Farr (2001: 108–9). On the role of pirates in the economy of Saint-Domingue, see Pétré-Grenouilleau (1998: 26–7, 34–5).

18   The metaphorical blood on the jewels is therefore not so much that of Red Rackham and his men, killed by Hadoque – as Apostolidès (1984: 151) asserts – but that of the slaves who mined the jewels in the Spanish colonies.

19   Hergé first serialized this story in the collaborationist press in Nazi-controlled Belgium during the Second World War. On collaborationism and antisemitism in Hergé's life and work, see especially Assouline (1998), Benoît-Jeannin (2001, 2007), Peeters (2002a) and Frey (2008a).

20   However, the protagonists had already gained the support of an American capitalist and industrialist, who more or less adopted the parentless boys and helps them out periodically.

21   This is true even when the attempt to claim a colonial inheritance backfires in colonial-era comics: in *Zig et Puce aux Indes*, but also in "L'héritage" [The Inheritance], a Spirou story by Franquin, serialized 1946–7 (Franquin 2006: 51). The comic loss of the inheritance there does not constitute a critique of colonialism (cf. Jannone 1995a: 402).

22   See Rigney (2005) for a useful model of the production of cultural memory.

23   For fascinating analyses and examples of the different ways in which the colonial inheritance of slavery has been critically examined – or not – in the formerly slave-trading port cities of Nantes and Bordeaux, see Pétré-Grenouilleau (1998), Chivallon (2005) and Guillet (2009).

24   Said (1994b) analyzes the "voyage in," which exists in an implicit parallel with the colonial "voyage out."

25   E.g., Les Editions Taupinambour [*sic*], based in Soissons, which specializes in reissuing old comics and recently republished some of the earlier adventures of "Tif et Tondu" [Hair and Shorn], by Fernand Dineur (1904–56), including a lengthy (62-page) episode set in the Belgian Congo (Dineur 2009), initially serialized in *Spirou* magazine, 1939–40 (cf. Delisle 2008; Lefèvre 2008).

26   The "Odilon Verjus" series, by Yann and Verron, is published in the "Troisième degré" collection of comics by Belgian publisher Le Lombard. It plays with colonial clichés about missionaries, savages and the like, and includes historical characters ranging from Margaret Mead to Josephine Baker.

27   Thierry Smolderen (1984: 63), quoted in Quella-Guyot (1991: 15).

28   Formerly the Centre National de la Bande Dessinée et de l'Image (CNBDI), and still very much a French national entity, in organization, funding and focus.

29 On   www.centrenationaldulivre.fr/Lacunes-bande-dessinee.html (consulted 1 February 2007).

30 For English-language scholarship on these hotly debated questions, see Frey (1999, 2002, 2004, 2008a), Grove (2005), Miller (2004, 2007), Screech (2005) and McKinney (2007b).

31 Billy Bunter was a popular character in children's prose fiction and then, beginning in 1939, appeared in a comic-strip version.

32 E.g., Craenhals (1970), Kunzle (1973, 1990a, 2007; cf. 1990b), Laval (1974), Pierre (1984, 1988, 1992, 1993, 2000), Servantie (1989), Basfao (1990), Douvry (1991), Quella-Guyot (1991), Jannone (1992, 1995a, 1995b), Gauthier (1993), Halen (1993a, 1993b, 1994), Holo (1993a, 1995), Douglas and Malti-Douglas (1994, 2008), Fratta (1994), Thiebaut (1994), Pigeon (1996), McKinney (1997a, 1997b, 1998, 2000, 2001, 2004a, 2004b, 2007a, 2008a, 2008b, 2008c, 2008d, 2009), Tribak-Geoffroy (1997), Tirefort (2001–2), Hunt (2002), Jobs (2003), Frey (2004, 2008b), Miller (2004, 2007, 2008, 2009a, 2009b), Danehy (2005, 2008), Pasamonik and Verhoest (2005), entries by Josette Liauzu ("Bande dessinée"; "Bécassine"; "Enfant et propagande coloniale") in Liauzu (2007b), Lefèvre (2008) and Macdonald (2008). I gratefully thank Paul Gravett for the copy of Pasamonik and Verhoest (2005).

33 For Guillot (1985) *Sam et Sap* is what "one can take to be, today and no doubt definitively, the *first* French *bande dessinée*" (original emphasis; cf. Patinax 1985). I am not using such a narrow definition of comics here: for example, I do not exclude graphic narratives that use text below the images. For an analysis of the serialized version of "Sam et Sap," see Pigeon (1996: 142–4). For the place of *Sam et Sap* in the debate over the origins of the French-language comic strip, see Miller (1999: 76); and on the emergence of the use of the speech balloon in European comics, see Lefèvre (2006).

34 Exceptions include Jannone (1992: 5–6), Holo (1993a: 75–6) and Delisle (2008: 13, 50).

35 Petitfaux (1985: 12), Groensteen (1996a: 10) and Peeters (2002b: 118, 120).

36 For example, he has been described as follows: "the founding father of French comics" (La rédaction 1985); "the inventor of French comics" (Gaumer and Moliterni 1994: 555); "undoubtedly the father of Francophone comics" (Petitfaux, in Saint-Ogan 1995a: 48); "this great man of French comics, who was the President of the first Angoulême festival" (Groensteen 2007a: 8). See also Petitfaux (1985, 1995), Groensteen (1996a), Moliterni, Mellot and Denni (1996: 34–5), Peeters (2002b: 118–20) and Jean-Pierre Mercier (2001: 166).

37 Later, their name was again changed, to the generic "Prix de..." (e.g., Prix du meilleur album [Prize for the best book]).

38 Blutch, Frédéric Boilet, Jean-Claude Denis, Denis Lapière, Johan de

Moor, Michel Plessix, Martin Veyron and Vink cite Hergé as an influence; Jochen Gerner cites Saint-Ogan; Boilet mentions Breysse's Oscar Hamel series.

39 For example, the artistic genealogy that Farid Boudjellal has sketched for, and sometimes in, his own comics lays out a different set of influential comics and cartoonists, with their own complicated colonial and imperialist ramifications (e.g., "Milton Caniff," featuring a military pilot, by American cartoonist Milton Caniff; and *Blek le roc*, a French Canadian pioneer strip by three Italian artists known collectively as Essegesse). On the latter, see Miller (2007: 173–4).

40 Benoît-Jeannin (2001, 2007), Hunt (2002) and Frey (2004, 2008a).

41 Charles Forsdick (2005b: 107 n2) makes a similar point about the Croisière jaune.

42 In his insightful article on "L'imaginaire colonial dans la bande dessinée," Yann Holo (1993a: 75) disregards the order of exhibition (first; *Zig et Puce aux Indes*) and expedition (second; *Zig, Puce et Furette*) episodes in Saint-Ogan's comic, instead analyzing them in the order of the historical events on which they were based: first the Croisière noire episode, then the Exposition coloniale one. On the other hand, a children's voyage out to a colony (Mysore) – and, before that, the colonial voyage and conquest by an ancestor – in the sequence analyzed above, does precede the exhibition episode in *Zig et Puce aux Indes*.

43 In 1997 the CNBDI republished his *Cinq-mars*, a *bande dessinée* adaptation of Alfred de Vigny's work, and the French Centre National du Livre (CNL) lists his *bande dessinée* version of Victor Hugo's *Quatre-vingt treize* as a lacuna, i.e., a classic comic in need of republication and eligible for a public "subvention à la publication" [publication support] of up to 60 percent (http://www.centrenationaldulivre.fr/?Lacunes-bande-dessinee; consulted 11 July 2009).

44 On the symbolism of the sedan chair, see below, pp. 125, 127, 194 n. 33.

45 A literary and cultural type from the French Caribbean; see Bachollet et al. (1994: 113), Chamoiseau and Confiant (1991: 88–92) and McKinney (2000: 91).

46 On some of the paradoxes and problems of traveling from colonial exhibitions in the European *métropole* out to the colonies, see Mitchell (2004).

Chapter One

1 Six volumes of Greg's version have been published (Greg 1974, 1994, 1995a, 1995b, 1995c, 1995d); see Petitfaux (in Saint-Ogan 1995e: 63; 1995f: 55–8); Petitfaux and Greg (in Saint-Ogan 2000: 52–5).

2 The publishing house of Etienne Robial and Florence Cestac was later taken over by Gallimard, which let it languish for several years, but it has more recently been reactivated as a joint venture with Mourad Boudjellal, the publisher of Soleil Editions and younger brother of Algerian-French cartoonist Farid Boudjellal. Cf. Cestac (2007) and Beaty (2008).

3 They include pages from the serialized version of the story that had been cut from the first book edition.

4 Cf. Groensteen and Morgan (2007). I consulted the critical dossier on Saint-Ogan held by the CIBDI, which included the following material in 2006 (plus a couple of publishers' descriptions of books): François (1974); Saint-Ogan (1974b, 1988); Petitfaux (1985, 1986, 1995); Lehideux (1995: 18–21) – includes the interview with Petitfaux (1995). Much of the CIBDI dossier consists of material by Petitfaux that was recycled in his afterwords to the Glénat version of the Zig et Puce series, so I have usually not provided duplicate references for such material.

5 My abbreviation "SOC" refers to Saint-Ogan's scrapbooks (*carnets*), consulted at the (then) CNBDI (May–June 2006) and then downloaded in their digitized form, on 16–24 March 2008, from its website, www.cnbdi. fr/_collections-numerisees/server2go_a2_psm_mini/www/_app_php_ mysql/cahiers/recherche_alpha_cles.php; now (4 August 2010) available at: http://collections.citebd.org/saint_ogan/www/_app_php_mysql/cahiers/ recherche_alpha_cles.php. The page numbering of these scrapbooks is tricky – they may contain larger numbers stamped in ink (but sometimes the order is backwards [e.g., SOC 39]); hand-written numbers in pencil; or even two, slightly differing, sets of pencil numbers, one at the top and the other at the bottom of the pages (e.g., SOC 20).

6 See also below, p. 56, 188 n. 107.

7 Cf. *Dictionnaire mondial de la bande dessinée* (Gaumer and Moliterni 1994: 555–6): Saint-Ogan "can be considered, for many reasons, to be the inventor of French *bande dessinée* [...] Preferring effectiveness and readability, his graphic style struck the imagination of his readers and influenced a great many authors, including the great Hergé."

8 But on European comics up through the nineteenth century, see Kunzle (1973, 1990a).

9 Francophone Canada may be somewhat of an exception in this regard.

10 On Rosaldo and imperialist nostalgia, including as these relate to the Croisière noire, see also Forsdick (2005b: 69, 91–2, 106–9).

11 See, for example, colonial nostalgia in statements by French presidents François Mitterrand (Smith 1993) and Jacques Chirac (Merchet 1996); and, for a critique of negationist French historiography on colonialism, see Benot (2001: 173–81). See also Blanchard and Bancel (1997: 101, 104). On the repetition, by Nicolas Sarkozy, of colonial-era clichés about Africa, see

Chrétien et al. (2008). Official French colonial nostalgia is exemplified by the law of 23 February 2005, including the abrogated fourth article (Liauzu and Manceron 2006). On French neo-imperialism, which is precisely what supports today's colonial nostalgia, see, for example, Verschave (2001).

12 His emphasis throughout. Johnson (in Strömberg 2003: 11–12) also calls for extensive analysis of similarly degrading cartoon and comics imagery "of all racial *Others*," including Jews, Irish, Chinese and Japanese. Cf. a revised version of Strömberg's study (2010), in French.

13 In *Zig et Puce cherchent Dolly* (Saint-Ogan 1995e: 50–6). Cayenne is the capital of French Guyana.

14 In *Zig, Puce et Furette* (Saint-Ogan 1996a: 19).

15 In *Zig, Puce et Furette* (Saint-Ogan 1996a: 19). Madagascar is off the eastern coast of Africa.

16 In *Zig et Puce aux Indes* (Saint-Ogan 1995f: 4, 15, 19).

17 In *Zig, Puce et Furette* (Saint-Ogan 1996a: 19). Located in the western Sahara.

18 In *Zig et Puce et le cirque* (Saint-Ogan 1999b: 41–51).

19 In *Zig, Puce et Furette* (Saint-Ogan 1996a: 19). Bangui is the capital of the République Centrafricaine. The Oubangui River, one of the tributaries of the Congo River, serves as a frontier between the Congo and the République Démocratique du Congo.

20 In *Zig et Puce millionnaires* (Saint-Ogan 1995b: 16–25); and in *Zig, Puce et Alfred* (Saint-Ogan 1995c: 9–15).

21 In *Zig, Puce et Furette* (Saint-Ogan 1996a: 19). Now Burkina, located just north of Ghana.

22 In *Zig, Puce et Furette* (Saint-Ogan 1996a: 19).

23 In *Zig et Puce en Ethiopie* (Saint-Ogan 1999c: 13–16), serialized 20 November 1949 to 28 May 1950. Djibouti is in the horn of East Africa. Formal colonization by the French was from approximately 1888–1977. French legionaries are still stationed there.

24 *Zig et Puce à New York* (Saint-Ogan 1995d: 30–2); *Zig, Puce et Furette* (Saint-Ogan 1996a: 17–18).

25 In *Zig et Puce Millionnaires* (Saint-Ogan 1995b: 7–11); *Zig et Puce et l'homme invisible* (Saint-Ogan 1998b: 44–5).

26 *Zig et Puce cherchent Dolly* (Saint-Ogan 1995e: 15–25).

27 *Zig et Puce aux Indes* (Saint-Ogan 1995f: 4).

28 *Zig et Puce au XXIe siècle* (Saint-Ogan 1997a: 4), serialized 1933–4. Lebanon was under French mandate at the time.

29 *Zig et Puce en Ethiopie* (Saint-Ogan 1999c: 11).

30 The most formidable leader of the Moroccan insurgents was the Emir Abd-el-Krim (Muhammad ben 'Abdul-Karim), who made great headway against the Spanish forces before fighting the Rif War against the French from April 1925 to May 1926, when he was finally defeated by a

Franco-Spanish force (Abun-Nasr 1990: 378–82; Pervillé 1993: 52). Saint-Ogan's serialized comic was appearing in the weekly *Dimanche-illustré* during approximately the same period (3 May 1925 to 30 January 1927).

31 This is a street in Toulon, extending northwest from the avenue de la République, which borders the harbor. On colonial streets and monuments in France today, see Amato (1979), Aldrich (2002, 2005) and Kidd (2002). The naming of public spaces in Toulon and other places has become the subject of debates over the nature of colonial history (Ould-Aoudia 2006).

32 Post-1962 French comics set in Southeast Asia are more likely to show Franco-American imperialist rivalry and continuity, whereas those set in Africa focus more on Franco-British rivalry. For comic-book references to the latter, specifically the 1898 incident at Fashoda and its sequels, including the Voulet and Chanoine expedition, see Saint-Michel and Le Honzec (1994: 24–8), Logez and Delannoy (2001) and Jarry and Otto T. (2007: n.p.). I analyze these below, pp. 104–11, 189 n. 18.

33 In Hergé (1973: 293). On this, see Met (1996). See also Hergé's depiction of fetishism in supposedly primitive cultures in *L'oreille cassée* (first ed. 1935; in Hergé 1979).

34 On this trope in *Tintin au Congo*, see Met (1996: 142).

35 Jijé, a well-known Belgian cartoonist, went so far as to name (in 1939) a black character "Cirage" [shoe polish], in the comics series entitled "Blondin et Cirage" [Blondy and Shoe-black]. For an analysis of the series, see Pigeon (1996: 151–3).

36 "If there are mores and customs to respect, there are also hatreds and rivalries that need to be untangled and turned to our profit, by setting some against others, while we rely on some to better vanquish the others" (quoted in Verschave 2001: 107).

37 Hervé de Charette (foreign minister 1995–7, under Alain Juppé and Chirac) wrote a biography of Lyautey and has cited him as a role model (Charette 1997).

38 This ridiculous name may be a parodic allusion to Paul Reboux's 1920 novel, *Romulus Coucou, roman nègre*. On the latter, see Berliner (2002: 38–45).

39 Cf. an entry in the first volume of Saint-Ogan's bio-bibliographical scrapbook and photo album (SOC I; CAI_FA_M_03386.pdf), for 6 April 1927: "Presentation of the Alfred fetish at Innovation (Josephine Baker, Spada, Fursy, [illegible abbreviations] Hefty [?] d'Autigny)."

40 Nederveen Pieterse (1992: 188–210), Bachollet et al. (1994) and McClintock (1995: 207–31).

41 The manichean, racialized representation of black and white difference is widespread in classic French-language comics, including "Les Schtroumpfs noirs" [The black Smurfs] (in Peyo and Delporte 2005; first ed. 1963). I thank Fabrice Leroy for having reminded me of this example.

42 *Zig et Puce millionnaires* (Saint-Ogan 1995b: 7–9); but see the pidgin French of Harikoko, the Haitian king, in the song "Zig et Puce chez les Nègres" [Zig and Puce among the Negroes] (in *Zig et Puce et l'homme invisible*, Saint-Ogan 1998b: 44–5), based on the Haitian episode from the comic strip. The king's name is a ridiculous pun on the foodstuffs produced by colonized and Third World peoples for the industrialized world: French "haricot" [bean] and English "cocoa." The name Harikoko suggests "chocolate [i.e., black] bean."

43 E.g., Saint-Ogan (1995a: 6; 1995b: 7, 16; 1995c: 16; 1995f: 18; 1997c: 14; 1999c: 14; 2000: 35). In *Zig et Puce en Ethiopie* one finds on the same page (1999c: 14) two Africans, in Djibouti, who speak pidgin French and a third one whose French is grammatically correct. However, the latter example is exceptional in the series.

44 E.g., Logez and Delannoy (2001); see pp. 104–10, below.

45 The editorial caption in Groensteen (2007b: 46) is "Appeared in *Le Petit Journal* (June 1931)."

Chapter Two

1 E.g., Fanon (1986: 27; first ed. 1952), Dorfman and Mattelart (1984) and Kunzle (1990b).

2 For a compendium of such arguments pertaining to *Tintin au Congo*, see Peeters (2002a: 79); and for similar claims about the Pieds-Nickelés, see Tulard (2008: 44–6, 62, 70–4). Peeters (2002a: 79) connects the production of *Tintin au Congo* to the Exposition coloniale in Paris, but gets the date wrong (1930 instead of 1931). Levine (2005: 87) states that the story was inspired by the earlier Croisière noire, which is more probable. Tulard (2008: 55) too gets the date of a colonial exhibition wrong: he claims that the one that inspired the Forton episode of the Pieds-Nickelés was held in 1937. There was an Exposition universelle in Paris that year, but the exhibition in *Attractions sensationnelles* (Forton 1931, 1935a), analyzed below, is the Exposition coloniale of 1931. Tulard also gives the wrong date (1938) for the first book publication of *Attractions sensationnelles*; in fact, it was first published in 1933, and the Exposition coloniale episode had been serialized 30 July–8 October 1931, in nos. 1200–10 (Tulard also mistakenly claims that *Pieds Nickelés en Amérique* was published in 1938, but it too first came out in book form in 1933).

3 On the mythification of Tintin and Hergé in Belgium, see Kotek (1995) and McKinney (2007b).

4 On the return to childhood as a disorienting experience, precisely when it brings readers face to face with the violence of colonialism and racism, see Dorfman (1983) and Benhaïm (2005).

5 There is a haunting, critical reference to a human zoo in Proust's *A la*

recherche du temps perdu that is analyzed by André Benhaïm (2005: 97–8). I thank Fabrice Leroy for having brought Benhaïm's article to my attention. The insulting terms that Proust's text critiques are found already in the title of *Négro et Négrette à l'Exposition* (Anonymous 1931a), for example. Its story is no improvement.

6 Christophe (1889), collected in Christophe (1981); see also Caradec (1981: 90–100), Ory (1989: 52) and Christophe (2004).

7 See below, and Lehembre (2005: 42, 50).

8 Quoted in Hodeir and Pierre (1991: 106). The same could be said for many colonialist comics: they were designed to enchant French youths and thereby inspire colonial vocations among them. The recent *Le roi noir n'est pas noir* (Logez and Delannoy 2001), analyzed below, suggests precisely the kind of connection expressed by Reynaud, but condemns it.

9 See Hodeir and Pierre (1991: 105–6) and Olivier (1932–4, vol. IV: 299–303). Hodeir and Pierre (1991: 30) also mention another, similar outreach to children, associated with the 1930 Centennial exhibition of the French conquest of Algeria. For the outreach to children and students by the organizers of the 1922 colonial exhibition in Marseilles, see Artaud (1923: 460–2).

10 Demaison (1931); cf. Findinier (2007: 57). Pinchon was paid 5,000 francs for this work, according to *arrêté* no. 1443, dated 31 December 1931 and signed by M. Olivier. André Demaison, the author of the guidebook text, was paid 20,000 francs (bill by Demaison, dated 20 February 1931; *bordereau* no. 664 from the Exposition, dated 24 February 1931 and signed by "Vatin-Pérignon"). CAOM (Centre des Archives d'Outre-Mer) FM ECI 23 ("Secrétariat général: Subventions").

11 See Bennett (1988) and McClintock (1995: 56–61); cf. Nederveen Pieterse (1992: 111, 2nd illus. on page).

12 Reproduced in *Désirs d'ailleurs: Les expositions coloniales de Marseille 1906 et 1922* (2006: 12); on this poster, see Boulanger (1995: 167), *Dans l'ombre de Bécassine* (2007: 61) and the online database (Ulysse) of the CAOM (consulted 12 July 2009): http://caom.archives-nationales.culture.gouv.fr/sdx/ulysse/notice?n=1&id=FR%20CAOM%20 9Fi490&qid=sdx_q1&p=1. Joseph de la Nézière (1873–1944) was a well-connected painter specializing in colonial themes (see Benjamin 2003). The de la Nézière brothers were childhood friends of Pinchon (*Dans l'ombre de Bécassine* 2007: esp. 12–13). According to the website of the de la Nézière family, R. de la Nézière "[p]articipates in the Colonial exhibition [1922, Marseilles], [and] there paints twins [?; "des jumeaux"] and the friezes of the Syrian pavilion" (http://delaneziere.free.fr/raymond.html; consulted 11 December 2006). I thank Bas Schuddeboom of www.lambiek. net for helpful leads to sources on Raymond de la Nézière.

13 "This description would not be complete if we forgot to point out

the dioramas of an artist of great talent, Mr. Pinchon, who livened up the technical documentation with images that were faithful and life-like. A scene of Algiers at night, the great landscapes of the Sahel and the High Plateaus, a mining site, orange-picking, the Test Garden of Hamma, the snow-covered cedars of the Aurès, the gorges of El Kantara, the ruins of Djemila were just so many colorful and accurate visions of the agricultural, forested, pastoral, mining, archeological and touristic Algeria, and constituted one of the most picturesque attractions of the Exhibition" (Artaud 1923: 94).

14 Findinier (2007: 51) explains that this government commission, which represented the pinnacle of his artistic career, fit logically into his previous artistic and colonial trajectory: "Though the intervention of Joseph de la Nézière counted in the receipt of such an artistic commission, one should also recall that Emile Pinchon is one of the first members of the Société coloniale des artistes français. It has been insufficiently noted that, at the colonial exhibition in Marseilles in 1906, which unofficially gives birth to the Société coloniale des artistes français, the two brothers, Joseph-Porphyre and Emile, win travel scholarships awarded by the Ministry of Colonies. Emile was then exhibiting among the artists competing for scholarships for travel to Tunisia. He then shows the fruit of his voyage at MM. Bernheim jeune et Cie in Paris, in 1908, in the exhibition *L'Algérie, la Tunisie et les Indes*."

15 A preliminary study of one of the bas-reliefs, in the sub-series on "colonial woods," may depict an *autochenille* [half-track], such as those used in the Croisière noire and other Citroën expeditions (cf. Findinier 2007: 54, figure 8), although it seems to have been titled "Transport par tracteur" [Transport by tractor] (Findinier 2007: 56).

16 Findinier (2007). Cf. www.artaujourdhui.info/article/5538 (consulted 12 July 2009) and the online French government culture databases named "Mobilier (Palissy)" and "Image (Mémoire)" (consulted 12 July 2009): http://www.culture.gouv.fr/public/mistral/palissy_fr?ACTION=RETROUVER&FIELD_4=AUTR%2cATEL&VALUE_4=PINCHON%20EMILE&NUMBER=5&GRP=0&REQ=%28%28PINCHON%20EMILE%29%20%3aAUTR%2cATEL%20%29&USRNAME=nobody&USRPWD=4%24%2534P&SPEC=9&SYN=1&IMLY=&MAX1=1&MAX2=200&MAX3=200&DOM=Tous.

17 Olivier (1932–4, vol. V, part 1: 436) and Findinier (2007).

18 "In addition, the graphic and photographic documents held by the Centre national des archives d'Outre-mer d'Aix-en-Provence reveal in often novel ways how Emile projected his work, a cycle whose logic is indeed located – for it involved conceiving a frieze – within a certain interdependence of each one of the works" (Findinier 2007: 53).

19 See Morton (2000: 120–1). The issue of *Le rire* contains visual and textual references to two songs, "Boudou Badabou" and "Nénuphar,"

the latter composed for the Exposition. Both are examples of the colonial grotesque in another popular medium (see Ruscio 2001: 202–4, 443–5, 448–9; Liauzu and Liauzu 2002: 91, 109; Borowice 2008). On blacks and the colonial grotesque in advertising, see Hale (2008: 92–9).

20 Artaud (1923: 109, 123, 133, 275, 357, 456, 485–6).

21 Textual descriptions and photographs of the dioramas are found in *Exposition coloniale internationale de Paris – 1931: Territoires africains sous mandat de la France: Cameroun et Togo* (1931).

22 In SOC [Saint-Ogan's Carnets (Scrapbooks)] I (CAI_FA_M_03386. pdf) – in 1931: 11, 15, 16, 19, 27 May; 29 June; 8, 13 July; 13 August; 12 September.

23 See pp. 55–6, below.

24 The Centenaire de l'Algérie française has received much less attention than the 1931 Exposition coloniale. Studies of the Centenaire include Ageron (1979), Hodeir and Pierre (1991: 29–32) and Benjamin (2003).

25 Cf. Groensteen (2007b: 44). He (42) also notes the "anticommunisme primaire" of some of the satirical articles illustrated by Saint-Ogan in *Le Charivari* around 1930.

26 *Le coup de patte* received 6,750 francs for the advertising, placed there by Havas: "18 1/4 de page (1 par numéro jusqu'au 20 Octobre) au prix de 375.– le quart de page)" [18 quarters of a page (1 per issue until 20 October) at the rate of 375.– the quarter page] (in "Additif au budget de propagande en faveur de l'Exposition coloniale internationale de Paris," Agence Havas, Service Commercial, 27 June 1931; CAOM ECI 26). I found quarter-page advertisements for the Exposition in the following sixteen issues of *Le coup de patte*: no. 7, 27 June 1931, p. 29; no. 8, 4 July, p. 29; no. 9, 11 July, p. 10; no. 10, 18 July, p. 29; no. 11, 25 July, p. 29; no. 12, 1 August, p. 29; no. 13, 8 August, p. 29; no. 14, 15 August, p. 29; no. 15, 22 August, p. 26; no. 16, 29 August, p. 19; no. 18, 12 September, p. 30; no. 20, 26 September, p. 30; no. 21, 3 October, p. 4; no. 22, 10 October, p. 4; no. 23, 17 October, p. 30; no. 24, 24 October 1931, p. 4 (issues 17 and 19 no doubt also had advertisements). The organizers of the Exposition contracted with Havas to have the agency place advertising in regional French newspapers (e.g., *L'avenir de la Touraine*), as well as specialized publications, including *Les potins de Paris*, *Les cahiers des droits de l'homme*, *Le scout de France* and the *Journal des nations américaines* (a Parisian publication). The sum allocated to *Le coup de patte* was one of the largest, and for one of the longest-running series of advertisements (most of the others were for between 1,500 to 3,000 francs, and for fewer paid insertions); see the other Havas-related documents in CAOM ECI 26.

The parody of *L'Humanité* is also pasted into Alain Saint-Ogan's scrapbooks (23.112–13). It was an early example in a series of parodies in *Le coup de patte* of other publications. The parody of *La dépêche métropolitaine et maritime*, published two weeks before the one of *L'Humanité*, is closely related to it: it purports to report on a fictional Exposition internationale métropolitaine, held in Dakar, simultaneously with the Exposition coloniale in Paris. It includes colonialist and racist humor about Léon Blum, Josephine Baker, Blaise Diagne (a black French government minister and mayor of Dakar), as well as Pierre Laval, then Président du Conseil (he is represented as an African "fétiche," i.e., a statuette, in a cartoon by Sennep).

27 A French colonial army unit based in North Africa.

28 Reproduced in Liauzu (1982: 243, original emphasis; cf. 38); cf. Pierre (1980: 194–5, 198–9). See also Thirion (1972: 319–21), Hodeir and Pierre (1991: 125–34), Andrew and Ungar (2005: 309–11) and Ruscio (2005: 131–9). Original documents and related material, including on French government surveillance of anti-colonial activists organizing around or against the Exposition, consulted at CAOM (in FM ECI 27 ["Propagande"]). Organizations spied on included the Ligue contre l'Impérialisme (or Ligue Anti-Impérialiste), the Ligue de Défense de la Race Nègre de Paris, the Parti Communiste Français and the Etoile Nord-Africaine.

29 Articles about the Exposition in the issues of *Le coup de patte* that I consulted included minor complaints (for example, about the early evening closing of a section, or the choice of paintings for an exhibition) but no substantive critiques of it.

30 E.g., Lebovics (1992: 104–10), Norindr (1996: 52–71), Morton (2000: 96–129), Ungar (2003: 210), Liauzu (2007b: 149) and Demeulenaere-Douyère (2010b: 159–61). See below, regarding a cartoon parody of the counter-Exposition, pp. 118–20.

31 See above, pp. 25, 28–33.

32 For an extensive investigation of anti-colonial critique in 1930s France, see the Groupe Interdisciplinaire d'Etudes Nizaniennes (2009); and on (anti-)colonialism and racism then, see Lebovics (1992) and Reynaud-Paligot (2007).

33 See above, pp. 39–40.

34 Glued into Saint-Ogan's scrapbooks, SOC 23.250 (CA23_FA_M_03328.PDF).

35 *Benjamin*, special issue (n.d. [1931]: 18); see an advertisement pasted into Saint-Ogan's scrapbook, SOC 23.51 (CA23_FA_M_03328.PDF). On the company and its history, see www.ovomaltine.ch (consulted 21 July 2009).

36 According to Groensteen (2007b: 49), Michel Lefebvre was a pseudonym used by Saint-Ogan.

37 See in SOC I (CAI_FA_M_03386.pdf), his entries for his activities related to the 1937 exhibition, on the following dates: 5 February; 3, 24, 26, 27 May; 2, 29 June; 3, 9, 14, 24, 26, 27, 30, 31 July; 18 August; 12, 13, 30 September; 3 October.

38 Although Assouline mistakenly gives the title as *Le coup de gratte*. Another cartoon about the same exhibition is reproduced by Groensteen (2007b: 47; cf. 44). On the right-wing press during the Exposition, see Blanchard (2003).

39 Cf. "A l'Exposition coloniale," an unsigned article in which the author uses irony to describe Friday visits to the exhibition by "des 'gens chics'" [chic people] (*Le coup de patte*, no. 6, 20 June 1931, p. 14).

40 I have not discovered any relationship between the racist insult "bicot" and this title.

41 Cf. Groensteen (2007b: 41): "The troupe [of Pierre Humble] will go on a triumphal tour of Algeria in early 1930." He also reproduces a newspaper photo from it (36), but does not mention the fact that the Algerian tour was part of the celebrations for the Centenaire de l'Algérie française. See also the entry in the second column across from the date of 27 May 1930, in the first volume of Saint-Ogan's bio-bibliographical scrapbook and photo album (SOC I; CAI_FA_M_03386.pdf): "'Zig et Puce' sont à Alger[,] Oran, Philippeville[,] etc." It is not clear whether that entry corresponds exactly to the date for the entry in the first column.

42 Letters between Pierre Humble and the Centenaire's organizers, in the archives of the Centenaire held by the CAOM (carton ALG GGA 64S/43 [Gouvernement général de l'Algérie; série 64; sous-série 43 ("Fêtes, théâtre, illuminations")]) state that a total of nine shows had been decided on initially (plus two more days of travel within Algeria, from Oran to Algiers and from Algiers to Constantine, for an 11-day stay there), for a remuneration of 70,000 francs, but with a supplement of 3,000 francs for each additional show and 1,500 francs per each additional day in Algeria without one. A 24,000-franc supplement was foreseen at one point, for eight additional shows (matinée or evening events), apparently including ones in Bône and Philippeville. Troupe personnel numbered twenty. For these sums the theater was to cover all expenses for travel (except the additional travel from Constantine to Bône and from there to Philippeville, for added shows), costumes, actors' fees, etc., whereas the Centenaire was to pay for all advertising and theater rental (see esp. a letter from Pierre Humble to "Monsieur le Commissaire général du 'Centenaire de l'Algérie,'" dated 18 February 1930, and a copy of the letter from [Gustave] Mercier [the Commissaire général du Centenaire] to Humble, dated 5 March 1930). The copy of a letter dated 6 March 1930 from L. Fouque, the Délégué du Commissariat Général for theatrical productions of the Centenaire in Oran to M. Armand, Conseiller de Gouvernement in Algiers (and Président de la Commission des fêtes et cérémonies), states that "The performances [of the Théâtre du Petit Monde] will take place on 23, 24, and 26 May at the Theater [of Oran]. The exhibition will cover the deficit of two performances. As for the third, I think that I can have the Department pick

up the tab, on the credit allocated for the Centennial celebrations." The participation of the Théâtre du Petit Monde in the Centenaire celebrations appears to have been an initiative of Humble (the copy of a letter from Mercier to Armand, dated 17 October 1929, refers to "a letter in which Mr. Pierre Humble, Director of the Théâtre du Petit Monde... offers to organize children's performances, on the occasion of the celebration of the Centennial").

    A letter (6 February 1930) outlining the artistic program of the Commission des fêtes et réceptions officielles describes the Algerian tour: "The tour of the Petit Monde (Humble theater) – 6 performances in Algiers, 4 in Oran, 2 in Constantine, one in Philippeville and 2 in Bône, expenditure 90,000 F[rancs]" (p. 1, by Armand to the Commissaire général, in CAOM ALG GGA 64S/44 ["Fêtes, manifestations, concerts"]). The letter goes on (p. 2) to describe expected revenue of 76,000 francs, with an expected deficit of "about 20,000 F." to be made up. Another official document ("Manifestations théâtrales et musicales du Centenaire auxquelles les tickets des bons seront reçus," undated, in ALG GGA 64S/44) lists the following performances, apparently 14 in total, by the Théâtre du Petit Monde: 23–4, 26 May (Oran); 28–31 May, plus matinée and soirée performances on 1 June (Algiers); 3–4 June (Constantine); matinée and soirée performances on 5 June (Bône); 6 June (Philippeville). An unsigned and undated copy of a contract between Mercier and M. Coste in Algiers stipulates a total of five performances ("having an educative and popular character") by the troupe in Algiers, for 10,000 francs per performance to be paid to Coste, and 5,000 francs per each additional performance, if any (ALG GGA 64S/44). The performances in Algiers were at the opera (letter of 18 March 1930, from Armand to the Commissaire général, in ALG GGA 64S/45 ["Fêtes et kermesses"]).

    43 Cf. the CNBDI (now CIBDI) Saint-Ogan bibliography (an entry for "1930, mercredi, 23 avril"), which mistakenly gives the location of these articles as scrapbook no. 20, whereas they are in SOC 21.34–5 (CA21_FA_M_03328.PDF). The Algerian tour of Humble's troupe is also mentioned in Gustave Mercier (1931, vol. 2: 334) and Arnaudiès (1941: 213). Humble had earlier produced a three-act play, *Le mariage du savant Cosinus*, based on the comic book by Christophe (Georges Colomb).

    44 SOC 23.105 (CA23_FA_M_03328.PDF); Saint-Ogan's bio-bibliographical scrapbooks contain no entry for 11 June 1931, so it is not clear whether he attended the show on that day.

    45 Its punning title obviously refers to the colonialist story *Around the World in 80 Days*, comparing it to the putative ability of the Exposition and of the performance to show visitors the cultures of the world in one day or show (Morton 2000: 3, 16–69). It also alludes to the Bois de Vincennes, where the Exposition was located.

46   The CAOM holds a photograph of "Le Théâtre du Petit Monde 1931 à l'Exposition coloniale" (FM ECI 28 ["Médailles et diplômes"]). A scan was placed online at http://www.archivesnationales.culture.gouv.fr/anom/fr/11_anc.documents/caom_documentsdumois.html (consulted 1 August 2010). I identify child actors playing Bécassine (in a Breton costume) and Zig or Puce (in a boating hat and bowtie). The balding man standing in the center background appears to be Saint-Ogan (cf. photos from the same period in his first scrapbook photo album [SOC I; CAI_FA_M_03386.pdf]). A man standing on the right may be a North African.

47   No. 8, 18 June 1931, p. 8. In *Aux colonies! Suivez le guide* (*Benjamin* n.d. [1931]: 31) a list of events at the Exposition coloniale that would be of interest to children states that a "Gala de l'enfance" dedicated to Bécassine was scheduled for the following dates: 4, 18 June; 9, 23 July. Presumably this was a different show from the one described by the playbill in Saint-Ogan's scrapbook. A *Calendrier provisoire des Fêtes de l'Exposition coloniale internationale de Paris 1931: Etabli au 1er avril 1931*, published by the Commissariat des fêtes of the Exposition (the commissioner of festivals was Fernand Rouget), lists the following children's gala events ("Galas de l'enfance"): "*Bécassine aux colonies* (avec danses et musiques coloniales)" [*Bécassine in the colonies* (with colonial dance and music], on Thursday, 4 June and 9 July ; "*Bécassine chez les noirs* (avec danses et musiques coloniales)" [*Bécassine among the blacks* (with colonial dance and music)], on Thursday, 18 June; "*Bécassine coloniale* (avec danses et musiques)" [*Colonial Bécassine* (with dance and music)], on Thursday, 23 July. It is not clear whether there was any difference between these four events, despite the variation in their titles. An accompanying booklet, entitled *Ce que seront les fêtes de l'Exposition coloniale internationale de Paris 1931: 1er avril 1931* (p. 2) also mentions the colonial Bécassine performance: "The Cinema of the Exposition Coloniale will be at once both instructive and attractive and the Commissariat has already seen to the organization, on Thursdays, of a show created with children in mind, and including a short presentation on the Colonies, and a children's review presenting '*Bécassine in the Colonies*' with native elements." Both booklets from the CAOM (FM ECI 5).

48   The show thereby used ordinary colonized soldiers to represent, as exotic spectacle, the elite of their nations who had been subjugated by French imperialist forces: Southeast Asians subdued by French imperialists such as Francis Garnier and Henri Rivière; a queen of Madagascar, perhaps Ranavalo(na) III, swept aside by Gallieni (assisted by Lyautey) and exiled to Algeria; and the Mossi conquered by the scorched earth policy of Paul Voulet. On Voulet, see below.

49   According to V. J., the reviewer in *Benjamin*. The Mme. Marchand cited here may have been the wife of Jean-Baptiste Marchand, of the

Fashoda incident, although he was a general by the time this article was published.

50 Spahis were a group of colonial troops. The connections between scouting and imperialism have been demonstrated, especially in British history (Warren 1986; Harlow and Carter 1999: 352–60; cf. Bancel 2003: 188–9). They are manifest in the life and work of Hergé (Hergé 1987; Van Opstal 1998).

51 According to various notices in *Benjamin*, it was also produced on 18 June; 9 and 23 July; 6, 20 and 27 August; and 10 and 24 September (except for 20 August, these correspond to dates given in the *Rapport général*; see below). The choice of Thursday, at least during September, was probably motivated in part by the fact that it was a day off from school, and a time when religious classes could be taken by children (e.g., Catholic catechism). The *Rapport général* of the Exposition coloniale internationale et des pays d'outre mer contains several references to the shows put on by Humble, but none that describe their relationship to comics. *Vie de l'Exposition* (Olivier 1932–4, vol. IV: 320) contains the following descriptions of the event: "A delicious evocation of the window display of Dolls at the Musée des colonies gave the opportunity to the troupe of the *Théâtre du Petit Monde* to put on a charming entertainment." This was part of the show "L'adieu des colonies à la métropole" [Farewell from the colonies to the *métropole*], first presented on 7 November 1931 and then throughout the final two weeks of the Exposition. The regular shows put on throughout the Exposition by Humble's troupe are also described, on the following page (321): "Children were not forgotten. For them were organized – on Thursday mornings – a bi-monthly show, as instructive as it was very amusing. The valiant troupe of the *Théâtre du Petit Monde*, directed by Mr. Pierre Humble, interpreted a review *Le tour du monde en quatre-vingts scènes* [Around the world in eighty scenes], that transported its young spectators to the diverse parts of our colonial empire, a clever pretext for the presentation of the colonial units [of troops]. This review met with the greatest success." The same volume of the report (Olivier 1932–4, vol. IV: 343–52) lists the box office receipts of the shows by the Théâtre du Petit Monde, totaling 236,308.25 francs: 5,980.00 (10 June, matinée); 7,909.75 (18 June); 7,678.00 (9 July); 9,009.50 (23 July); 2,914.50 (6 August, matinée); 6,964.50 (27 August); 10,075.00 (10 September); 26,125.00 (24 September); 24,630.00 (1 October); 22,915.00 (8 October); 13,677.00 (11 October); 24,115.00 (18 October); 26,290.00 (25 October); 48,025.00 (15 November). The following volume of the *Rapport général*, entitled *Sections coloniales*, mentions the contribution made by the colonial troops to some of these shows (Olivier 1932–4, vol. V, part 1: 242): "The processions for the public on Sunday evenings, and some plays/ pieces [pièces] by the *Théâtre du Petit Monde* also solicited the assistance of the Army."

52 To indicate their appreciation, organizers awarded a commemorative diploma to Humble for his participation in the 1931 Exposition, and he in turn thanked them for it. Emile Pinchon submitted an entry in the competition for the design of the diplomas and was awarded 1,000 francs for his submission. Documents in CAOM FM ECI 23 and 28.

53 However, Sandrine Lemaire (2002: 281–2) describes colonialist performances for children at the Exposition, based on Bécassine: "Thus, they were invited to a themed show with several versions, of which the first was *Bécassine aux colonies* then *Bécassine chez les Noirs* and finally *Bécassine coloniale* with colonial dance and music to accompany them in the hiatus between these episodes, which seemed to be an invitation to come back." Presumably, these were put on by Humble's troupe.

54 Copy of the "Arrêté portant répartition de la subvention de 8.000.000 de Frs allouée par l'Etat à l'Exposition Coloniale Internationale de Paris, en vue de son affectation aux Oeuvres de Retraites et de Pensions des Associations de la Presse," on 14 February 1931 (CAOM FM ECI 21 ["Convention avec la ville de Paris. Subventions à la presse"]). Cf. Blanchard (2003: 230), Andrew and Ungar (2005: 311).

55 Letter dated 6 May 1931 from the Fédération nationale des journaux français, charged with distributing the money to various publications, sent to M. Olivier, Commissaire général de l'Exposition, listing expenditures made for this purpose, including 50,400 francs due to *Le petit journal*, and requesting disbursement; an accompanying bill dated April 1931, from *Le petit journal*, requesting payment of that sum for a full-page advertisement; a copy of the *arrêté* no. 858, signed by Olivier on 6 June 1931, authorizing payment of the 200,000 francs; and a copy of an undated note for the Secrétaire général du Conseil supérieur, describing the communications strategy, including the imbalance between expenses of 500,000 francs of publicity at normal rates and the 200,000 francs actually allocated, as well as the allocation of additional money to the Havas agency, to fund publicity in other periodicals (all documents in CAOM ECI 23).

56 Contract no. 1767, dated 1 May 1931, in letter form, from "le Maréchal de France, Commissaire général de l'Exposition Coloniale Internationale" to "Monsieur Julien Coudy, Directeur de l'Office d'Annonces du Petit Parisien, d'Excelsior et des publications annexes"; see also the *bordereau* 1965, of 13 May 1931, from the Ministère des Colonies to the Direction des Finances, regarding this contract (among others) and the commitment to pay 400,000 francs (CAOM FM ECI 26).

57 For example, Herman Lebovics (1992: 51–97) includes a chapter on the exhibition in his historical critique of French cultural identity formations. Panivong Norindr (1996) critiques the place of French Indochina at the exhibition in his book on "phantasmatic Indochina." For Christopher Miller (1998) the exhibition was, similarly, a form of

collective hallucination. Important recent publications in English about the exhibition include the extensive architecture-based critique published by Patricia Morton (2000), and analyses by Elizabeth Ezra (2000) and Dudley Andrew and Steven Ungar (2005). In France, a ground-breaking study of French colonial exhibitions by Sylviane Leprun (1986) was followed by an important monograph on the exhibition by Hodeir and Pierre (1991). The ACHAC and BDIC have dedicated a great deal of critical attention to colonial exhibitions, e.g. Bancel, Blanchard and Gervereau (1993), Blanchard et al. (1995), Bancel et al. (2002) and Ungar (2003). Charles Forsdick (2002, 2005b) has analyzed exoticism and travel writing in and around the Exposition, including the novel *Mirages de Paris* by Senegalese writer Ousmane Socé (1964; first ed. 1937). The novel's main character, Fara, travels to the exhibition, where he meets Jacqueline, a young Frenchwoman, with whom he has a child. Jacqueline dies after delivering the child and Fara ultimately commits suicide. On the contemporary milieu that serves as the background of the novel, see Kaspi and Marès (1989) and Blévis et al. (2008). On the novel and its context, including the Exposition coloniale, cf. Miller (1998: 55–88), Thomas (2007: 66–75) and Malela (2008: esp. 147–55). Another earlier novel partially set at the Exposition is *Le prince Nikhil* by Eve Paul-Margueritte (1948; first ed. 1932). Both novels thematize exoticism and *métissage*, the former with respect to colonized West Africans and the latter in relationship to a wealthy Indian prince. André Hellé (1930), a celebrated book illustrator, also wrote and illustrated *La famille Bobichon à l'Exposition coloniale*, a short, incomplete children's story that ends abruptly and was to have a sequel ("Les remords de Miouset"). Its publication date is given as 1930, before the Exposition opened, but it anticipates key themes from the Exposition and after, including the stereotype of black Africans and New Caledonian Kanak as cannibals come to Paris; the transformation of French visitors to the Exposition into their colonized others; and the disappearance of a French child at the Exposition.

58 Orsenna was elected to the Académie française in 1998 and was appointed to the Conseil d'état in 1985.

59 The colonial museum was subsequently named the Musée de la France d'Outre-Mer (1935–60) and then the Musée des Arts africains et océaniens (1960). See Morton (2000: 272–312) and Blévis et al. (2008). It is also known as the Palais de la Porte dorée. The website of the new museum is www.histoire-immigration.fr.

60 Exceptions include Yann Holo, Pascal Blanchard and Nicolas Bancel.

61 On colonialism and carnivalesque in *Tintin au Congo*, see Met (1996: esp. 139–41).

62 For example, "The organizers had tried hard to keep out, from the presence of natives at the Exposition, everything that could give it

the character of a fairground exhibit [d'une exhibition foraine]" (Olivier 1932–4, vol. V, part 2: 299). See also Schneider (1982), Ageron (1984: 573–6) and Morton (2000: 71–4).

63 For brief mentions of this episode, see Lehembre (2005: 38) and Liauzu (2007b: 140–1), and, for a more substantial analysis, Couderc (2000: 228–31). On the treatment of colonial workers at the Exposition, see, e.g., Hodeir and Pierre (1991: 88–100), Dauphiné (1995), Hodeir (1995), Morton (2000: 113–14), Hodeir (2001), Blanchard, Bancel and Lemaire (2002: 68–9) and L'Estoile (2008).

64 On the special binding, see "Avertissement de l'éditeur," in *Zig, Puce et Alfred* (Saint-Ogan 1995c: 2).

65 On the wave of xenophobia and racism in France in 1937–8, see Schor (1985: 653–72).

66 See above, pp. 1–3.

67 The colonial metropolis, or colonizing center, i.e., mainland France; on an earlier map, see above, p. 3.

68 In the first volume, the boys criss-cross the globe in their attempt to reach America and become rich. At one point they land in black Africa, where they put on blackface to avoid being eaten by African cannibals (see above, p. 36). These activities and motivations are structurally different from those of the African cannibals, when they try to assimilate to French mores, whether through diet or dress. Representations of attempted assimilation by blacks (of whiteface) and of blackface by whites constitute different forms of colonial mimicry in the series.

69 Saint-Ogan (1999a: 23, 30, 51–2, 56); on cannibal jokes, see Nederveen Pieterse (1992: 113–22).

70 CAOM FM ECI 5 ("Secrétariat général: Arrêtés; Bulletin d'information. Congrès et fêtes"). A movie listed as *Mangeurs d'hommes*, probably *Chez les mangeurs d'hommes* (1928), was rented to the Exposition organizers in July 1931 (bill from Etablissements Roger Weil, 3 November 1931, in CAOM FM ECI 46 ["Fêtes et réceptions"]).

71 An Algerian indigenous soldier in a French colonial regiment.

72 The carnivalesque continues later in the story, at the bal de l'Opéra in Paris (pp. 43–5).

73 Yves Frémion kindly gave me a copy of his article about Manounou, the Senegalese wife of Ribouldingue, one of Forton's Pieds-Nickelés. He (2007) describes an episode in which Manounou dances under the name "Aoudja" in a fairground in Paris, a much later example of colonial masquerade at a sideshow.

74 In elegiac passages, she connects the popular forms to Baudelaire's vision of modernity; cf. Bennett (1988: 86–7, 92–3, 96).

75 Cf. Demeulenaere-Douyère (2010c: 26). Sébastien Rembert, archivist at the Archives départementales des Vosges, which has significant holdings

of *images d'Epinal*, kindly indicated (personal phone call, 22 July 2010) that its *dépôt légal* was 3 October 1867, and that the artist may have been André Chauffour.

76 A copy is held by The House of Alijn, Ghent, and accessible on their website (http://www.museuminzicht.be/public/collecties/obj_detail/index.cfm?id=hva2004-285-094; consulted on 24 July 2010). I am grateful to Greet Vanderhaegen and Sylvie Dhaene, of the museum, and to Pascal Lefèvre for their help with this document. Sébastien Rembert estimated (personal phone call, 22 July 2010), based on documentation available to him, that this edition might have been published between 1889 and 1900.

77 E.g., Bennett (1988: 80, 94–5), Lebovics (1992: 70, 86–7), McClintock (1995: 40–2, 56–61), Morton (2000: 195), MacKenzie (2002) and Hale (2008: 13–20, 86–9). In this comic, the rickshaw may prefigure this switch in focus and certainly looks forward to similar exotic, primitive machines, often associated with the Far East in later French comics set at exhibitions: "La famille Fenouillard à l'Exposition" (1889) by Christophe; and the Pieds-nickelés episode (1931), by Forton. On both, see below. On rickshaws [*pousse-pousse*] at French colonial exhibitions, see Morton (2000: 120), Ruscio (2002: 270–1), Blanchard and Deroo (2004: 56–7), Hale (2008: 18, 151, 191 n9) and Demeulenaere-Douyère (2010b: 178–9).

78 See, for example, McClintock (1995: 56–61) and Mitchell (2004).

79 Similarities between the exhibition visits by the Cocardeau and Fenouillard families include the loss and replacement of the bourgeois father's hat, and a rickshaw mishap.

80 See Caradec (1981: 77–80).

81 Suggesting *Tartarin de Tarascon* by Alphonse Daudet (1872), where a trip to Algeria leads to a tall tale, at the end, when the buffoonish anti-hero returns home to Tarascon and begins to recount his African adventures. For another tall tale about the Exposition, see O'Galop (1931), an illustrated children's story, whose narrator and protagonist is also a Marius from Marseilles.

82 Cf. Frantz Fanon, in *Peau noire, masques blancs* (1986: 27): "Le nègre doit, qu'il le veuille ou non, endosser la livrée que lui a faite le Blanc. Regardez les illustrés pour enfants, les nègres ont tous à la bouche le 'oui Missié' rituel." [The Negro must, whether he wants to or not, don the livery that the White made for him. Look at the illustrated magazines [i.e., magazines containing comics] for children, where Negroes all spout the ritual 'yes Mista.']

83 Cf. Nederveen Pieterse (1992: 217); McClintock (1995: 52–6).

84 I thank Michel Denni, owner of the Librairie Lutèce and an author of the BDM, for having kindly identified this author for me.

85 Hergé's *Tintin au Congo* was republished in the same magazine, 1932–3 (Van Opstal 1998: 129).

86 Banania is a well-known children's breakfast food, whose production and advertising have long been marked by French colonialism (Garrigues 1991; Bachollet et al. 1994; Donadey 2000).

87 E.g., a starched collar and tie, but no shirt, in Hergé (1973: 198, 215–19); see Met (1996) and Hunt (2002).

88 See Plate 2 (white man and woman on lower left); *L'Illustration* (1931), a photo of pith helmets worn and for sale in a collage titled "Le visage familier de l'Exposition"; Ezra (2000: 21–2).

89 I thank Michel Denni for having recommended that I consult the *Dico Solo* (Solo, Saint-Martin and Bertin 2004), which allowed me to identify the cartoonist.

90 Cf. Morton (2000: 120) and note 77, above.

91 The last panel includes a stylized signature "RN." It must have been drawn by Raymond de la Nézière, who contributed extensively to *La semaine de Suzette*. He signed some of the pages of *Miloula la négrillonne* (drawn by him) in the same manner (Hellèle and Nézière 1929: 11, 19, 27). This book was published by Gautier-Languereau, after having been serialized in its girls' magazine *La semaine de Suzette* (nouvellesuzette. canalblog.com/archives/auteur__hellele/index.html, and http://delaneziere. free.fr/livres.html, both consulted 31 July 2009). On the book and its young African protagonist, inspired by Claire de Duras's *Ourika*, see Couderc (2005: 43–4), and especially Gérard G. Pigeon (1996: 146–51), who describes Miloula as "the first true black female hero of the francophone comic strip" (146).

92 The panels are incrusted on the background, in a variant of what Groensteen (1999: 10–16) describes: an incrustation is one panel layered on top of, or nested within, another one.

93 The comic-strip images of carved African poles may have been inspired by the exhibition section for Cameroon and Togo, including its Grand Pavilion. See especially the photos of the exterior of the latter, featuring tall poles (possibly carved or painted), and interior (e.g., right-hand side) in the exhibition catalog, *Territoires africains sous mandat de la France: Cameroun et Togo* (1931). The interior featured large mural paintings with geometric patterns and statue heads, which strikingly resemble the cartoonist's poles. Below them stood dioramas (representing Africans) in two glass cases, which suggest comic-strip frames, like the ones in which the French children build their Africanist fantasy. Other objects inside the Grand Pavilion included carved wooden poles and masks. The catalog states that the paintings were by Voguet and the dioramas by the "peintre J. de la Nézière." On the architectural hybridity of the exhibition's architecture, see Morton (2000: esp. chs. 5–7). On the Cameronian and Togolese portion, see Morton (2000: 52–4, 209). On the human dioramas and "the native on display" at the exhibition, see Morton (2000:

esp. 79–95, 111–29). On other carvings [fétiches] at the Exposition, see Leprun (1986: 153).

94 And at least one exhibition worker from Guadeloupe was beaten by a French security guard (Morton 2000: 113–14). Cf. Dauphiné (1998: 29).

95 "Une croquignole" is a "petit biscuit croquant" [crunchy little biscuit] (*Petit Robert*). "Filocher" means "aller vite; se hâter" [go quickly; hurry up], "se défiler devant une corvée, s'y soustraire (soldats, prisonniers)" [get out of doing a chore (soldiers, prisoners)], and "suivre à la trace, un suspect, un véhicule, filer" [track a suspect or a vehicle]. "Une filoche" is "une bourse, portefeuille" [a wallet], or "une filature policière" [police tracking]. "Une ribouldingue" is a "partie de plaisir; débauche occasionnelle" [pleasure party; riotous time] (Cellard and Rey 1980). The names might also be read as portmanteau words that bring together terms suggesting a burlesque criminal lifestyle: "croquer" [bite] and "guignol" [puppet clown]; "ribouler" [to roll] and "dingue" [wacky]; "filou" [rogue] and "clochard" [bum].

96 Both this fire and the one lit at the exhibition by the African characters in Zig et Puce may have been inspired by real fires at the 1931 exhibition, including the one that burned down the Dutch Surinamese pavilion (Morton 2000: 60–2).

97 Cf. Morton (2000: 120) and note 77, above.

98 Morton (2000: 117–21) makes this point about a cartoon about belly dancing in a special issue of *Le rire* (1931: back cover) devoted to the 1931 Exposition. On belly dancing at and around French exhibitions, see also Leprun (1986: 18–21, 70–8), Çelik and Kinney (1990), Çelik (1992: 24–31), Hale (2002: 319), Demeulenaere-Douyère (2010a: 13, 16–17) and Décoret-Ahiha (2008: 147).

99 Cf. Barker (1989: 67–91).

100 Hodeir and Pierre (1991: 82–8), Lebovics (1992: 51, 92), Norindr (1996: 22) and Andrews and Ungar (2005: 306).

101 It had been serialized previously in *L'écho de Paris*, where Jaboune's father, Franc-Nohain (Maurice-Etienne Legrand), had worked as editor-in-chief (this paper is depicted on plate 29 of the book; see Gaumer and Moliterni [1994: 504]; Béra, Denni and Melot [2006: 289]). A website dedicated to Pinchon states that it was also serialized in *Le jour* (www.pinchon-illustrateur.info/pages/p03apag.html, consulted 12 July 2009).

102 A reference to "Riquet à la houppe," a character from a Mother Goose tale as retold by seventeenth-century French author Charles Perrault.

103 The Bécassine series deals with a similar dichotomy.

104 On colonial mimicry and hybridity, see Bhabha (1994), Young (1995) and Morton (2000: 12–14). For stimulating analyses of earlier cartoons (not comics) dealing with the disruption and transformation of European and non-European identities through cross-cultural encounters, when the

colonized entered the metropolis or when Europeans went to the colonies, see Gilman (1986) and Childs (2004), for example. For a fascinating study of (post-)colonial mimicry in comics by both Belgian and Congolese artists, see Hunt (2002).

105   Saint-Ogan 1997b.

106   The French department store; see Saint-Ogan (1999a: 61), SOC (16.2–3, 32–4, 46–7, 51, 101–2, etc.; CA16_FA_M_03328.PDF), Groensteen (2007b: 39) and Chapter 1, above.

107   According to Fourment (1987: 213), the sponsorship provided to *Cadet-revue* by the company that produced Ovomaltine was substantial: "This bimonthly [...] had a sponsor: the Wander company. The company purchased, for promotional purposes, between 15,000 and 20,000 copies of the publication, and gave them to clients who purchased Ovomaltine, its chocolate-flavored powder, in exchange for a certain number of proofs of purchase." In an interview with Petitfaux (1995: 19), Guy Lehideux (involved in several works commemorating Saint-Ogan; e.g., Lehideux 1995), remarks that "[a]nother very modern aspect of Saint-Ogan is his aptitude for using all the media of his time," to which Petitfaux replies: "Yes, his comic-strip heroes were transposed into [the media of] records, serialized radio show, theater, animated cartoon (*Prosper dans le concours de beauté* [Prosper in the Beauty Contest]), film-strip, film with actors. Saint-Ogan tried everything, before Hergé and quickly, whereas Tintin did not become a mass phenomenon until the fifties. The success that Saint-Ogan had with what one now calls spin-off products is equally astonishing. Through a curious reversal of things, it is his comics that appear to be spin-off products" (cf. Gordon 1998). These spin-off products could also contain noxious features: for example, in 1932 Saint-Ogan, Camille Ducray and Marius Zimmermann created various recorded songs and oral skits inspired by Zig et Puce (Groensteen 2007b: 48–9). Some of these had colonialist and racist features (cf. the reissued print versions in Saint-Ogan 1998b: 33–62). Seventy-two years later the set was transferred from the original 78 r.p.m. records to two compact discs and released in a limited edition of 1000 copies (Lehideux [n.d. (2004)]).

108   In *Zig et Puce au XXIe siècle*, "Zig et Puce en Atlantide" (republished in *Revoilà Zig et Puce*) and *Zig et Puce et le cirque*. On this repetition, see Chapter 1, above, and Petitfaux's afterword in Saint-Ogan (1998a).

Chapter Three

1   The story also borrows from Disney comics: their dog, named Micky [*sic*], resembles Pluto.

2   See above, pp. 22, 167 n. 24.

3   E.g., Deloncle (1931), Lyautey (1931) and *Exposition coloniale*

internationale de Paris – 1931: Territoires africains sous mandat de la France: Cameroun et Togo (1931).

4 For a trenchant critique of these, see Verschave (2001).

5 The fact that this type of visual reference is absent from colonial-era comics could be due to proprietary issues, such as the liability for copyright infringement by colonial-era cartoonists who reproduced exhibition posters.

6 Cf. Mercier (1931, vol.1, color plate between pp.144–5, center image).

7 My sources on Dinet include Dinet-Rollince (1938), Brahimi and Benchikou (1991), Pouillon (1997) and Benjamin (2003).

8 For the background of his collage, Ferrandez used a photo from *Le livre d'or du Centenaire de l'Algérie française* (2003; first ed. 1930: p. 357, left side); cf. Benjamin (2003: 254–5).

9 Fabrice Leroy kindly pointed out to me that this scene in Hergé is itself a reworking of an earlier, similar one in *Le Lotus bleu* (Hergé 1979: 153–4).

10 The Algerian shoe-shine boy was a widespread colonial type also found in children's prose fiction produced for the Centenaire: in *Le centenaire de l'Algérie: 2e livre* (Demousson and Pellier 1930b: front cover, 2–3). Cf. Demousson and Pellier (n.d. [1930a]) and Cheronnet (1931), both also produced for children for the Centenaire. For a critique of colonial ideology in postcards from North Africa, see, for example, Alloula (1981, 1986, 2001) – from whom Ferrandez directly borrowed certain images and created at least one character – and Bal (1996).

11 See above, p. 71.

12 Liauzu (1982: 105–30), Hô Chi Minh (1990), Blanchard and Deroo (2004: 95, 109) and Liauzu (2007a: 151–2).

13 For similarities with United States culture, see Paul Gilroy (1993: 117–24) and bell hooks (1992).

14 Cf. the accounts by those implicated: Joalland (1930) and Klobb and Meynier (2001). The latter is a critical edition with useful analysis and contextual material.

15 On Franco-British imperialist rivalry and the Mission Afrique Centrale, see also Mathieu (1995: esp. 24–37, 57–69, 128–9, 238–9).

16 Elsewhere, Mathieu (1995: 246) writes that "G. Tourot, wishing to rehabilitate the memory of his father and of Captain Voulet whom he admired, cites the names of numerous officers guilty of acts of violence comparable to those committed by the Central African mission (op. cit. p. 117)..." On Maréchal des logis Tourot, see Mathieu (1995: 46, etc.).

17 I thank Ann Miller for having kindly made me aware of this filmic connection.

18 In *L'empire* (2007), the second volume of their "Petite histoire des

colonies françaises," Grégory Jarry and Otto T. recount the Voulet and Chanoine episode across nine pages. Here, as always, they use biting satire. Tidjani Alou (2005), found after my book was completed, also compares Rolland (1976) to Mamani (1980).

19 Cf. *Apocalypse Now*, directed by Francis Ford Coppola, released in 1979. I thank Fabrice Leroy for having kindly suggested this connection.

20 See Schneider (1982: 125–51), Berliner (2002: 107–22) and Schneider (2002).

21 See, for example, Schneider (1982: 126–36, 146–9; 2002), Dauphiné (1998: 86–7), Bergougniou, Clignet and David (2001: 157–60) and Coutancier and Barthe (2002). Intriguingly, Michel Pierre (2000: 47) claims that the spectacle of colonial exhibitions had an effect contrary to the goals of their organizers: "during the Exposition of 1931, a great many children of the time were invited to come visit this great event organized to glorify the French empire. They would be fascinated by the African or Asian artifacts and later become anti-colonial militants. The shock that they felt will not have been that of the recurrent figures of colonialism, but of the artistic output of the countries in question. They will not become missionaries or camel-riding military men [*méharistes*][...] but will struggle against colonialism." However, Pierre provides no evidence to support his claim, so its basis remains unclear.

22 In fact, by having their fictional character Ratillon visit the Paris exhibition of Africans in 1883, the cartoonists were probably tinkering with the historical record. Historian William H. Schneider (1982: 128–30; cf. 2002) discusses two displays of Nubians in the Jardin d'acclimatation in 1877 and 1879, whereas for 1883 he lists exhibitions of Ceylonese, Araucans (Guyana), Kalmouks (Siberia) and American Indians. The change in dates helps the cartoonists to cast Ratillon's voyage to Chad with the Voulet and Chanoine expedition as an initiatory experience for a young 25-year-old man.

23 Unsurprisingly, in *La Croisière noire*, Haardt and Audouin-Dubreuil (1971: 69–73, 80–3, 85–6) omit this inglorious episode from their epic account of the conquest of Chad by supposedly heroic French forces, although they do praise Joalland, who participated in the Mission under the command of Voulet and Chanoine, and was one of its new leaders after their demise.

24 For example, Rigney (2005), which I found at the end of my work on this book.

25 See above, p. 170 n. 11.

26 On her induction into the Légion d'honneur, see Heliot (1998). She also served on the Haut Conseil des rapatriés [High Council for the Repatriated (i.e., former colonizers, for the most part)] (www.premier-ministre.gouv.fr; consulted 12 March 2004). On the militantly pro-colonial perspective and activities of the Cercle Algérianiste, see Morin, Nadiras

and Thénault (2006: 29–30, 41, 53, 56) and the website of the organization (www.cerclealgerianiste.asso.fr).

27 I thank Mr. Jean-Michel Creutzer for having generously given me a set of the entire series.

28 Di Martino and Baloup belong to a group of cartoonists that shares an artists' studio in Marseilles.

29 The structure was brought to New Caledonia after the exhibition, re-erected in Nouméa and turned into a public library, with funding from Lucien Bernheim, a mine owner (www.bernheim.nc; consulted 17 July 2008).

30 It is also possible that Berger and JAR chose not to depict the "human zoo" of Kanak for other reasons: for example, perhaps because the earlier historical period (of 1900) was more useful to their overall narrative in the series about the emergence of a multi-ethnic New Caledonia. I am very grateful to Amanda Macdonald for having introduced me to the work of Berger and JAR and having generously given me a set of the series. Berger (2003) does play with French stereotypes of New Caledonian cannibalism in 22 *mille lieues sur la mer,* the twelfth volume in his humor-based series "La brousse en folie." There, a multi-ethnic delegation from the islands travels to France to meet equally (but differently) caricatured "native" French people.

31 The Banania figure was drawn at the time by the cartoonist Vica (Garrigues 1991: 84–5) – among others – a cartoonist now remembered most for the antisemitic comics he drew during the Occupation (Tufts 2004).

32 African soldiers, including Senegalese, in the French colonial army were of course an important part of the Exposition (see, for example, L'Estoile [2008]); on Josephine Baker and the Exposition, see Ezra (2000: 19) and Borowice (2008); cf. Morton (2000: 308–9).

33 Charles-Robert Ageron, Catherine Coquery-Vidrovitch, Jacques Dalloz, Gilbert Meynier, Raphaël Nzabakomada-Yakoma, Benjamin Stora, Jacques Thobie, etc.

Chapter Four

1 Nguyên Ái Quôc, "Ménagerie," in *Le paria,* 1 February 1923; republished in Hô Chi Minh 1990. Quoted in Forsdick (2005b: 108 n5). Alain Ruscio, who edited the collection of Ho Chi Minh's writings from which this is taken, states that this alludes to the Croisière noire. However, the date of the article's original publication suggests that it is likely a reference to the first trans-Saharan expedition sponsored by Citroën.

2 Throughout this chapter I refer mostly to the 1971 edition, and to the original edition (1927a) only with respect to the iconography, because

the plates in the 1971 edition were significantly modified from the original (placement, cropping, etc.); see also the English translation (1927b), whose text is missing certain passages.

3 Used in precisely this manner by Haardt and Audouin-Dubreuil (1971: 310).

4 The racializing of this color typology is obvious.

5 Haardt and Audouin-Dubreuil (1923: 8–10, 45–6); cf. Haardt and Audouin-Dubreuil (1971: 43) and Deschamps (1999: 84).

6 The Citroën expeditions included an automotive crossing of the Sahara – "le raid Citroën" – in 1922–3 (Haardt and Audouin-Dubreuil 1923); the Croisière noire; the "Croisière jaune," a similar expedition across Asia (4 April 1931–12 February 1932), during which Haardt died of illness and exhaustion; and a later Croisière blanche, across Canada, which failed miserably.

7 On the idea of linking France's North and West African colonies, see also *Le roi noir n'est pas noir* (Logez and Delannoy 2001: n.p.; 10th plate after title), set in 1898–9.

8 For critical readings of the Croisière noire, related Citroën expeditions and the publicity surrounding them, see Murray (2000), Berliner (2002: 189–204), Forsdick (2005b), Levine (2005) and Bloom (2006).

9 For photos of the expedition, showing machine guns mounted on some of the vehicles, see Haardt and Audouin-Dubreuil (1971: 33–5) and Audouin-Dubreuil (2004: 46–7, 59, 122). Deschamps (1999: 110, 119) mentions them and Haardt's designation of the gunners. Cf. Wolgensinger (2002: 75–6).

10 The colonial ethnographic vision is also visible in the contrast that the authors of *La Croisière noire* (Haardt and Audouin-Dubreuil 1971: 257–8) drew between the supposedly aristocratic Mangbetou and the physically and morally inelegant Bantous.

11 Cf. Barthes (1987: esp. 64–7, 137–44, 193–247), Çelik and Kinney (1990) and Ageron (1993).

12 Ubiquitous in French and Belgian comics about Africa.

13 See below, my discussion of Greg's comic *Le prototype zéro-zéro* (1995b).

14 Cf. Wolgensinger (2002: 74). This fascination is also found in a comic by Bardet and Jusseaume (1987: 33–6). For a critique of the French mythologizing and sexual exploitation of the Ouled-Naïl, see Lazreg (1994: 29–35).

15 On Haardt and Audouin-Dubreuil's vision of the Vénus noire, see Berliner (2002: 194–204). Cf. Nederveen Pieterse (1992: 181–7) and Sharpley-Whiting (1999).

16 The list of recent French comics containing this theme is too long to mention here. A significant example is Ferrandez (1994a).

17 In *Le centenaire*, Ferrandez (1994b) implicitly critiques this ubiquitous French imperialist motif in the colonial Algerian context. For a critique of its use to justify French colonial rule over Indochina, see Norindr (1996: 26–9).

18 E.g., Cocoa and Cacao, in Zig et Puce. For an analysis of the Senegalese rifleman as child, see Berliner (2002: 9–36).

19 In Christin and Goetzinger's *La voyageuse de petite ceinture* (1985), analyzed above, pp. 95–6.

20 Among other comics, in *Tintin au Congo* (Hergé 1973: 236–9). For a critique of this motif in French and Belgian comics, see Halen (1993a) and Jannone (1995b). Cf. Rahier (2003: 60–1, 66–7, 72).

21 Cf. Berliner (2002: 117–22).

22 Cf. 225, 227, 310; and Halen (1993a). See also the hagiographic comic *Stanley* (Joly and Hubinon 1994). For a demystifying critique of the Stanley legend, see Hochschild (1998).

23 The episodes of the book were serialized in *Dimanche-Illustré*, from 27 March 1932 to 8 January 1933. The journey is referred to as a "raid" in the story (Saint-Ogan 1996a: 8–9).

24 Rocherand (1979), Deschamps (1999: 92–3, 106–7, 126), Murray (2000: 101), Wolgensinger (2002: 103–84) and Rouxel (2003).

25 On the American influence on Saint-Ogan's series, specifically his use of speech balloons under the influence of the series "Bicot" (the French title of "Winnie Winkle") by Martin M. Branner, see Petitfaux in Saint-Ogan (1995b: 43; 1996b: 56). A French version of Winnie Winkle, by French cartoonists, was eventually created (Gaumer and Moliterni 1994: 669–70).

26 Holo also comments briefly on the 1931 Exposition coloniale episode in Zig et Puce.

27 The *Thysville* – the colonial name of a Congolese city, now Mbanza Ngungu, on the Lower Congo.

28 For a possible model for this car, see Farr (2001: 25).

29 Peeters (2002a: 88; cf. 74–5); cf. Groensteen (1996a: 8–9; 2007b: 44–5), Assouline (1998: 90), Sadoul (2000: 101) and Goddin (2008: 82). There are contradictions between these accounts of his trip(s) to Paris.

30 Morton (2000: 20). In addition, the Section de Synthèse of the Musée des colonies had a portion dedicated to trans-African automobile expeditions (Olivier 1932–4, vol. V, part 1: 100–1; cf. 422–3). The 1922 Exposition nationale coloniale de Marseille also included Citroën half-tracks from the trans-Saharan crossings (Artaud 1923: 322).

31 Murray (2000), Berliner (2002: 189–204), Levine (2005) and Bloom (2006).

32 Other comics featuring half-tracks include a "Blondin et Cirage" story (Hubinon 1977; first ed. 1951) and an early "Tif et Tondu" episode.

Illustrated children's stories with half-tracks include Dorlys (1930; 1932), Jeanjean (1930–1) and Anonymous (1931b).

33 Cf. Farr (2001: 23). Nederveen Pieterse (1992: 90) notes that "[t]he carrying hammock [was] one of the symbols of colonial hierarchy."

34 Hergé was no doubt inspired by an exhibit in the Musée royal de l'Afrique centrale in Tervuren, Belgium. On this motif in and around *Tintin au Congo*, see Halen (1993a: 147–85; 1994), Jannone (1995b), Assouline (1998: 83), Farr (2001: 26–7) and Peeters (2002a: 79).

35 The term is used in an earlier colonialist story situated in the Belgian Congo and drawn by Hergé (1987: 82), "Popokabaka: Bananera chantée," serialized 1 March–26 July 1927 and republished later (Hergé 1987: 70–95). Cf. Van Opstal (1998: 210–11).

36 E.g. Assouline (1998: 85), Farr (2001: 22–5), Hunt (2002: 91, 93) and Peeters (2002a: 80).

37 A "mission automobile belge" in the Belgian Congo appears at the end of "Popokabaka: Bananera chantée," drawn by Hergé and scripted by René Verhaegen (Hergé 1987: 95).

38 *Le livre d'or du Centenaire de l'Algérie française* (2003: 303–19) and Rouxel (2003: 150–9).

39 The collaboration between Citroën and the organizers of the 1931 Exposition was substantial, and included a massive publicity campaign (films, fliers, posters, stamps, brochures, maps, etc., in many European languages) for the Exposition that was carried out by the car manufacterer, as shown by documents held in the CAOM (Centre des Archives d'Outre-Mer, Aix-en-Provence), carton FM ECI 26; consulted 22 June 2010. For this, the Citroën company was paid 300,000 francs (letter from André Citroën to the Gouverneur général Olivier, dated 5 March 1931; and signed contract between the Citroën company and the government, dated 30 March 1931). The initial project, described by Citroën in the copy of a letter (incompletely dated: handwritten annotation "Novembre" – of 1930?; ref. RA no. 15.354) to Olivier, points out that the Croisière jaune would be in progress during the Exposition and confirms Citroën's interest in their previously discussed plan for Citroën to build a pavilion at the Exposition coloniale: it would house the "Exposition Citroën de la Pénétration Coloniale en Afrique: 1ère traversée du Sahara-Alger Madagascar-(Croisière Noire) et en Asie: Beyrouth Saïgon par Pékin (Croisière jaune)." Cf. Andrew and Ungar (2005: 304–5).

40 This issue of *Automobilia* also features two articles referring to the same trans-Saharan Citroën expedition and a series of photos of it (pp. 23–5, 27).

41 The comic strip has been reproduced in a book about André Citroën and his company (Sabatès and Schweitzer 1980: 110–11). Fabien Sabatès (co-)authored or played a role in the publication of three books I refer

to, which celebrate car manufacturers and road expeditions during the colonial era.

42 Cf. Wolgensinger (2002: 128). In *Carnets d'Orient*, Ferrandez (1994a) uses a similar trope: a Frenchman is disappointed when a woman opens her veil [haïk] and reveals that she is not the woman that he had glimpsed in a harem.

43 Fabien Sabatès and Sylvie Schweitzer (1980: 110) suggest that the comic story is a parody of *L'Atlantide*, by Pierre Louÿs. In fact, it was by Pierre Benoît (1920; first ed. 1919), with a movie version made from it by Jacques Feyder; see Slavin (1996), Berliner (2002: 49, 202), Wolgensinger (2002: 59, 67–9, 86, 135, 191–2) and Andrew and Ungar (2005: 312).

44 Saint-Ogan (1995d: 40); see p. 124, above.

45 Http://www.citroen.com/NR/exeres/F1D2F57B-F66C-4492-9198-483B86C19B08,frameless.htm (consulted 2 January 2006); Wolgensinger (2002: 135). This was not the first time that Bruller had published a work related to Citroën cars. In 1926 Les Editions Enfantines Citroën published *Frisemouche fait de l'auto*, a humor-based story designed to foster children's interest in Citroën cars (cf. Wolgensinger 1996: 54–5). It was illustrated by Jean Bruller and perhaps written by him too (Bruller 1991). Sabatès was instrumental in getting the book republished.

46 In his introduction to the republished *Le mariage de M. Lakonik*, Thierry Groensteen (in Bruller 2000: 3–7) does not mention Bruller's use of this historical model in his comic.

47 See above, p. 34.

48 Benoît-Jeannin (2001: 47) suggests that we should probably view the colonial troops in North Africa in *Le crabe aux pinces d'or* as *pétainiste* collaborators with the Nazis, because it is likely set in Vichy-controlled North Africa, and because Hergé first serialized the book in collaborationist Belgian newspapers (*Le Soir*, in French; *Het Laatste Nieuws*, in Flemish) from October 1940–September 1941. Hergé also collaborated closely with prominent Belgian fascists and ultra-traditionalist Catholics, and included antisemitic and (other) collaborationist material in his comics during the Nazi occupation of Belgium (see Van Opstal 1998: 30–1, 56–9, 79–94, 130; Benoît-Jeannin 2001: 42–52). The collaborationist Vichy government controlled Algeria and Morocco until November 1942, when the Allies landed there (Abun-Nasr 1990: 337–8, 389). See also the raiding Berbers in Jijé's volume (1994: 135–44) on Charles de Foucauld, and in Breysse (1995: 13–17).

49 The North African bandits run off because they are frightened by the eclipse of the sun, much as Tintin and Haddock are saved when Incas are frightened by a solar eclipse in *Le temple du soleil*, serialized 19 December 1946–22 April 1948, in *Tintin* magazine in Belgium (and in *Coeurs vaillants* in France).

50   The trans-African episode in this edition, which I used, is identical to that of the pre-war editions of the book (they extend from pp. 3–31). As Béra, Denni and Melot (2006: 509) point out, the post Second World War editions of Pieds-Nickelés books by Forton are considerably shorter (48 pp.) than the interwar versions (64 pp.), because of post-war paper shortages. In this volume, cuts were made after the *autochenille* segment.

51   See also similar textual and visual representations by André Dahl and Albert Dubout in a special issue of *Le rire* (1931).

52   *Bec* [beak] can refer to a person's mouth, as in the expression "clouer le bec à quelqu'un" [shut someone up]. Here "claquer du bec" could be interpreted as "to jabber away."

53   E.g., in *Sam et Sap* (Candide and Le Cordier 1908).

54   For Greg's account of how and why he continued the series, see Saint-Ogan (2000: 52–5). For bibliographic details about the series and its continuation, see Saint-Ogan (1995f: 61–2). For Petitfaux's presentation of this transition, see Saint-Ogan (1995e: 63; 1995f: 55–8). On Hergé's unconvincing half-attempts to clean up the antisemitism and colonialist racism of his comics, see Benoît-Jeannin (2001: 21, 29–30, 33, 69–86).

55   Also on the cover of Wolgensinger (2002) and in Ageron (1993: 102, illus. 11).

56   See also <u>*L'aventure*</u> *de la Croisière noire* (Wolgensinger 2002; my emphasis) and my second epigraph in this chapter, above.

57   On the colonial nostalgia of Chirac, see Merchet (1996), cited in Blanchard and Bancel (1997: 101); on that of Le Pen, see esp. Stora (1999); for the colonial nostalgia of Foreign Minister Hervé de Charette, see his book on Lyautey (1997). For perspectives on the Croisière noire that are shot through with colonial nostalgia, see *La Croisière noire: Sur la trace des explorateurs du XIXe siècle* (2004), by Ariane Audouin-Dubreuil, a daughter of Louis Audouin-Dubreuil, and Deschamps (1999).

58   One finds the move from the seductive to the grotesque, in typically sexist terms, in the official *Bulletin d'informations* (no. 2, 31 May 1930, p. 13; in CAOM FM ECI 5; consulted 23 June 2010) of the Commissariat général de l'Exposition coloniale internationale de 1931, in an unsigned article entitled "La Mode 1931 sera-t-elle Coloniale?":

> A few years ago, the film about the 'Croisière noire' had made popular the gracious and thoughtful image of a young mangbétou negress whose head was adorned with a strange hairdo: a narrow headband atop which there perched, slightly thrown back, a pierced and very flared disc.
>
> Fashion got involved and, for several months, authentic Parisian women covered the napes of their necks, not yet shaven, with hats that were visibly inspired by the purest mangbetou style.
>
> We will not see, alas! at the Exposition, either the Mangbetou of

the 'Croisière Noire,' no doubt become a respectable matron with dangling breasts, as the Mangbetou esthetic requires, or one of her sisters.

59 Cf. Andrew and Ungar (2005: 314).

60 Haardt and Audouin-Dubreuil (1971: 257–9, 263–4), Hodeir, Pierre and Leprun (1993: 135, illus. 16), Bachollet et al. (1994: 148–9 [illus. no. 209], 166 [illus. no. 237], 208 [illus no. 308]), Palmenaer (2000) and Andrew and Ungar (2005: 304–5). Parisian hairstylists and clothing designers also apparently drew inspiration from the picture of Nobosodrou (Norroy 1973: 116–17; Berliner 2002: 196; Levine 2005).

61 According to the *Trésors de la bande dessinée* (Bera, Denni and Mellot 2006: 435), the booklet is a shortened version of the serialized original.

62 The English translation of the fifth French volume is collected in Sfar (2008: 49–130). In my analysis I refer to the French original.

63 He also refashioned African voyages by French Jewish scholars Joseph Halevy and Jacques Faitlovitch, as Marla Harris informed me toward the end of my work on this book. Her work on this dimension is forthcoming.

64 On his use of North African music in the series, see McKinney (2009).

65 Cf. the reference to Communists in Haardt and Audouin-Dubreuil (1971: 150).

66 See also pp. 96–9, 101–10.

67 E.g., soldiers' accounts of French military exploits in Africa (Haardt and Audouin-Dubreuil 1971: 80–3, 114), colonial ethnographers (110–11) and Stanley's memoirs (314).

68 See above, pp. 131–2.

69 Among the modifications that Sfar makes to this story is the following minor, but intriguing, one: a Ford car, given to Barmou, the sultan of Tessaoua (Haardt and Audouin-Dubreuil 1971: 54–5), is changed into a Renault instead (Sfar 2006: 65). Is this a reminder by Sfar of the rivalry between the two French automobile manufacturers, or an attempt to eliminate a possible reference by Haardt and Audouin-Dubreuil to imperialist rivalry between France and the United States? Or perhaps it is only designed to make the story more coherently focused on relations between Africa and France.

70 Sfar may have borrowed certain elements of his *Vénus noire* figure from Deschamps (1999), whose book is cited as a source by Sfar (2006: 4). Deschamps (1999: 50) tells a story about an abandoned African woman whom Citroën members pick up in the desert (cf. Sfar 2006: 69). See also photos in Deschamps (1999: 149) and Audouin-Dubreuil (2004: 55, 172), which may have supplied models for Sfar.

71 This tension – between hunting and observing wild animals – already existed in the Croisière noire (Audouin-Dubreuil 2004: 79–80).

72 Sfar's characters also observe cranes peacefully (71), but kill an attacking crocodile (78), thereby spicing up the story in a typical way – cf. similar episodes in Haardt and Audouin-Dubreuil (1971: 86, 327).

73 Sfar's characters also visit colonial cities (Sfar 2006: 68–71; cf. Haardt and Audouin-Dubreuil 1971: 114–15, 236–7, 332–3, 351–5, 368), see a French fort (Sfar 2006: 71; cf. Haardt and Audouin-Dubreuil 1971: 91) and visit Uganda (Sfar 2006: 76; cf. Haardt and Audouin-Dubreuil 1971: 297–306), where Sfar inserts an interesting episode with a racist French painter, who angers the Russian by telling him how to paint blacks. The Frenchman carries with him a "Traité physiognomonique de la figure" [Physiognomonic treatise of the face], which presents an evolutionary vision of humankind, with Africans halfway between apes and whites.

74 See Deschamps (1999: 70) and the following references to various forms of paradise in Haardt and Audouin-Dubreuil (1971), in the trans-Saharan leg of their journey: the garden of Armida (22); Haroun-al-Raschid, from the *1001 Nights* (24); the garden of Eden (24); mirages in the Tanezrouft (32); and Africa as an El Dorado for adventurers (147).

75 Like many American students, I first read Saint-Exupéry's colonial fable in my high-school French class. The physical depiction of the Russian Jewish painter in *Jérusalem d'Afrique* is reminiscent of Saint-Exupéry's drawings of the little prince, who – we may remember – appears in the Sahara desert, which Sfar's artist paints (Sfar 2006: 39–46), just as Saint-Exupéry himself did. At that same point in Sfar's story, the rabbi's cat is stung by a scorpion, almost dies, but is rescued by the painter and receives medical attention in time to be cured. This may remind us of the snake bite that kills the little prince. Gallimard published Sfar's comics adaptation of *Le petit prince* in 2008. Sfar's Africanist sources probably also include depictions of Ethiopian women by Italian cartoonist Hugo Pratt (1987). Vastenov, the Russian officer in *Jérusalem d'Afrique*, may have been inspired by Baron Von Ungern-Sternberg in Hugo Pratt's *Corto Maltese en Sibérie* (1980), based on a historical figure. Pratt's Raspoutine character (Pratt 1980) may also be a model for Sfar's Vastenov. For Sfar's vision of Pratt's work, see Sfar (2007: 166).

76 See www.autochenille-production.com; consulted 20 July 2010.

Conclusion

1 On mourning and the transmission of a colonial inheritance in film, see Durmelat (2000).

2 Another indication of this is the fact that the grandparents' house contains North African furniture (Alagbé and Stein 1997: 19).

3 Also, a photograph above the preface appears to represent German soldiers (Alagbé and Stein 1997: 16).

4 I do not mean to imply that the Nazis' genocidal final solution for Jews and Europeans' violent and even genocidal conduct in colonized nations are not distinct, with their own specific horrors. Nor do I believe that the cartoonists are implying such a thing.

APPENDIX I

Colonialism and imperialism in Alain Saint-Ogan's Zig et Puce series

The serialization and book publication dates below are gathered from the Glénat volumes, especially Petitfaux's bibliography in vol. 6 (Saint-Ogan 1995f: 59–62), which contains additional publication information.
An asterisk indicates: 'Ouvrage publié avec le concours du Centre National des Lettres' [Work published with the assistance of the National Center of Literature]

I   **Zig et Puce: En route pour l'Amérique** serialized 3 May 1925 to 30 January 1927; book 1927, 1995

Imperialist or colonialist episode
(1) cannibals and animals in Africa [6–7]
(2) Rif War in Morocco: gunrunners and Rifains [9–10]
French soldiers: 10, 19–20 (?)
Senegalese riflemen: 43
Other blacks: boxer in Antwerp [28]

2   **Millionnaires** serialized 6 February 1927 to 19 February 1928; book 1928, 1995

Imperialist or colonialist episode
(1) Haiti [7–11]
(2) Senegal: bandits [16–25]
French soldiers: 24
Senegalese riflemen: 24

3   Et Alfred serialized 26 February 1928 to 25 November 1928; book
     1929 [1930?], 1995

Senegal: bandits, part 2 [7–15]
Other blacks: 11, 16, 18, 31

4   A New York serialized 2 December 1928 to 2 February 1930; book
     1930, 1995

Imperialist or colonialist episode
(1) Africa crossed, from north to south [30–49]: Suez Canal [30];
    Cairo [31]; pyramids and Sphinx [31–2]; European tourists in
    Egypt [31–2]; references to Alexandria and Port-Saïd [32]; desert
    scenes, including a lion, which is tamed, and a caravan [32–9];
    black African villagers in desert oasis fear lion [37–9]; reference to
    autochenilles [halftracks] crossing the desert, which save the trio
    [40]; South Africa [40–9], with Afrikaner farmers and speculators,
    diamond-hunting, black child [41], money-lender [47–8].
(2) black Africans recalled [59]: probable reference to vol. 1.
• see vol. 7, *Zig, Puce et Furette*, for related, later episode of crossing
  of Africa, also based on the Citroën expeditions.
Other blacks: Africans in desert [37–9]; in South Africa [41]. African-
American servant of uncle of Dolly in NY [63]

5   Cherchent Dolly serialized 9 February 1930 to 22 March 1931;
     book 1931, 1995

Imperialist or colonialist episode
(1) Native Americans [9–11]
(2) Latin America [15–48]: Mexico (ranch), Honduras (cotton
    plantation), Nicaragua, Costa Rica, Panama Canal (US zone)
    [26–8].
(3) Cayenne, Martinique, Bermudas: bandits from Senegal, part 3
    [49–56]; deserted island [57–8].
Other blacks: 3, 22, 26–8, 59

6   Aux Indes serialized 29 March 1931 to 20 March 1932; book 1932,
     1995

Imperialist or colonialist episode
(1) Enthronement of Puce in Indian state [3–14]: Napoleonic
    imperialism [4]; Indian fakirs and snake charmers [7, 14]; sacred
    animals [4, 13–14]; corrupt local officials, including the French (?)
    lawyer.
(2) Colonial exhibition [15–29]: link between colonies and *métropole*

(maps: 4, 19); exotic locales abroad and at home; Marseilles as colonial port [17]; colonial newspaper [19]; conversion narratives (vegetarian missionary; cannibals into domestic servants)
Colonial administrators: 4
French soldiers: 4 (Napoleonic officer)
Cocoa and Cacao (African cannibals): First appearance [18–29], as Kacoco [18] and Radadou [22]

7   **Et Furette** serialized 27 March 1932 to 8 January 1933; book 1933, 1996*

Imperialist or colonialist episode
(1) African raid [3–23]: itinerary [9, 19]; Port Said [15-17]; côte des Somalis, Madagascar, Congo, Oubangui, Haute Volta, Mauritanie, New York [19].
• see vol. 4, *à New York* [40] for reference to *autochenilles* and crossing of desert, plus a trans-African crossing by trio.
(2) Clipperton Island expedition [27–37]: Robinson Crusoe episode [27–32]; arrival of explorer and inventor, Professor Médor [33–4]; deserted island claimed by French navy [34]; boys rescued by navy [35–6]; penguin Alfred as mascot of sailors [35–40]; rue d'Alger in Toulon, harbor of imperialist navy [37].
• see vol. 11, *Et le prof. Médor,* including preface by Petitfaux on Clipperton and French imperialism [2].
French soldiers: sailors save boys [34–6]
Senegalese riflemen: in crowd that greets boys in Toulon [36]
Cocoa and Cacao (African cannibals): 20
Other blacks: African-American family [26]; Antillais (?) servants on ship – Adonis Nicéphore and Napoléonne Ocarina [33]

8   **Et la petite princesse** serialized 15 January 1933 to 10 December 1933; book 1934, 1996*

Imperialist or colonialist episode
Summarize the story of their travels to English schoolmaster [6]
Cocoa and Cacao (African cannibals): 46, 48–9

9   **Au XXI siècle** serialized 17 December 1933 to 14 October 1934; book 1935, 1997*

Imperialist or colonialist episode
• Explore stratosphere and end up in 21st century [3–5]: balloon seen by people in Hebrides and Lebanon [4].
In 21st century:
(1) Boats from 16th century (colonization?) [20–4].

(2) Voyage to Mars ends up on Venus [25–44]: clearly inspiration for Hergé's Tintin (e.g., cf. p. 38, and *Temple du Soleil*); division of people in Venus into white race and superstitious black one (latter described as monkey-like [39, 41]).

• cf. vol. 17, *Sur Vénus*.

Cocoa and Cacao (African cannibals): 46 (after return to 20th century)

10   **Ministres** [33–62] not serialized; book 1938, 1997
("**Et le poulain**") [3–32] serialized 23 January 1936 to 13 August 1936; book 1989, 1997

Imperialist or colonialist episode
(1) Shipwrecked on coast of Africa [11–16]: African cannibals turn out to be civilized, because light cigarettes with lighter, ride motorcycle, drive car, speak French (*sabir*).
(2) Visit to Easter Island [17–32]: primitive religion; natives easily tricked, speak pidgin ("y'a bon" [it good]), and are beaten up by the boys; *évolué* policeman; colonial European administrator.

• cf. vol. 11, *Et le prof. Médor.*[†]

11   **Et le professeur Médor** [3–32] serialized 1 April 1939 to 15 August 1939; book 1941, 1997
(**Mécanos**) [33–48] book 1930, 1988, 1997

Imperialist or colonialist episode
(1) Summary of adventures, including colonial ones [3].
(2) Easter Island [11–32]: repeat of story in preceding vol. [10: 17–32]. Same elements as before; plus gunrunning pirates, finally beaten by Chilean warship [32]; and fantastic episode of prehistoric creatures on sister island [23–32]. Médor wants animals for Vincennes zoo [31]. Story of strange bird that led Médor on wild goose chase from account by Marseilles ship captain Marius (= fibber) [32].

• reference by Petitfaux to French imperialism and Clipperton island [2].
• see vols. 12, 15 for similar antediluvian stories.

Cocoa and Cacao (African cannibals): 3–4
Other blacks: a pirate [21]

[†] Petitfaux (in Saint-Ogan 1997b: 63–4) explains that he was in charge of Futuropolis version of the Zig et Puce series, in "Copyright," a collection directed by Florence Cestac (cf. Cestac 2007).

12   Revoilà Zig et Puce [3–32] serialized 3 May 1946 to 11 December
     1946; book 1947, 1998
     (En Atlantide) [33–45] serialized 18 December 1946 to 9 July 1947;
     book 1992, 1998

Imperialist or colonialist episode
- first version of Atlantide episode in Zig et Puce [33–45] shows a
  race of black people initially described as a black thing [38] and
  then as monkeys [39], before recognition as people who live at a
  lower level than the white race of Atlantes, with whom they do not
  get along [39] – civilizational hierarchy concretized in living space.
  Among the blacks, some are civilized and scientifically advanced,
  and are less black, with thinner lips [41]. War between the two
  races [43–5], ending in atomic bomb explosion [45], when blacks
  learn from document in Cpt. Nemo's ship how to become invisible
  [42–3].
- afterword mentions this as the "racisme 'tranquille' de l'époque"
  ['tranquil' racism of the time] [46] and suggests why this episode
  was never published in book form by Hachette.
- see later re-working of same episode in vol. 15, with similar racist
  structure.
- cf. novels with related themes mentioned here [47] and vol. 15.
  Here [47] Petitfaux also gives H. G. Wells, *La machine à explorer
  le temps* (1895) as Saint-Ogan's source for manichean structure.
  Petitfaux says occurs four times in Zig et Puce. For Saint-Ogan's
  ref. to Wells, see vol. 13 [23–4].

13   Et l'homme invisible [3–32] serialized 17 July 1947 to 12 February
     1948; book 1949, 1998
     (Scènes et chansons de) [33–62] booklet and records 1932 (1998,
     2004)

Imperialist or colonialist episode
- man with pith helmet in circus [4]
- Pudding couple said to be in Africa, Médor in Indies [5]
- summary of Médor's adventures [27]: Clipperton, blacks and
  bracelet, fakir from India.
- hotel named Malikoko XV [30–2]
- *Scènes et chansons de Zig et Puce* (1932), includes: "Zig et Puce
  chez les Nègres" [Z and P among the Negroes] (Haiti) [44–5]; "Zig
  et Puce dans la brousse" [Z and P in the bush] [46–7]; Senegalese
  fighter and cannibal joke in "Zig et Puce lutteurs" [Z and P
  wrestlers] [54–5]

- on history of publication of *Scènes et chansons* [64]; cf. *Et Furette*, vol. 7 [39–40].
- comment by Petitfaux in his afterword [64], defending Hergé and Saint-Ogan against accusations of racism.

Other blacks: African-American reads paper in NY [20]

14   **Et le complot** serialized 19 February 1948 to 5 December 1948; book 1950, 1999
     (**"Marche de"**) [58–60] 1952, 1954 [?], 1999

Imperialist or colonialist episode

- return of cannibal humor in 1948, long after first appearance of Cocoa and Cacao (1931–2).
- vol. has two versions of same story, serialized one after the other, in different magazines: 1–32; 33–58.
- important afterword by Petitfaux, comparing Hergé and Saint-Ogan [61–3]. Includes reproduction of ad for Le Printemps with images of Haitians [61], and Petitfaux's reasons for reading Saint-Ogan today [63].
- Followed by cartoon page of hommage by Hergé to Saint-Ogan [64].

Cocoa and Cacao (African cannibals): As Cacao and Cocoa: 20, 23, 30–1, 51–2, 56–7. Cannibal joke [23, 52]
Other blacks: Haitians in advertisement reproduced at end [61]. Cf. vols 2 [7]; 13 [44–5]

15   **Et le cirque** serialized 12 December 1948 to 13 November 1949; book 1951, 1999

Imperialist or colonialist episode

- Franco-Belgian circus travels to North Africa (mentioned [33]; represented [41–51]). In the Sahara, the boys stumble upon remainder of inhabitants of Atlantide/Atlantis, represented by an Englishman. Reproduces colonial ideology: black servants on bottom, then white Atlantides (natives), and European (English) colonizer as spokesman who makes decision for the group (expel Zig and Puce and make them forget).
- afterword discusses M. Poche as stereotype of Frenchman (cf. afterword to next vol. [53]).
- for earlier version of Atlantide episode, see vol. 12 [33–45] and its afterword [46–8], and prose texts cited here [47, 53] and in afterword of vol. 12.

French soldiers: in North African city [43]
Other blacks: dock-worker, speaks *sabir* [39]; some of the Atlantidéens [46–7]

16   En Ethiopie [3–33] serialized 20 November 1949 to 28 May 1950;
      book 1952, 1999
      (Et Alfred) "album rose" [35–42] book 1952, 1999
      (Alfred le pingouin volant) "album rose" [43–50] book 1953, 1999

Imperialist or colonialist episode
(1) voyage to Addis Abeba to give a fortune won in national lottery
    to inheritors [6]. Boat is named *Ali Baba Pacha*, and goes to
    Indochina via Djibouti (both French colonies; cf. Petitfaux,
    p. 52) [11] – boat based in Marseilles [12]. In Djibouti [13–16], a
    colonizer irritated by tourists searching for local color [13], talking
    African characters (two speak pidgin; one standard) [14], incl.
    two motivated by rewards of French governor; white and Africans
    afraid of ghost [15]. French trains [15] run from Djibouti to Addis
    Abeba. In Addis Abeba, scenes with Africans [16–19], then Prof.
    Medor disguised as Ras/Ethiopian chief arrives to collect animals
    for French government for Vincennes zoo [19].
(2) Médor tries to capture animals [20–2]; boys return to Marseilles.
• Afterword by Petitfaux discusses *pétainisme* and antisemitism of
  Saint-Ogan [51–5] and responds [53] to article by Groensteen
  (1996a: esp. 13–15), but without mentioning anti-black racism, to
  which Groensteen specifically refers.
Colonial administrators: French governor mentioned [13–14]
French soldiers: traffic police ? [14]
Cocoa and Cacao (African cannibals): 3
Other blacks: 13–22

17   Sur Vénus [3–36] serialized 4 June 1950 to 14 January 1951; book
      2000
      ("Au Far West") [37–51] serialized 21 January 1951 to 29 April
      1951; book 2000

Imperialist or colonialist episode
Voyage to Venus and back [5–36]: technologically advanced white
    Venusians live on sunlit side of planet [6–16, 30–4]; primitive black
    Venusians on unlit side of planet [16–17, 21–8] – called "blancs"
    [whites], "nègres" [Negroes] and "noirs" [blacks] by characters,
    and then narrator too [25, 27–8]. Various primitive practices
    interpreted by characters as ethnologists: funeral monuments [21],
    sacrifice [22], temple with idols [23–4], to whom white Venusians to
    be sacrificed, but saved by Puce [24–5], degree of savagery debated
    [26], beaten by plucky characters [25–8], Alfred mistaken for their
    god [27–8], of whom a rock carving had been shown earlier [25],
    panicked by light and by invention of white Venusian [28].

- title of book and second episode created by Petitfaux, who explains arbitrary nature of titles to Saint-Ogan's books [2].
- discussion by Petitfaux of racism in Saint-Ogan's depiction of black Venusians and reference to "integration-assimilation", and to Native Americans on warpath as anachronism in 1951 [2].
- quote by Petitfaux: Zig et Puce belong to History [52].
- reprinted preface by Greg to Futuropolis ed.: description of encounters between Hergé and Saint-Ogan [53]; quote, attributed to Saint-Ogan, comparing Josephine Baker to penguin Alfred [54].
- see vol. 9 for original version of voyage to Venus.

Cocoa and Cacao (African cannibals): 36, 51
Other blacks: sailor and others [35]

18   **Et Nenette et autres histoires**
      (**Nénette et la baronne Truffe**) serialized 15 December 1952 to 1 March 1954; book 2001
      (**Dans le pays souterrain**) serialized 15 March 1954 to 15 February 1955; book 2001
      (**Et la petite princesse**; 2nd vers.) serialized 1 December 1955 to 19 July 1956; book 2001

Imperialist or colonialist episode
Republication of various stories, often combined together, including *Zig et Puce sur Vénus* (in "Zig et Puce dans le pays souterrain" [38–43]); *Zig et Puce et la petite princesse* [45–9]

APPENDIX 2

French colonial exhibitions in comics[1]

Title (and author)	First published (in periodical)	Exhibition: date; title; city	Time of story (i.e., when set)
(1) "Visite de la famille Cocardeau à l'Exposition universelle de 1867" (Anonymous)	1867; image d'Epinal	1867; Exposition universelle; Paris	1867
(2) *Les mésaventures de M. Bêton* (Petit)	ca. 1868[7]	?; "Grand théâtre des merveilles de la nature" (cf. Fête de Montrouge); Paris	ca. 1868
(3) "La famille Fenouillard à l'exposition" (Christophe)	(1889; *Le petit Français illustré*)[9]	1889; Exposition universelle; Paris	1889
(4) *Bécassine chez les Turcs* (Caumery and Pinchon)	1919[11]	1900; Exposition universelle; Paris	1900–19
(5) *Bécassine, son oncle et leurs amis* (Caumery and Pinchon)	1926[13]	1925; Exposition internationale des arts décoratifs; Paris	1925
(6) "Monsieur Flan fait une folie!" (Saint-Ogan)[14]	(1930?; *Le petit journal*)	1930; Centenaire de l'Algérie française	1930
(7) "Marius Galéjade à l'Exposition coloniale" (S. Pania [Espagnat])	(1931; *La jeunesse illustrée*)[15]	1931; Exposition coloniale internationale; Paris	1931

Visit to the exhibition[2]	*Ethnic others and colonized groups at exhibition or elsewhere*[3]	*Exhibition poster shown*	*Republished after 1962*	*Exhibition episode*[4]	*Total story length*[5]
yes	Cochin-chinois?; Germans; Russians; Spaniards; Persians; Chinese; Indians; Mexicans; Arabs; etc.	no	yes[6]	1 page (17 frames)	1 page
yes	"sauvages"	no	no	7+ pp.[8]	52 pp.
yes	Muslims; white Frenchman as Muslim	no	yes[10]	5 pp.	5 pp.
yes	Bretonne; Turks; Muslim (Turkish?)[12]	no	yes	esp. 4 frames (p. 15)	61 pp.
yes (much of the book)	Bretons; Hindu	no	yes	most of book, but esp. 33 pp.	60 pp.
no	Algerian	no	probably not	5 frames	5-frame strip
yes	Tarasconnais as king of Africans; blacks from central Africa	no	probably not	2 pp. (12 frames ea.)	2 pp.

Title (and author)	First published (in periodical)	Exhibition: date; title; city	Time of story (i.e., when set)
(8) "A l'Exposition coloniale: Jeannot-Lapin-dromadaire entre sans payer…" (Touchet)	(1931; *Benjamin*)[16]	1931; Exposition coloniale internationale; Paris	1931
(9) "Coco, Banania et les poissons volants (Conte de l'exposition coloniale)" (Caouissin)	(1931; *Coeurs vaillants*)[17]	1931; Exposition coloniale internationale; Paris	1931
(10) "Koko, grand chef des becs rouges" (Dharm)	(1931; *Le petit journal illustré*)[19]	1931; Exposition coloniale internationale; Paris	1931
(11) *Le mariage de M. Lakonik* (Bruller)	1931	1931; unspecified; Paris	1931 (but cf. Citroën episode)
(12) "Les nouvelles aventures des Pieds-Nickelés" (Forton)	(1931; *L'épatant*)[22]	1931; Exposition coloniale internationale; Paris	1931
(13) "Un palais nègre" (RN [de la Nézière])	(1931; *La semaine de Suzette*)[24]	1931; Exposition coloniale internationale; Paris	1931
(14) *Bécassine aux bains de mer* (Caumery and Pinchon)	1932 (1931; *La semaine de Suzette*)[25]	1931; Exposition coloniale internationale; Paris	1931
(15) *Zig et Puce aux Indes* (Saint-Ogan)	1932 (1931–2; *Dimanche-illustré*)	1931; Exposition coloniale internationale; Paris	1931
(16) *Frimousset: Directeur de jardin zoologique* (Pinchon and Jaboune)	1933[27]	?; "Jardin privé des bêtes"[28] (cf. Jardin zoologique d'acclimatation); Paris	1933
(17) "A l'exposition" (Lefebvre)[29]	(1937; *Cadet-revue*)	1937; Exposition universelle; Paris	1937

Visit to the exhibi-tion[2]	Ethnic others and colonized groups at exhibition or elsewhere[3]	Exhibition poster shown	Republished after 1962	Exhibition episode[4]	Total story length[5]
yes	dromedary	no	probably not	11 frames	11-frame strip
yes	blacks	no	yes[18]	8 frames	8-frame strip
yes[20]	Arab (?) with a camel.	no	no	1 frame[21]	18 pp.
yes	white Frenchman as black	no	yes	3 pp. (16–18)	38 pp.
yes	white Frenchmen as various other groups	yes	probably not[23]	20 pp.	NA
no	white French children as blacks	no	probably not	9 frames	9-frame story
no	Dutch; indigenous other(s)	no	yes	1 frame	60 pp.
yes (15–29)	sub-Saharan black Africans	no	yes	15 pp. (15–29)	52 pp. in book[26]
yes	sub-Saharan black Africans ("la tribu Tsé-Tsé" [the Tse-tse tribe]); white Parisians	no	no	6 pp.	37 pp.
yes	none (white French only)	no	probably not	3 frames	3-frame strip

Title (and author)	First published (in periodical)	Exhibition: date; title; city	Time of story (i.e., when set)
(18) *Les merveilleuses aventures du P'tit Quinquin* (Marylis and Dupuich)	ca. 1950?	1900; Exposition universelle; Paris	ca. 1950?
(19) "L'expo" (Larbi and Santi)	(1983; *Viper*)	1989; Exposition universelle; Belleville (Paris)	1989
(20) *La voyageuse de petite ceinture* (Christin and Goetzinger)	1985 (1984–5; *Pilote*)	1931; Exposition coloniale internationale; Paris	1984
(21) *Le centenaire* (Ferrandez)	1994 (1993; *(A Suivre)* [sic])	1930; Centenaire de l'Algérie française; Algiers	1930
(22) *Les bâtisseurs d'empire* (Saint-Michel and Le Honzec)	1994	1931; Exposition coloniale internationale; Paris	1871–1931
(23) *Soldats de la liberté* (Saint-Michel and Le Honzec)	1995	1931; Exposition coloniale internationale; Paris	1931–95
(24) *Le roi noir n'est pas noir* (Logez and Delannoy)	2001	1883; Grande exhibition de Nubiens; Paris (Jardin zoologique d'acclimatation)	1883–99
(25) *Ecorces* (Berger and JAR)	2001	1900; Exposition universelle; Paris	1895, 1900
(26) *A un de ces quatre* (Falba and Di Martino)	2001	1906; Exposition coloniale; Marseilles	2082
(27) *Un ange passe* (Moncomble and Grand)	2001	1922; Exposition coloniale nationale; Marseilles	1922

Visit to the exhibition[2]	Ethnic others and colonized groups at exhibition or elsewhere[3]	Exhibition poster shown	Republished after 1962	Exhibition episode[4]	Total story length[5]
no	black African	no	probably not	1 frame	32 pp.
yes	mix: post-colonial + Cold War groups and ethnicities	no	NA	2 pp.	2 pp.
no[30]	mix of women: Asian, black, Maghrebi	yes[31] (37–9)	NA	poster in 1 frame (p. 36)	62 pp.
yes	mix of white French (Christians, Jews) and Algerian	yes[32] (5)	NA	entire book	77 pp.
yes	mix of French colonial troops and colonies	no	NA	1.3 pp. (43–4)	44 pp.
no	mix of French colonial troops and colonies	yes[33] (1)	NA	2 frames (p. 1)	44 pp.
yes (2–4)	British; black Africans	yes[34] (2–3)	NA	3 pp. (6–8)[35]	82 pp.
yes	Europeans (amid New Caledonian artifacts)	no	NA	2 pp. (1–2)	52 pp.
no	mix: Marseillais and Maghrebi-French	yes[36] (24)	NA	poster in 1 frame (p. 24)	46 pp.
yes[37] (43–4)	mix: various colonial others	no	NA	4 frames (p. 44)	46 pp.

Title (and author)	First published (in periodical)	Exhibition: date; title; city	Time of story (i.e., when set)
(28) *Les rivages amers: L'Algérie, 1920–62* (Joyaux-Brédy and Joux)	2003?	1930; Centenaire de l'Algérie française; Algiers	1930
(29) *Le chemin de Tuan* (Baloup and Jiro)	2005	(1) 1922; Exposition coloniale internationale; Marseilles (2) 1925; human zoo; Grenoble (3) 1930; Centenaire de l'Algérie française; Paris	sometime between 1922 and 1930
(30) *Kia Ora*, 3 vols: (1) *Le départ*; (2) *Zoo humain*; (3) *Coney Island* (Jouvray, Ollagnier and Efa)	3 vols.: (1) 2007, (2) 2008, (3) 2009	(vol. 2) in England (Crystal Palace, Victoria Palace Theatre, etc.); in France (Jardin d'acclimatation); (vol. 3) in USA (Coney Island)	ca. 1910
(31) *Le diable amoureux et autres films jamais tournés par Méliès* (Vehlmann and Duchazeau)	2009	1900; Exposition universelle; Paris	1900
(32) *Petite histoire des colonies françaises*, vol. 3: *La décolonisation* (Jarry and Otto T.)	2009	1931; Exposition coloniale internationale and La vérité sur les colonies; Paris	1931, etc.

Notes

1   This list of exhibition comics is very probably incomplete: for example, there are almost certainly more colonial-era comics about colonial exhibitions, or exhibitions with a colonial sub-theme. On the other hand, my list does cover many of the major exhibitions and comics. It includes exhibitions whose major focus was not the colonies, but which included a colonial facet. I have not included Belgian colonial exhibitions in my study. (Two more recent comic books depicting French colonial exhibitions of different sorts came to my attention after the completion of this volume: *Cannibale* [Paris: Emmanuel Proust, 2009], an adaptation by cartoonist Emmanuel Reuzé of the prose novel with the same title by Didier Daeninckx, set in and around the 1931 Exposition coloniale internationale in Paris; and *Vénus noire*, scripted by Abdellatif Kechiche and drawn by Renaud Pennelle [Paris: Emmanuel Proust, 2010]. The publication of the latter, about Saartjie Baartman, coincided with the release of the movie of the same title directed by Kechiche.)

Visit to the exhibition[2]	Ethnic others and colonized groups at exhibition or elsewhere[3]	Exhibition poster shown	Republished after 1962	Exhibition episode[4]	Total story length[5]
yes (30–2)	mix of French colonizers and Algerians	no	NA	3 pp. (30–2)	80 pp.
yes (as flash -back; 77–8)	mix of colonized; focus on Indochinese	no	NA	approx. 2 pp. total (22, 77–8, 121)	110 pp.
yes	Maoris (principally); African-Americans; Chinese	no	NA	three vols.	146 pp. total (3 vols.)
yes	blacks; French as colonized	no	NA	12 pp.	80 pp.
yes	New Caledonians (Kanak)	no	NA	3 pp.	125 pp.

2 I.e., a visit to an exhibition that takes place by the main characters within the comic strip story. In some instances where this is not the case, there is the representation of a trip to the exhibition made by other characters that is depicted in the strip (e.g., by the Princess of Holland in one frame in *Bécassine aux bains de mer*) or that has been made by the main characters before the fictional time of the strip (e.g., in "Un palais nègre").

3 The ethnic groups may be at the exhibition or elsewhere, depending on the story. Even if not stated in this chart, there are almost always white French depicted in the comic.

4 Page locations have been given with the artists' numbering, or with the publishers' numbers if the former do not exist. When the book is completely unpaginated, my own numbering begins with the title page as page 1.

5 The form of some older, serialized stories is often rather free-flowing and variable in length: some episodes have no definite beginnings or ends, because the

main narrative structure was derived from the serial form, not from a subsequent, coherently delimited book version. Partly as a result, the transfer from serial to book format (generally with a standard number of pages) was often rather arbitrary, so that, for example, the tail end of one episode could end up at the beginning of a book that focused on one or more other episodes. This was often the case for Zig et Puce (Petitfaux 1995: 19) and the Pieds-Nickelés. Moreover, some book versions of both series were arbitrarily shorn of pages: the post Second World War versions of Forton's Pieds-Nickelés stories were cut down from 64 to 48 pages (Béra, Denni and Melot 2006: 509), and early book versions of Zig et Puce also lost pages from the serialized version. In the Glénat book republications of Zig et Puce, Petitfaux reintroduced the missing pages from the serialized versions.

6   In Demeulenaere-Douyère (2010b: 116).

7   According to comics historian David Kunzle (1990a: 154 n16).

8   After the episode, throughout much of the remainder of the story, characters from the theater go around Paris still in their theater costumes (as "savages" or "femme à barbe" [bearded woman]).

9   Serialized 31 August–28 September; cf. Christophe (1981: 22).

10   E.g., in Christophe (1981: 37–41).

11   I have not been able to consult the serialized version of this episode. It very probably appeared in *La semaine de Suzette*, in 1918 and/or 1919.

12   On his enigmatic national origin, see Marie-Anne Couderc (2000: 228–31). Elsewhere she (2005: 46–7) describes him as "Maghrébin"; cf. Servantie (1989: 40).

13   I have not been able to consult the serialized version of this episode. It very probably appeared in *La semaine de Suzette*, in 1925 and/or 1926.

14   A five-frame printed strip by Saint-Ogan pasted into one of his scrapbooks (no. 21, pp. 12–13, cote Am-02602, inventaire 16145; CNBDI [now CIBDI], Angoulême). It is subtitled "A l'occasion du centenaire de la conquête, M. Flan a décidé de faire connaître l'Algérie à sa famille."

15   Issue no. 1440, 10 May 1931, pp. 1–2.

16   Issue of 21 May 1931, p. 1.

17   Issue of 31 May, page 8.

18   In Hodeir, Pierre and Leprun (1993: 137, illus. no. 20).

19   Serialized in 18 episodes, 14 June 1931 (no. 2112) through 11 October 1931 (no. 2129).

20   In the twelfth episode (30 August 1931; no. 2123; p. 412)

21   Only one frame is actually set at the Exposition; however, the visit then inspires an episode that lasts several pages, through the end of the story.

22   The original version was serialized in *L'épatant*, no. 1200, 30 July 1931 through no. 1210, 8 October 1931. It was republished in the booklet *Les nouvelles aventures des Pieds Nickelés*, no. 8: *Attractions sensationnelles* (1933, 1946 [abridged]).

23   There has been an extensive recent republication of the Pieds Nickelés strips drawn by René Pellos, but not so much for the earlier ones by Louis Forton, the initiator of the series.

24   Issue of 24 September 1931, pp. 193–4 (i.e., the first and second pages of the issue).

25   The exhibition is mentioned and visually depicted only in the final frame of

a two-page serial episode, "III: Le coeur gros," of "Bécassine aux bains de mer" (17 December 1931); republished in *Bécassine aux bains de mer* (Caumery and Pinchon 1982: 9; first ed. 1932).

26 See note 5, above.

27 I have not yet been able to consult the serialized version of this episode, which appeared in *L'écho de Paris* (see Gaumer and Moliterni [1994: 504]; Béra, Denni and Melot [2006: 289]). A website dedicated to Pinchon states that it was also serialized in *Le jour* (www.pinchon-illustrateur.info/pages/p03apag.html, consulted 12 July 2009).

28 "Jardin privé des bêtes, célèbre parc d'acclamation situé près du bois de Montmartre" (episode III, "Au jardin privé des bêtes").

29 The strip by Michel Lefebvre was published on 1 August 1937, in *Cadet-revue*, of which Saint-Ogan was editor in chief, and is included on p. 29 of Saint-Ogan's scrapbook no. 33. There are at least two (other) colonialist drawings by Lefebvre in one of Saint-Ogan's scrapbooks (no. 30, pp. 121, 252), both apparently also from *Cadet-revue*. Groensteen (2007b: 49) plausibly suggests that Michel Lefebvre was probably a pseudonym used by Saint-Ogan.

30 But the bordello in the present (1980s) serves as a neo-colonial exhibition space.

31 For a reproduction of one of the posters, see Hodeir, Pierre and Leprun (1993: 133) and Blanchard and Bancel (1998: 41).

32 A poster commemorating the centennial is reproduced as a full page at the beginning of *Le centenaire*, the fourth book in the cartoonist's series entitled "Carnets d'Orient" (Ferrandez 1994b: 5). A figure from the poster reappears as a character in a drawing in *Le cimetière des princesses*, the fifth book, with no explanation (Ferrandez 1995: 63).

33 The same poster is reproduced in Blanchard and Bancel (1998: 40).

34 Pagination mine. The model poster appears to be the one reproduced in Gervereau (1993: 36), Bachollet et al. (1994: 45 [ill. 41]) and Blanchard and Bancel (1998: 18). If this is indeed the model, the cartoonists have creatively redrawn and titled it "Jardin zoologique d'acclimatation [de Paris]: Grande exhibition de Nubiens" [Zoological Garden of Acclimatation [of Paris]: Great exhibit of Nubians]. That Gervereau (1993) was a source for the cartoonists is strongly suggested by the reproduction in *Le roi noir n'est pas noir* of a paper cut-out model of "La hutte des sauvages" [The hut of savages], also found in Gervereau's chapter ("Hutte de sauvages," p. 32, ill. 15). Here too the cartoonists freely modified their model. For analysis of such "human zoos" and the publicity surrounding them, see especially Schneider (1982: 125–51; 2002), Blanchard et al. (1995), Bancel et al. (2002) and Blanchard et al. (2008).

35 Unpaginated book. Counting from title page (as p. 1).

36 Reproductions of the same poster appear in Holo (1993b: 64), Blanchard and Bancel (1998: 25) and Bachollet et al. (1994: 53 [ill. 53]).

37 Dates given for the story, pp. 1, 15; ref. to the exhibition in Marseilles, p. 43; a visit to the exhibition, p. 44.

APPENDIX 3

French trans-African expeditions in comics

Title (and author)	First published (in periodical)	Name of real (or fictional) expedition	Reason for expedition	African itinerary
(1) "Elle??..." (Routier)	(15 January 1923; *Automobilia*)	Mission Haardt–Audoin-Dubreuil, 1922–3	search for "Elle"	Ouargla; Inifel; middle of desert/ Tanezrouff
(2) *Zig et Puce à New York* (Saint-Ogan)	1930 (serialized in *Dimanche-illustré*, 2 December 1928 to 2 February 1930)	none	attempt to reach New York (boarded wrong boat)	Egyptian pyramids; Sahara desert; South Africa (Pretoria, etc.)
(3) *Le mariage de M. Lakonik* (Bruller)	1931	Croisière noire or preceding Citroën expedition ("Mission John Citron. Traversée du Sahara Tunis-Lac Tchad")	repeatedly frustrated attempts to return home to Paris	Tunis; tropical jungle; coast
(4) *Les nouvelles aventures des Pieds-Nickelés*, vol. 9: *Les PN ont le filon*; vol. 10: *La vie est belle* (Forton)	1933	none	temporarily replace French Minister of Colonies; acquire wealth by defrauding Africans	Abyssinia; Bangui; "un important centre indigène"; "un port du golfe de Guinée"

Means of transport	Ethnic others and colonized groups	Encounter European expedition or troops	Republished after 1962	Expedition episode length[1]	Total story length[2]
train; camel; foot; Citroën *autochenilles* [half-tracks]	Targui	rescued in desert by Citroën expedition	yes (1980)	2 pl.	2 pl.
camel; foot; half-tracks	black Africans	rescued in desert by caravan of half-tracks	yes (1995)	1 frame [p. 40] in a trans-African voyage of 19 pl. [pp. 30–48]	61 pl.
half-track + wheel barrow; camel; foot	Arab; Bedouins; Berbers; Touaregs; black African cannibals	Lakonik abandoned in desert by Citron expedition [33–4]; French spahis [36]; French soldier [36]	yes (2000)	7 pl. [pp. 33–9; = pl. 23–9, artist's nos.]	39 pl.
caterpillar vehicle	black Africans: Abyssinians; central Africans.	encounter European adminis-trators and colonized troops	probably not	35 pl. [pp. 3–37]	46 pl.

Title (and author)	First published (in periodical)	Name of real (or fictional) expedition	Reason for expedition	African itinerary
(5) *Zig, Puce et Furette* (Saint-Ogan)	1933 (serialized in *Dimanche-illustré*, 27 March 1932 to 8 January 1933)	(le raid de l'auto-amphibie de Zig et Puce [no real title])	advertise vehicles built by the American adult friend of Zig and Puce	France (Paris?); Corsica; Athens; Port Saïd; Somalia; Mada-gascar; Congo; Mauritania
(6) *L'idole aux yeux d'émeraude* (Breysse)	(serialized in *Coeurs vaillants*, nos. 3–13, 1948–9)	(Mission Orionus)	scientific expeditions	Marseilles; Saint-Louis (Senegal); Sahara; Saint-Louis
(7) *Les Pieds-Nickelés et le raid Paris-Tombouctou* (Pellos and Tibéri)	1981 (serialized 1979)	Paris–Dakar (Raid Paris–Tombouctou)[3]	promotion of spaghetti brand Lasauce	Paris, Dakar, Bamako, Tombouctou (also, New York, Tahiti, Brittany)
(8) *Couleur café* (Berthet and Andrieu)	1983 (serialized in *Spirou*, 1981)[4]	Croisière noire, 1924–5	not stated (but same as in actual Citroën expedition)	segment in the Belgian Congo (by the Congo river, 100 km. from Léopoldville)
(9) *L'oublié de la Croisière noire* (Armand and Bergouze)	1986 (serialized in *Métal aventure*, no. 9, 1985)	Croisière noire, 1924–5	investigative report on abandoned half-track from Croisière noire for *Métal aventure*	Colomb-Béchar[5]; Beni-Abbes; La Hamada; Gao; Niger; Chad; Mount Kilimanjaro

Means of transport	Ethnic others and colonized groups	Encounter European expedition or troops	Republished after 1962	Expedition episode length[1]	Total story length[2]
"auto-amphibie" [amphibious vehicle]	several African groups	new vehicle brought by expedition agent to Port Saïd [18]	yes (1996)	18 pl. [pp. 3–20]	41 pl.
"chenillette" [caterpillar vehicle]; foot; camel; plane; car	Moors	expedition rescued in desert by French colonial soldiers.	yes (first book edition, 1995)	22 pl. [pp. 3–24; = pl. 1–22, artist's nos.]	62 pl.
sailboat; camel-drawn carriage; camel; donkey; sand yacht; truck; etc.	Senegalese; Tahitians; Touaregs; Malians	no (African customs agents; Malian army)	NA	39 pl. [58–96; = 6–44, artist's nos.]	44 pl.
Citroën half-tracks	Congolese	*Croisière noire* rescues the white protoganist	NA	3 pl. [pp. 46–8]	46 pl.
Citroën half-tracks	several African groups	driver rescued in savannah by Africans; later found by French journalists	NA	8 pl.[6]	8 pl.

Title (and author)	First published (in periodical)	Name of real (or fictional) expedition	Reason for expedition	African itinerary
(10) *Les aventures de Jeannette Pointu, reporter photographe*, vol. 2: *Quatre x quatre* (Wasterlain)	1986	Rallye Paris–Alger–Dakar	press report on, and participation in, the car rally	Paris; Algiers; Dakar; etc.[7]
(11) *Les autos de l'aventure*, vol. 1: *La passion des défis* (Follet and Royère)[8]	1996	a. Mission Haardt–Audoin-Dubreuil, 1922–3; b. Croisière noire, 1924–5; c. Croisière jaune, 1931–2; d. Croisière blanche, 1934; etc.	Citroën advertising campaigns and colonial objectives of French government	Same as real expeditions
(12) "La Croisière noire" (Dieter and Malès)	(1 February 2004; *Okapi*)	Croisière noire, 1924–5	test half-tracks of Citroën; connect African colonies of France; etc.	same as real expedition
(13) *Le chat du rabbin*, vol. 5: *Jérusalem d'Afrique* (Sfar)	2006	Croisière noire, 1924–5	search for an African Jerusalem	Tanezrouft (Sahara); Maradi (Niger); Belgian Congo; Uganda; Asmara (Eritrea); Jerusalem of Africa

Means of transport	Ethnic others and colonized groups	Encounter European expedition or troops	Republished after 1962	Expedition episode length[1]	Total story length[2]
four-wheel-drive trucks (esp. Land Rover); helicopter	several African groups	rescued in desert and savannah by various expedition vehicles.	NA	19 pl. [pp. 30–48; = pl. 28–46]	46 pl.
Citroën half-tracks	several African groups	same as real-life expeditions: e.g., Croisière noire encounters unit of colonized troops in Belgian Congo	NA	a. 4.5 pl. b. 5 pl. c. 7 pl. d. 1 pl.	46 pl. + maps on end-papers
Citroën half-tracks	various African groups	no	NA	12 pl.	12 pl.
Citroën half-track previously used in Croisière noire	Muslim nomads in Sahara; Touaregs; various black African groups, including one with "femmes à plateaux" (Oubangui-Chari? [C.A.R.]); Eritrean Jews	the primary expedition encounters Tintin and Snowy on big-game hunting expedition (with car) in the Belgian Congo	NA	44 pl.	80 pl.

Notes

1 Length is given in frames, pages and plates (pl.). The trans-African expeditions in comics almost always include an initial trans-Mediterranean or Atlantic leg and sometimes even a prior crossing of France, for example, when the expedition begins in Paris (e.g., in "Les Pieds-Nickelés et le raid Paris-Tombouctou" and *Quatre x quatre*). I have included the pre-African leg(s) of these trips in my calculation of the length of the expedition, in pages or frames. However, in some cases ("Elle??..." and *Zig et Puce à New York*), the characters are making trans-African voyages when they encounter a half-track expedition that rescues them. In other examples, the protagonists are making their own vehicular trans-African expedition in a half-track, caterpillar or multiple use (land and amphibious) vehicle. It is also important to note that the trans-African episode may be immediately followed by another (leg of the) voyage, especially in picaresque, colonial-era comics such as les Pieds-Nickelés. I do not include such subsequent travels in my analysis or in this table.

2 The form of some older, serialized stories is often rather free-flowing and variable in length: some episodes have no definite beginnings or ends, because the main narrative structure was derived from the serial form, not from a subsequent, coherently delimited book version. Partly as a result, the transfer from serial to book format (generally with a standard number of pages) was often rather arbitrary, so that, for example, the tail end of one episode could end up at the beginning of a book that focused on one or more other episodes. This was often the case for Zig et Puce (Petitfaux 1995: 19) and the Pieds-Nickelés. Moreover, some book versions of both series were arbitrarily shorn of pages: the post Second World War versions of Forton's Pieds-Nickelés stories were cut down from 64 to 48 pages (Béra, Denni and Melot 2006: 509), and early book versions of Zig et Puce also lost pages from the serialized version. In the Glénat book republications of Zig et Puce, Petitfaux reintroduced the missing pages from the serialized versions.

3 In his introduction to the republished book edition that I used, the scriptwriter Tibéri (in Pellos 1990: 52) also points out that in this story he and Pellos had parodied trans-Atlantic boat trips (which have their own colonial heritage) and the beach sport of land yachting or sand yachting [char à voile].

4 Jannone (1992: 6 n9) states that the work was serialized in 1981 in *Spirou* magazine: nos. 2233 (29 January), 2234 (5 February), 2245 (23 April), 2248 (14 May), 2261 (13 August), 2266 (17 September).

5 Now Béchar.

6 The serialized version is 8 pp. long (4 strips/page), but the book version is double (16 pp.; 2 strips/page), because of the small format of the book in the "Collection X" of Futuropolis.

7 In France, the itinerary includes Orléans, Toulouse and Nîmes. In Africa, the itinerary includes Algeria (Algiers, Touggourt, Ouargla, H. Messaoud, Djanet, Tamanrasset), Niger (Chirfa, Dirkou, Agades, Tahoua, Niamey), Mali (Gao, Timbuktu, Mopti), Burkina (Ouagadougou), Ivory Coast (Korhogo), Mali (Bamako, Nioro, Kayes), Senegal (Tambacounda, Kongheuil, Louga, Saint-Louis, Dakar).

8 The second volume, *Les fruits de la passion* (Follet and Royère 1998), also depicts many other road trips and "raids," including the Paris–Dakar, in which Citroën cars participated.

Bibliography

Archive Sources

Benjamin (CNBDI, cote AA-6018), nos. 60–81, 84, 88–91, 93, 95–109, 112 (1931), and special issue titled *Aux colonies! Suivez le guide* (n.d. [1931])

Cadet-revue (CNBDI, cote +R4448), nos. 97–9, 101–7, 109–15, 120–2, 125–41, 144–6, 148, 150–1, 153–5, 157 (1937–1939)

Coeurs vaillants, no. 22 (31 May 1931)

Le coup de patte, nos. 1–16, 18, 20–4, 27, 29–30, 33–5, 40, 43–4, 50–2, 54 (1931–1932)

Dimanche-illustré (CNBDI, cote AA-6108), nos. 359, 364–6, 368–9, 373, 375–6, 379–83, 385, 388, 391, 393–8, 401–5, 407–9 (1930), nos. 410, 437, 442–5, 447–8, 455 (1931)

L'Epatant (CNBDI, cote AA-4124), nos. 1123–30, 1132, 1135–40, 1143–51, 1153–4, 1157–68 (1930), nos. 1171–88, 1190–8, 1200–22 (1931)

Lisette: Journal des fillettes (CNBDI, cote +R4226), 443e livraison–494e livraison (nos. 1–52, 1930)

Métal aventure 1 (September 1983), 2–9, 10–11 (double issue, June 1985)

Okapi no. 88, with special dossier on the 50th anniversary of the Croisière noire (15–31 July 1975)

Le rire no. 642, special issue on the 1931 Exposition coloniale in Paris, by Albert Dubout (drawings) and André Dahl (text) (23 May 1931)

Saint-Ogan, Alain (n.d.), artist's eighty bound scrapbooks and two photo albums (consulted at the CNBDI [Angoulême] summer 2006; subsequently made available on the CNBDI website, respectively as CA01_FA_M03306. PDF through CA80_FA_M_03385.PDF, and CAI_FA_M_03386.PDF, CAII_FA_M_03386.PDF; downloaded from www.cnbdi.fr/_collections-numerisees/ on 17–24 March 2008; now [4 August 2010] at http://collections. citebd.org/saint_ogan/www/_app_php_mysql/cahiers/recherche_alpha_cles.php).

La semaine de Suzette (CNBDI, cote +R4077), nos. 1–48 (1930), nos. 5–43, 45–52 (1931), nos. 1–5 (December 1931), nos. 6–16 (1932)

Works Cited

Abelé, Christine (1988), *J. P. Pinchon (1871–1953): Peintre et dessinateur*, Noyon: Amis du Musée du Noyonnais

Abun-Nasr, Jamil M. (1990), *A History of the Maghrib in the Islamic Period*, Cambridge: Cambridge University Press

Ageron, Charles-Robert (1979), "La célébration du centenaire de l'Algérie française," chapter 2 of *Histoire de l'Algérie contemporaine*, vol. 2: *De l'insurrection de 1871 au déclenchement de la guerre de libération (1954)*, Paris: PUF, pp. 403–11

— (1984), "L'exposition coloniale de 1931: Mythe républicain ou mythe impérial?", in Pierre Nora, ed., *Les lieux de mémoire*, vol. 1: *La république*, Paris: Gallimard, pp. 561–91

— (1993), "L'empire et ses mythes," in Nicolas Bancel, Pascal Blanchard and Laurent Gervereau, eds., *Images et colonies: Iconographie et propagande coloniale sur l'Afrique française de 1880 à 1962*, Nanterre: BDIC/Paris: ACHAC, pp. 98–110

Ahounou, Chantal (2001), "L'affaire Voulet et Chanoine," in Colonel Klobb and Lieutenant Meynier, *A la recherche de Voulet: Sur les traces sanglantes de la mission Afrique centrale, 1898–9*, Paris: Cosmopole, pp. 141–55

Ainsa, Fernando (1982), "Utopia, promised lands, immigration and exile," *Diogenes*, no. 119, Fall, pp. 49–64

Alagbé, Yvan (1995), *Nègres jaunes*, Wissous: Amok

Alagbé, Yvan (art) and Eléonore Stein (script) (1997), "Le deuil," *Le cheval sans tête*, vol. 4: *Un héritage*, November, pp. 16–31

Aldrich, Robert (1996), *Greater France: A History of French Overseas Expansion*, London: Macmillan

— (2002), "Putting the colonies on the map: colonial names in Paris streets," in Tony Chafer and Amanda Sackur, eds., *Promoting the Colonial Idea: Propaganda and Visions of Empire in France*, New York: Palgrave, pp. 211–23

— (2005) *Vestiges of the Colonial Empire in France: Monuments, Museums and Colonial Memories*, New York: Palgrave Macmillan

Alloula, Malek (1981), *Le harem colonial: Images d'un sous-érotisme*, Geneva: Slatkine

— (1986), *The Colonial Harem*, trans. Myrna Godzich and Wlad Godzich, intro. Barbara Harlow, Minneapolis, MN: University of Minnesota Press

— (2001), *Le harem colonial: Images d'un sous-érotisme*, Paris: Séguier

Amato, Alain (1979), *Monuments en exil*, Paris: Editions de l'Atlanthrope

Anderson, Benedict (1991), *Imagined Communities: Reflections on the Origin and Spread of Nationalism*, New York: Verso, rev. ed.

Andrew, Dudley, and Steven Ungar (2005), *Popular Front Paris and the Poetics of Culture*, Cambridge, MA: Harvard University Press

Anonymous (n.d. [ca. 1889–1900]), "Visite de la famille Cocardeau à l'Exposition universelle," Epinal: Imagerie Pellerin, no. 484 [1867]

— (1931a), *Négro et Négrette à l'exposition*, Paris: Editions enfantines ("Albums de la quinzaine," no. 9)

— (1931b), *Les belles aventures de Pierrot, Marisette et Négro: Un voyage mouvementé*, Paris: Editions enfantines ("Albums de la quinzaine," no. 16)

Apostolidès, Jean-Marie (1984), *Les métamorphoses de Tintin*, Paris: Seghers

Armand, Jacques [Martin, Jean-Jacques] (art) and Bergouze [Bernalin, Philippe] (script) (1985), "Ric Brio: L'oublié de la Croisière noire," *Métal aventure*, no. 9, January, pp. 39–46

— (1986), *Ric Brio*, Paris: Futuropolis

Arnaudiès, Fernand (1941), *Histoire de l'opéra d'Alger: Episodes de la vie théâtrale algéroise, 1830–1940*, intro. A. Rogis, pref. F. Gauthier, Algiers: V. Heintz

Artaud, Adrien (1923), *Rapport général: Exposition nationale coloniale de Marseille, 16 avril–19 novembre 1922*, Marseilles: Commissariat général

Assouline, Pierre (1998), *Hergé*, Paris: Gallimard [1996]

Audouin-Dubreuil, Ariane (2004), *La Croisière noire: Sur la trace des explorateurs du XIXe siècle*, Grenoble: Glénat

— (2008), *La première traversée du Sahara en autochenille: Sur les pistes de Tombouctou*, Grenoble: Glénat/Paris: La Société de géographie

Bachollet, Raymond, Jean-Barthélemi Debost, Anne-Claude Lelieur and Marie-Christine Peyrière (1994), *Négripub: L'image des Noirs dans la publicité*, pref. Kofi Yamgnane, Paris: Somogy

Bal, Mieke (1996), *Double Exposures: The Subject of Cultural Analysis*, London: Routledge

Balibar, Etienne (1998), *Droit de cité*, La Tour d'Aigues: Editions de l'Aube

Balibar, Etienne, and Immanuel Wallerstein (1991), *Race, Nation, Class: Ambiguous Identities*, trans. Chris Turner, London: Verso

Baloup, Clément (2008), telephone interview, 6 August

Baloup, Clément (script) and Mathieu Jiro (art) (2005), *Chính Tri*, vol. 1: *Le chemin de Tuan*, pref. Pascal Blanchard, Paris: Le Seuil

Bancel, Nicolas (2003), "Le bain colonial: Aux sources de la culture coloniale populaire," in Pascal Blanchard and Sandrine Lemaire, eds., *Culture coloniale: La France conquise par son empire, 1871–1931*, Paris: Autrement, pp. 179–89

Bancel, Nicolas, Pascal Blanchard, Gilles Boëtsch, Eric Deroo and Sandrine Lemaire, eds. (2002), *Zoos humains: XIXe et XXe siècles*, Paris: La Découverte

Bancel, Nicolas, Pascal Blanchard and Laurent Gervereau, eds. (1993), *Images et colonies: Iconographie et propagande coloniale sur l'Afrique française de 1880 à 1962*, Nanterre: BDIC/Paris: ACHAC

Barbier, Alex, et al. (2001), *Jeux d'influences: Trente auteurs de bandes dessinées parlent de leurs livres fétiches*, Montrouge: P.L.G.

Bardet, Daniel (script) and Patrick Jusseaume (art) (1987), *Chronique de la maison Le Quéant*, vol. 3: *Les fils du Chélif*, colors J. J. and Y. Chaguard, Grenoble: Glénat.

Barker, Martin (1989), *Comics: Ideology, Power and the Critics*, Manchester: Manchester University Press

Barthes, Roland (1985), "L'effet de réel," in Roland Barthes et al., *Littérature et réalité*, Paris: Le Seuil, pp. 81–90

— (1987), *Mythologies*, Paris: Le Seuil

Basfao, Kacem (1990), "Arrêt sur images: Les rapports franco-maghrébins au miroir de la bande dessinée," *Annuaire de l'Afrique du Nord*, no. 29, pp. 225–35

Beaty, Bart (2007), *Unpopular Culture: Transforming the European Comic Book in the 1990s*, Toronto: University of Toronto Press

— (2008), "The concept of 'patrimoine' in contemporary Franco-Belgian comics production," in Mark McKinney, ed., *History and Politics in French-Language Comics and Graphic Novels*, Jackson, MS: University Press of Mississippi, pp. 69–93

Bellanger, Claude, Jacques Godechot, Pierre Guiral and Fernand Terrou, eds. (1972), *Histoire générale de la presse française*, 4 vols., Paris: PUF

Bellefroid, Thierry (2005), *Les éditeurs de bande dessinée: Entretiens avec Thierry Bellefroid*, Niffle

Benhaïm, André (2005), "From Baalbek to Baghdad and beyond: Marcel Proust's foreign memories of France," *Journal of European Studies*, vol. 35, no. 1, pp. 87–101

Benjamin, Roger (2003), *Orientalist Aesthetics: Art, Colonialism, and French North Africa, 1880–1930*, Berkeley, CA: University of California Press

Bennett, Tony (1988), "The exhibitionary complex," *New Formations*, no. 4, Spring, pp. 73–102

Benoît, Pierre (1920), *L'Atlantide*, Paris: Albin Michel [1919]

Benoît-Jeannin, Maxime (2001), *Le mythe Hergé*, Villeurbanne: Golias

— (2007), *Les guerres d'Hergé: Essai de paranoïa-critique*, Brussels: Aden

Benot, Yves (2001), *Massacres coloniaux, 1944–50: La IVe République et la mise au pas des colonies françaises*, pref. François Maspero, Paris: La Découverte, 2nd ed.

Béra, Michel, Michel Denni and Philippe Melot (2006), *Trésors de la bande dessinée: BDM, catalogue encyclopédique*, Paris: Editions de l'Amateur

Berger, Bernard (2003), *La brousse en folie*, vol. 12: *22 mille lieues sur la mer*, Nouméa: Brousse en folie

Berger, Bernard, and JAR (2001), *Le sentier des hommes*, vol. 4: *Ecorces*, Nouméa: Brousse en folie

Bergougniou, Jean-Michel, Rémi Clignet and Philippe David (2001), *"Villages noirs" et autres visiteurs africains et malgaches en France et en Europe (1870–1940)*, Paris: Karthala

Berliner, Brett A. (2002), *Ambivalent Desire: The Exotic Black Other in Jazz-Age France*, Amherst, MA: University of Massachusetts Press

Berthet, Philippe (art) and Antoine Andrieu (script) (1990), *Couleur café*, Marcinelle: Dupuis

Bhabha, Homi K. (1994), *The Location of Culture*, New York: Routledge

Bibliothèque municipale de Toulouse (n.d.), *Exposition: Des incunables à Zig et Puce, 28 mai–4 juin 1973*, Toulouse: Bibliothèque municipale de Toulouse

Biondi, Jean-Pierre, and Gilles Morin (1993), *Les anticolonialistes (1881–1962)*, Paris: Hachette ("Pluriel" no. 8368)

Blanchard, Pascal (2003), "L'union nationale: La 'rencontre' des droites et des gauches à travers la presse et autour de l'Exposition de Vincennes," in Pascal Blanchard and Sandrine Lemaire, eds., *Culture coloniale: La France conquise par son empire, 1871–1931*, Paris: Autrement, pp. 213–31

Blanchard, Pascal, and Nicolas Bancel (1997), "De l'indigène à l'immigré, le retour du colonial," *Imaginaire colonial, figures de l'immigré*, special issue of *Hommes et Migrations*, no. 1207, May–June, pp. 100–13

— (1998), *De l'indigène à l'immigré*, Paris: Gallimard ("Découvertes," no. 345)

Blanchard, Pascal, Nicolas Bancel, Gilles Boëtsch, Eric Deroo, Sandrine Lemaire and Charles Forsdick, eds. (2008), *Human Zoos: Science and Spectacle in the Age of Colonial Empires*, trans. Teresa Bridgeman, Liverpool: Liverpool University Press

Blanchard, Pascal, Nicolas Bancel and Sandrine Lemaire (2002), "Les zoos humains: Le passage d'un 'racisme scientifique' vers un 'racisme populaire et colonial' en Occident," in Nicolas Bancel, Pascal Blanchard, Gilles Boëtsch, Eric Deroo and Sandrine Lemaire, eds., *Zoos humains: XIXe et XXe siècles*, Paris: La Découverte, pp. 63–71

Blanchard, Pascal, Stéphane Blanchoin, Nicolas Bancel, Gilles Boëtsch and Hubert Gerbeau, eds. (1995), *L'autre et nous: "Scènes et types,"* Paris: ACHAC/Syros

Blanchard, Pascal, and Gilles Boëtsch (1993), "La révolution impériale: Apothéose coloniale et idéologie raciale," in Nicolas Bancel, Pascal Blanchard and Laurent Gervereau, eds., *Images et colonies: Iconographie et propagande coloniale sur l'Afrique française de 1880 à 1962*, Nanterre: BDIC/Paris: ACHAC, pp. 186–214

Blanchard, Pascal, and Eric Deroo, eds. (2004), *Le Paris Asie: 150 ans de présence de la Chine, de l'Indochine, du Japon... dans la capitale*, Paris: La Découverte/ACHAC

Blévis, Laure, Hélène Lafont-Couturier, Nanette Jacomijn Snoep and Claire Zalc, eds. (2008), *1931: Les étrangers au temps de l'Exposition coloniale*, pref. Jacques Toubon, foreword Jacques Hainard and Olivier Schinz, Paris: Gallimard/Cité Nationale de l'Histoire de l'Immigration

Bloom, Peter J. (2006), "Trans-Saharan automotive cinema: Citroën-, Renault- and Peugot-sponsored documentary interwar crossing films," in Jeffrey Ruoff, ed., *Virtual Voyages: Cinema and Travel*, Durham, NC: Duke University Press, pp. 139–56

Bogdan, Robert (1994), "Le commerce des monstres," *Actes de la recherche en sciences sociales*, no. 104, September, pp. 34–46

Boltanski, Luc (1975), "La constitution du champ de la bande dessinée," *Actes de la recherche en sciences sociales*, no. 1, pp. 37–59

Borowice, Yves (2008), "L'indigène au prisme de la chanson," in Laure Blevis, Hélène Lafont-Couturier, Nanette Jacomijn Snoep and Claire Zalc, eds., *1931: Les étrangers au temps de l'Exposition coloniale*, Paris: Gallimard/Cité Nationale de l'Histoire de l'Immigration, pp. 154–9

Boulanger, Patrick (1995), "Des danseuses cambodgiennes aux cavaliers algériens, visions d'empire: Les affiches des expositions coloniales de Marseille (1906–22)," in Pascal Blanchard, Stéphane Blanchoin, Nicolas Bancel, Gilles Boëtsch and Hubert Gerbeau, eds., *L'autre et nous: "Scènes et types,"* Paris: ACHAC/Syros, pp. 167–70

Brahimi, Denise, and Koudir Benchikou (1991), *La vie et l'oeuvre de Etienne Dinet*, Courbevoie: ACR [1984]

Breysse, Frédéric-Antonin (1995), *Les aventures d'Oscar Hamel: L'idole aux yeux d'émeraude*, Paris: Editions du Triomphe [serialized 1948–9]

Bruller, Jean (1991), *Frisemouche fait de l'auto*, pref. Fabien Sabatès, Paris: Charles Massin [1926]

— (2000), *Le mariage de M. Lakonik*, pref. Thierry Groensteen, Angoulême: Centre National de la Bande Dessinée et de l'Image [1931]

Cadilhac, Paul-Emile (1931), "Promenade à travers les cinq continents," illus. Georges Scott, *L'Exposition coloniale*, special issue of *L'Illustration*, July, n.p.

Candide, Rose (art) and Georges Le Cordier (script) (1908), *Sam et Sap: Aventures surprenantes d'un petit nègre et de son singe*, Paris: Delagrave

Caouissin, Henry (1931), "Coco, Banania et les poissons volants (Conte de l'exposition coloniale)," *Coeurs vaillants*, no. 22, 31 May, p. 8

Caradec, François (1981), *Christophe*, pref. Raymond Queneau, Paris: Pierre Horay

Caumery [Languereau, Maurice] (script) and J[oseph]-P[orphyre] Pinchon (1926), *Bécassine, son oncle et leurs amis*, Paris: Gautier-Languereau

— (1982), *Bécassine aux bains de mer*, Paris: Gautier-Languereau [1932]

— (1986), *Les mésaventures de Bécassine*, Paris: Club France Loisirs [1939]

— (1991), *Bécassine chez les Turcs*, Paris: Gautier-Languereau [1919]

Çelik, Zeynep (1992), *Displaying the Orient: Architecture of Islam at Nineteenth-Century World's Fairs*, Berkeley, CA: University of California Press

Çelik, Zeynep, and Leila Kinney (1990), "Ethnography and exhibitionism at the Expositions universelles," *Assemblage*, no. 13, December, pp. 34–59

Célimène, Fred, and André Legris, eds. (2002), *L'économie de l'esclavage colonial: Enquête et bilan du XVII au XIXe siècle*, Paris: CNRS

Cellard, Jacques, and Alain Rey (1980), *Dictionnaire du français non-conventionnel*, Paris: Hachette

Cenci, Philippe (art) and Louis-Bernard Koch (script) (2007), *Avec Lyautey de Nancy à Rabat*, Paris: Editions du Triomphe

Cestac, Florence (2007), *La véritable histoire de Futuropolis: 1972–94*, Paris: Dargaud.

Chamoiseau, Patrick, and Raphaël Confiant (1991), *Lettres créoles: Tracées antillaises et continentales de la littérature: Haïti, Guadeloupe, Martinique, Guyane, 1635–1975*, Paris: Hatier

Charette, Hervé de (1997), *Lyautey*, Paris: J. C. Lattès

Chauvaud, Frédéric (2009), "De la malle à l'entrepôt: Les prisons de papier dans la bande dessinée au tournant des années 1930," in Michel Porret, ed., *Objectif bulles: Bande dessinée et histoire*, Geneva: Georg ("L'Equinoxe")/ Médecine et Hygiène, pp. 111–35

Cheronnet, Louis (1931), *Algérie*, illus. Maurice Tranchant, Paris: Duchartre

Childs, Elizabeth C. (2004), *Daumier and Exoticism: Satirizing the French and the Foreign*, New York: Peter Lang

Chivallon, Christine (2005), "L'émergence récente de la mémoire de l'esclavage dans l'espace public: enjeux et significations," *Revue d'histoire moderne et contemporaine*, vol. 52, no. 4 bis, supplement: *Bulletin de la Société d'histoire moderne et contemporaine*, pp. 64–81

Chrétien, Jean-Pierre, Pierre Boilley, Achille Mbembe, Ibrahima Thioub and Jean-François Bayart (2008), *L'Afrique de Sarkozy: Un déni d'histoire*, Paris: Karthala

Christin, Pierre (script) and Annie Goetzinger (art) (1985), *La voyageuse de petite ceinture*, Paris: Dargaud

— (1996), personal interview, Paris, 22 July

Christophe [Colomb, Georges] (1889), "La famille Fenouillard à l'Expo-sition," *Le petit Français illustré*, nos. 27–31, 31 August–28 September

— (1981), *Le baron de Cramoisy; La famille Fenouillard (inédits); Histoires en images; Ombres, jeux et découpages*, ed. François Caradec, Paris: Pierre Horay

— (2004), *La famille Fenouillard*, Paris: Armand Colin [1893]

Coquery-Vidrovitch, Catherine (2003), "Vendre: Le mythe économique colonial," in Pascal Blanchard and Sandrine Lemaire, eds., *Culture coloniale: La France conquise par son empire, 1871–1931*, Paris: Autrement, pp. 163–75

Couderc, Marie-Anne (2000), *Bécassine inconnue*, pref. Jean Perrot, Paris: CNRS

— (2005) La Semaine de Suzette: *Histoires de filles*, Paris: CNRS

Coutancier, Benoît, and Christine Barthe (2002), "'Exhibition' et médiatisation de l'autre: Le Jardin zoologique d'acclimatation (1877–90)," in Nicolas Bancel, Pascal Blanchard, Gilles Boëtsch, Eric Deroo and Sandrine Lemaire, eds., *Zoos humains: XIXe et XXe siècles*, Paris: La Découverte, pp. 306–14

Craenhals, G. (1970), "Les préjugés et stéréotypes raciaux et nationaux dans les principales bandes dessinées belges," Mémoire de licence en Communications sociales, Institut des sciences politiques et sociales, Université catholique de Louvain

Crépin, Thierry (2001), *"Haro sur le gangster!": La moralisation de la presse enfantine, 1934–54*, pref. Pascal Ory, Paris: CNRS

La Croisière noire: Edition spéciale (1974), illus. René Follet, Paris: Citroën

Daeninckx, Didier (1998), *Cannibale*, Lagrasse: Verdier

— (2001), *Le retour d'Ataï*, Lagrasse: Verdier

— (2004), *L'enfant du zoo*, illus. Laurent Corvaisier, Rue du Monde

Danehy, Cécile Vernier (2005), "*Le bar du vieux Français* ou la question de l'Autre," in Adelaide Russo and Fabrice Leroy, eds., *Dossier thématique: Bande dessinée belge*, spec. issue of *Etudes francophones*, vol. 20, no. 1, pp. 92–104

— (2008) "Textual absence, textual color: A journey through memory – Cosey's *Saigon-Hanoi*," in Mark McKinney, ed., *History and Politics in French-Language Comics and Graphic Novels*, Jackson, MS: University Press of Mississippi, pp. 212–36

Dans l'ombre de Bécassine: L'oeuvre méconnu de Joseph Porphyre (1871–1953) et Emile (1872–1933) Pinchon (2007), Noyon: Conservation des musées de Noyon

Dauphiné, Joël (1995), "Les Canaques et l'exposition coloniale de 1931," in Pascal Blanchard, Stéphane Blanchoin, Nicolas Bancel, Gilles Boëtsch and Hubert Gerbeau, eds., *L'autre et nous: "Scènes et types,"* Paris: ACHAC/Syros, pp. 163–6

— (1998), *Canaques de la Nouvelle-Calédonie à Paris en 1931: De la case au zoo*, Paris: L'Harmattan

Dauphiné, Joël, and Alice Bullard (2002), "Les Canaques au miroir de l'Occident," in Nicolas Bancel, Pascal Blanchard, Gilles Boëtsch, Eric Deroo and Sandrine Lemaire, eds., *Zoos humains: XIXe et XXe siècles*, Paris: La Découverte, pp. 118–26

Dayan, Joan (1996), "Paul Gilroy's slaves, ships and routes: the middle passage as metaphor," *Research in African Literatures*, vol. 27, no. 4, pp. 7–14

Dayez, Hugues (2000), *Tintin et les héritiers: Chronique de l'après-Hergé*, Paris: Editions du Félin

Décoret-Ahiha, Anne (2008), "Danseurs et danseuses exotiques dans le Paris des années 1930," in Laure Blévis, Hélène Lafont-Couturier, Nanette Jacomijn Snoep and Claire Zalc, eds., *1931: Les étrangers au temps de l'Exposition coloniale*, Paris: Gallimard/Cité Nationale de l'Histoire de l'Immigration, pp. 146–53

Delavignette, Robert (1941), *Petite histoire des colonies françaises*, Paris: PUF

Delisle, Philippe (2008), *Bande dessinée franco-belge et imaginaire colonial: Des années 1930 aux années 1980*, Paris: Karthala

Deloncle, Pierre (1931), "La continuité de l'action coloniale française," *L'Exposition coloniale*, special issue of *L'Illustration*, July, n.p.

Delporte, Christian (1993), *Les crayons de la propagande*, Paris: CNRS

Demaison, André (1931), *Exposition coloniale internationale: Guide officiel*, illus. Joseph-Porphyre Pinchon, Paris: Mayeux

Demeulenaere-Douyère, Christiane (2010a), "Exotiques expositions...," in Christiane Demeulenaere-Douyère, ed., *Exotiques expositions...: Les expositions universelles et les cultures extra-européennes. France, 1855–1937*, Paris: Somogy éditions d'art/Archives nationales, pp. 7–21

—, ed. (2010b), *Exotiques expositions...: Les expositions universelles et les cultures extra-européennes. France, 1855–1937*, pref. Isabelle Neuschwander, Paris: Somogy éditions d'art/Archives nationales

—, ed. (2010c) *Exotiques expositions...: Les expositions universelles et les cultures extra-européennes. France, 1855–1937. Livret d'exposition*, Paris: Archives nationales

Demousson, Pierre, and Henri Pellier (n.d. [1930a]), *Le centenaire de l'Algérie: 1er livre*, illus. M. Toussaint, Paris: Larousse ("Les livres roses pour la jeunesse," no. 488)

— (1930b), *Le centenaire de l'Algérie: 2e livre*, illus. M. Toussaint, Paris: Larousse ("Les livres roses pour la jeunesse," no. 489)

Deschamps, Eric (1999), *Croisières Citroën: Carnets de route africains*, Boulogne: E.T.A.I.

Désirs d'ailleurs: Les expositions coloniales de Marseille 1906 et 1922 (2006), Marseilles: Alors Hors du Temps

Dewitte, Philippe (1989), "Le Paris noir de l'entre-deux-guerres," in André Kaspi and Antoine Marès, eds., *Le Paris des étrangers depuis un siècle*, Paris: Imprimerie nationale

— (1995), "Le 'noir' dans l'imaginaire français," in Pascal Blanchard, Stéphane Blanchoin, Nicolas Bancel, Gilles Boëtsch and Hubert Gerbeau, eds., *L'autre et nous: "Scènes et types,"* Paris: ACHAC/Syros, pp. 27–32

Dharm, Georges Simon (1931), "Koko, grand chef des becs rouges," *Le petit journal illustré*, nos. 2112–29, 14 June–11 October

Dieter [Teste, Didier] (script) and Marc Malès (art) (2004), "La croisière noire," *Okapi*, no. 753, 1 February, pp. 56–67

Dinet-Rollince, Jeanne (1938), *La vie de E. Dinet*, Paris: G.-P. Maisonneuve

Dineur, Fernand (2009), *Tif et Tondu au Congo Belge*, Soissons: Le Topinambour

Donadey, Anne (2000), "'Y'a bon Banania': ethics and cultural criticism in the colonial context," *French Cultural Studies*, vol. 11, part 1, no. 31, pp. 9–29

Dorfman, Ariel (1983), *The Empire's Old Clothes: What the Lone Ranger, Babar, and Other Innocent Heroes Do to Our Minds*, trans. Clark Hansen, New York: Pantheon

Dorfman, Ariel, and Armand Mattelart (1984), *How to Read Donald Duck: Imperialist Ideology in the Disney Comic*, intro. David Kunzle, New York: International General [1971]

Dorlys, Michel (1930), "L'oiseau de malheur," illus. Etienne Le Rallic, serialized in *Guignol: Cinéma de la jeunesse*, nos. 143 [second installment]–144, 20 April–4 May

— (1932), "C'est ma faute!," illus. E. Dot, serialized in *Guignol: Cinéma de la jeunesse*, nos. 219–221, 11–25 December

Douglas, Allen, and Fedwa Malti-Douglas (1994), *Arab Comic Strips: Politics of an Emerging Mass Culture*, Bloomington, IN: Indiana University Press

— (2008) "From the Algerian War to the Armenian massacres: memory, trauma and medicine in *Petit Polio* of Farid Boudjellal," *International Journal of Comic Art*, vol. 10, no. 2, pp. 282–307

Douvry, Jean-François (1991), *Le grand atlas des pays imaginaires de la bande dessinée*, illus. Claude Serriere and Marc Maldera, Grenoble: Phoenix

— (2006) "Saint-Ogan écrivain," *Le collectionneur de bandes dessinées*, no. 107, pp. 44–7

Dufay, François (2008), "Epatants Pieds Nickelés!," interview Jean Tulard, *L'Express*, no. 2972, 19 June, p. 116

Durmelat, Sylvie (2000), "Transmission and mourning in *Mémoires d'immigrés: L'héritage maghrébin*: Yamina Benguigui as 'Memory Entrepreneuse,'" in Jane Freedman and Carrie Tarr, eds., *Women, Immigration and Identities in France*, Oxford: Berg, pp. 171–88

Exposition coloniale internationale de Paris – 1931: Territoires africains sous

mandat de la France: Cameroun et Togo (1931), Mulhouse-Dornach: Les presses de Braun et cie

Ezra, Elizabeth (2000), *The Colonial Unconscious: Race and Culture in Interwar France*, Ithaca, NY: Cornell University Press

Falba, Bruno (script) and Richard Di Martino (art) (2001), *Malek Sliman*, vol. 2: *A un de ces quatre*, colors Arnaud Boutle, Issy-les-Moulineaux: Vents d'ouest

Fanon, Frantz (1986), *Peau noire masques blancs*, Paris: Le Seuil ("Points" no. 26) [1952]

— (2002), *Les damnés de la terre*, pref. Jean-Paul Sartre, pref. Alice Cherki, postf. Mohammed Harbi, Paris: La Découverte/Syros [1961]

Farr, Michael (2001), *Tintin: The Complete Companion*, London: John Murray/ Brussels: Moulinsart

Ferrandez, Jacques (1994a), *Carnets d'Orient*, vol. 1, Tournai: Casterman [1987; partially ser. in *Corto*, nos. 8–10, May–July 1986; also published as *Djemilah*]

— (1994b), *Carnets d'Orient*, vol. 4: *Le centenaire*, pref. Benjamin Stora, Tournai: Casterman [ser. in *A Suivre*, nos. 187–9, August–October 1993]

— (1995), *Carnets d'Orient*, vol. 5: *Le cimetière des princesses*, pref. Louis Gardel, Tournai: Casterman [ser. in *A Suivre*, nos. 201–4, October 1994– January 1995]

— (1996), personal interview, Col du Loup, 30 July

Ferré, Jean-François (1985), "Le rhum aux Antilles," in A. Huetz de Lemps and Ph. Roudié, eds., *Eaux-de-vie et spiritueux: Colloque de Bordeaux-Cognac, octobre 1982*, Paris: CNRS, pp. 409–37

Ferro, Marc (1992), *Comment on raconte l'histoire aux enfants*, Paris: Payot [1981]

— (1994), *Histoire des colonisations: Des conquêtes aux indépendances, XIIIe– XXe siècle*, Paris: Le Seuil

Filliol, Jean (1999), "L'oeuvre coloniale," *Le Monde*, 14 October

Findinier, Benjamin (2007), "Les bas-reliefs de l'*Exposition coloniale internationale* de 1931: L'oeuvre ultime d'Emile Pinchon," in *Dans l'ombre de Bécassine: L'oeuvre méconnu de Joseph Porphyre (1871–1953) et Emile (1872–1933) Pinchon*, Noyon: Conservation des musées de Noyon, pp. 49–58

Follet, René (art) and Jean-Claude de la Royère (script) (1996), *Les autos de l'aventure*, vol. 1: *La passion des défis*, Editions de l'Yser

— (1998) *Les autos de l'aventure*, vol. 2: *Les fruits de la passion*, Editions Chevrons

Forsdick, Charles (2002), "Sa(l)vaging exoticism: new approaches to 1930s travel literature in French," in Charles Burdett and Derek Duncan, eds., *Cultural Encounters: European Travel Writing in the 1930s*, New York: Berghahn Books, pp. 29–45

— (2005a), "Exoticising the *domestique*: Bécassine, Brittany and the beauty of the dead," in Charles Forsdick, Laurence Grove and Libbie McQuillan, eds., *The Francophone Bande Dessinée*, New York: Rodopi, pp. 23–37

— (2005b), *Travel in Twentieth-Century French and Francophone Cultures: The Persistence of Diversity*, Oxford: Oxford University Press

— (2007), "'Ceci n'est pas un conte, mais une histoire de chair et de sang': representing the colonial massacre in Francophone literature and culture," in Lorna Milne, ed., *Postcolonial Violence, Culture and Identity in Francophone Africa and the Antilles*, New York: Peter Lang, pp. 31–57

Forton, Louis (1931), "Les nouvelles aventures des Pieds-Nickelés," *L'Epatant*, nos. 1200–10, 30 July–8 October

— (1935a), *Les nouvelles aventures des Pieds-Nickelés*, vol. 8: *Attractions sensationnelles*, Paris: Société parisienne d'édition [1933]

— (1935b), *Les nouvelles aventures des Pieds-Nickelés*, vol. 9: *Les Pieds-Nickelés ont le filon*, Paris: Société parisienne d'édition [1933]

— (1949), *Les nouvelles aventures des Pieds-Nickelés*, vol. 10: *La vie est belle*, Paris: Société parisienne d'édition [1933]

Fourment, Alain (1987), *Histoire de la presse des jeunes et des journaux d'enfants (1768–1988)*, Paris: Eole

François, E. (1974), "Alain Saint-Ogan," obituary, in *Phénix*, no. 40, p. 52

Franquin, André (2006), *Spirou et Fantasio*, vol. 1: *Les débuts d'un dessinateur, 1946–50*, ed. Patrick Pinchart and Thierry Martens, Marcinelle: Dupuis

Fratta, Anna Soncini, ed. (1994), *Tintin, Hergé et la "belgité,"* Bologna: Cooperativa Libraria Universitaria Editrice Bologna

Frémion, Yves (2007), "Manounou, le 4ème Pied-Nickelé," *Papiers nickelés*, no. 14, pp. 12–14

Fresnault-Deruelle, Pierre (1979), "L'effet d'histoire," in Jean-Claude Faur, ed., *Histoire et bande dessinée: Actes du deuxième Colloque international éducation et bande dessinée, La Roque d'Antheron, 16–17 février 1979*, La Roque d'Antheron [France]: Objectif Promo-Durance/Colloque international Education et Bande dessinée, pp. 98–104

Frey, Hugo (1999), "Tintin: the extreme right-wing and the 70th anniversary debates," *Modern and Contemporary France*, vol. 7, no. 3, pp. 361–3

— (2002), "History and memory in Franco-Belgian bande dessinée (BD)," in Hugo Frey and Benjamin Noys, eds., *History in the Graphic Novel*, spec. issue of *Rethinking History*, vol. 6, no. 3, pp. 293–304

— (2004), "Contagious colonial diseases in Hergé's *The Adventures of Tintin*," *Modern and Contemporary France*, vol. 12, no. 2, pp. 177–88

— (2008a), "Trapped in the past: anti-semitism in Hergé's *Flight 714*," in Mark McKinney, ed., *History and Politics in French-Language Comics and Graphic Novels*, Jackson, MS: University Press of Mississippi, pp. 27–43

— (2008b), "'For all to see': Yvan Alagbé's *Nègres jaunes* and the representation of the contemporary social crisis in the *banlieue*," in Jan Baetens and Ari J. Blatt, eds., *Writing and the Image Today*, special issue of *Yale French Studies*, no. 114, pp. 116–29

Frostin, Charles (1972), "Histoire de l'autonomisme colon de la partie française de St. Domingue aux XVIIe et XVIIIe siècles," 2 vols., thesis, Université de Paris, 28 June

Garrigues, Jean (1991), *Banania: Histoire d'une passion française,* Paris: Du May

Gaumer, Patrick, and Claude Moliterni (1994), *Dictionnaire mondial de la bande dessinée*, Paris: Larousse

Gauthier, Guy (1993), "De l'imagerie d'une époque à sa représentation aujourd'hui," in Odette Mitterrand and Gilles Ciment, eds., *L'histoire... par la bande: Bande dessinée, histoire et pédagogie*, Paris: Ministère de la jeunesse et des sports/Syros, pp. 55–61

Germain, Yvonne (1992), *Notre ami Jean Nohain*, pref. Charles Trenet, Paris: L'Harmattan

Gervereau, Laurent (1993), "L'exotisme," in Nicolas Bancel, Pascal Blanchard and Laurent Gervereau, eds., *Images et colonies: Iconographie et propagande coloniale sur l'Afrique française de 1880 à 1962*, Nanterre: BDIC/Paris: ACHAC, pp. 26–47

Gilman, Sander L. (1986), "Black bodies, white bodies: toward an iconography of female sexuality in late nineteenth-century art, medicine, and literature," in Henry Louis Gates, Jr., ed., *"Race," Writing and Difference*, Chicago: University of Chicago Press, pp. 223–61

Gilroy, Paul (1993), *The Black Atlantic: Modernity and Double Consciousness*, Cambridge, MA: Harvard University Press

Girardet, Raoul (1995), *L'idée coloniale en France de 1871 à 1962*, Paris: Hachette [1972]

Goddin, Philippe (2008), *The Art of Hergé, Inventor of Tintin*, vol. 1: *1907–37*, trans. Michael Farr, San Francisco: Last Gasp

Goerg, Odile (2002), "The French provinces and 'greater France,'" in Tony Chafer and Amanda Sackur, eds., *Promoting the Colonial Idea: Propaganda and Visions of Empire in France*, New York: Palgrave, pp. 82–101

Gordon, Ian (1998), *Comic Strips and Consumer Culture, 1890–1945*, Washington, D.C.: Smithsonian Institution Press

Gough, J. B. (1998), "Winecraft and chemistry in 18th-century France: chaptal and the invention of chaptalization," *Technology and Culture*, vol. 39, no. 1, pp. 74–104

Greg [Regnier, Michel] (1974), *Zig et Puce: Le voleur fantôme*, Neuilly sur Seine: Dargaud

— (1994), *Zig et Puce*, vol. 2: *Les frais de la princesse,* Grenoble: Glénat

— (1995a), *Zig et Puce*, vol. 3: *S.O.S. Sheila*, Grenoble: Glénat

— (1995b), *Zig et Puce*, vol. 4: *Le prototype zéro zéro*, Grenoble: Glénat

— (1995c), *Zig et Puce*, vol. 5: *Et la pierre qui vole*, Grenoble: Glénat

— (1995d), *Zig et Puce*, vol. 6: *Contre le légume boulimique*, Grenoble: Glénat

Groensteen, Thierry (1996a), "Hergé débiteur de Saint-Ogan," *9e art*, no. 1, pp. 8–17

— (1996b), "L'amour en France," rev. of Yvan Alagbé, *Nègres jaunes*, in *9e art*, no. 1, p. 123

— (1999), *Système de la bande dessinée*, Paris: PUF

— (2007a), "Saint-Ogan l'enchanteur," in Thierry Groensteen and Harry Morgan, *L'art d'Alain Saint-Ogan*, Arles: Actes Sud–L'an 2, pp. 6–13

— (2007b), "Vie et oeuvre d'Alain Saint-Ogan," in Thierry Groensteen and Harry Morgan, *L'art d'Alain Saint-Ogan*, Arles: Actes Sud–L'an 2, pp. 19–85

Groensteen, Thierry, and Harry Morgan (2007), *L'art d'Alain Saint-Ogan*, Arles: Actes Sud–L'an 2

Groupe Interdisciplinaire d'Etudes Nizaniennes (2009), *Anticolonialistes des années 30 et leurs héritages*, spec. issue of *Aden: Paul Nizan et les années 30*, no. 8, October

Grove, Laurence (2005), *Text/Image Mosaics in French Culture: Emblems and Comic Strips*, Aldershot: Ashgate

Guillet, Bertrand (2009), *La Marie-Séraphique: Navire négrier*, Nantes: Musée d'Histoire de Nantes/Editions MeMo

Guillot, Claude (1985), editorial, *Le collectionneur de bandes dessinées*, no. 46, p. 3

Guyotat, Régis (1999), "La colonne infernale de Voulet-Chanoine," *Le Monde*, 27 September

Haardt, Georges-Marie, and Louis Audouin-Dubreuil (1923), *Le raid Citroën: La première traversée du Sahara en automobile, de Touggourt à Tombouctou par l'Atlantide*, intro. André Citroën, illus. Bernard Boutet de Monvel, Paris: Plon

— (1927a), *La croisière noire: Expédition Citroën Centre-Afrique*, Paris: Plon

— (1927b), *The Black Journey: Across Central Africa with the Citroën Expedition*, New York: Cosmopolitan Book Corporation

— (1971), *La croisière noire: Expédition Citroën Centre-Afrique*, pref. Pierre Sabbagh, Geneva: Le Cercle du Bibliophile

Hale, Dana S. (2002), "L''indigène' mis en scène en France, entre exposition et exhibition (1880–1931)," in Nicolas Bancel, Pascal Blanchard, Gilles Boëtsch, Eric Deroo and Sandrine Lemaire, eds., *Zoos humains: XIXe et XXe siècles*, Paris: La Découverte, pp. 315–22

— (2008), *Races on Display: French Representations of Colonized Peoples, 1886–1940*, Bloomington, IN: Indiana University Press

Halen, Pierre (1993a), *Le petit Belge avait vu grand: Une littérature coloniale*, Brussels: Labor

— (1993b), "Le Congo revisité: Une décennie de bandes dessinées 'belges' (1982–92)," *Textyles*, no. 9, pp. 365–82

— (1994), "Tintin, paradigme du héros colonial belge? (A propos de *Tintin au Congo*)," in Anna Soncini Fratta, ed., *Tintin, Hergé et la "belgité*," Bologna: Cooperativa Libraria Universitaria Editrice Bologna, pp. 39–56

Hargreaves, Alec G., and Mark McKinney (1997), "Introduction: the post-colonial problematic in contemporary France," in Alec G. Hargreaves and Mark McKinney, eds., *Post-Colonial Cultures in France*, New York: Routledge, pp. 3–25

Harlow, Barbara, and Mia Carter, eds. (1999), *Imperialism and Orientalism: A Documentary Sourcebook*, Oxford: Blackwell

Haudrère, Philippe (1995a), "La compagnie des Indes," in Philippe Le Tréguilly and Monique Morazé, eds., *L'Inde et la France: Deux siècles d'histoire commune, XVIIe–XVIIIe siècles: Histoire, sources, bibliographie*, Paris: CNRS, pp. 11–21

— (1995b), "Le commerce," in Philippe Le Tréguilly and Monique Morazé, eds.,

L'Inde et la France: Deux siècles d'histoire commune, XVIIe–XVIIIe siècles: Histoire, sources, bibliographie, Paris: CNRS, pp. 23–31

Heliot, Armelle (1998), "La promotion de Paques," *Le Figaro*, 13 April

Hellé, André (1927), *Le tour du monde en 80 pages*, pref. Gaston Chérau, Paris: J. Ferenczi et fils

— (1930), *La famille Bobichon à l'Exposition coloniale*, Paris: Berger-Levrault

Hellèle (script) and R[aymond] de la Nézière (art) (1929), *Miloula la négrillonne*, Paris: Gautier-Languereau

Henry, Jean-Robert (1997), "Des filiations plus que des continuités," in *Imaginaire colonial, figures de l'immigré*, special issue of *Hommes et Migrations*, no. 1207, May–June, pp. 87–9

Hergé [Remi, Georges] (1973), *Archives Hergé*, vol. 1: "Totor, c.p. des Hannetons," *Tintin au pays des Soviets* (1929), *Tintin au Congo* (1930), *Tintin en Amérique* (1931), Tournai: Casterman

— (1974), *Le secret de la licorne*, Tournai: Casterman

— (1979), *Archives Hergé*, vol. 3: *Les cigares du pharaon* (1932), *Le lotus bleu* (1934), *L'oreille cassée* (1935), Tournai: Casterman

— (1980), *Archives Hergé*, vol. 4: *L'île noire* (1937), *Le sceptre d'Ottokar* (1938), *Le crabe aux pinces d'or* (1940), Tournai: Casterman

— (1986), *Coke en stock*, Tournai: Casterman

— (1987), *Hergé 1922–32: Les débuts d'un illustrateur*, ed. Benoît Peeters, Tournai: Casterman

— (2006), *Les vrais secrets de la Licorne*, ed. Daniel Couvreur, Frédéric Soumois and Philippe Goddin, Brussels: Moulinsart

— (2007), *A la recherche du trésor de Rackham le rouge*, ed. Daniel Couvreur and Frédéric Soumois, pref. Dominique Maricq, Brussels: Moulinsart/ Tournai: Casterman

Hô Chi Minh (1990), *Hô Chi Minh: Textes, 1914–69*, ed. Alain Ruscio, Paris: L'Harmattan

Hobsbawm, Eric, and Terence Ranger, eds. (1989), *The Invention of Tradition*, New York: Cambridge University Press

Hochschild, Adam (1998), *King Leopold's Ghost: A Story of Greed, Terror and Heroism in Colonial Africa*, New York: Houghton Mifflin

Hodeir, Catherine (1995), "Etre 'indigène' aux expositions: Paris 1931 et Paris 1937," in Pascal Blanchard, Stéphane Blanchoin, Nicolas Bancel, Gilles Boëtsch and Hubert Gerbeau, eds., *L'autre et nous: "Scènes et types,"* Paris: ACHAC/Syros, pp. 157–62

— (2001), "Une journée à l'exposition coloniale," *Les collections de l'Histoire*, no. 11: *Le temps des colonies*, April, pp. 60–3

Hodeir, Catherine, and Michel Pierre (1991), *L'exposition coloniale*, Brussels: Complexe

Hodeir, Catherine, Michel Pierre and Sylviane Leprun (1993), "Les expositions coloniales: Discours et images," in Nicolas Bancel, Pascal Blanchard and Laurent Gervereau, eds., *Images et colonies: Iconographie et propagande coloniale sur l'Afrique française de 1880 à 1962*, Nanterre: BDIC/Paris: ACHAC, pp. 129–39

Holo, Yann (1993a), "L'imaginaire colonial dans la bande dessinée," in Pascal Blanchard and Armelle Chatelier, eds., *Images et colonies: Nature, discours et influence de l'iconographie coloniale liée à la propagande coloniale et à la représentation des Africains et de l'Afrique en France, de 1920 aux indépendances*, Paris: Syros/ACHAC, pp. 73–6

— (1993b), "L'oeuvre civilisatrice de l'image à l'image," in Nicolas Bancel, Pascal Blanchard and Laurent Gervereau, eds., *Images et colonies: Iconographie et propagande coloniale sur l'Afrique française de 1880 à 1962*, Nanterre: BDIC/Paris: ACHAC, pp. 58–65

— (1995), "Les représentations des Africains dans l'imagerie enfantine," in Pascal Blanchard, Stéphane Blanchoin, Nicolas Bancel, Gilles Boëtsch and Hubert Gerbeau, eds., *L'autre et nous: "Scènes et types,"* Paris: ACHAC/Syros, pp. 201–4.

hooks, bell (1992), "Representing whiteness in the black imagination," in Lawrence Grossberg, Cary Nelson and Paula A. Treichler, eds., *Cultural Studies*, London: Routledge, pp. 338–46

Hubinon, Victor (1977), *Les nouvelles aventures de Blondin et Cirage*, Brussels: Michel Deligne [1951]

Hunt, Nancy Rose (2002), "Tintin and the interruptions of Congolese comics," in Paul S. Landau and Deborah D. Kaspin, eds., *Images and Empires: Visuality in Colonial and Postcolonial Africa*, Berkeley, CA: University of California Press, pp. 90–123

L'Illustration (1930), *L'Algérie française, 1830–1930*, no. 4551, 24 May

L'Illustration (1931), *L'Exposition coloniale internationale de Paris, 1931*, July, 2nd ed.

Jannone, Christian (1992), "La vision de l'Afrique coloniale dans la bande dessinée franco-belge: Le journal *Spirou* (1938–90)," *Ultramarines*, no. 6, pp. 3–8

— (1995a), "La vision de l'Afrique coloniale dans la bande dessinée franco-belge des années trente à nos jours: *Spirou, Tintin, Vaillant, Pif* (1938–93)," doctoral thesis, Université d'Aix-Marseille

— (1995b) "Les hommes-léopards et leurs dérivés dans la bande dessinée," in Pascal Blanchard, Stéphane Blanchoin, Nicolas Bancel, Gilles Boëtsch and Hubert Gerbeau, eds., *L'autre et nous: "Scènes et types,"* Paris: ACHAC/Syros, pp. 197–200

Jarry, Grégory (script) and Otto T. (art) (2006), *Petite histoire des colonies françaises*, vol. 1: *L'Amérique française*, colors Guillaume Heurtault, Poitiers: FLBLB

— (2007), *Petite histoire des colonies françaises*, vol. 2: *L'empire*, colors Guillaume Heurtault and Thomas Tudoux, Poitiers: FLBLB

— (2009), *Petite histoire des colonies françaises*, vol. 3: *La décolonisation*, colors Lucie Castel et Guillaume Heurtault, Poitiers: FLBLB

Jeanjean, Marcel (1930–1), "A travers la jungle," serialized in *Pierrot: Journal des garçons*, nos. 31–4, 3 August 1930–25 January 1931

Jennequin, Jean-Paul (1996), "Amok: Un éditeur fou furieux," *9e art*, no. 1, pp. 122–3

Jijé [Gillain, Joseph] (1990), *Baden Powell*, Marcinelle: Dupuis [1950]
— (1994), "Charles de Foucauld: Conquérant pacifique du Sahara," in *Tout Jijé, 1958–9*, Marcinelle: Dupuis, pp. 101–44 [ser. 9 April–10 September 1959, in *Spirou*]
Joalland, General Paul (1930), *Le drame de Dankori: Mission Voulet-Chanoine, Mission Joalland-Meynier*, Paris: Nouvelles Editions Argo
Jobs, Richard I. (2003), "Tarzan under attack: youth, comics and cultural reconstruction in postwar France," *French Historical Studies*, vol. 26, no. 4, pp. 687–725
Joly, Octave (script), and Victor Hubinon (art) (1994), *Stanley*, Marcinelle: Dupuis [1955]
Jouvray, Olivier, Virginie Ollagnier and Efa (2007), *Kia Ora*, vol. 1: *Le départ*, Issy-les-Moulineaux: Vents d'ouest
— (2008), *Kia Ora*, vol. 2: *Zoo humain*, Issy-les-Moulineaux: Vents d'ouest
— (2009), *Kia Ora*, vol. 3: *Coney Island*, Issy-les-Moulineaux: Vents d'ouest
Joyaux-Brédy, Evelyne (script) and Pierre Joux (art) (n.d.), *Les rivages amers: L'Algérie – 1920–62*, Aix-en-Provence: Cercle Algérianiste d'Aix-en-Provence
Joyeux, André (1912), *La vie large aux colonies*, pref. Jean Ajalbert, Paris: Maurice Bauche
Kaspi, André, and Antoine Marès, eds. (1989), *Le Paris des étrangers depuis un siècle*, Paris: Imprimerie nationale
Kidd, William (2002), "Representation or recuperation? The French colonies and 1914–18 war memorials," in Tony Chafer and Amanda Sackur, eds., *Promoting the Colonial Idea: Propaganda and Visions of Empire in France*, New York: Palgrave, pp. 184–94
Klobb, Colonel Arsène, and Lieutenant Octave Meynier (2001), *A la recherche de Voulet: Sur les traces sanglantes de la mission Afrique centrale, 1898–9*, pref. A. Maitrot de la Motte-Capron, ed. Chantal Ahounou, Paris: Cosmopole
Kotek, Joël (1995), "Tintin, un mythe belge de remplacement," in Anne Morelli, ed., *Les grands mythes de l'histoire de Belgique, de Flandre et de Wallonie*, Brussels: Vie ouvrière, pp. 281–9
Kunzle, David (1973), *History of the Comic Strip*, vol. 1: *The Early Comic Strip: Narrative Strips and Picture Stories in the European Broadsheet from c. 1450 to 1825*, Berkeley, CA: University of California Press
— (1990a), *The History of the Comic Strip: The Nineteenth Century*, Berkeley, CA: University of California Press
— (1990b), "Dispossession by ducks: the imperialist treasure hunt in Southeast Asia," *Art Journal*, vol. 49, no. 2, pp. 159–66
— (2007), *Father of the Comic Strip: Rodolphe Töpffer*, Jackson, MS: University Press of Mississippi
Lafont, Jean-Marie (2001), "The *Mémoires* of Lieutenant-Colonel Russel concerning Mysore: in the Service Historique de l'Armée de Terre, Château de Vincennes, Paris," in Irfan Habib, ed,. *State and Diplomacy under Tipu Sultan: Documents and Essays*, New Delhi: Tulika, pp. 82–107

Larbi [Mechkour] (art and script) and [Gérard] Santi (script) (1983), "L'expo," *Viper*, no. 8, pp. 54–5

Larguèche, Dalenda (2004), "La Tunisie à Paris: Les Expositions universelles de 1867 et 1878, de la mise en scène de l'exotique à celle du projet colonial," in Colette Zytnicki and Chantal Bordes-Benayoun, eds., *Sud-Nord: Cultures coloniales en France (XIXe–XXe siècles)*, Toulouse: Privat, pp. 207–17

Lassus, Alexandra de (2006), *Africains et Asiatiques dans la littérature de jeunesse de l'entre-deux-guerres*, Paris: L'Harmattan

Laurent, Yves, and Serge Moati (2006), *Capitaines des ténèbres*, Paris: Fayard

Laval, Henri (1974), "Du 'fait colonial' chez Hergé et de la théorie hergéenne de la guerre," *Haga*, nos. 16–17, Winter, pp. 14–16

Law, Robin (1994), "The slave trade in seventeenth-century Allada: a revision," *African Economic History*, no. 22, pp. 59–92

Lazreg, Marnia (1994), *The Eloquence of Silence: Algerian Women in Question*, London: Routledge

Lebovics, Herman (1992), *True France: The Wars Over Cultural Identity, 1900–45*, Ithaca, NY: Cornell University Press

— (2002), "Les zoos de l'Exposition coloniale internationale de Paris en 1931," in Nicolas Bancel, Pascal Blanchard, Gilles Boëtsch, Eric Deroo and Sandrine Lemaire, eds., *Zoos humains: XIXe et XXe siècles*, Paris: La Découverte, pp. 367–73

Le Breton, David (1996), "L'extrême-ailleurs: Une anthropologie de l'aventure," in David Le Breton, ed., *L'aventure: La passion des détours*, Paris: Autrement, pp. 15–71

Lecigne, Bruno (1983), *Les héritiers d'Hergé*, Brussels: Magic Strip

Lefebvre, Michel [Saint-Ogan, Alain] (1937), "A l'exposition," *Cadet-revue*, no. 111, 1 August, p. 4

Lefèvre, Pascal (2006), "The battle over the balloon: The conflictual institutionalization of the speech balloon in various European cultures," *Image [&] Narrative*, no. 14, http://www.imageandnarrative.be/painting/lefevre_scholars.htm; accessed 22 September 2006

— (2008), "The Congo drawn in Belgium," in Mark McKinney, ed., *History and Politics in French-Language Comics and Graphic Novels*, Jackson, MS: University Press of Mississippi, pp. 166–85

Lehembre, Bernard (2005), *Bécassine: Une légende du siècle*, Paris: Hachette/Gautier-Languereau

Lehideux, Guy (1995), dossier on Alain Saint-Ogan, in *Le collectionneur de bandes dessinées*, no. 77, pp. 18–23

—, ed. (n.d. [2004]), *Zig et Puce*, Big Beat records, no. 00083

Lemaire, Sandrine (2002), "Le 'sauvage' domestiqué par la propagande coloniale," in Nicolas Bancel, Pascal Blanchard, Gilles Boëtsch, Eric Deroo and Sandrine Lemaire, eds., *Zoos humains: XIXe et XXe siècles*, Paris: La Découverte, pp. 275–83

Leprun, Sylviane (1986), *Le théâtre des colonies: Scénographie, acteurs et discours de l'imaginaire dans les expositions, 1855–1937*, Paris: L'Harmattan

L'Estoile, Benoît de (2008), "Les indigènes des colonies à l'Exposition coloniale de 1931," in Laure Blévis, Hélène Lafont-Couturier, Nanette Jacomijn Snoep and Claire Zalc, eds., *1931: Les étrangers au temps de l'Exposition coloniale*, Paris: Gallimard/Cité Nationale de l'Histoire de l'Immigration, pp. 36–43

Le Tréguilly, Philippe (1995), "Les aventuriers," in Philippe Le Tréguilly and Monique Morazé, eds., *L'Inde et la France: Deux siècles d'histoire commune, XVIIe–XVIIIe siècles: Histoire, sources, bibliographie*, Paris: CNRS, pp. 51–63

Le Tréguilly, Philippe, and Monique Morazé, eds. (1995), *L'Inde et la France: Deux siècles d'histoire commune, XVIIe–XVIIIe siècles: Histoire, sources, bibliographie*, Paris: CNRS

Levine, Alison Murray (2005), "Film and colonial memory: *La croisière noire* 1924–2004," in Alec G. Hargreaves, ed., *Memory, Empire and Postcolonialism: Legacies of French Colonialism*, Lanham, MD: Lexington Books, pp. 81–97

— (2009), "Les automobiles, le désert africain et le cinéma: Un tourisme imaginaire," in Colette Zytnicki and Habib Kazdaghli, eds., *Le tourisme dans l'empire français: Politiques, pratiques et imaginaires (XIXe–XXe siècles): Un outil de la domination coloniale?*, Paris: Publications de la Société française d'histoire d'outre-mer, pp. 181–91

Liauzu, Claude (1982), *Aux origines des tiers-mondismes: Colonisés et anticolonialistes en France (1919–39)*, Paris: L'Harmattan

— (2007a), *Histoire de l'anticolonialisme en France du XVIe siècle à nos jours*, Paris: Armand Colin

—, ed. (2007b), *Dictionnaire de la colonisation française*, Paris: Larousse

Liauzu, Claude, and Josette Liauzu (2002), *Quand on chantait les colonies: Colonisation et culture populaire de 1830 à nos jours*, Paris: Syllepse

Liauzu, Claude, and Gilles Manceron, eds. (2006), *La colonisation, la loi et l'histoire*, pref. Henri Leclerc, Paris: Syllepse

Lionnet, Françoise (1995), "Immigration, poster art and transgressive citizenship: France 1968–88," in Lawrence D. Kritzman, ed., *France's Identity Crises*, spec. issue of *SubStance*, vol. 24, nos. 1–2, pp. 93–108

Le livre d'or du Centenaire de l'Algérie française (2003), Nice: Jacques Gandini [1930]

Logez, Frédéric (art) and Pierre Alban Delannoy (script) (2001), *Le roi noir n'est pas noir*, Tourcoing: Brûle Maison

Luce et Colas aux colonies (n.d. [1931]), illus. René Giffey, Paris: Delagrave

Lyautey, Maréchal (1931), "L'exposition coloniale internationale de Paris: Le sens d'un grand effort," *L'Exposition coloniale*, special issue of *L'Illustration*, July, n.p.

Macdonald, Amanda (2008), "Distractions from history: redrawing ethnic trajectories in New Caledonia," in Mark McKinney, ed., *History and Politics in French-Language Comics and Graphic Novels*, Jackson, MS: University Press of Mississippi, pp. 186–211

MacKenzie, John M., ed. (1986), *Imperialism and Popular Culture*, Manchester: Manchester University Press

— (2002), "Les expositions impériales en Grande Bretagne," in Nicolas Bancel, Pascal Blanchard, Gilles Boëtsch, Eric Deroo and Sandrine Lemaire, eds., *Zoos humains: XIXe et XXe siècles*, Paris: La Découverte, pp. 193–202

Malela, Buata B. (2008), *Les écrivains afro-antillais à Paris (1920–60): Stratégies et postures identitaires*, Paris: Karthala

Mamani, Abdoulaye (1980), *Sarraounia: Le drame de la reine magicienne*, Paris: L'Harmattan

Marylis and J. A. Dupuich (n.d. [ca. 1950]), *Les merveilleuses aventures du P'tit Quinquin*, Tourcoing: Artima

Mathieu, Muriel (1995), *La mission Afrique centrale*, Paris: L'Harmattan

M'Bokolo, Elikia (1999), "La terreur, élément constitutif du système colonial," interview by Thérèse-Marie Deffontaines and Régis Guyotat, *Le Monde*, 27 September

McClintock, Anne (1995), *Imperial Leather: Race, Gender and Sexuality in the Colonial Contest*, New York: Routledge

McKinney, Mark (1997a), "Haunting figures in contemporary discourse and popular culture in France," *Sites*, vol. 1, no. 1, pp. 51–76

— (1997b), "*Métissage* in post-colonial comics," in Alec G. Hargreaves and Mark McKinney, eds., *Post-Colonial Cultures in France*, New York: Routledge, pp. 169–88

— (1998), "Beur comics," in Alex Hughes and Keith Reader, eds., *Encyclopedia of Contemporary French Culture*, pref. Malcolm Bowie, London: Routledge, p. 66

— (2000), "The representation of ethnic minority women in comic books," in Jane Freedman and Carrie Tarr, eds., *Women, Immigration and Identities in France*, New York: Berg, pp. 85–102

— (2001), "'Tout cela, je ne voulais pas le laisser perdre': colonial *lieux de mémoire* in the comic books of Jacques Ferrandez," *Modern and Contemporary France*, vol. 9, no. 1, pp. 43–53

— (2004a), "Framing the *banlieue*," in Roger Célestin, Eliane DalMolin and Alec G. Hargreaves, eds., *Banlieues, part 2*, special issue of *Con- temporary French and Francophone Studies*, vol. 8, no. 2, pp. 113–26

— (2004b), "Histoire et critique sociale dans les bandes dessinées africaines-américaines et franco-africaines," in Alec G. Hargreaves, ed., *Minorités ethniques anglophones et francophones: Etudes culturelles comparatives*, Paris: L'Harmattan, pp. 199–218

— (2007a), "La frontière et l'affrontière: La bande dessinée et le dessin algériens de langue française face à la nation," in Mireille Rosello, ed., *Images, imagination: Algérie*, spec. issue of *Expressions maghrébines*, vol. 6, no. 1, pp. 113–33

— (2007b), "Georges Remi's legacy: between half-hidden history, modern myth and mass marketing," *International Journal of Comic Art*, vol. 9, no. 2, pp. 68–80

— (2008a), "Representations of history and politics in French-language comics and graphic novels: an introduction," in Mark McKinney, ed., *History and Politics in French-Language Comics and Graphic Novels*, Jackson, MS: University Press of Mississippi, pp. 3–24

— (2008b), "The Algerian War in *Road to America* (Baru, Thévenet, Ledran)," in Mark McKinney, ed., *History and Politics in French-Language Comics and Graphic Novels*, Jackson, MS: University Press of Mississippi, pp. 139–65

— (2008c), "The frontier and the affrontier: French-language Algerian comics and cartoons confront the nation," trans. Ann Miller, *European Comic Art*, vol. 1, no. 2, pp. 177–201

—, ed. (2008d), *History and Politics in French-Language Comics and Graphic Novels*, Jackson, MS: University Press of Mississippi

— (2009), "'On connaît la chanson…': Le colonialisme français au Maghreb en chansons et en musique dans la bande dessinée," *Etudes francophones*, vol. 24, nos. 1–2, pp. 70–95

Memmi, Albert (1985), *Portrait du colonisé, précédé de Portrait du colonisateur*, pref. Jean-Paul Sartre, Paris: Gallimard [1957]

Merchet, Jean-Dominique (1996), "Chirac ou la nostalgie des colonies," *Libération*, 12 November, p. 13

Mercier, Gustave (1931), *Gouvernement général de l'Algérie: Commissariat Général du Centenaire: Le Centenaire de l'Algérie: Exposé d'ensemble*, Algiers: Editions P. & G. Soubiron, 2 vols.

Mercier, Jean-Pierre (2001), "Notices bio-bibliographiques des auteurs," in Alex Barbier et al., *Jeux d'influences: Trente auteurs de bandes dessinées parlent de leurs livres fétiches*, Montrouge: P.L.G., pp. 153–68

Met, Philippe (1996), "Of men and animals: Hergé's *Tintin au Congo*, a study in primitivism," *Romanic Review*, vol. 87, no. 1, pp. 131–44

Michel, Franck (1996), "L'Asie exotique: Aventures coloniales et littéraires," in David Le Breton, ed., *L'aventure: La passion des détours*, Paris: Autrement, pp. 119–39

Miller, Ann (1999), "*Bande dessinée*: a disputed centenary," *French Cultural Studies*, vol. 10, part 1, no. 28, pp. 67–87

— (2003), "*Bande dessinée*," in Hugh Dauncey, ed., *French Popular Culture: An Introduction*, London: Arnold, pp. 135–49

— (2004), "*Les héritiers d'Hergé*: the figure of the *aventurier* in a postcolonial context," in Yvette Rocheron and Christopher Rolfe, eds., *Shifting Frontiers of France and Francophonie*, New York: Peter Lang, pp. 307–23

— (2007), *Reading* Bande dessinée: *Critical Approaches to French-Language Comic Strip*, Bristol: Intellect

— (2008), "Citizenship and city spaces: *Bande dessinée* as reportage," in Mark McKinney, ed., *History and Politics in French-Language Comics and Graphic Novels*, Jackson, MS: University Press of Mississippi, pp. 97–116

— (2009a), "The astonishing return of Blake and Mortimer: Francophone fantasies of Britain as imperial power and retrospective rewritings," in Liedeke Plate and Anneke Smelik, eds., *Technologies of Memory in the Arts*, New York: Palgrave Macmillan, pp. 74–85

— (2009b), "Enfants de la bulle," in Driss El Yazami, Yvan Gastaut and Naïma Yahi, eds., *Générations: Un siècle d'histoire culturelle des Maghrébins en France*, Paris: Génériques/CNHI; Gallimard, pp. 183–8

Miller, Christopher L. (1985), *Blank Darkness: Africanist Discourse in French*, Chicago: University of Chicago Press

— (1998), *Nationalists and Nomads: Essays on Francophone African Literature and Culture*, Chicago: University of Chicago Press

Mitchell, Timothy (1991), *Colonising Egypt*, Berkeley, CA: University of California Press

— (2004), "Orientalism and the exhibitionary order," in Donald Preziosi and Claire Farago, ed., *Grasping the World: The Idea of the Museum*, Aldershot: Ashgate, pp. 442–61

Moliterni, Claude, Philippe Mellot and Michel Denni (1996), *Les aventures de la BD*, Paris: Gallimard ("Découvertes" no. 273)

Moncomble, Gérard, and Alain Grand (2001), *Les chroniques de Zilda T.: Un ange passe*, colors Catherine Simoni, Les 400 coups

Morin, Valérie Escanglon, François Nadiras and Sylvie Thénault (2006), "Les origines et la genèse d'une loi scélérate," in Claude Liauzu and Gilles Manceron, eds., *La colonisation, la loi et l'histoire*, Paris: Syllepse, pp. 23–58

Morton, Patricia A. (2000), *Hybrid Modernities: Architecture and Representation at the 1931 Colonial Exposition, Paris*, Cambridge, MA: MIT Press

Murray, Alison (2000), "Le tourisme Citroën au Sahara (1924–5)," *Vingtième Siècle*, no. 68, October–December, pp. 95–107

Nederveen Pieterse, Jan (1992), *White on Black: Images of Africa and Blacks in Western Popular Culture*, New Haven, CT: Yale University Press

Nézière, Raymond de la (1931), "Un palais nègre," *La semaine de Suzette*, no. 43, 24 September, pp. 193–4

Nora, Pierre, ed. (1984–92), *Les lieux de mémoire*, Paris: Gallimard

Norindr, Panivong (1996), *Phantasmatic Indochina: French Colonial Ideology in Architecture, Film and Literature*, Durham, NC: Duke University Press

Norroy, Maurice (1973), *André Citroën, le précurseur*, Evreux: Hérissey

O'Galop [Rossillon, Marius] (1931), *Le tour du monde en 80 minutes: Les aventures drolatiques de Marius à l'Exposition coloniale*, Paris: Albin Michel

Olivier, Marcel (1932–4), *Exposition coloniale internationale de 1931: Rapport général, présenté par le gouverneur général Olivier, rapporteur général, délégué général à l'exposition*, Paris: Ministère des colonies; Imprimerie nationale [vol. I, *Conception et organisation*; vol. II, *Construction*; vol. III, *Exploitation technique*; vol. IV, *La vie de l'exposition*; vol. V, part 1, *Les sections coloniales*; vol. V, part 2, *Les sections coloniales françaises*; vol. VI, part 1, *La section métropolitaine*; vol. VI, part 2, *La section métropolitaine*; vol. VII, *Les sections étrangères*]

Orsenna, Erik (1988), *L'exposition coloniale*, Paris: Seuil

Ory, Pascal (1989), *L'expo universelle*, Brussels: Complexe

Ould-Aoudia, Jean-Philippe (2006), "Les stèles de la honte et la mémoire des enseignants victimes de l'OAS," in Claude Liauzu and Gilles Manceron, eds., *La colonisation, la loi et l'histoire*, Paris: Syllepse, pp. 139–44

Paape, Eddy (art) and Yvan Delporte (script) (1987), *Jean Valhardi et les êtres de la forêt*, Marcinelle: Dupuis [1950]

Palmenaer, Els de (2000), "Mangbetu hairstyles and the art of seduction: *Lipombo*," in Roy Sieber and Frank Herreman, eds., *Hair in African Art and Culture*, New York: Museum for African Art/Prestel, pp. 117–23

Pania, S. [Espagnat, Paul d'] (1931), "Marius Galéjade à l'Exposition coloniale," *La jeunesse illustrée*, no. 1440, 10 May, pp. 1–2.

Pasamonik, Didier, and Eric Verhoest, eds. (2005), *White Man's Remorse*, trans. Paul Gravett, exhibition catalog, Charleroi: Charleroi Images

Patinax, M. (1985), "Sam et Sap et les influences américaines," *Le collectionneur de bandes dessinées*, no. 46, pp. 20–1

Paul-Margueritte, Eve (1948), *Le prince Nikhil*, Paris: S.E.P.E. [1932]

Peeters, Benoît (1984), *Les bijoux ravis*, Brussels: Magic Strip

— (2002a), *Hergé: Fils de Tintin*, Paris: Flammarion

— (2002b), *Lire la bande dessinée*, Paris: Flammarion ("Champs")

— (2004), *Le monde d'Hergé*, Tournai: Casterman, 3rd ed.

— (2007), *Lire Tintin: Les bijoux ravis*, Brussels: Les Impressions Nouvelles

Pellier, Henri (1928a, 1928b), *Avec la Croisière noire*, parts 1 and 2, Paris: Librairie Larousse ("Les livres roses pour la jeunesse," nos. 449, 453) [fictionalized adaptation of Georges-Marie Haardt and Louis Audouin-Dubreuil, *La croisière noire: Expédition Citroën Centre-Afrique*, Paris: Plon, 1927]

Pellos, René (1990), *Les Pieds-Nickelés de René Pellos, collection intégrale*, vol. 1: *Les Pieds-Nickelés banquiers; Les Pieds-Nickelés et le raid Paris-Tombouctou; Les Pieds Nickelés et le chanvre berrichon*, intro. Jean-Paul Tibéri, Issy-les-Moulineaux: Vents d'ouest

Pervillé, Guy (1993), *De l'empire français à la décolonisation*, Paris: Hachette

Petit, Léonce (ca. 1868), *Les mésaventures de M. Bêton*, [Paris?]: [Librairie internationale?]

Petitfaux, Dominique (1985), part 1 of dossier on Zig et Puce, *Le collectionneur de bandes dessinées*, no. 48, pp. 12–22

— (1986) part 2 of dossier on Zig et Puce, *Le collectionneur de bandes dessinées*, no. 49, pp. 32–41

— (1995), "Alain Saint-Ogan revisité," interview by Guy Lehideux, *Le collectionneur de bandes dessinées*, no. 77, pp. 18–21

Pétré-Grenouilleau, Olivier (1998), *Nantes au temps de la traite des Noirs*, Paris: Hachette Littératures

Peyo [Culliford, Pierre] and Yvan Delporte (2005), *3 Histoires de Schtroumpfs: Les Schtroumpfs noirs; Le Schtroumpf volant; Le voleur de Schtroumpfs*, Marcinelle: Dupuis [1963]

Pierre, José, ed. (1980), *Tracts surréalistes et déclarations collectives, 1922–39*, Paris: Le Terrain Vague

Pierre, Michel (1984), "Un certain rêve africain," *Les cahiers de la bande dessinée*, no. 56, February–March, pp. 83–6

— (1988), "La B.D., terre des grands fantasmes," *Notre librairie*, no. 91, January–February, pp. 116–19

— (1992), "Les mille et une bulles: L'orient imaginaire dans la bande dessinée," *A Suivre*, no. 170, March, pp. 25–9

— (1993), "L'Afrique en bande dessinée," in Nicolas Bancel, Pascal Blanchard and Laurent Gervereau, eds., *Images et colonies: Iconographie et propagande coloniale sur l'Afrique française de 1880 à 1962*, Nanterre: BDIC/Paris: ACHAC, pp. 241–5

— (2000), "L'Afrique dans la bande dessinée européenne: Un continent décor!," interview by Emmanuelle Mahoudeau, in a dossier on "BD d'Afrique," ed. Sébastien Langevin, *Africultures*, no. 32, November, pp. 43–7

— (2001), "L'affaire Voulet-Chanoine," *Les collections de l'Histoire*, no. 11: *Le temps des colonies*, April, pp. 18–21

Pigeon, Gérard G. (1996), "Black icons of colonialism: African characters in French children's comic strip literature," *Social Identities*, vol. 2, no. 1, pp. 135–59

Pinchon, Joseph-Porphyre (art) and Jaboune [Nohain, Jean; born Jean-Marie Legrand] (script) (n.d. [1933]), *Frimousset directeur de jardin zoologique*, Paris: J. Ferenczi et fils

Porterfield, Todd (1998), *The Allure of Empire: Art in the Service of French Imperialism, 1798–1836*, Princeton, NJ: Princeton University Press

Potts, Lydia (1990), *The World Labour Market: A History of Migration*, trans. Terry Bond, London: Zed Books

Pouillon, François (1997), *Les deux vies d'Etienne Dinet, peintre en Islam*, Paris: Balland

Pratt, Hugo (1980), *Corto Maltese en Sibérie*, Tournai: Casterman

— (1987), *Corto Maltese in Africa*, pref. Didier Platteau, New York: N.B.M.

Quella-Guyot, Didier (1991), "Cases exotiques," *Les carnets de l'exotisme*, nos. 7–8, July–December, pp. 7–16

Rahier, Jean Muteba (2003), "The ghost of Leopold II: the Belgian Royal Museum of Central Africa and its dusty colonialist exhibition," *Research in African Literatures*, vol. 34, no. 1, pp. 58–84

La rédaction (1985), "Les premières bulles en France," *Le collectionneur de bandes dessinées*, no. 46, p. 12

Reynaud-Paligot, Carole (2007), *Races, racisme et antiracisme dans les années 1930*, Paris: PUF

Rigney, Ann (2005), "Plenitude, scarcity and the circulation of cultural memory," *Journal of European Studies*, vol. 35, no. 1, pp. 11–28

Robbins, Bruce (1995), "Foreword," in Raymond Williams, *The Sociology of Culture*, Chicago: University of Chicago Press

Rocherand, Charles (1979), *L'histoire d'André Citroën: Souvenirs d'une collaboration, 1922–34*, Paris: Editions Christian [1938]

Rodinson, Maxime (1989), *La fascination de l'Islam, suivi de, Le seigneur bourguignon et l'esclave sarrasin*, Paris: La Découverte

Rolland, Jacques-Francis (1976), *Le grand capitaine*, Paris: Bernard Grasset

Rosaldo, Renato (1989), "Imperialist nostalgia," in Natalie Zemon Davis and

Randolph Starn, eds., *Memory and Counter-Memory*, spec. issue of *Representations*, no. 26, Spring, pp. 107–22

Rosello, Mireille (1998), *Declining the Stereotype: Ethnicity and Representation in French Cultures*, Hanover, NH: University Press of New England

Ross, Andrew (1989), *No Respect: Intellectuals and Popular Culture*, London: Routledge

Routier, J. [Jean] (1923), "Elle??...," *Automobilia*, no. 136, 15 January, pp. 28–9

Rouxel, Marie-Christine (2003), *Renault en Afrique: Croisières automobiles et raids aériens, 1901–39*, with Claude Rouxel, Boulogne-Billancourt: ETAI

Ruedy, John (1992), *Modern Algeria: The Origins and Development of a Nation*, Bloomington, IN: Indiana University Press

Ruscio, Alain (2001), *Que la France était belle au temps des colonies...: Anthologie de chansons coloniales et exotiques françaises*, Paris: Maisonneuve & Larose

— (2002), "Du village à l'exposition: Les Français à la rencontre des *Indochinois*," in Nicolas Bancel, Pascal Blanchard, Gilles Boëtsch, Eric Deroo and Sandrine Lemaire, eds., *Zoos humains: XIXe et XXe siècles*, Paris: La Découverte, pp. 267–74

— (2005), *La question coloniale dans* L'Humanité, *1904–2004*, Paris: La Dispute

Sabatès, Fabien, François-Xavier Baudet and Martine de Cortanze (n.d.), *Les raids: De la Croisière noire au rallye Paris–Alger–Dakar*, Paris: Editions de Messine

Sabatès, Fabien, and Sylvie Schweitzer (1980), *André Citroën: Les chevrons de la gloire*, E.P.A.

Sadoul, Numa (2000), *Tintin et moi: Entretiens avec Hergé*, Tournai: Casterman

Said, Edward W. (1994a), *Orientalism*, New York: Vintage Books [1978]

— (1994b), *Culture and Imperialism*, New York: Vintage Books

— (2001), "Homage to Joe Sacco," in Joe Sacco, *Palestine*, Seattle, WA: Fantagraphics, pp. i–v

Saint-Exupéry, Antoine de (1992), *Le petit prince, avec les dessins de l'auteur*, Paris: Gallimard [1946]

Saint-Michel, Serge (script) and René Le Honzec (art) (1994), *Histoire des troupes de Marine*, vol. 2 (1871–1931): *Les bâtisseurs d'empire*, Paris: Mémoire d'Europe/ Crépin-Leblond

— (1995), *Histoire des troupes de Marine*, vol. 3 (1931–95): *Soldats de la liberté*, Paris: Mémoire d'Europe/Crépin-Leblond

Saint-Ogan, Alain (1946), *Sans tambours ni trompettes*, Paris: Arthème Fayard

— (1961), *Je me souviens de Zig et Puce et de quelques autres*, Paris: La Table Ronde

— (1974a), *Alain Saint-Ogan, dessinateur de presse: Dessins d'Alain Saint-Ogan pour Le Parisien libéré*, pref. Eric Leguèbe, Ivry: Serg

— (1974b), "Le dernier interview d'Alain Saint-Ogan," by Jean-Louis Durher, *Phénix*, no. 40, pp. 54–6

— (1988), "Alain Saint-Ogan," interview by Gérard Dôle, *Le collectionneur de bandes dessinées*, no. 56, pp. 34–9

— (1995a),* *Zig et Puce*, vol. 1: *En route pour l'Amérique!*, Grenoble: Glénat [1927; ser. 3 May 1925–30 January 1927]

— (1995b), *Zig et Puce millionnaires*, vol. 2, Grenoble: Glénat [1928; ser. 6 February 1927–19 February 1928]

— (1995c), *Zig, Puce et Alfred*, vol. 3, Grenoble: Glénat [1929; ser. 26 February 1928–25 November 1928]

— (1995d), *Zig et Puce à New York*, vol. 4, Grenoble: Glénat [1930; ser. 2 December 1928–2 February 1930]

— (1995e), *Zig et Puce cherchent Dolly*, vol. 5, Grenoble: Glénat [1931; ser. 9 February 1930–22 March 1931]

— (1995f), *Zig et Puce aux Indes*, vol. 6, Grenoble: Glénat [1932; ser. 29 March 1931–20 March 1932]

— (1996a), *Zig, Puce et Furette*, vol. 7, Grenoble: Glénat [1933; ser. 27 March 1932–8 January 1933]

— (1996b), *Zig, Puce et la petite princesse*, vol. 8, Grenoble: Glénat [1934; ser. 15 January 1933–10 December 1933]

— (1997a), *Zig et Puce au XXIe siècle*, vol. 9, Grenoble: Glénat [1935; ser. 17 December 1933–14 October 1934]

— (1997b), *Zig et Puce ministres*, vol. 10, Grenoble: Glénat [1938; not serialized]

— (1997c), *Zig et Puce et le professor Médor*, vol. 11, Grenoble: Glénat [1941; ser. 1 April 1939–15 August 1939]

— (1998a), *Revoilà Zig et Puce*, vol. 12, Grenoble: Glénat [1947; ser. 3 May 1946–11 December 1946]

— (1998b), *Zig et Puce et l'homme invisible*, vol. 13, Grenoble: Glénat [1949; ser. 17 July 1947–12 February 1948]

— (1999a), *Zig et Puce et le complot*, vol. 14, Grenoble: Glénat [1950; ser. 19 February 1948–5 December 1948]

— (1999b), *Zig et Puce et le cirque*, vol. 15, Grenoble: Glénat [1951; ser. 12 December 1948–13 November 1949]

— (1999c), *Zig et Puce en Ethiopie*, vol. 16, Grenoble: Glénat [1952; ser. 20 November 1949–28 May 1950]

— (2000), *Zig et Puce sur Vénus*, vol. 17, Grenoble: Glénat [ser. 4 June 1950–14 January 1951]

— (2001), *Zig et Puce et Nénette, et autres histoires*, vol. 18, Grenoble: Glénat [ser. 15 December 1952–1 March 1954]

— (2008), *Je me souviens de Zig et Puce et de quelques autres*, pref. José-Louis Bocquet, Paris: La Table Ronde

* The information for serial and first book edition publication of Saint-Ogan's Zig et Puce series is from Dominique Petitfaux's bibliography, in Saint Ogan, *Zig et Puce aux Indes* (1995f: 59–61), which contains other useful bibliographical information too. For example, a few volumes listed here contain additional serialized episodes collected together by Petitfaux, and virtually all the Glénat volumes include pages from the serialized version that were cut from the first book edition.

Savarese, Eric (1995), "La femme noire en image: Objet érotique ou sujet domestique," in Pascal Blanchard, Stéphane Blanchoin, Nicolas Bancel, Gilles Boëtsch and Hubert Gerbeau, eds., *L'autre et nous: "Scènes et types,"* Paris: ACHAC/Syros, pp. 79–84

Schneider, William H. (1982), *An Empire for the Masses: The French Popular Image of Africa, 1870–1900*, Westport, CT: Greenwood Press

— (2002), "Les expositions ethnographiques du Jardin zoologique d'acclimatation," in Nicolas Bancel, Pascal Blanchard, Gilles Boëtsch, Eric Deroo and Sandrine Lemaire, eds., *Zoos humains: XIXe et XXe siècles*, Paris: La Découverte, pp. 72–80

Schodt, Frederik L. (1986), *Manga! Manga!: The World of Japanese Comics*, foreword. Osamu Tezuka, Tokyo: Kodansha International

Schor, Ralph (1985), *L'opinion française et les étrangers en France, 1919–1939*, Paris: Publications de la Sorbonne

Screech, Matthew (2005), *Masters of the Ninth Art: Bandes dessinées and Franco-Belgian Identity*, Liverpool: Liverpool University Press

Servantie, A. (1989), "Les médias modernes à grande diffusion, véhicules de stéréotypes politiques: Bandes dessinées sur la Turquie," *Cahiers d'études sur la Méditerranée orientale et le monde turco-iranien*, no. 8, pp. 25–75

Sfar, Joann (2003), *Le chat du rabbin*, vol. 2: *Le malka des lions*, pref. Fellag, colors Brigitte Findakly, Paris: Dargaud

— (2005a), *Le chat du rabbin*, vol. 4: *Le paradis terrestre*, pref. Jean Giraud, colors Brigitte Findakly, Paris: Dargaud

— (2005b), *The Rabbi's Cat*, colors Brigitte Findakly, trans. Alexis Siegel and Anjali Singh, New York: Pantheon

— (2006), *Le chat du rabbin*, vol. 5: *Jérusalem d'Afrique*, pref. Philippe Val, colors Brigitte Findakly, Paris: Dargaud

— (2007), *Les carnets de Joann Sfar: Greffier*, Paris: Guy Delcourt

— (2008), *The Rabbi's Cat*, vol. 2, colors Brigitte Findakly, trans. Alexis Siegel, New York: Pantheon

Sharpley-Whiting, Tracy Denean (1999), *Black Venus: Sexualized Savages, Primal Fears and Primitive Narratives*, Durham, NC: Duke University Press

Sherzer, Dina (1996), "Race matters and matters of race: interracial relationships in colonial and postcolonial films," in Dina Sherzer, ed., *Cinema, Colonialism, Postcolonialism: Perspectives from the French and Francophone World*, Austin, TX: University of Texas Press

Shohat, Ella, and Robert Stam (1994), *Unthinking Eurocentrism: Multiculturalism and the Media*, London: Routledge

Siblot, Paul (1991), "Représentations de la langue et production d'ethnotype," in Jean-Claude Bouvier and Claude Martel, eds., *Les Français et leurs langues*, Aix-en-Provence: Publications de l'Université de Provence Aix-Marseille 1, pp. 371–99

Slavin, David H. (1996), "Heart of darkness, heart of light: the civilizing mission in *L'Atlantide*," in Steven Ungar and Tom Conley, eds., *Identity Papers: Contested Nationhood in Twentieth-Century France*, Minneapolis, MN: University of Minnesota Press, pp. 113–35

Smith, Stephen (1993), "La 'plus grande France' à la rescousse," *Libération*, 18 October, p. 3

Smolderen, Thierry (1984), "La vie des revues: Le dernier cri de l'aventure," *Cahiers de la bande dessinée*, no. 56, March, pp. 62–5

Socé, Ousmane (1964), *Mirages de Paris*, Paris: Nouvelles Editions Latines [1937]

Solé, Robert (1997), *L'Egypte, passion française*, Paris: Le Seuil

Solo [Solot, François], Catherine Saint-Martin and Jean-Marie Bertin (2004), *Dico Solo: Plus de 5,000 dessinateurs de presse et 600 supports en France, de Daumier à l'an 2,000*, Vichy: Aedis

Stoler, Ann Laura (2006), "Colonial archives and the arts of governance: On the content in the form," in Francis X. Blouin Jr. and William G. Rosenberg, eds., *Archives, Documentation, and Institutions of Social Memory: Essays from the Sawyer Seminar*, Ann Arbor, MI: University of Michigan Press, pp. 267–79

Stora, Benjamin (1989), "Les Algériens dans le Paris de l'entre-deux-guerres," in André Kaspi and Antoine Marès, eds., *Le Paris des étrangers depuis un siècle*, Paris: Imprimerie nationale, pp. 141–55

— (1999), *Le transfert d'une mémoire: De l'"Algérie française" au racisme anti-arabe*, Paris: La Découverte

— (2004), *Histoire de l'Algérie coloniale (1830–1954)*, Paris: La Découverte

Strömberg, Fredrik (2003), *Black Images in the Comics: A Visual History*, afterword Charles Johnson, Seattle, WA: Fantagraphics Books

— (2010), *Images noires: La représentation des noirs dans la bande dessinée mondiale*, postf. Charles Johnson, Montrouge: P.L.G.

Sylvander, Erik (1999), "La colonne infernale," *Le Monde*, 7 October

Tardi, Jacques (art) and Daniel Pennac (script) (2000), *La débauche*, Paris: Futoropolis/Gallimard

Thiébaut, Michel (1994), *Les chantiers d'une aventure: Autour des* Passagers du vent *de François Bourgeon*, Tournai: Casterman

Thirion, André (1972), *Révolutionnaires sans révolution*, Paris: Robert Laffont

Thode-Arora, Hilke (2002), "Hagenbeck et les tournées européennes: L'élaboration du zoo humain," in Nicolas Bancel, Pascal Blanchard, Gilles Boëtsch, Eric Deroo and Sandrine Lemaire, eds., *Zoos humains: XIXe et XXe siècles*, Paris: La Découverte, pp. 81–9

Thomas, Dominic (2007), *Black France: Colonialism, Immigration and Transnationalism*, Bloomington, IN: Indiana University Press

Tidjani Alou, Antoinette (2005), "Sarraounia et ses intertextes: Identité, intertextualité et émergence littéraire," *Sud Langues*, no. 5, December, www.sudlangues.sn/spip.php?article91 (accessed 24 December 2010)

Tirefort, Alain (2001–2), "Les petites Suzette aux colonies: *La semaine de Suzette* et la culture coloniale pendant l'entre-deux-guerres," *Afrika Zamani*, nos. 9–10, pp. 102–25

Töpffer, Rodolphe (1996), *Le docteur Festus; Histoire de monsieur Cryptogame: Deux odysées*, pref. Thierry Groensteen, Paris: Seuil

— (2007), *Rodolphe Töpffer: The Complete Comic Strips*, compiled, translated and annotated by David Kunzle, Jackson, MS: University Press of Mississippi

Touchet, Jacques (1931), "A l'Exposition coloniale: Jeannot-Lapin-dromadaire entre sans payer...," *Benjamin*, no. 80, 21 May, p. 1

Tribak-Geoffroy, Nabila (1997), "Carnets d'Orient: Jacques Ferrandez et l'histoire de l'Algérie, réalité ou mythologie," in Nicolas Gaillard, ed., *La bande dessinée: Histoire, développement, signification*, spec. issue of *Contre-champ: Littérature, culture et société*, no. 1, pp. 115–29

Tufts, Clare (2004), "Vincent Krassousky – Nazi collaborator or naïve cartoonist?," *International Journal of Comic Art*, vol. 6, no. 1, pp. 18–36

Tulard, Jean (2008), Les Pieds Nickelés *de Louis Forton*, Paris: Armand Colin

Ungar, Steven (2003), "La France impériale exposée en 1931: Une apothéose," in Pascal Blanchard and Sandrine Lemaire, eds., *Culture coloniale: La France conquise par son empire, 1871–1931*, Paris: Autrement, pp. 201–11

Van Opstal, Huibrecht (1998), *Tracé RG: Le phénomène Hergé*, Brussels: Claude Lefrancq

— (2006), personal communication regarding *Tintin au Congo*, 26 December

Vann, Michael G. (2009), "Caricaturing 'the colonial good life' in French Indochina," *European Comic Art*, vol. 2, no. 1, pp. 83–108

Vann, Michael G., and Joel Montague (2008), *The Colonial Good Life: A Commentary on André Joyeux's Vision of French Indochina*, Bangkok: White Lotus Press

Vehlmann, Fabien (script) and Frantz Duchazeau (art) (2009), *Le diable amoureux et autres films jamais tournés par Méliès*, Paris: Dargaud

Verschave, François-Xavier (2001), *La Françafrique: Le plus long scandale de la république*, Paris: Stock [1998]

Warren, Allen (1986), "Citizens of the empire: Baden-Powell, scouts and guides, and an imperial ideal," in John M. MacKenzie, ed., *Imperialism and Popular Culture*, Manchester: Manchester University Press, pp. 232–56

Wasterlain, Marc (1986), *Les aventures de Jeannette Pointu, reporter photographe*, vol. 2: *Quatre x quatre*, Charleroi: Dupuis

Weiland, Isabelle (2010), "Entre Tunisie fantasmée et Tunisie réelle: La présence tunisienne dans les expositions universelles Paris, 1855–1900," in Christiane Demeulenaere-Douyère, ed., *Exotiques expositions...: Les expositions universelles et les cultures extra-européennes. France, 1855–1937*, Paris: Somogy éditions d'art/Archives nationales, pp. 36–47

Williams, Raymond (1975), *The Country and the City*, New York: Oxford University Press

— (1995), *The Sociology of Culture*, foreword Bruce Robbins, Chicago: University of Chicago Press

Willis, Susan (1991), *A Primer for Daily Life*, New York: Routledge

Wolgensinger, Jacques (1974), *Raid Afrique*, Paris: Flammarion

— (1996), *Citroën: Une vie à quitte ou double*, Paris: Arthaud

— (2002), *L'aventure de la Croisière noire*, Paris: Robert Laffont

Young, Robert J. C. (1995), *Colonial Desire: Hybridity in Theory, Culture and Race*, London: Routledge

Zemon Davis, Natalie (1975), *Society and Culture in Early Modern France*, Stanford, CA: Stanford University Press

Index

Note: Each of the following headings groups together several related entries not
duplicated elsewhere in the index:
- character types in colonial comics
- colonial and imperial
- colonial army and police in comics and cartoons
- colonialism and colonization
- ethnic or racialized groups in comics and cartoons
- exhibition comics and cartoons
- exhibitions
- expedition comics
- expeditions
- humor and jokes
- ideologies and practices of exclusion and domination
- imperialism
- periodicals with comics and cartoons
- publishers of comics
- scholars, critics and editors of/on comics
- scholarship on comics
- tropes in (post-)colonial comics and critical concepts for reading them